Muirhead Library of Philosophy

PHILOSOPHICAL PAPERS

MUIRHEAD

20TH CENTURY PHILOSOPHY
In 22 Volumes

PHILOSOPHICAL PAPERS

GEORGE EDWARD MOORE

First published in 1959

Reprinted in 2002 by
Routledge
2 Park Square, Milton Park, Abingdon, Oxon, OX14 4RN
or
270 Madison Avenue, New York, NY 10016

First issued in paperback 2010

Routledge is an imprint of the Taylor & Francis Group

British Library Cataloguing in Publication Data
A CIP catalogue record for this book
is available from the British Library

Philosophical Papers
ISBN 978-0-415-29551-2 (hbk)
ISBN 978-0-415-60657-8 (pbk)
20th Century Philosophy: 22 Volumes
ISBN 978-0-415-29526-0
Muirhead Library of Philosophy: 95 Volumes
ISBN 978-0-415-27897-3

MUIRHEAD LIBRARY OF PHILOSOPHY

An admirable statement of the aims of the Library of Philosophy was provided by the first editor, the late Professor J. H. Muirhead, in his description of the original programme printed in Erdmann's *History of Philosophy* under the date 1890. This was slightly modified in subsequent volumes to take the form of the following statement:

'The Muirhead Library of Philosophy was designed as a contribution to the History of Modern Philosophy under the heads: first of different Schools of Thought—Sensationalist, Realist, Idealist, Intuitivist; secondly of different Subjects—Psychology, Ethics, Aesthetics, Political Philosophy, Theology. While much had been done in England in tracing the course of evolution in nature, history, economics, morals and religion, little had been done in tracing the development of thought on these subjects. Yet "the evolution of opinion is part of the whole evolution".

'By the co-operation of different writers in carrying out this plan it was hoped that a thoroughness and completeness of treatment, otherwise unattainable, might be secured. It was believed also that from writers mainly British and American fuller consideration of English Philosophy than it had hitherto received might be looked for. In the earlier series of books containing, among others, Bosanquet's *History of Aesthetic*, Pfleiderer's *Rational Theology since Kant*, Albee's *History of English Utilitarianism*, Bonar's *Philosophy and Political Economy*, Brett's *History of Psychology*, Ritchie's *Natural Rights*, these objects were to a large extent effected.

'In the meantime original work of a high order was being produced both in England and America by such writers as Bradley, Stout, Bertrand Russell, Baldwin, Urban, Montague, and others, and a new interest in foreign works, German, French and Italian, which had either become classical or were attracting public attention, had developed. The scope of the Library thus became extended into something more international, and it is entering on the fifth decade of its existence in the hope that it may contribute to that mutual understanding between countries which is so pressing a need of the present time.'

The need which Professor Muirhead stressed is no less pressing today, and few will deny that philosophy has much to do with enabling us to meet it, although no one, least of all Muirhead himself, would regard that as the sole, or even the main, object of philosophy. As Professor Muirhead continues to lend the distinction of his name to the Library of Philosophy it seemed not inappropriate to allow him to recall us to these aims in his own words. The emphasis on the history of thought also seemed to me very timely; and the number of important works promised for the Library in the near future augur well for the continued fulfilment, in this and other ways, of the expectations of the original editor.

H. D. LEWIS

PHILOSOPHICAL PAPERS

BY

GEORGE EDWARD MOORE
O.M.

LITT.D., HON. LL.D., F.B.A.

*Emeritus Professor of Philosophy
and Fellow of Trinity College
in the University of Cambridge*

Routledge
Taylor & Francis Group

LONDON AND NEW YORK

FIRST PUBLISHED IN 1959
SECOND IMPRESSION 1963

in 11 on 12 pt Imprint type

G. E. MOORE

(The following notice is reprinted, with corrections and additions, from *The Manchester Guardian* of October 25, 1958, by kind permission of the Editor.)

George Edward Moore was born in London in 1873 and died at Cambridge on October 24, 1958. He was the third son of D. Moore, M.D., and Henrietta Sturge, and was a brother of Sturge Moore, the poet.

Moore was at school at Dulwich College, and he entered Trinity College, Cambridge, in 1892. He took a First in Part I of the Classical Tripos, and then turned to the study of Moral Science, to which he devoted the rest of his life. In 1896 he was placed in the first class of Part II of the Moral Sciences Tripos, and in 1898 he was awarded a prize-fellowship at Trinity. His dissertation dealt with two main topics, viz. the notion of the 'empirical' and the 'noumenal' self in Kant's ethical writings, and the notions of 'reason' and 'idea', with special reference to Bradley's *Logic*. The substance of both parts of the dissertation was afterwards published in *Mind* in two articles, entitled 'Freedom' and 'The Nature of Judgment'. His first book, *Principia Ethica*, was published in 1903.

He was away from Cambridge until 1911, holding no teaching post. In 1911 he returned to take up the office of University Lecturer in Moral Science. He held this for the next fourteen years, lecturing on Psychology and on Metaphysics. In 1921 he became editor of *Mind*, on the retirement of G. F. Stout. In 1925 he succeeded James Ward as Professor of Philosophy in Cambridge, and in the same year he again became Fellow of Trinity. In 1951 he was appointed to the Order of Merit. Moore married Miss Dorothy Ely in 1916 and had two sons.

Beside *Principia Ethica* Moore published three books, *Ethics* (1912) in the Home University Series, *Philosophical Studies* (1922), and *Some Main Problems of Philosophy* (1953). He contributed many extremely important articles, in his earlier years to *Mind* and other philosophical periodicals, and later to the *Proceedings* and the annual *Supplementary Volumes* of the Aristotelian Society.

Moore's philosophical interests were wholly analytic and critical. He had not the slightest belief in the possibility of any system of constructive metaphysics, and he was a devastating critic of the fallacies and confusions inherent in such systems. By his own writings, and the influence which he exercised on contemporaries like Bertrand Russell, and (as Keynes has testified) on a whole series of able men of a younger generation, he did more than any other person to undermine the hitherto predominant influence of Kantianism and Hegelianism in England. One essay of his, 'A Defence of Common Sense', contributed to *Contemporary British Philosophy* (Second Series 1925), had and has continued to have an immense influence on British philosophy. The 'Autobiography' and 'Reply to my Critics', which he contributed to *The Philosophy of G. E. Moore* in Schilpp's 'Library of Living Philosophers' (1942), throw much light on his personality and on his philosophical position in his later years.

Though his published works are all absolutely first-rate contributions to philosophy, his influence on English philosophic thought was out of all proportion to his comparatively small literary output. It was by his lectures, his discussion-classes, his constant and illuminating contributions to discussion at the Cambridge Moral Science Club and the Aristotelian Society, and his private conversations with his colleagues and pupils that he mainly produced his effects on the thought of his time.

It is doubtful whether any philosopher known to history has excelled or even equalled Moore in sheer power of analysing problems, detecting and exposing fallacies and ambiguities, and formulating and working out alternative possibilities. He knew his own limitations, and within the field of absolutely fundamental problems to which he confined himself, he illuminated and transformed every subject which he treated. His literary style is fundamentally simple, lucid, and direct: though sometimes it seems involved because of his determination to state and reiterate every needful qualification and to remove every possibility of misunderstanding.

Apart from his immense analytic power Moore's most noticeable characteristic was his absolutely single-minded desire to discover truth and avoid error and confusion. Fundamentally he was a man of simple tastes and character, absolutely devoid of all affectation, pose, and flummery. He thoroughly enjoyed the simple human pleasures of eating and drinking, walking, gardening, talking to his friends, playing with his children, and so on. It is because ordinary, unpretending Englishmen are so often muddle-headed, and intellectuals so often cracked and conceited, that Moore, who combined the virtues of both and had the vices of neither, was so exceptional and lovable a personality.

C. D. BROAD

PREFACE

All the papers contained in this volume, except the two on 'Certainty' and 'Four Forms of Scepticism', have been previously published; and of those which have been previously published all are reprinted, with only a small number of corrections, in the order in which they were written. I know that some of these papers contain mistakes; but they seem to me, even as they stand, to say some things which are worth saying, and I hope that readers may find it convenient to have them collected in one volume.

The paper on 'Certainty' was given as the Howison lecture at the University of California in 1941. And I wish now to express my gratitude to the University at being appointed Howison Lecturer, and my regret that the publication of the paper has been so long delayed. There are bad mistakes in it which I cannot yet see how to put right. 'Four Forms of Scepticism', which has been only partly revised, was delivered as a lecture to various universities during my sojourn in the United States of America during 1940–44, a sojourn which I owe primarily to my good friends Alice and Morris Lazerowitz whose interest and encouragement are largely responsible for the publication of this volume now. My thanks are also due to the Committee of the Aristotelian Society for permission to reprint the large number of papers contained in the various supplementary volumes of their Proceedings; to the Editor of 'The Library of Living Philosophers' for permission to reprint 'Russell's "Theory of Descriptions" from *The Philosophy of Bertrand Russell*; to the Editor of *Mind* for permission to reprint the articles on Wittgenstein; to the Council of the British Academy for permission to reprint 'Proof of an External World' from Volume XXV of their Proceedings; and to Casimir Lewy and my wife and my son Timothy for the immense amount of trouble they have taken in preparing this book for the press while I was in hospital.

G. E. MOORE

Cambridge
September 1958

Those of the papers in this volume which have been previously published originally appeared as follows:

CONTENTS

I

ARE THE CHARACTERISTICS OF PARTICULAR THINGS UNIVERSAL OR PARTICULAR?

I understand that the object of this Symposium is to discuss a view advocated by Professor Stout in his Hertz Lecture to the British Academy on 'The Nature of Universals and Propositions'.[1] He there advocates some view, which he seems to think can be properly expressed by the words: 'Every character which characterizes either a concrete thing or a concrete individual is particular and not universal.' And I understand that what we are wanted to do is to discuss the view which *he* expresses by those words. We are not to give to the words the sense or senses which *we* may think they ought to bear, and then to discuss whether the view or views they would *then* express is true or false. What we have to do is to try to discover what Professor Stout means by them, and then merely to discuss whether the view which *he* uses them to express is true or false, even though we may think that the view in question is one which cannot be properly expressed by them at all.

Now I confess that I think it extremely difficult to be sure what Professor Stout does mean by those words. All that I can do, therefore, is to try to state as clearly as possible the only views which, so far as I can see, he might mean by them, and to discuss whether those are true or false. It is, of course, possible that I may have overlooked just the view which is what he really does mean; but, if so, I hope that what I shall say will at least have the use of making it easier for him to point out to us what he does mean.

There are two main points as to which I feel doubt. The first is as to what precisely he means by the expression '*is particular*' (or '*is a particular*'; for he sometimes uses this latter expression also as equivalent to the former, e.g. page 8) in the sentence, 'Every character which characterizes a concrete thing *is particular*'. And the second is as to how, precisely, he uses the term 'character'.

[1] *Proceedings of the British Academy*, Vol. X, 1921–22.

As regards the first point, I feel no doubt whatever that *part, at least,* of what he means by 'is particular' is 'characterizes one thing only'. Part, at least, of what he means to assert with regard to every entity of which it can be truly said that it is 'a character of a concrete thing', in the sense (whatever it may be) in which he is using the term 'character', is, quite clearly, that every such entity *characterizes one thing only*; or (what is equivalent to this) that no such entity characterizes more than one thing—no such entity is a 'common character' of two or more things. This notion, of characterizing one thing only, seems to me to be a perfectly clear conception; and hence, if only we can discover what Professor Stout means by 'characters', we shall have one perfectly clear proposition, which is certainly part at least of what he means to assert, and which we can discuss. My only doubt is as to whether 'characterizes one thing only' can be *all* that he means by 'is particular' or 'is a particular'. But here I have to confess that, if Professor Stout does mean anything else, I have not been able to form the faintest notion of what else he does mean. I shall, therefore, have to content myself with discussing, with regard to certain classes of entities, whether it is or is not true of them that every such entity *characterizes one thing only*, although I recognize that this is probably only a part of what Professor Stout means to assert.

It seems to me, I may explain, a wholly indefensible misuse of language, to use the expressions 'is particular' or 'is a particular' in such a way that the proposition 'P is particular' or 'P is a particular' implies 'P characterizes one thing only'. None of the various senses in which 'is particular' can be properly used seems to me to carry with them this implication. But I think there is no doubt that Professor Stout is using them in some sense which does carry this implication; and, as I have said, I understand that we are to discuss only views which he does mean, and not views which we may think his words ought to mean.

But there is one meaning which might be attached to the expressions 'is particular' or 'is a particular', with regard to which I think it is very important to point out that Professor Stout cannot, consistently with statements of his own, be using the expressions with *that* meaning. In the formulation of our question the phrase 'particular things' is apparently used as a synonym for the phrase 'concrete things', which Professor Stout uses on pages 4 and 5;

and Professor Stout himself so uses it at the top of page 5. And I think that undoubtedly one correct usage of 'is particular' or 'is a particular' is as a synonym for 'is a particular thing' or 'is a concrete thing'. If Professor Stout were using the expressions in this sense, his statement 'Every character of a concrete thing is particular' would, of course, mean the same as 'Every character of a concrete thing is itself a concrete thing'. And it might perhaps be thought that this is what he does mean. But he certainly cannot *consistently* mean this; since on page 7 he declares that a sneeze certainly is 'particular', while he implies that nevertheless it is *not* a 'substance'—the expression 'is a substance' being one which he uses throughout from page 7 onwards as equivalent to 'is a concrete thing or individual'. He implies, therefore, that a sneeze, while it is 'particular' in the sense (whatever that may be) in which he maintains that all 'characters' of concrete things are 'particular', is *not* itself a 'concrete thing'. And in the same passage he employs a useful mark for distinguishing 'characters' from 'concrete things' or 'concrete individuals'. Nothing, he implies, can be a 'character', *unless* it is *predicable of something else*; and nothing can be a 'concrete thing' or 'concrete individual' or 'substance' *if* it is *predicable of something else*; from which it would again follow that, according to him, *no* character can be 'particular' in the sense of being a concrete thing. It seems to me that the notion of being *predicable of something else* is a clear one, and that it is undoubtedly in accordance with usage to confine the term 'character' to what is predicable of something else, and the terms 'concrete thing', 'concrete individual' and 'substance' to what is *not*. I should myself be inclined to use the term 'is a character' as *equivalent to* 'is predicable of something else'; so that not only would every 'character' be predicable of something else, but everything that is predicable of anything else would be a 'character': I fully recognize, however, that it is legitimate to use the term 'character' in a more restricted sense, so that some only of the entities which are predicable of something else would be 'characters'. But that nothing can be properly called a 'character' *unless* it is predicable of something else, I do agree with Professor Stout; and that is why, by the way, I wholly dissent from his proposition that a sneeze *is* a 'character'. I may say of a given individual A: 'It was A that sneezed that sneeze'; and here the words 'sneezed that sneeze' may, I think, express a 'character', since they may express something which is predicable of A. But that the sneeze itself is predicable of anything whatever, I wholly deny. What we mean by 'sneezed that sneeze' is *not* the same as what we mean by 'that sneeze'. The sneeze itself is, I should say, quite clearly an *event*; and every event is quite as incapable of being predicated of anything else, as is a concrete thing or concrete individual or substance. All events, including sneezes and flashes of lightning, are, I should agree with Mr Johnson, what he calls 'substantives proper'—a category which excludes their being 'characters', for the very reason that no 'substantive proper' is predicable of anything else. But though all events are 'substantives proper', it appears to me, as I gather it does to Mr Johnson, a mere misuse of language to call events, as Dr McTaggart does, 'substances'. When he asserted on page 7 that Mr Johnson says that a flash of lightning is a substance, Professor Stout must, I suppose, have been assuming that Mr Johnson would use the term 'substance' as a synonym for 'substantive proper'; whereas, while Mr Johnson does hold that a flash of lightning is *not* a 'character', he also holds that it is not a 'substance', since he recognizes a category of entities which he calls 'occurrences', which, though they share with 'substances' the characteristic that they are not predicable of anything, and are therefore not 'characters', differ from 'substances' in other respects.

To return from this digression. The only meaning which I can see Professor Stout to be attaching to the expressions 'is particular' or 'is a particular' is the meaning 'characterizes one thing only', and hence the only possible meanings of his sentence 'Every character of a concrete thing or a concrete individual is particular', which I can discuss, will be meanings obtained by understanding 'is particular' in this sense.

But there remains the question: In what sense is he using the term 'character'?

The sentence 'Every character of a concrete thing characterizes one thing only', would, I think, be naturally understood in a sense from which it would follow that, if A and B are two different concrete things, then it cannot be true, e.g. both that A is round, and that B is round; both that A is red, and that B is red, etc. This is what would be naturally implied by saying that two concrete things never have a common character. But these propositions are obviously monstrously false, and I think it is quite plain that

Professor Stout does not mean to assert that they are true. He is obviously willing to allow that, where 'A' and 'B' are names of two different concrete things, the expressions 'A is round' and 'B is round', may, nevertheless, each of them express a true proposition. But what, then, does he mean by saying that, if A and B are two different concrete things, *every* character which belongs to A belongs to A only, and every character which belongs to B, to B only?

So far as I can see, there are only two possible alternatives as to his meaning. (1) He might possibly be meaning to say that, if, where 'A' and 'B' are names of two different concrete things, the expressions 'A is round' and 'B is round' both express true propositions, the sense in which 'is round' is used in the one must be *different* from that in which it is used in the other. Or (2) he may be using the term 'character' in a quite indefensibly restricted sense; so that, while admitting that what is predicated of A in a true proposition expressed by 'A is round' may be exactly the same as what is predicated of B in a true proposition expressed by 'B is round', he would maintain that what is, in such cases, predicated of both, cannot properly be called a 'character'.

As regards (1), I think it is just possible that Professor Stout does mean to say this, because, in a former publication of his on the same subject[1] he has said something which seems to imply it. 'When I assert', he there says, 'that the sense-datum is red, I mean just that particular red with which I am immediately acquainted.' This ought to mean, I take it, that if I have two different sense-data, one of which, A, presents to me one particular shade of red, R_1, while the other, B, presents to me a different particular shade, R_2, then what I should mean by the expression 'is red', if I said of A 'A is red', would be 'A is characterized by R_1', while what I should mean by 'is red', if I said of B 'B is red', would be 'B is characterized by R_2', and that, therefore, I should be using 'is red', in the two cases, in different senses. But if Professor Stout does mean this, then I think what he means is obviously false. If I merely tell somebody that one of my sense-data is red, I am obviously *not* telling him what particular shade of red it is of. That is to say, I am *not* using 'is red' as a name for the particular shade which it, in fact, presents to me. Suppose the shade in question is R_1. I am *not*, as Professor Stout seems to imply, using 'is red' as a name for R_1. And what I am using it as a

---

[1] *Proceedings of the Aristotelian Society*, 1914–15, p. 348.

name for, is, I think, pretty obvious. I perceive with regard to R1
that it has a certain character, P, which belongs also to the shade
R2 and to an immense number of other particular shades, and
what I mean by 'is red' is simply 'has *some* character of the kind
P'. And what I am telling anybody, if I tell him, with regard to
another sense-datum, B, which presents to me the shade R2,
that it also is red, is *precisely the same thing*, namely, that B also
'has *some* character of the kind P'. It is true that how I know, in
the case supposed, that the sense-datum A has *some* character
of the kind P, and that the sense-datum B also has *some* character
of the kind P, is because I know in the case of A that it has R1,
and that R1 has the character P, and in the case of B that it has
R2, and that R2 has the character P. But is it not obvious that this
extra knowledge, which I, in fact, have with regard to A and B,
namely, that A has the shade R1, and B the shade R2, forms no
part of what I *express* by 'A is red' or by 'B is red'? The opposite
view that what I express by 'is red' in the one case is 'has R1',
and in the other 'has R2', and is therefore something different in
the two cases, can, I think, be refuted by a *reductio ad absurdum*
as follows. Suppose R1 and R2 are not only shades of red, but also
shades of scarlet. I can then truly use the words 'A and B are both
scarlet' as well as the words 'A and B are both red'. But if what I
meant by 'A is red and B is red' were 'A has R1 and B has R2',
then obviously what I shall mean by 'A is scarlet and B is scarlet'
would also be 'A has R1 and B has R2'. That is to say, the view
that what I mean by 'A is red' is something different from what
I mean by 'B is red', namely, in the one case 'A has R1' and in
the other 'A has R2', involves the absurd consequence that what
I mean by 'A is scarlet' is the *same* as what I mean by 'A is red'.
Quite obviously this consequence is absurd, and therefore the
view which entails it is false.

I doubt whether Professor Stout would really disagree with
what I have just been saying. On the contrary, my contention
that what we do mean by 'is red' is just 'has *some* character of
the kind P' is, I think, *part* (*not* the whole) of what he himself,
on page 14, is asserting to be true and taking Mr Johnson to deny,
when he says that 'colour' and 'redness' *are* 'general kinds of
quality' and are *not* 'both singular, each standing for a single
positive quality'. *Part* of what he means by this is, I think, just
that what 'A is red' stands for is merely something of the form

'A has *some* character of the kind P', and what 'A is coloured' stands for is merely something of the form 'A has *some* character of the kind Q'; though this is not the whole, since he conjoins with this contention a further view, which I think certainly false, as to the analysis of propositions of the form 'A has *some* character of the kind P'. What I want to insist on is that the view that 'A is red' is to be analysed in this way, so far from supporting, is definitely incompatible with the view that, when I truly say, of two different concrete things, A and B, both 'A is red' and 'B is red', what I express by 'is red' in the one sentence must be different from what I express by 'is red' in the other. On the contrary, the character for which I use 'is red' as a name is, in each case, precisely the same, namely, 'has *some* character of the kind P'.

It follows that the first of the two alternatives as to Professor Stout's meaning, which seemed to me to be the only possible ones, is such that, if he does mean what it would suppose him to mean, then what he means is certainly false. It is false that what we express by 'is red' is something which cannot characterize more than one concrete thing. And since what we express by 'is red' certainly is a character, in any legitimate sense of the term 'character', Professor Stout's sentence, 'Every character of a concrete thing characterizes only one thing', can only be true if he is using 'character' in some quite improperly restricted sense.

That he is doing this—that just as he means by 'is particular' something which nobody ought to mean by 'is particular', so he means by 'Every character' something which nobody ought to mean by 'Every character'—was the second alternative as to his meaning which I distinguished above. And we can now see, I think, what the unduly restricted sense in which he is using the term 'character' is. He is using it in such a sense that no *generic* character such as those which are expressed by 'is red', 'is round', 'is coloured', etc., is, in his terminology, a character at all. Of such generic characters it is perfectly obvious that they may characterize two or more concrete things; and we saw that Professor Stout does not seem really to wish to deny this. It remains that when he says 'Every character', what he really means must be 'Every *absolutely specific* character'; where by 'absolutely specific' we mean the same as 'not generic'. In other words, he is talking, quite unjustifiably, as if absolutely specific characters could alone be properly called 'characters'. And the proposition he

really wants to maintain is this: 'Every absolutely specific character, which characterizes a concrete thing or individual, characterizes one thing only.'

This, so far as I can see, is the only proposition which Professor
Stout's arguments, if sound, could have any tendency to show.
And I will try first, briefly, to explain my own attitude towards it,
and then to deal with his arguments.

That it is certainly false I see no way of proving. But the
contention that it is *true* can, I think, obviously only be justified
by the contention that it *must* be true; since it is obviously impossible to justify it by comparing every concrete thing in turn
with every other concrete thing, and seeing that every absolutely
specific character which belongs to each does in fact belong to no
other. Professor Stout, therefore, must be holding that we can see,
a priori, that an absolutely specific character, which characterizes
a concrete thing, *must* characterize one thing only, or *cannot* be a
common character. And *this* proposition, I think, I can see to be
certainly false. In the case of two sense-data, A and B, both of
which appear to me to be red, I often cannot tell that the most
specific shade of red which A presents to me is not exactly the
same as the most specific shade which B presents to me. I also
cannot tell that the most specific shade which A presents to me is
not an absolutely specific shade. And I think I *can* see quite
clearly that it is *logically possible* both that it is an absolutely
specific shade, and that it does in fact characterize both A and B.
While I allow, therefore, that it *may, as a matter of fact,* be true
that the same absolutely specific shade never does in such cases
characterize both A and B, I contend that Professor Stout cannot
possibly have any good reason for saying that it is so; and that, if
he holds that it *must* be so, he is certainly wrong.

Let us now turn to Professor Stout's arguments in favour of
his proposition, which are given on pages 7–9. With the first
argument on page 7, since it only professes to prove that *some*
absolutely specific characters of concrete things 'are particular',
we need not trouble ourselves. I have already explained that I
think it fails to prove even this, because what Professor Stout there
takes to be 'characters', namely, such entities as 'a sneeze, the
flight of a bird, the explosion of a mine', are, in my view, clearly
not 'characters' at all, but events or occurrences. But even if
Professor Stout had proved that *some* absolutely specific characters

of concrete things characterize one thing only, this would clearly by itself have no tendency to prove that the same is true of *all*.

The arguments which concern us, therefore, are only those beginning at the bottom of page 7, where Professor Stout expressly sets out to prove that '*all* qualities and relations' 'are particulars'. And, so far as I can make out, he has only two such arguments.

The first is that developed on page 8; and, so far as I can make out, the point of it is this. Professor Stout urges that, in the case of any two perceived concrete things, which I 'know or suppose' to be 'locally separate', I must also 'know or suppose' that the specific colour or shape, which the one presents to me, is also 'locally separate' from that which the other presents to me. And I suppose he infers that if the specific colour of A is 'known or supposed' to be 'locally separate' from the specific colour of B, it cannot be identical with the specific colour of B.

But this inference seems to me to be a mere mistake. I admit the premiss that if A is locally separate from B, and if A really has the colour which it presents to me, and B really has the colour which it presents to me, then the colour which A presents to me really is 'locally separate' from that which B presents to me. But I deny that, even if this is so, it follows that the colour of A is not identical with the colour of B. Professor Stout's whole point seems to me to rest on supposing that there is no distinction between the sense in which two *concrete things* can be said to be 'locally separate', and that in which two *characters* can be said to be so. Of local separation or mutual externality, in the sense in which we use this term of concrete things, it does seem to me to be self-evident (though this is sometimes disputed) that it is a relation which nothing can have to itself. In other words, I admit, as Professor Stout seems to assume, that it is impossible for one and the same concrete thing to be in two different places at the same time. But when we speak of two qualities as 'locally separate' we seem to me to be using the phrase in an entirely different sense. All that we mean, or can mean, by it, is, I think, that the first belongs to a concrete thing which is locally separate (in our first sense) from a concrete thing to which the second belongs. And with *this* sense of 'locally separate', it seems to me perfectly obvious that a quality can be 'locally separate' from itself: one and the same quality *can* be in two different places at the same time. Indeed, to deny that it can be is simply to beg the original question at issue. For if to say 'the specific colour of A is locally separate from the specific colour of B' merely *means* that the specific colour of A belongs to a concrete thing which is locally separate from a concrete thing to which the specific colour of B belongs, it follows that the specific colour of A *can* be 'locally separate' from itself, provided only it is true that the specific colour of A *can* belong to each of two concrete things.

This answer, if sound, is, so far as I can see, an absolutely complete answer to Professor Stout's first argument, and makes it unnecessary for me to examine the argument on page 8 by which he tries to show that the 'same indivisible quality cannot appear separately in different times and places', unless it really *is* locally or temporally separate. For I maintain that the same indivisible quality can really *be* locally or temporally separate; maintaining that all this means is that it can really belong to both of two concrete things or events which are, in the fundamental sense appropriate to concrete things or events, locally or temporally separate. Professor Stout must be assuming that absolutely specific characters can really be 'locally separate' in the *same* sense in which 'concrete things' are so, and 'temporally separate' in the *same* sense in which events are so; and that, as a matter of fact, in a case where A and B are two 'locally separate' coloured concrete things, the absolutely specific colour of A must always, in *that* sense, be 'locally separate' from the absolutely specific colour of B. I admit that, if this were so, it would follow that the absolutely specific colour of A cannot be identical with that of B. But I deny that any two characters can ever be 'locally separate' in the sense in which two concrete things can be, or 'temporally separate' in the sense in which two events can be.

Professor Stout's second argument is that which begins at the bottom of page 8 and is continued on page 9. And it is clear, with regard to this argument, that he starts with some premiss (1) which he expresses by the words 'A substance is nothing *apart from* its qualities'; that he infers from this premiss some proposition (2) which he expresses by the words 'to know a substance without knowing its qualities is to know nothing'; and that from (2), in its turn, he states that there follows a proposition (3) which he expresses by the words 'we cannot distinguish substances from each other without discerning a corresponding distinction between their qualities'. It is clear also that it is only by the help of

(3) that he professes, in *this* argument, to be able to reach the conclusion that every absolutely specific character of a concrete thing characterizes one thing only.

What, precisely, then, does (3) assert?

It is clear that, whatever Professor Stout may mean by '*discerning* a corresponding distinction between their qualities', he means something which we cannot do, unless there *is* 'a corresponding distinction between their qualities'. He is, therefore, here asserting at least this: that we cannot ever distinguish two concrete things unless there *is* 'a corresponding distinction between their qualities'. But what exactly does he mean by this? I take it that what he must mean is at least this: that we can never distinguish two concrete things, A and B, unless A has at least one quality which is *not* possessed by B, and B at least one quality which is *not* possessed by A. He may, of course, mean more than this: he may mean that *every* quality which is possessed by A must be a quality which is not possessed by B, and *vice versa*. But he must mean, *at least*, what I have said: that, if we can distinguish A and B, then A must have at least one quality not possessed by B, and B at least one not possessed by A.

But, then, returning to the question what he means by '*discerning* a corresponding distinction between their qualities', I think it is clear that he must at least mean this further thing by (3): namely, that we cannot ever distinguish two concrete things, A and B, unless at least one quality, which we *perceive* to belong to A, is not possessed by B, and at least one, which we *perceive* to belong to B, is not possessed by A. For you certainly cannot be said to 'discern a distinction' between two qualities, unless you perceive both of them. What I am in doubt about is whether he also means to assert or not this further thing: that we cannot distinguish between A and B, unless, with regard to at least one quality, which we *perceive* to belong to A, we *perceive* that it does not belong to B, and, with regard to at least one quality, which we *perceive* to belong to B, we *perceive* that it does not belong to A. I think very likely he does *not* mean to assert this. But it is on the question, whether he does or does not, that my attitude towards his proposition (3) depends. If he *does*, then I wish to maintain that his proposition (3) is false. If he does *not*, I only wish to maintain that it is a proposition which there is no reason whatever to believe.

First, then, I wish to maintain: That I certainly do, in some cases, distinguish between two concrete things, A and B, without *perceiving*, with regard to any *quality*, which I perceive to belong to A, that it does *not* belong to B, or *vice versa*. But I want to emphasize that it is only of *qualities*, strictly so-called, as opposed to relational properties, that I wish to maintain this. That I can ever distinguish between two concrete things, A and B, without perceiving, with regard to some *relational property*, which I perceive to belong to A, that it does not belong to B, I do *not* wish to assert. But I think it is clear that Professor Stout, if he is to prove his point, must maintain that his proposition (3) *is* true of *qualities*, strictly so-called, as opposed to relations: since his conclusion is that *every* absolutely specific character of a concrete thing, including, therefore, absolutely specific *qualities*, characterizes one thing only; and plainly this conclusion cannot be proved by any premiss which makes no assertion about *qualities*.

This being understood, I should propose to prove my proposition by reference to cases of the very kind to which Professor Stout immediately goes on to refer. He insists (and I fully agree) that there are cases in which I can distinguish between two concrete things, A and B (as, for instance, when I distinguish between two different parts of a sheet of white paper), although I cannot perceive that A is *qualitatively unlike* B in any respect whatever—either in shape, or size, or colour. But to say that I cannot perceive A to be *qualitatively unlike* B in any respect whatever is, according to me, the same thing as to say that whatever quality I take, which A appears to me to possess, I cannot perceive that just that quality does not *also* belong to B, and that whatever quality I take, which B appears to me to possess, I cannot perceive that just that quality does not *also* belong to A. And if these two propositions *are* identical, then my proposition is proved. Does Professor Stout mean to dispute that they are identical? I cannot tell. But if he does, I think it is clear that his only ground for doing so must be that he is assuming the truth of the peculiar doctrine as to the relation between a concrete thing and its qualities, which he goes on to expound on page 11. If that peculiar doctrine of his were true, it would, I think, really follow that where, in a case like that we are considering, I perceive that A is other than B, what I am doing is to perceive with regard to some quality or set of qualities P, and some *other* quality or set of qualities Q, that *the* 'complex' to which P is related in a certain way is other than *the* 'complex' to which Q is related in the same way. My perception that A is other than B would be *identical* with a perception, that *the* complex to which P has the relation in question is other than *the* complex to which Q has the same relation. I should, that is to say, be perceiving, *ex hypothesi*, that P had the relation in question to only one complex, and that Q had it also to only one complex, and that the one to which P had it was *other* than that to which Q had it; and, perceiving all this, I could hardly fail to perceive also that P had *not* got the relation in question to the complex to which Q had it, and *vice versa*; which would, *ex hypothesi*, be the same thing as perceiving that P did not belong to B, and that Q did not belong to A. If, therefore, this peculiar doctrine of Professor Stout's were true, it would, I think, really follow that I could not perceive A to be other than B, without perceiving, with regard to some quality which I perceived to belong to A, that it did *not* belong to B, and *vice versa*. But one reason why I think that that peculiar doctrine of his cannot be true, is just that it has this consequence. It seems to me quite plain (1) that I can distinguish an A from a B, where I cannot perceive A to be in any respect *qualitatively unlike* B, and (2) that this means that I can do it, without perceiving with regard to any quality, which I perceive to belong to A, that it does *not* belong to B, or *vice versa*. And, since, if Professor Stout's peculiar doctrine were true, it would follow that I couldn't, I infer that his doctrine is false.

If, on the other hand, all that Professor Stout means to assert in his proposition (3) is that I cannot distinguish A from B, unless some quality which I perceive A to possess, does not in fact belong to B, and *vice versa*, then I have to confess I see no way of proving that he is wrong. All that I then maintain is that there is no reason whatever to suppose that he is right. For, so far as I can see, the only reason for supposing so would be, if, in every such case as I have been considering, I could *perceive* that some quality, which I perceived to belong to A, did not belong to B. This, for the reasons I have given, I think I cannot do. It remains, therefore, a bare possibility that though I cannot *perceive* that any quality, which I perceive to belong to A, does not belong to B, there may nevertheless really *be* some quality, which I perceive to belong to A, and which does not belong to B.

It seems to me, finally, that Professor Stout is in any case mistaken in supposing that his proposition (3) follows either from (1) or from (2). I am perfectly willing to admit both (1) that a concrete thing *must* have some qualities; which is all that I take Professor Stout to mean by saying that it is nothing *apart from* its qualities, since he himself holds that it is certainly *other* than any one of its qualities or all of them put together. And also (2) that I never do, and even never *can*, perceive any concrete thing without its appearing to me to have some absolutely specific quality—that to say that I perceive it is the same thing as to say that there is some such quality which it appears to me to have; and I even think it quite likely that I never can perceive any concrete thing without *perceiving* it to have some absolutely specific quality. But none of these admissions seems to compel me to admit any probability whatever in favour of (3). So far as I can see, they have nothing whatever to do with (3), nor, therefore, with the question we were asked to discuss. It is true that, if we grant the premiss that I cannot perceive any concrete thing without perceiving, with regard to some absolutely specific quality, that it has that quality, it will follow that I cannot *distinguish* two concrete things, A and B, both of which I perceive, without perceiving, with regard to *some* absolutely specific quality, that A has it, and with regard to *some* absolutely specific quality, that B has it. But how can the premiss in question possibly prove any more than this? How can it prove that it is not possible that when I distinguish A from B, every absolutely specific quality which I perceive to belong to A should *also* be one which I perceive to belong to B, and *vice versa?* Our premiss only tells us that, in the case of every concrete thing which I perceive, there must be *some* absolutely specific quality which I perceive to belong to it, and cannot possibly, therefore, imply anything at all, as to whether, when I perceive *two*, it may or may not be the case that every absolutely specific quality which I perceive to belong to the one is also perceived by me to belong to the other.

My answer to our question is, then: That if (as we must do, if we are to deal with any question raised by Professor Stout) we understand the expression 'is particular' in some sense which logically implies 'characterizes one thing only', then, quite certainly, *many* characters of concrete things are *not* particular; and that there is no reason to suppose that absolutely specific characters are any exception to the rule.

As for the question whether *any* characters of concrete things do characterize one thing only, that will depend upon what is meant by 'characters'; and it seems to me possible that there may be some legitimate sense of the term 'character', such that, in that sense, *none* do—that *all* characters of concrete things are common characters. If, however, the term 'character' is used in the wide sense in which whatever is truly predicable of anything is a character of it, then, in this sense, it is quite certain that many characters of concrete things do belong, each of them, to one thing only. If we use 'character' in this sense, then, it is quite certain both that many characters of concrete things *are* common characters, and also that many are *not*. And if (as Professor Stout must be doing) we use the phrase 'is a universal' in a sense which logically implies 'is a common character', it follows, of course, that, with the same wide sense of 'character', we shall have to say that many characters of concrete things are universals, and many are not. It is, however, I think, worth emphasizing that there is one well-established usage of the expression 'is a universal', which is such that, in that sense, every character without exception—characters which belong to only one thing, just as much as common characters—is quite certainly a universal: that sense, namely, in which 'is a universal' is simply logically equivalent to 'is either predicable of something or is a relation'.

II

A DEFENCE OF COMMON SENSE

In what follows I have merely tried to state, one by one, some of the most important points in which my philosophical position differs from positions which have been taken up by *some* other philosophers. It may be that the points which I have had room to mention are not really the most important, and possibly some of them may be points as to which no philosopher has ever really differed from me. But, to the best of my belief, each is a point as to which many have really differed; although (in most cases, at all events) each is also a point as to which many have agreed with me.

I. The first point is a point which embraces a great many other points. And it is one which I cannot state as clearly as I wish to state it, except at some length. The method I am going to use for stating it is this. I am going to begin by enunciating, under the heading (1), a whole long list of propositions, which may seem, at first sight, such obvious truisms as not to be worth stating: they are, in fact, a set of propositions, every one of which (in my own opinion) I *know*, with certainty, to be true. I shall, next, under the heading (2), state a single proposition which makes an assertion about a whole set of *classes* of propositions—each class being defined, as the class consisting of all propositions which resemble *one* of the propositions in (1) in a certain respect. (2), therefore, is a proposition which could not be stated, until the list of propositions in (1), or some similar list, had already been given. (2) is itself a proposition which may seem such an obvious truism as not to be worth stating: and it is also a proposition which (in my own opinion) I *know*, with certainty, to be true. But, nevertheless, it is, to the best of my belief, a proposition with regard to which many philosophers have, for different reasons, differed from me; even if they have not directly denied (2) itself, they have held views incompatible with it. My first point, then, may be said to be that (2), together with all its implications, some of which I shall expressly mention, is true.

(1) I begin, then, with my list of truisms, every one of which

(in my own opinion) I *know*, with certainty, to be true. The propositions to be included in this list are the following:

There exists at present a living human body, which is *my* body. This body was born at a certain time in the past, and has existed continuously ever since, though not without undergoing changes; it was, for instance, much smaller when it was born, and for some time afterwards, than it is now. Ever since it was born, it has been either in contact with or not far from the surface of the earth; and, at every moment since it was born, there have also existed many other things, having shape and size in three dimensions (in the same familiar sense in which it has), from which it has been *at various distances* (in the familiar sense in which it is now at a distance both from that mantelpiece and from that bookcase, and at a greater distance from the bookcase than it is from the mantelpiece); also there have (very often, at all events) existed some other things of this kind with which it was *in contact* (in the familiar sense in which it is now in contact with the pen I am holding in my right hand and with some of the clothes I am wearing). Among the things which have, in this sense, formed part of its environment (i.e. have been either in contact with it, or at *some* distance from it, however *great*) there have, at every moment since its birth, been large numbers of other living human bodies, each of which has, like it, (a) at some time been born, (b) continued to exist from some time after birth, (c) been, at every moment of its life after birth, either in contact with or not far from the surface of the earth; and many of these bodies have already died and ceased to exist. But the earth had existed also for many years before my body was born; and for many of these years, also, large numbers of human bodies had, at every moment, been alive upon it; and many of these bodies had died and ceased to exist before it was born. Finally (to come to a different class of propositions), I am a human being, and I have, at different times since my body was born, had many different experiences, of each of many different kinds: e.g. I have often perceived both my own body and other things which formed part of its environment, including other human bodies; I have not only perceived things of this kind, but have also observed facts about them, such as, for instance, the fact which I am now observing, that that mantelpiece is at present nearer to my body than that bookcase; I have been aware of other facts, which I was not at the time observing, such as, for instance, the fact, of which I am now aware, that my body existed yesterday and was then also for some time nearer to that mantelpiece than to that bookcase; I have had expectations with regard to the future, and many beliefs of other kinds, both true and false; I have thought of imaginary things and persons and incidents, in the reality of which I did not believe; I have had dreams; and I have had feelings of many different kinds. And, just as my body has been the body of a human being, namely myself, who has, during his lifetime, had many experiences of each of these (and other) different kinds; so, in the case of very many of the other human bodies which have lived upon the earth, each has been the body of a different human being, who has, during the lifetime of that body, had many different experiences of each of these (and other) different kinds.

(2) I now come to the single truism which, as will be seen, could not be stated except by reference to the whole list of truisms, just given in (1). This truism also (in my own opinion) I *know*, with certainty, to be true; and it is as follows:

In the case of *very many* (I do not say *all*) of the human beings belonging to the class (which includes myself) defined in the following way, i.e. as human beings who have had human bodies, that were born and lived for some time upon the earth, and who have, during the lifetime of those bodies, had many different experiences of each of the kinds mentioned in (1), it is true that each has frequently, during the life of his body, known, with regard to *him*self or *his* body, and with regard to some time earlier than any of the times at which I wrote down the propositions in (1), a proposition *corresponding* to each of the propositions in (1), in the sense that it asserts with regard to *him*self or *his* body and the earlier time in question (namely, in each case, the time at which he knew it), just what the corresponding proposition in (1) asserts with regard to *me* or *my* body and the time at which I wrote that proposition down.

In other words what (2) asserts is only (what seems an obvious enough truism) that each of *us* (meaning by 'us', very many human beings of the class defined) has frequently *known*, with regard to *him*self or *his* body and the time at which he knew it, everything which, in writing down my list of propositions in (1), I was claiming to know about *my*self or *my* body and the time at which I wrote that proposition down, i.e. just as *I* knew (when I wrote it down) 'There exists at present a living human body which is my body', so each of us has frequently known with regard to himself and some other time the different but corresponding proposition, which *he* could *then* have properly expressed by, 'There exists *at present* a human body which is *my* body'; just as *I* know 'Many human bodies other than mine have before now lived on the earth', so each of us has frequently known the different but corresponding proposition 'Many human bodies other than *mine* have before *now* lived on the earth'; just as *I* know 'Many human beings other than myself have before now perceived, and dreamed, and felt', so each of *us* has frequently known the different but corresponding proposition 'Many human beings other than *myself* have before *now* perceived, and dreamed, and felt'; and so on, in the case of *each* of the propositions enumerated in (1).

I hope there is no difficulty in understanding, so far, what this proposition (2) asserts. I have tried to make clear by examples what I mean by 'propositions *corresponding* to each of the propositions in (1)'. And what (2) asserts is merely that each of us has frequently known to be true a proposition *corresponding* (in that sense) to each of the propositions in (1)—a *different* corresponding proposition, of course, at each of the times at which he knew such a proposition to be true.

But there remain two points, which, in view of the way in which some philosophers have used the English language, ought, I think, to be expressly mentioned, if I am to make quite clear exactly how much I am asserting in asserting (2).

The first point is this. Some philosophers seem to have thought it legitimate to use the word 'true' in such a sense that a proposition which is partially false may nevertheless also be true; and some of these, therefore, would perhaps *say* that propositions like those enumerated in (1) are, in their view, true, when all the time they believe that every such proposition is partially false. I wish, therefore, to make it quite plain that I am not using 'true' in any such sense. I am using it in such a sense (and I think this is the ordinary usage) that if a proposition is partially false, it follows that it is *not* true, though, of course, it may be *partially* true. I am maintaining, in short, that all the propositions in (1), and also many propositions corresponding to each of these, are *wholly* true; I am asserting this in asserting (2). And hence any philosopher, who does in fact believe, with regard to any or all of these classes of propositions, that every proposition of the class in question is partially false, is, in fact, disagreeing with me and holding a view incompatible with (2), even though he may think himself justified in *saying* that he believes some propositions belonging to all of these classes to be 'true'.

And the second point is this. Some philosophers seem to have thought it legitimate to use such expressions as, e.g. 'The earth has existed for many years past', as if they expressed something which they really believed, when in fact they believe that every proposition, which such an expression would *ordinarily* be understood to express, is, at least partially, false; and all they really believe is that there is some *other* set of propositions, related in a certain way to those which such expressions do actually express, which, unlike these, really are true. That is to say, they use the expression 'The earth has existed for many years past' to express, not what it would ordinarily be understood to express, but the proposition that some proposition, related to this in a certain way, is true; when all the time they believe that the proposition, which this expression would ordinarily be understood to express, is, at least partially, false. I wish, therefore, to make it quite plain that I was not using the expressions I used in (1) in any such subtle sense. I meant by each of them precisely what every reader, in reading them, will have understood me to mean. And any philosopher, therefore, who holds that any of these expressions, if understood in this popular manner, expresses a proposition which embodies some popular error, is disagreeing with me and holding a view incompatible with (2), even though he may hold that there is some *other*, true, proposition which the expression in question might be legitimately used to express.

In what I have just said, I have assumed that there is some meaning which is *the* ordinary or popular meaning of such expressions as 'The earth has existed for many years past'. And this, I am afraid, is an assumption which some philosophers are capable of disputing. They seem to think that the question 'Do you believe that the earth has existed for many years past?' is not a plain question, such as should be met either by a plain 'Yes' or 'No', or by a plain 'I can't make up my mind', but is the sort of question which can be properly met by: 'It all depends on what you mean by "the earth" and "exists" and "years": if you mean so and so, and so and so, and so and so, then I do; but if you mean so and so, and so and so, and so and so, or so and so, and so and so, and so and so, or so and so, and so and so, and so and so, then I don't, or at least I think it is extremely doubtful.' It seems to me that such a view is as profoundly mistaken as any view can be. Such an expression as 'The earth has existed for many years past' is the very type of an unambiguous expression, the meaning of which we all understand. Anyone who takes a contrary view must, I suppose, be confusing the question whether we understand its meaning (which we all certainly do) with the entirely different question whether we *know what it means*, in the sense that we are able to *give a correct analysis* of its meaning. The question what is the correct analysis of *the* proposition meant *on any occasion* (for, of course, as I insisted in defining (2), a different proposition is meant at every different time at which the expression is used) by 'The earth has existed for many years past' is, it seems to me, a profoundly difficult question, and one to which, as I shall presently urge, no one knows the answer. But to hold that we do not know what, in certain respects, is the analysis of what we understand by such an expression, is an entirely different thing from holding that we do not understand the expression. It is obvious that we cannot even raise the question how what we do understand by it is to be analysed, unless we do understand it. So soon, therefore, as we know that a person who uses such an expression is using it in its ordinary sense, we understand his meaning. So that in explaining that I was using the expressions used in (1) in their ordinary sense (those of them which have an ordinary sense, which is not the case with quite all of them), I have done all that is required to make my meaning clear.

But now, assuming that the expressions which I have used to express (2) are understood, I think, as I have said, that many philosophers have really held views incompatible with (2). And the philosophers who have done so may, I think, be divided into two main groups. A. What (2) asserts is, with regard to a whole set of *classes* of propositions, that we have, each of us, frequently *known* to be true propositions belonging to *each* of these classes. And one way of holding a view incompatible with this proposition is, of course, to hold, with regard to one or more of the classes in question, that *no* propositions of that class *are* true—that all of them are, at least partially, false; since if, in the case of any one of these classes, *no* propositions of that class *are* true, it is obvious that nobody can have *known* any propositions of that class to be true, and therefore that *we* cannot have known to be true propositions belonging to *each* of these classes. And my first group of philosophers consists of philosophers who have held views incompatible with (2) for this reason. They have held, with regard to one or more of the classes in question, simply that no propositions of that class *are* true. Some of them have held this with regard to *all* the classes in question; some only with regard to *some* of them. But, of course, whichever of these two views they have held, they have been holding a view inconsistent with (2). B. Some philosophers, on the other hand, have not ventured to assert, with regard to *any* of the classes in (2), that no propositions of that class *are* true, but what they have asserted is that, in the case of some of these classes, no human being has ever *known*, with certainty, that any propositions of the class in question are true. That is to say, they differ profoundly from philosophers of group A, in that they hold that propositions of *all* these classes *may* be true; but nevertheless they hold a view incompatible with (2) since they hold, with regard to some of these classes, that none of us has ever *known* a proposition of the class in question to be true.

A. I said that some philosophers, belonging to this group, have held that no propositions belonging to *any* of the classes in (2) are wholly true, while others have only held this with regard to *some* of the classes in (2). And I think the chief division of this kind has been the following. Some of the propositions in (1) (and, therefore, of course, all propositions belonging to the corresponding classes in (2)) are propositions which cannot be true, unless some *material things* have existed and have stood *in spatial relations* to one another: that is to say, they are propositions which, *in a certain sense*, imply *the reality of material things*, and *the reality of Space*. E.g. the proposition that my body has existed for many years past, and has, at every moment during that time been either in contact with or not far from the earth, is a proposition which implies both the *reality of material things* (provided you use 'material things' in such a sense that to deny the reality of material things implies that no proposition which asserts that human bodies have existed, or that the earth has existed, is wholly true) and also the *reality of Space* (provided, again, that you use 'Space' in such a sense that to deny the reality of Space implies that no proposition which asserts that anything has ever been in contact with or at a distance from another, in the familiar senses pointed out in (1), is wholly true). But others among the propositions in (1) (and, therefore, propositions belonging to the corresponding classes in (2)), do not (at least obviously) imply either the reality of material things or the reality of Space: e.g. the propositions that I have often had dreams, and have had many different feelings at different times. It is true that propositions of this second class do imply one thing which is also implied by all propositions of the first, namely that (*in a certain sense*) *Time is real*, and imply also one thing not implied by propositions of the first class, namely that (*in a certain sense*) *at least one Self is real*. But I think there are some philosophers, who, while denying that (in the senses in question) either material things or Space are real, have been willing to admit that Selves and Time are real, in the sense required. Other philosophers, on the other hand, have used the expression 'Time is not real', to express some view that they held; and some, at least, of these have, I think, meant by this expression something which is incompatible with the truth of *any* of the propositions in (1)— they have meant, namely, that *every* proposition of the sort that is expressed by the use of 'now' or 'at present', e.g. 'I am now both seeing and hearing' or 'There exists at present a living human body', or by the use of a *past* tense, e.g. 'I *have* had many experiences in the past', or 'The earth *has* existed for many years', are, at least partially, false.

All the four expressions I have just introduced, namely, 'Material things are not real', 'Space is not real', 'Time is not real', 'The Self is not real', are, I think, unlike the expressions I used in (1), really ambiguous. And it may be that, in the case of each of them, some philosopher has used the expression in question to express some view he held which was not incompatible with (2). With such philosophers, if there are any, I am not, of course, at present concerned. But it seems to me that the most natural and proper usage of each of these expressions is a usage in which it *does* express a view incompatible with (2); and, in the case of each of them, some philosophers have, I think, really used the expression in question to express such a view. All such philosophers have, therefore, been holding a view incompatible with (2).

All such views, whether incompatible with *all* of the propositions in (1), or only with *some* of them, seem to me to be quite certainly false; and I think the following points are specially deserving of notice with regard to them:

(*a*) If *any* of the classes of propositions in (2) is such that no proposition of that class is true, then no philosopher has ever existed, and therefore none can ever have held with regard to any such class, that no proposition belonging to it is true. In other words, the proposition that some propositions belonging to each of these classes are true is a proposition which has the peculiarity, that, if any philosopher has ever denied it, it follows from the fact that he has denied it, that he must have been wrong in denying it. For when I speak of 'philosophers' I mean, of course (as we all do), exclusively philosophers who have been human beings, with human bodies that have lived upon the earth, and who have at different times had many different experiences. If, therefore, there have been any philosophers, there have been human beings of this class; and if there have been human beings of this class, all the rest of what is asserted in (1) is certainly true too. Any view, therefore, incompatible with the proposition that many propositions corresponding to each of the propositions in (1) are true, can only be true, on the hypothesis that no philosopher has ever held any such view. It follows, therefore, that, in considering whether this proposition is true, I cannot consistently regard the fact that many philosophers, whom I respect, have, to the best of my belief, held views incompatible with it, as having any weight at all against it. Since, if I know that they have held such views, I am, *ipso facto*, knowing that they were mistaken; and, if I have no reason to believe that the proposition in question is true, I have still less reason to believe that they have held views incompatible with it; since I am more certain that they have existed and held *some* views, i.e. that the proposition in question is true, than that they have held any views incompatible with it.

(*b*) It is, of course, the case that all philosophers who have held such views have repeatedly, even in their philosophical works, expressed other views inconsistent with them: i.e. no philosopher has ever been able to hold such views consistently. One way in which they have betrayed this inconsistency, is by alluding to the existence of other philosophers. Another way is by alluding to the existence of the human race, and in particular by using 'we' in the sense in which I have already constantly used it, in which any philosopher who asserts that 'we' do so and so, e.g. that '*we* sometimes believe propositions that are not true', is asserting not only that he himself has done the thing in question, but that *very many other human beings, who have had bodies and lived upon the earth*, have done the same. The fact is, of course, that all philosophers have belonged to the class of human beings which exists only if (2) be true: that is to say, to the class of human beings who have frequently *known* propositions corresponding to each of the propositions in (1). In holding views incompatible with the proposition that propositions of all these classes are true, they have, therefore, been holding views inconsistent with propositions which they themselves *knew* to be true; and it was, therefore, only to be expected that they should sometimes betray their knowledge of such propositions. The strange thing is that philosophers should have been able to hold sincerely, as part of their philosophical creed, propositions inconsistent with what they themselves *knew* to be true; and yet, so far as I can make out, this has really frequently happened. My position, therefore, on this first point, differs from that of philosophers belonging to this group A, not in that I hold anything which they don't hold, but only in that I don't hold, as part of my philosophical creed, things which they do hold as part of theirs—that is to say, propositions inconsistent with some which they and I both hold in common. But this difference seems to me to be an important one.

(*c*) Some of these philosophers have brought forward, in favour of their position, arguments designed to show, in the case of some or all of the propositions in (1), that no propositions of that type can possibly be wholly true, because every such proposition entails both of two incompatible propositions. And I admit, of course, that if any of the propositions in (1) did entail both of two incompatible propositions it could not be true. But it seems to me I have an absolutely conclusive argument to show that none of them does entail both of two incompatible propositions. Namely this: All of the propositions in (1) are true; no true proposition entails both of two incompatible propositions; therefore, none of the propositions in (1) entails both of two incompatible propositions.

B*

(d) Although, as I have urged, no philosopher who has held with regard to any of these types of proposition that no propositions of that type are true, has failed to hold also other views inconsistent with his view in this respect, yet I do not think that the view, with regard to any or all of these types, that no proposition belonging to them is true, is *in itself* a self-contradictory view, i.e. entails both of two incompatible propositions. On the contrary, it seems to me quite clear that it *might* have been the case that Time was not real, material things not real, Space not real, selves not real. And in favour of my view that none of these things, which might have been the case, *is* in fact the case, I have, I think, no better argument than simply this— namely, that all the propositions in (1) are, in fact, true.

B. This view, which is usually considered a much more modest view than A, has, I think, the defect that, unlike A, it really is self-contradictory, i.e. entails both of two mutually incompatible propositions.

Most philosophers who have held this view, have held, I think, that though each of us knows propositions corresponding to *some* of the propositions in (1), namely to those which merely assert that *I* myself have had in the past experiences of certain kinds at many different times, yet none of us knows *for certain* any propositions either of the type (a) which assert the existence of *material things* or of the type (b) which assert the existence of *other* selves, beside myself, and that *they* also have had experiences. They admit that we do in fact *believe* propositions of both these types, and that they *may* be true: some would even say that we know them to be highly probable; but they deny that we ever know them, *for certain*, to be true. Some of them have spoken of such beliefs as 'beliefs of Common Sense', expressing thereby their conviction that beliefs of this kind are very commonly entertained by mankind: but they are convinced that these things are, in all cases, only *believed*, not known for certain; and some have expressed this by saying that they are matters of Faith, not of Knowledge.

Now the remarkable thing which those who take this view have not, I think, in general duly appreciated, is that, in each case, the philosopher who takes it is making an assertion about 'us'—that is to say, not merely about himself, but about *many other human beings as well*. When he says 'No human being has ever *known* of the existence of other human beings', he is saying: 'There have been many other human beings beside myself, and none of them (including myself) has ever known of the existence of other human beings.' If he says: 'These beliefs are beliefs of Common Sense, but they are not matters of *knowledge*', he is saying: 'There have been many other human beings, beside myself, who have shared these beliefs, but neither I nor any of the rest has ever known them to be true.' In other words, he asserts with confidence that these beliefs *are* beliefs of Common Sense, and seems often to fail to notice that, *if* they are, they must be true; since the proposition that they are beliefs of Common Sense is one which logically entails propositions both of type (*a*) and of type (*b*); it logically entails the proposition that many human beings, beside the philosopher himself, have had human bodies, which lived upon the earth, and have had various experiences, including beliefs of this kind. This is why this position, as contrasted with positions of group A, seems to me to be self-contradictory. Its difference from A consists in the fact that it is making a proposition about *human knowledge* in general, and therefore is actually asserting the existence of many human beings, whereas philosophers of group A in stating their position are not doing this: they are only contradicting *other* things which they hold. It is true that a philosopher who says 'There have existed many human beings beside myself, and none of us has ever known of the existence of any human beings beside himself', is only contradicting himself if what he holds is 'There have *certainly* existed many human beings beside myself' or, in other words, '*I* know that there have existed other human beings beside myself'. But this, it seems to me, is what such philosophers have in fact been generally doing. They seem to me constantly to betray the fact that they regard the proposition that those beliefs *are* beliefs of Common Sense, or the proposition that they themselves are not the only members of the human race, as not merely true, but *certainly* true; and *certainly* true it cannot be, unless one member, at least, of the human race, namely themselves, has *known* the very things which that member is declaring that no human being has ever known.

Nevertheless, my position that I *know*, with certainty, to be true all of the propositions in (1), is certainly not a position, the denial of which entails both of two incompatible propositions.

If I do *know* all these propositions to be true, then, I think, it is quite certain that other human beings also have known corresponding propositions: that is to say (2) also *is* true, and *I* know it to be true. But do I really *know* all the propositions in (1) to be true? Isn't it possible that I merely believe them? Or know them to be highly probable? In answer to this question, I think I have nothing better to say than that it seems to me that I *do* know them, with certainty. It is, indeed, obvious that, in the case of most of them, I do not know them *directly*: that is to say, I only know them because, in the past, I have known to be true *other* propositions which were evidence for them. If, for instance, I do know that the earth had existed for many years before I was born, I certainly only know this because I have known other things in the past which were evidence for it. And I certainly do not know exactly what the evidence was. Yet all this seems to me to be no good reason for doubting that I do know it. We are all, I think, in this strange position that we do *know* many things, with regard to which we *know* further that we must have had evidence for them, and yet we do not know *how* we know them, i.e. we do not know what the evidence was. If there is any 'we', and if we know that there is, this must be so: for that there is a 'we' is one of the things in question. And that I do know that there is a 'we', that is to say, that many other human beings, with human bodies, have lived upon the earth, it seems to me that I do know, for certain.

If this first point in my philosophical position, namely my belief in (2), is to be given any name, which has actually been used by philosophers in classifying the positions of other philosophers, it would have, I think, to be expressed by saying that I am one of those philosophers who have held that the 'Common Sense view of the world' is, in certain fundamental features, *wholly* true. But it must be remembered that, according to me, *all* philosophers, without exception, have agreed with me in holding this: and that the real difference, which is commonly expressed in this way, is only a difference between those philosophers, who have *also* held views inconsistent with these features in 'the Common Sense view of the world', and those who have not.

The features in question (namely, propositions of any of the classes defined in defining (2)) are all of them features, which have this peculiar property—namely, that *if we know that they are features in the 'Common Sense view of the world', it follows that they are true*: it is self-contradictory to maintain that *we* know them to be features in the Common Sense view, and that yet they are not true; since to say that *we* know this, is to say that they are true. And many of them also have the further peculiar property that, *if they are features in the Common Sense view of the world (whether 'we' know this or not), it follows that they are true*, since to say that there is a 'Common Sense view of the world', is to say that they are true. The phrases 'Common Sense view of the world' or 'Common Sense beliefs' (as used by philosophers) are, of course, extraordinarily vague; and, for all I know, there may be many propositions which may be properly called features in 'the Common Sense view of the world' or 'Common Sense beliefs', which are not true, and which deserve to be mentioned with the contempt with which some philosophers speak of 'Common Sense beliefs'. But to speak with contempt of those 'Common Sense beliefs' which I have mentioned is quite certainly the height of absurdity. And there are, of course, enormous numbers of other features in 'the Common Sense view of the world' which, if these are true, are quite certainly true too: e.g. that there have lived upon the surface of the earth not only human beings, but also many different species of plants and animals, etc. etc.

II. What seems to me the next in importance of the points in which my philosophical position differs from positions held by *some* other philosophers, is one which I will express in the following way. I hold, namely, that there is no good reason to suppose either (A) that *every* physical fact is *logically* dependent upon some mental fact or (B) that *every* physical fact is *causally* dependent upon some mental fact. In saying this, I am not, of course, saying that there *are* any physical facts which are wholly independent (i.e. both logically and causally) of mental facts: I do, in fact, believe that there are; but that is not what I am asserting. I am only asserting that there is *no good reason* to suppose the contrary; by which I mean, of course, that none of the human beings, who have had human bodies that lived upon the earth, have, during the lifetime of their bodies, had any good reason to suppose the contrary. Many philosophers have, I think, not only believed either that *every* physical fact is *logically* dependent upon some mental fact ('physical fact' and 'mental fact' being understood in the sense in which I am using these terms) or that *every* physical fact is *causally* dependent upon some mental fact, or both, but also that they themselves had good reason for these beliefs. In this respect, therefore, I differ from them.

In the case of the term 'physical fact', I can only explain how I am using it by giving examples. I mean by 'physical facts', facts *like* the following: 'That mantelpiece is at present nearer to this body than that bookcase is', 'The earth has existed for many years past', 'The moon has at every moment for many years past been nearer to the earth than to the sun', 'That mantelpiece is of a light colour'. But, when I say 'facts *like* these', I mean, of course, facts like them *in a certain respect*; and what this respect is I cannot define. The term 'physical fact' is, however, in common use; and I think that I am using it in its ordinary sense. Moreover, there is no need for a definition to make my point clear; since among the examples I have given there are some with regard to which I hold that there is no reason to suppose *them* (i.e. these particular physical facts) either logically or causally dependent upon any mental fact.

'Mental fact', on the other hand, is a much more unusual expression, and I am using it in a specially limited sense, which, though I think it is a natural one, does need to be explained. There may be many other senses in which the term can be properly used, but I am only concerned with this one; and hence it is essential that I should explain what it is.

There may, possibly, I hold, be 'mental facts' of three different kinds. It is only with regard to the first kind that I am sure that there are facts of that kind; but if there were any facts of either of the other two kinds, they would be 'mental facts' in my limited sense, and therefore I must explain what is meant by the hypothesis that there are facts of those two kinds.

(*a*) My first kind is this. I am conscious now; and also I am seeing something now. These two facts are both of them mental facts of my first kind; and my first kind consists exclusively of facts which resemble one or other of the two *in a certain respect*.

(α) The fact that I am conscious now is obviously, in a certain sense, a fact, with regard to a particular individual and a particular time, to the effect that that individual is conscious at that time. And every fact which resembles this one in that respect is to be included in my first kind of mental fact. Thus the fact that I was also conscious at many different times yesterday is not itself a fact of this kind: but it entails that there *are* (or, as we should commonly say, because the times in question are past times, 'were') many other facts of this kind, namely each of the facts, which, at each of the times in question, I could have properly expressed by 'I am conscious *now*'. *Any* fact which is, in this sense, a fact with regard to an individual and a time (whether the individual be myself or another, and whether the time be past or present), to the effect that that individual *is* conscious at that time, is to be included in my first kind of mental fact: and I call such facts, facts of class (α).

(β) The second example I gave, namely the fact that I am seeing something now, is obviously related to the fact that I am conscious now in a peculiar manner. It not only *entails* the fact that I am conscious now (for from the fact that I am seeing something it *follows* that I am conscious: I *could* not have been seeing anything, unless I had been conscious, though I might quite well have been conscious without seeing anything) but it also is a fact, with regard to a *specific way* (or mode) of being conscious, to the effect that I am conscious in that way: in the same sense in which the proposition (with regard to any particular thing) 'This is red' both entails the proposition (with regard to the same thing) 'This is coloured', and is also a proposition, with regard to a *specific way* of being coloured, to the effect that that thing is coloured in that way. And any fact which is related in this peculiar manner to any fact of class (α), is also to be included in my first kind of mental fact, and is to be called a fact of class (β). Thus the fact that I am hearing now is, like the fact that I am seeing now, a fact of class (β); and so is any fact, with regard to myself and a past time, which could at that time have been properly expressed by 'I am dreaming now', 'I am imagining now', 'I am at present aware of the fact that . . .', etc. etc. In short, any fact, which is a fact with regard to a particular individual (myself or another), a particular time (past or present), and *any particular kind of experience*, to the effect that that individual is having at that time an experience of that particular kind, is a fact of class (β): and only such facts are facts of class (β).

My first kind of mental facts consists exclusively of facts of classes (α) and (β), and consists of *all* facts of either of these kinds.

(*b*) That there are many facts of classes (α) and (β) seems to me perfectly certain. But many philosophers seem to me to have held a certain view with regard to the *analysis* of facts of class (α), which is such that, if it were true, there would be facts of another kind, which I should wish also to call 'mental facts'. I don't feel at all sure that this analysis is true; but it seems to me that it *may* be true; and since we can understand what is meant by the supposition that it is true, we can also understand what is meant by the supposition that there are 'mental facts' of this second kind.

Many philosophers have, I think, held the following view as to the analysis of what each of us knows, when he knows (at any time) 'I am conscious now'. They have held, namely, that there is a certain intrinsic property (with which we are all of us familiar and which might be called that of 'being an experience') which is such that, at any time at which any man knows 'I am conscious now', he is knowing, with regard to that property and himself and the time in question, 'There is occurring now an event which has this property (i.e. "is an experience") and which is an experience of *mine*', and such that this fact is what he expresses by 'I am conscious now'. And if this view is true, there must be many facts of each of three kinds, each of which I should wish to call 'mental facts'; viz. (1) facts with regard to some event, which has this supposed intrinsic property, and to some time, to the effect that that event is occurring at that time, (2) facts with regard to this supposed intrinsic property and some time, to the effect that *some* event which has that property is occurring at that time, and (3) facts with regard to some property, which is a *specific way* of having the supposed intrinsic property (in the sense above explained in which 'being red' is a specific way of 'being coloured') and some time, to the effect that some event which has that specific property is occurring at that time. Of course, there not only are not, but *cannot* be, facts of any of these kinds, unless there is an intrinsic property related to what each of us (on any occasion) expresses by 'I am conscious now', in the manner defined above; and I feel very doubtful whether there is any such property; in other words, although I know for certain both that I have had many experiences, and that I have had experiences of many different kinds, I feel very doubtful whether to say the first is the same thing as to say that there have been many events, each of which was an experience and an experience of mine, and whether to say the second is the same thing as to say that there have been many events, each of which was an experience of mine, and each of which also had a different property, which was a specific way of being an experience. The proposition that I have had experiences does not necessarily entail the proposition that there have been any events which were experiences; and I cannot satisfy myself that I am acquainted with any events of the supposed kind. But yet it seems to me possible that the proposed analysis of 'I am conscious now' is correct: that I am really acquainted with events of the supposed kind, though I cannot see that I am. And *if* I am, then I should wish to call the three kinds of facts defined above 'mental facts'. Of course, if there are 'experiences' in the sense defined, it would be possible (as many have held) that there *can* be no experiences which are not *some individual's* experiences; and in that case any fact of any of these three kinds would be logically dependent on, though not necessarily identical with, some fact of class (α) or class (β). But it seems to me also a possibility that, if there are 'experiences', there might be experiences which did not belong to any individual; and, in that case, there would be 'mental facts' which were neither identical with nor logically dependent on any fact of class (α) or class (β).

(*c*) Finally some philosophers have, so far as I can make out, held that there are or may be facts which are facts with regard to some individual, to the effect that he is conscious, or is conscious in some specific way, but which differ from facts of classes (α) and (β), in the important respect that they are not facts *with regard to any time*: they have conceived the possibility that there may be one or more individuals, who are *timelessly* conscious, and timelessly conscious in specific modes. And others, again, have, I think, conceived the hypothesis that the intrinsic property defined in (*b*) may be one which does not belong only to *events*, but may also belong to one or more wholes, which do *not* occur at any time: in other words, that there may be one or more *timeless* experiences, which might or might not be the experiences of some individual. It seems to me very doubtful whether any of these hypotheses are even possibly true; but I cannot see for certain that they are not possible: and, if they are possible, then I should wish to give the name 'mental fact' to any fact (if there were any) of any of the five following kinds, viz. (1) to any fact which is the fact, with regard to any individual, that he is *timelessly* conscious, (2) to any fact which is the fact, with regard to any

individual, that he is *timelessly* conscious in any specific way,
(3) to any fact which is the fact with regard to a *timeless* experience
that it exists, (4) to any fact which is the fact with regard to the
supposed intrinsic property 'being an experience', that something
timelessly exists which has that property, and (5) to any fact
which is the fact, with regard to any property, which is a specific
mode of this supposed intrinsic property, that something timelessly
exists which has that property.

I have, then, defined three different kinds of facts, each of
which is such that, if there *were* any facts of that kind (as there
certainly *are*, in the case of the first kind), the facts in question
would be 'mental facts' in my sense; and to complete the definition
of the limited sense in which I am using 'mental facts', I have
only to add that I wish also to apply the name to one *fourth* class
of facts: namely to any fact, which is the fact, with regard to any
of these three kinds of facts, or any kinds included in them,
that there are facts of the kind in question; i.e. not only will each
individual fact of class (α) be, in my sense, a 'mental fact', but
also the general fact 'that there are facts of class (α)', will itself be a
'mental fact'; and similarly in all other cases: e.g. not only will the
fact that I am now perceiving (which is a fact of class(β)) be a
'mental fact', but also the general fact that *there are* facts, with
regard to individuals and times, to the effect that the individual in
question is perceiving at the time in question, will be a 'mental fact'.

A. Understanding 'physical fact' and 'mental fact' in the senses
just explained, I hold, then, that there is no good reason to suppose
that *every* physical fact is *logically* dependent upon some mental
fact. And I use the phrase, with regard to two facts, F_1 and F_2,
'F_1 is *logically dependent* on F_2', wherever and only where F_1 *entails*
F_2, either in the sense in which the proposition 'I am seeing now'
entails the proposition 'I am conscious now', or the proposition
(with regard to any particular thing) 'This is red' entails the
proposition (with regard to the same thing) 'This is coloured',
or else in the more strictly logical sense in which (for instance)
the conjunctive proposition 'All men are mortal, and Mr Baldwin
is a man' entails the proposition 'Mr Baldwin is mortal'. To say,
then, of two facts, F_1 and F_2, that F_1 is *not* logically dependent
upon F_2, is only to say that F_1 *might* have been a fact, even if there
had been no such fact as F_2; or that the conjunctive proposition
'F_1 is a fact, but there is no such fact as F_2' is a proposition which

is not self-contradictory, i.e. does not entail both of two mutually incompatible propositions.

I hold, then, that, in the case of *some* physical facts, there is no good reason to suppose that there is some mental fact, such that the physical fact in question could not have been a fact unless the mental fact in question had also been one. And my position is perfectly definite, since I hold that this is the case with all the four physical facts, which I have given as examples of physical facts. For example, there is no good reason to suppose that there is any mental fact whatever, such that the fact that that mantel-piece is at present nearer to my body than that bookcase could not have been a fact, unless the mental fact in question had also been a fact; and, similarly, in all the other three cases.

In holding this I am certainly differing from some philosophers. I am, for instance, differing from Berkeley, who held that that mantelpiece, that bookcase, and my body are, all of them, either 'ideas' or 'constituted by ideas', and that no 'idea' can possibly exist without being perceived. He held, that is, that this physical fact is logically dependent upon a mental fact of my fourth class: namely a fact which is the fact that there is at least one fact, which is a fact with regard to an individual and the present time, to the effect that that individual is now perceiving something. He does not say that this physical fact is logically dependent upon any fact which is a fact of any of my first three classes, e.g. on any fact which is the fact, with regard to a particular individual and the present time, that *that* individual is now perceiving something: what he does say is that the physical fact couldn't have been a fact, unless it had been a fact that there was *some* mental fact of this sort. And it seems to me that many philosophers, who would perhaps disagree either with Berkeley's assumption that my body is an 'idea' or 'constituted by ideas', or with his assumption that 'ideas' cannot exist without being perceived, or with both, never-theless would agree with him in thinking that this physical fact is logically dependent upon *some* 'mental fact': e.g. they might say that it could not have been a fact, unless there had been, at some time or other, or, were timelessly, *some* 'experience'. Many, indeed, so far as I can make out, have held that *every* fact is logically dependent on every other fact. And, of course, they have held in the case of their opinions, as Berkeley did in the case of his, that they had good reasons for them.

B. I also hold that there is no good reason to suppose that *every* physical fact is *causally* dependent upon some mental fact. By saying that F_1 is *causally* dependent on F_2, I mean only that F_1 *wouldn't* have been a fact unless F_2 had been; *not* (which is what 'logically dependent' asserts) that F_1 *couldn't conceivably* have been a fact, unless F_2 had been. And I can illustrate my meaning by reference to the example which I have just given. The fact that that mantelpiece is at present nearer to my body than that book-case, is (as I have just explained) so far as I can see, not *logically* dependent upon any mental fact; it *might* have been a fact, even if there had been no mental facts. But it certainly is *causally* dependent on many mental facts: my body *would* not have been here unless I had been conscious in various ways in the past; and the mantelpiece and the bookcase certainly *would* not have existed, unless other men had been conscious too.

But with regard to two of the facts, which I gave as instances of physical facts, namely the fact that the earth has existed for many years past, and the fact that the moon has for many years past been nearer to the earth than to the sun, I hold that there is no good reason to suppose that these are *causally* dependent upon any mental fact. So far as I can see, there is no reason to suppose that there is any mental fact of which it could be truly said: unless this fact had been a fact, the earth would not have existed for many years past. And in holding this, again, I think I differ from some philosophers. I differ, for instance, from those who have held that all material things were created by God, and that they had good reasons for supposing this.

III. I have just explained that I differ from those philosophers who have held that there is good reason to suppose that all material things were created by God. And it is, I think, an important point in my position, which should be mentioned, that I differ also from all philosophers who have held that there is good reason to suppose that there is a God at all, whether or not they have held it likely that he created all material things.

And similarly, whereas some philosophers have held that there is good reason to suppose that we, human beings, shall continue to exist and to be conscious after the death of our bodies, I hold that there is no good reason to suppose this.

IV. I now come to a point of a very different order.

As I have explained under I., I am not at all sceptical as to the *truth* of such propositions as 'The earth has existed for many years past', 'Many human bodies have each lived for many years upon it', i.e. propositions which assert the existence of material things: on the contrary, I hold that we all know, with certainty, many such propositions to be true. But I am very sceptical as to what, in certain respects, the correct *analysis* of such propositions is. And this is a matter as to which I think I differ from many philosophers. Many seem to hold that there is no doubt at all as to their *analysis*, nor, therefore, as to the analysis of the proposition 'Material things have existed', in certain respects in which I hold that the analysis of the propositions in question is extremely doubtful; and some of them, as we have seen, while holding that there is no doubt as to their *analysis*, seem to have doubted whether any such propositions are *true*. I, on the other hand, while holding that there is no doubt whatever that many such propositions are wholly true, hold also that no philosopher, hitherto, has succeeded in suggesting an analysis of them, as regards certain important points, which comes anywhere near to being certainly true.

It seems to me quite evident that the question how propositions of the type I have just given are to be analysed, depends on the question how propositions of another and simpler type are to be analysed. I know, at present, that I am perceiving a human hand, a pen, a sheet of paper, etc.; and it seems to me that I cannot know how the proposition 'Material things exist' is to be analysed, until I know how, in certain respects, these simpler propositions are to be analysed. But even these are not simple enough. It seems to me quite evident that my knowledge that I am now perceiving a human hand is a deduction from a pair of propositions simpler still—propositions which I can only express in the form 'I am perceiving *this*' and '*This* is a human hand'. It is the analysis of propositions of the latter kind which seems to me to present such great difficulties, while nevertheless the whole question as to the *nature* of material things obviously depends upon their analysis. It seems to me a surprising thing that so few philosophers, while saying a great deal as to what material things *are* and as to what it is to perceive them, have attempted to give a clear account as to what precisely they suppose

themselves to *know* (or to *judge*, in case they have held that we
don't *know* any such propositions to be true, or even that no
such propositions *are* true) when they know or judge such things
as 'This is a hand,' 'That is the sun', 'This is a dog', etc. etc. etc.

Two things only seem to me to be quite certain about the
analysis of such propositions (and even with regard to these I am
afraid some philosophers would differ from me) namely that
whenever I know, or judge, such a proposition to be true, (1)
there is always some *sense-datum* about which the proposition in
question is a proposition—some sense-datum which is *a* subject
(and, in a certain sense, the principal or ultimate subject) of the
proposition in question, and (2) that, nevertheless, *what* I am
knowing or judging to be true about this sense-datum is not
(in general) that it is *itself* a hand, or a dog, or the sun, etc. etc.,
as the case may be.

Some philosophers have I think doubted whether there are
any such things as other philosophers have meant by 'sense-
data' or 'sensa'. And I think it is quite possible that some philosophers (including myself, in the past) have used these terms in
senses such that it is really doubtful whether there are any
such things. But there is no doubt at all that there are sense-
data, in the sense in which I am now using that term. I am at
present seeing a great number of them, and feeling others. And
in order to point out to the reader what sort of things I mean by
sense-data, I need only ask him to look at his own right hand.
If he does this he will be able to pick out something (and, unless
he is seeing double, *only* one thing) with regard to which he will
see that it is, at first sight, a natural view to take that that thing
is identical, not, indeed, with his whole right hand, but with that
part of its surface which he is actually seeing, but will also (on
a little reflection) be able to see that it is doubtful whether it can be
identical with the part of the surface of his hand in question.
Things *of the sort* (in a certain respect) of which this thing is,
which he sees in looking at his hand, and with regard to which
he can understand how some philosophers should have supposed
it to *be* the part of the surface of his hand which he is seeing,
while others have supposed that it can't be, are what I mean by
'sense-data'. I therefore define the term in such a way that it is
an open question whether the sense-datum which I now see
in looking at my hand and which is a sense-datum of my hand is

or is not identical with that part of its surface which I am now actually seeing.

That what I know, with regard to this sense-datum, when I know 'This is a human hand', is not that it is *itself* a human hand, seems to me certain because I know that my hand has many parts (e.g. its other side, and the bones inside it), which are quite certainly *not* parts of this sense-datum.

I think it certain, therefore, that the analysis of the proposition 'This is a human hand' is, roughly at least, of the form 'There is a thing, and only one thing, of which it is true both that it is a human hand and that *this surface* is a part of its surface'. In other words, to put my view in terms of the phrase 'theory of representative perception', I hold it to be quite certain that I do not *directly* perceive *my hand*; and that when I am said (as I may be correctly said) to 'perceive' it, that I 'perceive' it means that I perceive (in a different and more fundamental sense) something which is (in a suitable sense) *representative* of it, namely, a certain part of its surface.

This is all that I hold to be *certain* about the analysis of the proposition 'This is a human hand'. We have seen that it includes in its analysis a proposition of the form 'This is part of the surface of a human hand' (where 'This', of course, has a different meaning from that which it has in the original proposition which has now been analysed). But this proposition also is undoubtedly a proposition about the sense-datum, which I am seeing, which is a sense-datum *of* my hand. And hence the further question arises: *What*, when I know '*This* is *part of the surface of* a human hand', am I knowing about the sense-datum in question? Am I, in this case, really knowing about the sense-datum in question that it *itself* is part of the surface of a human hand? Or, just as we found in the case of 'This is a human hand', that what I was knowing about the sense-datum was certainly not that it *itself* was a human hand, so, is it perhaps the case, with this new proposition, that even here I am not knowing, with regard to the sense-datum, that it is *itself* part of the surface of a hand? And, if so, what is it that I am knowing about the sense-datum itself?

This is the question to which, as it seems to me, no philosopher has hitherto suggested an answer which comes anywhere near to being *certainly* true.

There seem to me to be three, and only three, alternative

types of answer possible; and to any answer yet suggested, of any of these types, there seem to me to be very grave objections.

(1) Of the first type, there is but one answer: namely, that in this case what I am knowing really is that the sense-datum *itself* is part of the surface of a human hand. In other words that, though I don't perceive *my hand* directly, I do *directly* perceive part of its surface; that the sense-datum itself *is* this part of its surface and not merely something which (in a sense yet to be determined) 'represents' this part of its surface; and that hence the sense in which I 'perceive' this part of the surface of my hand, is not in its turn a sense which needs to be defined by reference to yet a third more ultimate sense of 'perceive', which is the only one in which perception is direct, namely that in which I perceive the sense-datum.

If this view is true (as I think it may just possibly be), it seems to me certain that we must abandon a view which has been held to be certainly true by most philosophers, namely the view that our sense-data always really have the qualities which they sensibly appear to us to have. For I know that if another man were looking through a microscope at the same surface which I am seeing with the naked eye, the sense-datum which he saw would sensibly appear to him to have qualities very different from and incompatible with those which my sense-datum sensibly appears to me to have: and yet, if my sense-datum is identical with the surface we are both of us seeing, his must be identical with it also. My sense-datum can, therefore, be identical with this surface only on condition that it is identical with his sense-datum; and, since his sense-datum sensibly appears to him to have qualities incompatible with those which mine sensibly appears to me to have, his sense-datum can be identical with mine only on condition that the sense-datum in question either has not got the qualities which it sensibly appears to me to have, or has not got those which it sensibly appears to him to have.

I do not, however, think that this is a fatal objection to this first type of view. A far more serious objection seems to me to be that, when we see a thing double (have what is called 'a double image' of it), we certainly have *two* sense-data each of which is *of* the surface seen, and which cannot therefore both be identical with it; and that yet it seems as if, if any sense-datum is ever identical with the surface *of* which it is a sense-datum, each of these so-called 'images' must be so. It looks, therefore, as if every sense-datum is, after all, only 'representative' of the surface, *of* which it is a sense-datum.

(2) But, if so, what relation has it to the surface in question?

This second type of view is one which holds that when I know 'This is part of the surface of a human hand', what I am knowing with regard to the sense-datum which is *of* that surface, is, *not* that it is *itself* part of the surface of a human hand, but something of the following kind. There is, it says, *some* relation, R, such that what I am knowing with regard to the sense-datum is either 'There is one thing and only one thing, of which it is true both that it is a part of the surface of a human hand, and that it has R to this sense-datum', or else 'There are a set of things, of which it is true both that that set, taken collectively, *are* part of the surface of a human hand, and also that each member of the set has R to this sense-datum, and that nothing which is not a member of the set has R to it'.

Obviously, in the case of this second type, many different views are possible, differing according to the view they take as to what the relation R is. But there is only one of them, which seems to me to have any plausibility; namely that which holds that R is an ultimate and unanalysable relation, which might be expressed by saying that 'xRy' means the same as 'y is an appearance or manifestation of x'. I.e. the analysis which this answer would give of 'This is part of the surface of a human hand' would be 'There is one and only one thing of which it is true both that it is part of the surface of a human hand, and that this sense-datum is an appearance or manifestation of it'.

To this view also there seem to me to be very grave objections, chiefly drawn from a consideration of the questions how we can possibly *know* with regard to any of our sense-data that there is one thing and one thing only which has to them such a supposed ultimate relation; and how, if we do, we can possibly *know* anything further about such things, e.g. of what size or shape they are.

(3) The third type of answer, which seems to me to be the only possible alternative if (1) and (2) are rejected, is the type of answer which J. S. Mill seems to have been implying to be the true one when he said that material things are 'permanent possibilities of sensation'. He seems to have thought that when I know such a fact as 'This is part of the surface of a human hand',

what I am knowing with regard to the sense-datum which is
the principal subject of that fact, is not that it is itself part of the
surface of a human hand, nor yet, with regard to any relation, that
the thing which has to it that relation is part of the surface of a
human hand, but a whole set of hypothetical facts each of which
is a fact of the form 'If *these* conditions had been fulfilled, I
should have been perceiving a sense-datum intrinsically related to
this sense-datum in *this* way', 'If *these* (other) conditions had been
fulfilled, I should have been perceiving a sense-datum intrinsically related to *this* sense-datum in *this* (other) way', etc. etc.

With regard to this third type of view as to the analysis of
propositions of the kind we are considering, it seems to me, again,
just *possible* that it is a true one; but to hold (as Mill himself and
others seem to have held) that it is *certainly*, or nearly certainly,
true, seems to me as great a mistake, as to hold with regard either
to (1) or to (2), that they are *certainly*, or nearly certainly, true.
There seem to me to be very grave objections to it; in particular
the three, (*a*) that though, in general, when I know such a fact as
'This is a hand', I certainly do know some hypothetical facts of
the form 'If *these* conditions had been fulfilled, I should have been
perceiving a sense-datum of *this* kind, which would have been a
sense-datum of the same surface of which *this* is a sense-datum',
it seems doubtful whether any conditions with regard to which I
know this are not themselves conditions of the form 'If this and
that *material thing* had been in those positions and conditions . . . ',
(*b*) that it seems again very doubtful whether there is any intrinsic
relation, such that my knowledge that (under *these* conditions) I
should have been perceiving a sense-datum of *this* kind, which
would have been a sense-datum of the same surface of which *this*
is a sense-datum, is equivalent to a knowledge, with regard to
that relation, that I should, under those conditions, have been
perceiving a sense-datum related by it to *this* sense-datum, and
(*c*) that, if it were true, the sense in which a material surface
is 'round' or 'square', would necessarily be utterly different from
that in which our sense-data sensibly appear to us to be 'round' or
'square'.

V. Just as I hold that the proposition 'There are and have been
material things' is quite certainly true, but that the question how
this proposition is to be analysed is one to which no answer that

has been hitherto given is anywhere near certainly true; so I hold that the proposition 'There are and have been many Selves' is quite certainly true, but that here again all the analyses of this proposition that have been suggested by philosophers are highly doubtful.

That I am now perceiving many different sense-data, and that I have at many times in the past perceived many different sense-data, I know for certain—that is to say, I know that there are mental facts of class (β), connected in a way which it is proper to express by saying that they are all of them facts about *me*; but how this kind of connection is to be analysed, I do not know for certain, nor do I think that any other philosopher knows with any approach to certainty. Just as in the case of the proposition 'This is part of the surface of a human hand', there are several extremely different views as to its analysis, each of which seems to me *possible*, but none nearly certain, so also in the case of the proposition 'This, that and that sense-datum are all at present being perceived by *me*', and still more so in the case of the proposition '*I* am now perceiving this sense-datum, and *I* have in the past perceived sense-data of these other kinds'. Of the *truth* of these propositions there seems to me to be no doubt, but as to what is the correct analysis of them there seems to me to be the gravest doubt—the true analysis may, for instance, *possibly* be quite as paradoxical as is the third view given above under IV as to the analysis of 'This is part of the surface of a human hand'; but whether it *is* as paradoxical as this seems to me to be quite as doubtful as in that case. Many philosophers, on the other hand, seem to me to have assumed that there is little or no doubt as to the correct analysis of such propositions; and many of these, just reversing my position, have also held that the propositions themselves are not true.

III

FACTS AND PROPOSITIONS

I should like, first of all, to get as clear as possible as to what the class of entities is, with the logical analysis of which Mr Ramsey is concerned. In his first sentence he tells us that he proposes to discuss the logical analysis of *judgment*; but in his second he goes on to give an illustration, from which it would appear that the class of entities with the logical analysis of which he really is concerned is a certain class of *facts*. He does not, by way of illustration, mention any actual member of the class in question, but only tells us that, *if* at a particular moment he were judging that Caesar was murdered, then the fact that he was doing so *would* be a member of that class. That is to say, he only tells us that, if there *were* any fact of a certain kind, any such fact would belong to the class with which he is concerned. And the *kind* of fact, with regard to which he does tell us this, can, I think, be defined as follows: We all know that if, at a particular moment, Mr Ramsey were to utter the words 'I am now judging that Caesar was murdered', he *might*, by uttering those words at that moment, be expressing a *fact*. He *would*, in any case, be expressing a *proposition*; but if, at the moment in question, he happened to be really judging that Caesar was murdered, then, and then only, he would, by uttering those words at that moment, be *also* expressing a fact. The fact in question would be a fact, with regard to the particular moment in question, to the effect that he was at that moment judging that Caesar was murdered. But he might, of course, actually be judging that Caesar was murdered, at moments at which he did not utter the words 'I am now judging that Caesar was murdered'; and, in the case of any such moment, there would *be* a fact, of the kind he means, which was a fact with regard to that moment, although he would not be actually expressing it in this way. Of any such fact, however, it would still be true that it was *the* fact, such that, *if* at the moment in question he *had* uttered the words 'I am now judging that Caesar was murdered', then, by uttering those words at that moment, he *would* have expressed it; or, in other words, it would be *the* fact which he *could* have expressed by uttering those words at that moment. The *kind* of fact, therefore, with regard to which he implies that, if there were any facts of that kind, they would belong to the class of entities which he is concerned to analyse, can, I think, be defined as follows: An actual fact, F, is of the kind in question, if and only if there is *some* particular moment, such that F is the only fact of which it is true that, by uttering at that moment the words 'I am now judging that Caesar was murdered', Mr Ramsey *could* have expressed F. Obviously there may be no actual facts which are of this kind. There is a fact of this kind, if and only if there is a moment with regard to which it is true that Mr Ramsey did judge at it that Caesar was murdered; and there are several facts of this kind, if and only if there are several such moments.

But, supposing there were any facts of this kind, to what class would they belong? Obviously they would belong to ever so many different classes; but there can be no doubt, I think, as to which of these classes must have been *the* class of which Mr Ramsey intended to give them as an illustration. It can, I think, be defined as follows. Consider the class of sentences consisting of the sentence 'I am now judging that Caesar was murdered', together with all other sentences which resemble it in that they begin with the words 'I am now judging that', and are completed by a set of words which resemble the words 'Caesar was murdered' in that, if uttered by themselves, they would constitute a significant sentence. And next consider the class consisting of every fact of which it is true that there are a moment, a particular individual, and a sentence of the class defined, such that, *if* that individual had uttered or were to utter at that moment the sentence in question, then, by uttering that sentence at that moment, he would have expressed or would express the fact in question. This, I think, is the required class. Put more shortly, it is the class consisting of all facts which could have been or could be expressed by the utterance, on the part of some particular individual at some particular moment, of a sentence of the form 'I am now judging that *p*'. Obviously Mr Ramsey's sub-class, consisting of all facts which *he* could have expressed or could express by uttering at a particular moment the sentence 'I am *now* judging that Caesar was murdered', would, if there were any members of this sub-class, belong to the class in question. And I think there can be no doubt that this must have been the class which he meant to indicate, if we make one, rather important, proviso. The proviso I mean is as follows: Mr Ramsey assumes, later on (and his whole view of negation depends upon the truth of this assumption), that there are two fundamentally distinct, though, in a certain sense, 'equivalent', kinds of fact, the one a kind such that any fact of the kind might be expressed by using a sentence of the form 'I am *dis*believing that p', and the other a kind such that any fact of the kind might be expressed by using a sentence of the form 'I am believing that not-p'. It seems to me that this view is very likely true, though I have never been able to find any evidence that it is so which seemed to me at all cogent. And, if it is true, I think there is no doubt that Mr Ramsey would wish to include among the objects of his analysis all facts which could be expressed by 'I am *dis*believing that p', just as much as those which could be expressed by 'I am believing that p'. And if so, then the class of facts I have just defined could only be identified with the class intended by him, if any fact of the sort which might be expressed by 'I am disbelieving that p' could *also* be properly expressed in English by 'I am believing that not-p'. This may, of course, quite well be the case; even if there are the two fundamentally distinct kinds of negation which Mr Ramsey assumes, it is quite possible that it is correct English to express the fact that *either* kind is occurring by 'I am believing that not-p'. But it is only *if* this is the case that the class I have defined could be identified with the class intended by him; if it is not, then to define the class he intends, we should have to say that it is the sum of the two classes: facts which could be expressed by 'I am now judging that p', *and* facts which could be expressed by 'I am now *dis*believing that p'. As regards the latter phrase, it is, of course, not in fact good English; it is not good English to say, e.g. 'I disbelieve that Mr Ramsey intended to analyse judgments'. The way in which we actually express facts of the class which he describes by this phrase, if there are such facts at all, is by 'I don't believe that p'.

The class of facts which I have just defined, and which I will hereafter refer to as my first class, seems to me to be a very definite one, and one of which there is no doubt whatever that there are members. There certainly are facts, each of which is a fact with regard to a particular individual and a particular time, such that if at the time in question the individual in question had uttered a sentence of the form 'I am judging that p', he would have expressed the fact in question. If, therefore, as he implies in his second sentence, it were facts of this class, with regard to the analysis of which Mr Ramsey intends to make certain propositions, the question whether these propositions were true or false would be a definite one. But is it really facts of this class which he intends to analyse? There are two other classes of entities, each of which can be defined by reference to facts of this class (and, as far as I can see, in no other way), with regard to each of which it might be suggested that it was entities of that class, and *not* of my first class, with the analysis of which he really is concerned; and my own view is that it is one of these other classes that he really is concerned with. Both of these other classes are very apt to be confused both with my first class and with one another, and it seems to me very important to distinguish them clearly.

The first of these two classes is the class of *judgments*; and I see no way of defining this class except as follows. Let F be a fact of my first class; let A be the individual of whom it is true that by uttering at a certain moment a sentence of the form 'I am now judging that p' he would have expressed F; and let T be the moment in question. For instance, if Mr Ramsey ever did judge that Caesar was murdered, as he probably may have done the first time he was told so, F might be the fact which he would have expressed by uttering at that moment the words 'I am now judging that Caesar was murdered', if he had then uttered them. We so use the term 'judgment' that we should say: if A really did judge at T that p, then there must have been an event in A's history (one and only one) which occurred at T, and which was a *judgment* that p. Indeed, we so use it that F is either identical with or equivalent to the fact which A might have expressed by saying at T 'There is *some* event (one and only one), which is occurring now, which is an event in my history, and which is a *judgment* that p'. And I see no way of defining what is meant by a 'judgment', in that sense of the term in which every judgment is an event or occurrence, except by saying that it is an event of the sort (whatever that may be) which is such that this equivalence holds. We all understand what is meant by a sentence of the form 'A judged at T that p', and we so use 'judgment' that, in the case of every such sentence, a sentence of the form "There was an event in A's history, which occurred at T, and was a judgment that *p*', where A, T and *p* have the same values as in the original sentence, will either express the same proposition which the original sentence expressed or a proposition equivalent to it, in the sense that it both entails and is entailed by it. This, of course, does not tell us what would be the analysis of the proposition, with regard to a particular event, E, 'E is a judgment'; still less does it tell us how, if at all, any particular event E, which was a judgment, could be analysed. But it does make certain points clear. It makes clear (1) that no fact of my first class *is* a judgment, since every such fact is either identical with or equivalent to some fact, with regard to a particular individual, time and proposition, to the effect that there was one and only one event in that individual's history which occurred at that time and was a judgment that *p*. Clearly no such fact will itself be a judgment. A judgment is an event and occurs *at* a time; no such fact is an event, and none occurs *at* a time, though each is a fact *about* a time. But (2) though no fact of my first class *is* a judgment, yet to every fact of my first class there will *correspond* one and only one judgment, since every such fact is or is equivalent to a fact, with regard to a certain description, to the effect that there is one and only one judgment which satisfies that description; and hence each such fact will have to the judgment which does in fact satisfy the description, and to nothing else, the relation constituted by the double fact that *it* is, or is equivalent to, a fact, to the effect stated, *about* that description, while the judgment is the only thing to which the description in question applies. The fact and the corresponding judgment will be distinguished from and related to one another in some such way as that in which Mr Ramsey maintained that the fact *that Caesar died* is distinguished from and related to the event *Caesar's death*. And, finally (3) (what seems to me a very important point, almost universally overlooked), although it follows that to every fact of my first class there will correspond one and only one judgment, it by no means follows that to every judgment there will correspond *only* one fact of my first class. Suppose I am making two judgments simultaneously: e.g. that I am *both* judging that *p* and also, simultaneously, that *q*, where *p* and *q* are different propositions. We shall then have two different facts of my first class. And to each there will correspond one and one only judgment: namely, to the first the event in my mental history, occurring at that time, which is a judgment that p, and to the second the event in my mental history, occurring at that time, which is a judgment that q. But there is nothing whatever in the definition of a judgment to show that these two descriptions may not both apply to the *same* event; that the very same event in my history which is a judgment that p, may not also be a judgment that q. And if this should be so, then to one and the same judgment there will correspond two different facts of my first class. It seems to me to be constantly assumed that an event which is a judgment that p cannot also be a judgment that q, but I do not know of any solid grounds for this assumption; it seems to me to rest merely upon a confusion between judgment, in the sense in which only *events* are judgments, and a certain class of *facts*. It is quite obvious that the fact that I am judging that p cannot be identical with the fact that I am judging that q, if p and q are different; but it is by no means equally obvious that the event which is my present judgment that p may not be identical with the event which is my present judgment that q. Suppose at a given moment I am judging with regard to two objects A and B, both of which I am perceiving, that A has to B the relation R. It seems to me quite obvious that the event which is my judgment that A has R to B, must also have two very different characters—the very same event must also be both a perception of A, and a perception of B. But if the same event, which is a judgment that A has R to B, is also both a perception of A and a perception of B, why should it not also have other characters as well? Suppose I am also judging, with regard to another relation S, that A has S to B, why should not the same event which has the character of being a judgment that A has R to B, also have the character of being a judgment that A has S to B? For my part, I see no reason to think that more than *one* event ever occurs in my mental history at any one time. It is perfectly certain that there are an immense number of different *characters* of which it is true that some event having each of those characters is occurring in my mental history at a given time; but so far as I can see, it may be always one and the same event which has all these different characters. And if you say that it is not, I do not see on what principle you are to determine which among the characters in question belong to different events and which to the same.

c

Is it, possibly, with the analysis of *judgments*, in this sense which I have tried to explain, and *not* with that of facts of my first class, that Mr Ramsey is concerned? He constantly speaks, of course, as if it were *judgments*, but all such expressions of his can, I think, easily be interpreted as merely a loose and abbreviated way of referring to *facts* of a certain class. And I cannot help thinking that it is not really to judgments, in this sense, that he means his propositions to apply at all. If it were of judgments that he is speaking, all we could say, I think, is that every single proposition which he makes about their analysis is in the last degree dubious. It is utterly doubtful, in the first place, whether judgments can be analysed at all. Even if they can, it is utterly doubtful whether they ever contain any 'objective' factors; whereas he is assuming throughout that the entities, with the analysis of which he is concerned, certainly always do contain 'objective' factors. And, thirdly, if he were dealing with judgments, he would be making throughout the highly doubtful assumption, of which I have just spoken, that a judgment that p cannot be identical with a judgment that q, if p and q be different. I cannot believe that he really means to make any of these highly doubtful propositions. I think that what he implies in his second sentence so far expresses his real purpose, that it is a class of *facts* of a certain sort, each of which, though not identical with any judgment, has a certain special relation to one and only one judgment, that he really intends to analyse.

But is the class of facts in question really the one which he has indicated? That is to say, is it my first class of facts? I cannot believe that it is, for the following reason, among others. Every fact of my first class is, it seems to me, quite plainly a *general* fact; and, whereas Mr Ramsey assumes throughout and expressly states to begin with that every entity, with the analysis of which he is concerned, consists *in holding of some relation or relations between certain factors*, he would, if I understand rightly the latter part of his paper, deny that any *general* fact so consisted. Of course, it is possible that he may think that facts of my first class are *not* general facts, and that therefore they may really be capable of analysis in the way he says. But there seem to me to be many other indications that it is not really facts of this first class that he is trying to analyse; and what I want now to do is to state what seems to me to be the true alternative. I hold that what he is really trying to analyse are *neither* judgments *nor* facts of my first class, but a second class of facts, which I will hereafter call my second class, related in a peculiar way to both; and what I want to do is to try to make clear what this second class is.

Suppose that Mr Ramsey were now uttering the words 'I am now judging that Caesar was murdered', and were, by uttering them now, expressing a fact; as he would be doing if and only if he were actually judging now that Caesar was murdered. I say that the fact which he would thus express would, quite certainly, be merely a *general* fact; that it would be either identical with or equivalent to a fact, with regard to a certain description which could only apply to a *non-general* fact, to the effect that there was one and only one fact which answered to that description; and that hence there would necessarily be one and only one non-general fact, which was *the* non-general fact corresponding to it— corresponding, in the sense, that it was *the* non-general fact answering to the description in question. I hold that, similarly, in the case of *every* fact of my first class, there is one and only one non-general fact, which is *the* non-general fact corresponding to it. I shall hereafter suggest that it is possible that, in the case of some or all of these non-general facts, there may be one or more other facts *equivalent* to each of them, in the sense that they both entail and are entailed by the fact in question. And my second class of facts consists of all those non-general facts which correspond to facts of my first class, together with all those facts (if any) which are equivalent to any such non-general fact. This I believe to be the class of entities with the analysis of which Mr Ramsey is really concerned.

Consider what fact Mr Ramsey would express by saying now 'I am now judging that Caesar was murdered', if he expressed a fact at all. It seems to me quite plain that all he would be expressing would be a fact to the effect that he was making *some* judgment of a certain kind, i.e. for this reason alone, a *general* fact. There are many different ways of judging that Caesar was murdered, and all he would be telling us would be that he was so judging *in some way or other*. There are, for instance, an immense number of different descriptions, by which we can think of Caesar: we can think of him as the author of the *De Bello Gallico*; as the original of a certain bust in the British Museum; as the brother of the Julia who was a grandmother of Augustus, etc.

etc. And anybody who was judging, with regard to any such
description, which does actually apply to Caesar, that *the* person
who answered to it was murdered, would be *ipso facto* judging
that Caesar was murdered. It is surely quite plain that, if Mr
Ramsey were judging now that Caesar was murdered, he must be
judging, with regard to *some* such description, that the person
who answered to it was murdered; and no less plain that by
merely saying 'I am now judging that Caesar was murdered',
he would *not* be expressing, with regard to the particular proposition, of this form, which he would in fact be believing, the fact
that he was believing that particular proposition. All that he
would be *expressing* would be the fact that he was believing
some proposition, which was a proposition to the effect that
Caesar was murdered. I do not see how this can be disputed.
And this is not all: the fact which he would be expressing might
be a fact which would be *general* for yet other reasons. It is, for
instance, possible that, whenever one judges, one judges with
some particular degree of conviction, with some particular degree
of vagueness, etc. etc.; and, if so, then the fact which he would be
expressing by his words would only be a fact to the effect that he
was believing with *some* degree of conviction, *some* degree of
clearness or vagueness, etc., *some* proposition of a certain kind;
the fact, with regard to the particular degree of conviction,
vagueness, etc., with which he would in fact be believing the
proposition of the kind in question, which he was in fact believing,
to the effect that he was believing it with *that* degree of conviction,
vagueness, etc., would certainly not be expressed by his mere
use of the words 'I am now judging that Caesar was murdered'.
And, finally, it is perfectly possible that the use of the word 'I'
may conceal yet another element of generality; indeed, on Mr
Ramsey's own view, if I understand him rightly, it certainly
would. For he holds apparently that certain instances of certain
kinds of word would necessarily be related in a certain way
to the 'objective' factors in the fact, of the kind he wishes to
analyse, which there would be if he were making the judgment
now; and though, by merely saying 'I am now judging that
Caesar was murdered', he might possibly be expressing the fact,
with regard to the *kinds* of words in question, that *some* instances
of words of that kind were related in the necessary way to *some*
'objective' factors of a certain kind, the fact, with regard to the

particular instances of those kinds of words, which were in fact so related, to the effect that *those particular instances* were so related, is, it seems to me, one which he would certainly *not* be expressing. For these reasons it seems to me that every fact of my first class is, quite certainly, a *general* fact, which is, or is equivalent to, a fact, with regard to a certain description, to the effect that there is one and only one non-general fact answering to that description; and that it is only if we consider these non-general facts, each of which corresponds to one and only one fact of my first class, together with any other non-general facts which may be equivalent to any one of these, that we get the class of entities with the analysis of which Mr Ramsey really is concerned. If his class really is some other class, I have not the least idea how it can be defined.

With regard to this second class of facts, which I have tried to define, it is, I think, worth noticing that none of them, so far as I can see, could possibly be expressed in any actual language; perhaps, even none could be expressed in any possible language. This is one characteristic which distinguishes them sharply from facts of my first class, all of which, *ex hypothesi*, could be expressed in English. And surely it is, in fact, obvious that in the case of every, or nearly every, fact which could be expressed by using words of the form 'I am now judging that *p*,' there always is some other unexpressed and inexpressible fact of a sort, such that what you are expressing is only the fact that there is *some* fact of that sort.

Assuming, then, that it is these inexpressible facts of my second class with the analysis of which Mr Ramsey is really concerned, what propositions does he make about their logical analysis?

There are, first of all, two such propositions, which, if I understand him rightly, he means to assert to be 'hardly open to question' in his very first paragraph. The first is (1) some proposition which might be expressed by the words 'Every such fact contains at least one "mental" and at least one "objective" factor'; and the second, (2) some proposition which might be expressed by the words 'Every such fact consists in the holding of some relation or relations between the "mental" and "objective" factors which it contains'.

Now I must confess I feel some doubt as to what Mr Ramsey is here asserting. As regards (1) I think the words *can* be given a meaning such that the proposition they express really is 'hardly open to question'; but I am not certain that Mr Ramsey is really asserting this proposition and nothing more. As regards (2) I think it is not possible to give them any natural meaning such that the proposition they express would be 'hardly open to question', though I do not wish to deny that one or more of the questionable propositions they might express may *possibly* be true. I will try to explain the chief doubts and difficulties I feel with regard to them.

As regards (1) I think the following proposition really is not open to question, viz. that every fact of my second class both contains at least one 'objective' factor, and also contains at least one factor which is not *merely* 'objective'. And what is here meant by an 'objective' factor can, I think, be defined as follows: Let F be a fact of my second class, and A be a factor contained in F. A will then be an 'objective' factor of F, if and only if *either* (1) both (*a*) F entails that A is being believed, and also (*b*) if F entails with regard to any other entity, B, that B is being believed, then B is contained in A; *or* (2) there is some sense of the word 'about', such that F entails that, in that sense, something is being believed *about* A. To say of A that it fulfils the first of these conditions is equivalent to saying of it that it is *the* proposition, *p*, which is such that, if you were to assert F, then *p* would *either* be the *only* proposition which, in asserting F, you would be asserting to be believed, *or*, if not, would contain all other propositions which you were asserting to be believed—a proposition with regard to A, which would be usually expressed by saying that A is *what*, in asserting F, you would be asserting to be believed, or *the* 'content' which you would be asserting to be believed, or (as Mr Ramsey puts it) *the* proposition which you would be asserting to be 'judged'. And hence, no factor which F contains, will be an 'objective' factor which satisfies the first condition, unless F contains a factor which is a proposition: and F will not do this unless, as Mr Johnson puts it,[1] propositions are 'genuine entities'. I understand Mr Ramsey to be so using the term 'objective' factor, that, *if* propositions are 'genuine entities', then every fact of our class will contain one and only one 'objective' factor which satisfies this first condition; whereas, if they are *not* (as he goes on to maintain), then the only 'objective' factors

[1] *Logic*, Part I (Cambridge, 1921), p. 126.

contained in any fact of our class will be 'objective' factors which satisfy our second condition.

But, to return to my proposition that: Every fact of my second class both contains at least one 'objective' factor and also contains at least one factor which is not *merely* objective. The language used implies that *every* factor contained in such a fact may possibly be 'objective', but that, if so, one at least among them must be not *merely* objective. And it seems to me that if you are to give to (1) any meaning whatever, which is really not open to question, it must be a meaning which allows this possibility— which allows, therefore, that there may be some facts of this class, such that every 'mental' factor of them is *also* an 'objective' factor of them. To say this is to say that one and the same factor may possibly enter into the same fact in two different ways; and it is a well-known puzzle about facts of the class we are concerned with that this does *prima facie* seem to be true of some of them. To give what I regard as the strongest instance. Suppose Mr Ramsey really were judging now that Caesar was murdered. Then in the fact of my second class corresponding to the fact that he was so judging, it seems to me quite clear that the present moment (or something corresponding to it) would be an 'objective' factor; since it seems to me quite clear that he would be judging, with regard to or *about* this time, that an event of a certain kind took place before *it*. As a general rule, whenever we use a past tense to express a proposition, the fact that we use it is a sign that the proposition expressed is *about* the time at which we use it; so that if I say twice over 'Caesar was murdered', the proposition which I express on each occasion is a different one—the first being a proposition with regard to the earlier of the two times at which I use the words, to the effect that Caesar was murdered before *that* time, and the second a proposition with regard to the later of the two, to the effect that he was murdered before *that* time. So much seems to me hardly open to question. But, if so, then in the hypothetical fact with regard to Mr Ramsey which we are considering, the time at which he was making the judgment would certainly be an 'objective' factor; but also, *ex hypothesi*, the very same moment would also be a factor in this fact in another way, since it would also be the time, with regard to which the fact in question would be a fact to the effect that he was making that judgment *at* that time. I do not say that some view according to which the very same time (or something corresponding to it) would *not* be a factor in the fact in question in both of these two different ways may not possibly be *true*; but I do say that no such view can be properly described as 'hardly open to question'. And this is a doubt which would clearly affect the immense majority of facts of my second class; if, in this case, the same time would be a factor in the supposed fact in both of two different ways, then, in the immense majority of facts of this class, some one time *is* a factor in both of the two ways at once; since (1) by definition, some time always *is* a factor in such a fact in the non-objective way; (2) the immense majority of our judgments are judgments to the effect that something was, is, or will be the case, and (3) in all such cases the same time would (if it would be so in the case supposed) be also an 'objective' factor in the fact in question. But there is another familiar doubt of the same kind, which affects a much smaller, but important, class among the facts we are considering. Suppose I were now judging that I am seeing a human being. Here it seems, *prima facie*, as if not only would the present time enter in both ways into the fact of my second class corresponding to the fact that I was making this judgment, but also as if I myself (or something corresponding to me) should enter in both ways into the fact in question; *prima facie*, I should both be an 'objective' factor in the fact in question, because the judgment made would be a judgment *about* me, and should also be not *merely* an 'objective' factor in it, because the fact in question would be a fact to the effect that I was making the judgment. The questions whether this really is the case, involves, of course, the familiar puzzle as to what the sense is in which I can be an object to myself. And, of course, I do not say that no view, according to which, in such cases, I (or something corresponding to me) am *not* both an 'objective' factor in the fact in question and also a factor in a non-objective way, is *true*; but I do say that no such view can be properly described as 'hardly open to question'.

I think, therefore, that if we are to find for (1) any meaning which really is hardly open to question, it must be a meaning such that to say of a given factor, B, that it is a 'mental' factor in a fact, F, of the class in question, is not inconsistent with saying of B that it is *also* an 'objective' factor in F, but is inconsistent with saying of B that it is *merely* an 'objective' factor in F. And the meaning of 'mental factor' which I suggest as sufficient for this purpose, and as also giving (so far as I can discover) the sense in which Mr Ramsey is really using the term, is the following: Let F be a fact of my second class, and B a factor in F. Then B will be a 'mental' factor in F, if and only if both (1) B is not *merely* an 'objective' factor in F and also (2) B is not the time (or whatever factor in F corresponds to this time) *about* which F is a fact to the effect that a certain judgment is being made at that time.

Let us now turn to consider what proposition Mr Ramsey can be expressing by the words (2): 'Every such fact consists in the holding of some relation or relations between the "mental" and "objective" factors which it contains.' It seems to me that any proposition which these words could properly express is questionable for both of two different reasons. (*a*) It seems to me that one of the factors, which are such that a fact of this class will always consist in the holding of some relation or relations between that factor and other factors, is always *the time* (or whatever corresponds to it) which is such that the fact in question is a fact, with regard to that time, to the effect that a certain judgment is being made *at* it; and I think it is questionable whether this factor is not sometimes neither an 'objective' nor a 'mental' factor. We have seen that very frequently it does seem to be an 'objective' factor; but it would be rash to maintain that there are no cases in which it is not. And as for its being a 'mental' factor, I have expressly defined 'mental' in such a way that it will *never* be a 'mental' factor. Of course, it always will be a factor which is not *merely* objective; and it might be suggested that Mr Ramsey is using 'mental' merely to mean 'not merely objective'; in which case I should agree that the proposition expressed by (2) is not questionable for this first reason. I do not, however, believe that he is so using 'mental'. (*b*) It seems to me also questionable whether such a fact may not contain factors which are 'objective', but which are not among the factors such that the fact *consists* in the holding of some relation or relations between those factors. I fancy Mr Ramsey would maintain that no relational fact can contain any factors except factors which are such that the fact consists in the holding of some relation or relations between those factors; and I do not say that this view of his is not *true*, but only that it is questionable. He might, of course, so define 'factor'

C*

that it would be necessarily true; but I do not think that he is actually using the term 'factor' in such a way.

Having laid down these two preliminary propositions about the logical analysis of all facts of our second class, as 'hardly open to question', Mr Ramsey next goes on to express his belief in certain propositions about the 'objective' factor or factors in any such fact. And I think we can distinguish three propositions of this class, in which he expresses belief, though he himself does not distinguish them. The first is: (1) Every such fact contains more than one 'objective' factor; the second (2) In every such fact, among the factors, which are such that the fact consists in the holding of some relation or relations between those factors, there are more 'objective' factors than one; or in other words: In the case of no such fact is there any objective factor, which is the *only* objective factor which is a member of that class among the factors of the fact, which are such that the fact consists in the holding of some relation or relations between them; the third (3) In no such fact is there ever any objective factor, such that all the other objective factors of that fact are contained in it.

In the case of none of these three propositions does he, so far as I can see, offer any argument whatever in its favour. What he does do is to mention two different views, which are such that if *either* of them were true, then (2) and (3) would be false, and with regard to which he supposes (mistakenly, I think) that, if either of them were true, (1) would be false too. In the case of the first of these views, he himself offers no argument against it, but refers us to arguments which Mr Russell has brought against it, and contents himself with telling us that he agrees with Mr Russell's conclusion that (2) and (3) are both true. In the case of the second, he does bring arguments against it, which raise very important questions, which I shall have to discuss. But it is clear that even if these arguments were successful, they could not prove (2) and (3) in the absence of cogent arguments against the first view; and not even then, unless these two views are the *only* alternatives to (2) and (3).

I do not intend to argue these three propositions any more than Mr Ramsey has done. With regard to (1) it seems to me unquestionably true. But with regard to (2) and (3), I doubt both these propositions, though it seems to me very likely that both are true. (2) seems to me to raise a very important question

as to whether a principle which Mr Ramsey believes in, and to
which we shall have to refer again, is true; namely, the principle:
There cannot be two different facts, each of which entails the other.
If this principle were true, then, it seems to me, if we accept (1),
we should have to accept (2) also. For suppose I were now making
some judgment with regard to two objects, *a* and *b*, and a relation
R, to the effect that *a* has R to *b*. There must, it seems to me, in
such a case, certainly be some fact of my second class which
consists in the holding of some relation or relations between the
three objective factors, *a*, R, *b*, and some not merely objective
factors; and this fact could not possibly be identical with any
fact which consisted in the holding of some relation or relations
between the proposition *aRb* and some not merely objective
factors, since the same fact cannot possibly consist *both* in the
holding of some relation or relations between *one* set of factors
(*a*, R, *b* and some not merely objective factors), and *also* in the
holding of some relation or relations between another different
set of factors (the proposition *aRb*, and some not merely objective
factors). There could, therefore, if Mr Ramsey's principle were
true, be no fact of my second class which consisted in the holding
of some relation or relations between a proposition and some not
merely objective factors. For any fact, which so consisted, would,
if (1) is true, be *either* identical with *or* equivalent to (i.e. both
entailing and entailed by), some fact which consisted in the
holding of some relation or relations between a *plurality* of
objective factors and some not merely objective factors; and we
have seen it could not be identical with any such fact, whereas,
by Mr Ramsey's principle, it could not *either* be equivalent to it.
The same argument would apply to any other sort of single
objective factor, with regard to which it might be suggested that
some facts of our class consist in the holding of some relation or
relations between one and only one objective factor of the sort and
some not merely objective ones. If (1) is true, i.e. if every such
fact would actually contain a plurality of objective factors, it
must necessarily be *either* identical with or equivalent to some
fact consisting in the holding of some relation or relations between
a plurality of objective factors and some not merely objective
ones; and, if Mr Ramsey's principle were true, it could be neither.
If, therefore, Mr Ramsey's principle were true I should say (2)
must be true, but I can see no conclusive reason for thinking

that his principle is true, nor any other conclusive reason for thinking that (2) is true. As for (3), I should say that it might possibly be false, even if (2) were true, the question here raised being merely the question whether a given fact may not *have* factors which do not belong to the class of factors such that it *consists* in the holding of some relation or relations between them. Thus, in our case, it might be held that the fact which consisted in the holding of some relation or relations between *a*, R, *b* and some 'mental' factors, also had for a factor the proposition *aRb*; although, *ex hypothesi*, this proposition is not one of the factors in the holding of a relation or relations between which this fact consists, and although it might also be true that there is no equivalent fact which does consist in the holding of a relation between this proposition and some not merely objective factors. As for the arguments which Mr Russell has brought forward to show that propositions are not genuine entities, and that therefore (3), and consequently (2) also, cannot be true, it seems to me perfectly certain that neither any one of them singly, nor all of them taken together, is by any means conclusive; nor can I find any which does seem to me conclusive. I am not persuaded, therefore, that either (3) or (2) are true, though it seems to me quite likely that they are.

As for the second view, incompatible with (2) and (3), which Mr Ramsey goes on to discuss, it seems to me perfectly certain that this view is false; but for a reason quite different from, and much simpler than, those which he gives. The view in question is as follows. Suppose S1 were judging now that Caesar was murdered, and S2 were judging now that Caesar was not murdered. There would then be two different facts of my second class, one corresponding to each of these two general facts. And what the view in question suggests is that each of these two facts of my second class has for an objective factor *the fact* that Caesar was murdered; according to Mr Ramsey, it even goes further than this, and suggests that this fact is the *only* objective factor in each of them, thus constituting a view which is incompatible with (1) as well as with (2) and (3). It holds, of course similarly, that wherever we have a general fact of the form 'S is now judging that *p*', where *p* is false, the fact corresponding to not-*p* (or some fact equivalent to it) is an objective factor in the fact of my second class corresponding to this general fact; and that, wherever we have a general fact of the form 'S is now judging that p', where p is true, the fact corresponding to p is an objective factor in the fact of my second class corresponding to this one.

My simple objection to this view is that the fact that Caesar was murdered could not possibly be a factor at all, either objective or otherwise, in any fact corresponding to a fact of the form 'S is now judging that Caesar was not murdered'; for the simple reason that, if it were, then from the mere fact that S was making the particular judgment he was making to the effect that Caesar was *not* murdered, it would *follow* that Caesar *was* murdered. From any fact whatever in which the fact that Caesar was murdered was a factor, it would, of course, follow that Caesar *was* murdered. And nothing seems to me more certain than that from a fact from which there follows a fact of the form 'S is now judging that p', it cannot possibly follow *also* that p is false. If, as this view says, it always *did* follow, then from the fact from which I was able to infer, in a particular case, that I *was* judging that p, I should always, if p happened in fact to be false, be able to infer with certainty that p was false. The very same fact of my second class which enabled a person who was judging that Caesar was *not* murdered, to know that he was making this judgment, would at the same time enable him to know with certainty that Caesar *was* murdered! It seems to me that this is an absolutely conclusive *reductio ad absurdum* of the view in question; and that hence, instead of saying, as this view says, that *wherever* we have a general fact of the form 'S is now judging that p', and p happens to be false, then the fact corresponding to not-p (or some equivalent fact) is a factor in the corresponding second-class fact, we must say, not merely the contradictory, but the contrary of this— namely, that in *no* such case can the fact corresponding to not-p be a factor in the corresponding second-class fact.

With regard to the second half of what it asserts, namely, that wherever we have a general fact of the form 'S is judging that p', and p is *true*, then the fact corresponding to p is a factor in the second-class fact corresponding to our general fact, the case is, I think, different; we are able here to assert with certainty the contradictory of this proposition, but not its contrary. This is because, if we use 'judge' in the very wide sense in which philosophers often do use it, i.e. a sense such that every case of *knowing* that p is also a case of *judging* that p, then there will be *some* general facts of the form 'S is judging that p', where p is true, such that from the corresponding second-class fact it really does follow that p, namely, those in which the corresponding second-class fact is a case of *knowing*. But here, too, we are able to assert with certainty the *contradictory* of the view in question, since it is quite certain that, even where p is in fact true, the second-class fact which enables us to know that we are judging that p does not *always* enable us to know that p.

The discussion of this view illustrates very clearly the importance of the distinction between facts of my first class and facts of my second. If, as Mr Ramsey implied in his second sentence, the kind of facts he was trying to analyse were really facts of my *first* class, then we should have to understand this view as asserting that the fact that Caesar was murdered is a factor both in any general fact of the form 'S is judging that Caesar was murdered' and in any general fact of the form 'S is judging that Caesar was not murdered'. And to this view we should be able to make the absolutely conclusive and general objection that from a fact of the form 'S is judging that p', there *never* follows either p or not-p. Nothing is more certain than that we so use the word 'judge' in English, that the proposition expressed by a sentence of the form 'S is judging that p, and p' is never a tautology; and the proposition expressed by a sentence of the form 'S is judging that p, but not-p' is never a contradiction. This is the great distinction between the use of the words 'judge' and 'believe', and the use of the words 'know' and 'perceive' (in that sense of 'perceive' in which we speak of 'perceiving', not things, but *that* so and so is the case). 'S knows that p, and p' or 'S perceives that p, and p' do express tautologies;[1] and 'S knows that p, but not-p' or 'S perceives that p, but not-p' do express contradictions. Mr Ramsey speaks of the view that 'perception is infallible', as if there were some doubt about it. I cannot see how there can be any doubt. To say that 'perception is infallible' is only an awkward way of saying that any proposition of the form 'S is perceiving that p' entails p. And if you are using

[1] This is a mistake which Moore later acknowledged but did not correct. Using the phrase 'if . . . then . . . ' truth-functionally, his point can be stated correctly by saying that while 'If S knows that p, then p' and 'If S perceives that p, then p' do express tautologies, 'If S is judging that p, then p' does not express a tautology. A similar mistake occurs later in this paragraph when Moore says that 'S is judging *truly* that p, and p' is a tautology.—C. L.

'perceives' in any way in which it can be correctly used in English, it is perfectly certain that the proposition expressed by any sentence of the form 'S is perceiving that p' *does* entail p; every expression of the form 'S is perceiving that p, but not-p' is quite certainly a contradiction in terms. Of course, this by itself tells us nothing as to the analysis of 'S is perceiving that p'; for it is equally true that 'S is judging *truly* that p, and p' is a tautology, and 'S is judging *truly* that p, but not-p' a contradiction. The doctrine that perception is infallible is, therefore, perfectly consistent with the view that 'perceives' merely means the same as 'judges truly'. But how anybody can doubt that perception always *is* infallible, and judgment always fallible, passes my comprehension. The first merely means 'S is perceiving that p, but not-p' is *always* a contradiction; the second merely means 'S is judging that p, but not-p' is *never* a contradiction. And both of these statements seem to me quite certainly true.

For these reasons it seems to me that the argument which Mr Ramsey actually brings against this view is quite irrelevant to the analysis of judgment, since the view is, in any case, quite untenable for the reasons I have given. But his argument is, I think, highly relevant to the subject of 'facts and propositions', and, therefore, I must try to consider it. Unfortunately, it seems to me very obscure both *what* the conclusion of it is supposed to be, and how the argument is supposed to yield that conclusion. The conclusion which he seems to draw is that what Mr Russell held to be true of judgment, i.e. that (1), (2) and (3) are all true, is true not only of judgment, but also of any form of knowledge, including perception; in which case it would seem to follow that he is maintaining that *facts* are not 'genuine entities' any more than propositions are. But he never expressly says so. All that he expressly says is that any analysis of the non-general fact corresponding to a fact of the form 'S is perceiving that p', which says that it *consists* in the holding of some relation or relations between the fact corresponding to p and some not merely objective factors, 'cannot be accepted as ultimate'. If he merely means by this that (1) is true, i.e. that in such a non-general fact there is always a *plurality* of objective factors—that it is *not* true that the only objective factor in it is the fact corresponding to p—then I should completely agree with him. If he means, further, that such a non-general fact is always *either* identical with *or* equivalent to a fact which consists in the holding of some relation or relations between a plurality of objective factors and some not merely objective factors, I should agree with him again. If he means, further still, that no such fact is either identical with or equivalent to a fact which does consist in the holding of some relation or relations between the fact corresponding to p and some not merely objective factors, then I feel very doubtful. And if he means, lastly, that in no such fact, nor in any fact equivalent to such a fact, is the fact corresponding to p a factor at all, I feel more doubtful still.

But how does he suppose his arguments to support any of these conclusions? He begins the argument by giving reasons, which I do not dispute, for saying that phrases of the form 'the fact that p' in sentences of the form 'S is perceiving the fact that p' are not names. He goes on to state that, in his opinion, such phrases are not descriptions either, but in favour of this opinion he offers no argument whatever. He merely suggests that those who hold the contrary opinion may have been led to hold it by confusing that usage of the phrase, 'the death of Caesar', in which, according to him, it really is a description (a description of an *event*), with another usage—that in which it has the same meaning as the phrase 'the fact that Caesar died', this latter being a usage in which, according to him, it is *not* a description. But even if it were true that those who hold that 'the fact that Caesar died' is a description, always hold it only because of this confusion, it would still remain possible that their opinion was a true one; and, so far as I can see, he gives no ground whatever for supposing that it is *not* a true one. But, even if a phrase of the form 'the fact that p' never is a description, what would follow from this? The only conclusion he directly draws is that, if such a phrase is neither a name nor a description, then such a proposition as 'I know the fact that Caesar died' must be analysed into 'Caesar died and p', where p is a proposition in which neither the fact that Caesar died, nor any character which belongs to that fact and that fact only, is a constituent. But does it follow that, supposing 'I know that Caesar died' also expresses a *fact*, then neither in the non-general fact corresponding to this general fact, nor in any fact equivalent to it, is the fact that Caesar died a factor? This is the conclusion he seems ultimately to draw, and I cannot see that it follows.

I will just state briefly the only clear point I can see about all this. I do see an objection, which I imagine Mr Ramsey would consider conclusive, to the view that expressions of the form 'the fact that *aRb*' ever are descriptions. If they ever are, then, if '*aRb*' does express a fact, there must be some character, ϕ, which belongs to that fact and to nothing else, which is such that the *proposition aRb* is *either* identical with *or* equivalent to a proposition, with regard to ϕ, to the effect that one and only one thing possesses it. And it seems, at first sight, to be perfectly obvious that every proposition, without exception, *is* either identical with or equivalent to some proposition, with regard to a certain character, to the effect that there is one fact, and one only, which has that character; this being, I imagine, why Mr Johnson holds that propositions *are* characters of facts;[1] although, of course, the mere fact that in the case of every *true* proposition, there is some character of a fact such that the proposition in question is either identical with or equivalent to a proposition to the effect that *there is a fact which has that character*, gives no justification whatever for the view that any proposition whatever, true or false, *is* a character of a fact. But now consider the hypothesis, with regard to the *fact aRb*, that there is some character ϕ, belonging to it and to nothing else, such that the *proposition aRb* is either identical with or equivalent to the proposition that there is one and only one fact which has ϕ. The only *constituents* of the proposition in question are *a*, R, and *b*, none of which is identical with ϕ; hence the proposition *aRb*, cannot be identical with the proposition 'There is one and only one thing which has ϕ'. But, on Mr Ramsey's principle, that two *different* facts or propositions cannot possibly be equivalent, there also cannot possibly be any character ϕ, such that the proposition *aRb* is *equivalent* to the proposition 'There is one and only one thing which has ϕ'. It would seem to follow, then, from this principle, that there cannot possibly be any character which belongs to the fact *aRb* and to nothing else; and hence that there cannot be any phrase which is a description of it. Hence, if I accepted Mr Ramsey's principle, I should think that a phrase of the form 'the fact that *aRb*' never can be a description. But, in fact, I do not see how we can possibly do justice to the facts without supposing that there are genuinely different propositions and

[1] *Logic*, Part I, p. 14.

genuinely different facts, which nevertheless mutually entail one another. And hence, I should say that phrases of the form 'the fact that *aRb*' *are* descriptions. And I think that my view on this point, whether true or false, is certainly not due to confusion between the two different usages of 'the death of Caesar', which Mr Ramsey points out. I was at one time habitually guilty of this confusion, but I discovered many years ago that it was a confusion.

Mr Ramsey next proceeds to an excursus, which is confessedly quite irrelevant to the analysis of judgment, but which is again highly relevant to the subject of 'facts and propositions'. In this excursus, he says two things: (1) that 'it is true that *p*' means no more than '*p*', and (2) that there is no problem of truth, separate from the problem of the analysis of judgment; that to analyse judgment is the same thing as to solve the problem of truth; and that it is only through a 'linguistic muddle' that anyone holds the contrary opinion.

I cannot help dissenting from both these opinions, although Mr Ramsey thinks their truth so obvious; and I will try to give quite clearly my reasons for dissent. Both points are very closely connected, and it will appear that the question whether I am right or he, again depends on whether his principle that there cannot be two different propositions or two different facts, each of which entails the other, is true; if it is true, then I think he must be right on this point also; but I think that what I am going to say is a good reason for supposing that principle of his to be false.

As regards (1), I admit that 'it is true that *p*' can be properly used in such a way that it means no more than '*p*'. But I hold that there is *another* usage of it, such that, in this usage, 'it is true that *p*' always means something *different* from *p*, although something which is *equivalent* to it, i.e. both entails and is entailed by it. And my reasons for this can best be given by considering (2).

As regards (2), I hold that a certain particular 'correspondence' theory of truth is a correct theory; that the question whether this theory is correct or not certainly forms a part of anything which could properly be called '*the* problem of truth'; but that it does not form any part of the problem of the analysis of judgment, but raises at least one quite distinct question. The particular 'correspondence' theory in question is as follows: In the case of facts of my first class—facts which could be expressed by the

use of a sentence of the form 'I am now judging that p', it sometimes happens that the particular p in question would also express
a fact, and sometimes that it would *not*. For instance, I sometimes
judge that it will be fine tomorrow, and it *is* fine the next day;
but sometimes when I so judge, it is *not* fine the next day. In
the first case, we should say that, in judging that p, I was judging
truly; in the second that, in judging that p, I was judging *falsely*.
Now it seems to me that, in many cases, where *both* expressions
of the form 'I am now judging that p' *and* the particular p in
question *would* express facts, we notice a certain relation which
holds between the first and the second of these two facts—a
relation which *only* holds between facts of my first class and other
facts, and which only holds between a fact of my first class and
another fact, where the particular p in question does express a
fact. Let us call this relation 'correspondence'. What I believe is,
that sometimes when we say 'In judging that p, I was judging
truly', we are thinking of this particular relation, and mean by
our expression: 'The fact that I was judging that p, *corresponds*
to *some* fact'. And my particular 'correspondence' theory of
truth is only a theory to the effect that some of the ways in which
we use 'true', are such that the meaning of 'true' is to be defined
by reference to this particular relation which I have called
'correspondence', and that *all* our usages of 'true' are such that a
proposition expressed by the help of that word is *equivalent* to
some proposition in which this relation occurs. It is obvious that
what 'corresponds' in my sense is never itself true; only facts of my
first class 'correspond', and these are never true. But many
usages of 'true' are, I hold, to be defined by reference to this
relation; and, in particular, *one* of the meanings of 'It is *true*
that p' is a meaning in which this means 'If anyone were to believe
that p, then the fact (of my first class) in question would *correspond*
to a fact'. To say this is, I hold, *equivalent* to saying 'p'—each
proposition entails the other; but they are not identical, since in
the one the relation of correspondence is a constituent, in the
other not.

Surely the question whether this particular 'correspondence'
theory is true or not forms a part of 'the problem of truth'?
And how can it form a part of the problem of the analysis of
judgment? I fancy what Mr Ramsey may have been meaning
to say is that the further problem as to the *analysis* of the relation

which I call 'correspondence' is identical with that of the analysis of judgment. But even this, it seems to me, cannot possibly be true, although obviously the analysis of judgment will have an extremely important bearing on the other problem.

Mr Ramsey next proceeds to consider what he calls the 'mental factors' in a belief; that is to say, if my former interpretation was right, those *not merely objective* factors in facts of my second class, which cannot be identified with that particular not merely objective factor which is the *time* about which the fact in question is a fact.

And here I confess I am in a great difficulty, because he goes on to say that it is only to one particular sub-class among facts of my second class that his remarks are intended to apply, and I cannot understand, from his language, *what* particular sub-class it is that he does intend them to apply to. He describes the sub-class in question as 'beliefs which are expressed in words, or possibly images or other symbols, consciously asserted or denied'. That is to say, it looks at first sight as if he meant to confine himself to cases in which he not only judges, e.g. that Caesar was murdered, but actually *expresses* his belief, by uttering aloud, or writing down, the words 'Caesar was murdered' or other equivalent words, or by using some other physical symbols. But his 'possibly images' seems inconsistent with this supposition; he cannot suppose that any belief could be *expressed*, in this sense, by the use of images. But what, then, does he mean by 'expressed'?

However, he goes on to say that he takes the 'mental factors of such a belief to be words spoken aloud, or to one's self, or merely imagined, connected together, and accompanied by a feeling or feelings of belief or disbelief'. This looks as if he meant to say that even if the belief in question is 'expressed' in images or other symbols and *not* in words, yet words are always present; but I suppose this is not what he means, but only that he is going to consider only those cases in which it is 'expressed' in words, and to assume that, where, if ever, it is 'expressed' in images or other symbols and *not* in words, the same will apply, *mutatis mutandis*, to the images or symbols as to the words in other cases. It looks also as if he meant to say that the feeling or feelings of belief or disbelief are *not* 'mental factors', but I suppose he really means to say that they are.

He next tells us that he will 'suppose for simplicity that the thinker with whom we are concerned uses a systematic language without irregularities and with an exact logical notation like that of *Principia Mathematica*'. That is to say, he proposes to give up the problem of the analysis of actual beliefs altogether, and to consider only what *would* be the analysis of a certain sub-class among facts of my second class, if the individual about whom they were facts used a language such as nobody does use. He goes on to say something about the manner in which the words which were 'mental factors' in such a fact *would* be related to the objective factors in it. And I gather part of his view to be that the only objective factors in it would be factors such that for each of them there was a 'name' among the mental factors.

I find it very difficult to extract from all this any definite propositions at all about actual beliefs. But I will mention three points as to which it seems to me (perhaps wrongly) that Mr Ramsey is implying something with which I should disagree. (1) It seems to me quite doubtful whether, even if we confine ourselves to cases of belief in which the proposition believed is what Mr Ramsey calls 'expressed' in words, the words in question are always, or even ever, factors in the fact of my second class at all. I cannot see why they should not merely *accompany* the mental factors in such a fact, and not themselves *be* such factors. Any words with which I *express* a belief do seem to me to be subsequent to the belief, and not, therefore, to be factors in it. (2) An enormous number of our actual beliefs seem to me to be beliefs in which some of the objective factors are sense-data or images presented to us at the moment; and I imagine this would be the case with many even of Mr Ramsey's sub-class, which are, in the sense he means, 'expressed' in words. In the case of these objective factors it seems to me there are no words which are 'names' for them or which represent them in any way, so that Mr Ramsey's 'feelings' of belief or disbelief would have to be related *directly* to these objective factors—not, as he implies, only related to them by being related to words which were 'names' for them or related to them in some other way. I do not see why Mr Ramsey's individual with the ideal language should not have such beliefs: but perhaps he would reply that such beliefs would not belong to his sub-class of beliefs 'expressed' in words. (3) Even if Mr Ramsey were right as to the last two points, there seems to me to be one very important relation between the mental and objective .factors, which he has entirely omitted to mention. He speaks as if it were sufficient that his ideal individual should have belief feelings attached to words, which were in fact *names which meant* the objective factors. It would surely be necessary also, not merely that those names should *mean* those objective factors, but that he should *understand* the names.

There are two other topics in Mr Ramsey's paper, about which I should like to say something, though I have not space to say much—namely his explanation of 'the mode of significance' of the word 'not', and of the words 'all' and 'some'.

As regards the first, I am by no means convinced that Mr Chadwick's view is not the true one; and Mr Ramsey's ground of objection to it (for I can only find *one*, though he speaks as if there were several) does not appeal to me at all. He points out that on Mr Chadwick's view 'not-not-*p*' would be a *different* proposition from '*p*', although, admittedly, 'not-not-*p*' follows formally from '*p*', and also '*p*' from 'not-not-*p*'; and he says he 'feels' that the conclusion of a formal inference must be 'contained' in the premisses in such a sense, that if *both* '*p*' is contained in 'not-not-*p*', *and also* 'not-not-*p*' is contained in '*p*', then '*p*' and 'not-not-*p*' must be identical. This is the proposition to which I have referred so often before: That there cannot be two *different* propositions which mutually entail one another. I have no feeling that it must be true, and have given a reason for dissenting from it.

Nevertheless, I am, of course, not convinced that Mr Chadwick's view is true, and I have a 'feeling' against it, to the effect that 'the mode of significance' of 'not' must be somehow derived from the relation of *dis*believing. I do not trust this feeling very much, because, as I have said, I cannot find any evidence that there are two fundamentally distinct occurrences—*dis*believing that *p* and believing that not-*p*. But the feeling inclines me to think that some such view as Mr Ramsey's is very likely true. The only point I should like to raise about that view is one which will perhaps show that I have misunderstood it. It seems to me that, on any view, there certainly are negative *facts*. It certainly is a fact, for instance, that King George is not at this moment in this room; or that the earth is not larger than the sun. On Mr Ramsey's view, would it be possible to give any analysis of such facts? I should have thought it would; and that the analysis would be of some such kind as that the first fact would be the fact that, if anyone were to disbelieve that King George is in this room, then this disbelief would, under certain circumstances, produce certain consequences: that if, for instance, it were to lead to certain expectations, these expectations would be realized. If Mr Ramsey's view would lead to the result that such a fact was to be analysed in some such way, I see no conclusive reason why it should not be true.

The other point is the 'mode of significance' of 'all' and 'some'.

In support of his view on this question, Mr Ramsey urges, among other arguments, that it is the only view which explains (1) how '*fa*' can be inferred from 'for all *x*, *fx*', and (2) how 'there is an *x* such that *fx*' can be inferred from '*fa*'. And with regard to these two arguments, I want to say that the first does not seem to me a strong one, because the supposed fact, which Mr Ramsey's view would explain, does not seem to me to be a fact. 'Can be inferred from' must plainly be understood to mean 'can be *formally* inferred from' or 'is entailed by': and I entirely deny that *fa is* entailed by 'for all *x*, *fx*'; *fa is* entailed by the conjunction 'for all *x*, *fx*' and '*a* exists'; but I see no reason to think that 'for all *x*, *fx*' *by itself* entails it. The fact, therefore, that Mr Ramsey's view would explain, and in fact render necessary, this supposed fact, seems to me not an argument in its favour, but against it.

But in the case of the second argument, I admit I do feel force in his contention that Mr Chadwick's theory as to the analysis of 'There is an *x* such that *fx*' gives no intelligible connection between 'This is red' and 'Something is red'. I do not know, however, that Mr Chadwick's theory is the only alternative to his, though I can think of no other. And I must admit that I feel a stronger objection to his than I do to Mr Chadwick's.

Mr Ramsey then goes on to answer supposed objections to his view.

The first objection is one which he puts in the form: 'It will be said that *a* cannot enter into the meaning of "for all *x*, *fx*", because I can assert this without ever having heard of *a*.' And to this he gives two answers. His first answer does not seem to me to meet the objection, since what the objection denies is *not* that, when we judge 'for all *x*, *fx*', we are making a judgment '*about* things we have never heard of and so have no names for'; obviously, in *some* sense of 'about' we are. By saying that *a* does not *enter into the meaning of* 'for all *x, fx*', what it means is that, in judging that 'for all *x, fx*', we are not judging *about a* in the *same sense* as if we were judging *fa*—that, in short, *a, b, c, d*, etc., are not all of them *factors* in a fact of my second class corresponding to 'I am judging that for all *x, fx*'. I must own it seems to me obvious that they are not: and this answer of Mr Ramsey's goes no way to meet my objection. Nor does his second answer. This is that *a* certainly is 'involved in the meaning of' 'for all *x, fx*', because 'not-*fa*' is certainly inconsistent with 'for all *x, fx*'. This answer seems to me to make two separate assumptions, both of which I should dispute. Namely (1) that if '*fa*' is entailed by 'for all *x, fx*', then '*fa*' must be *contained* in it. I have already said that this proposition does not appeal to me as self-evident. And (2) that, since 'not-*fa*' is inconsistent with 'for all *x, fx*', therefore 'for all *x, fx*' must entail '*fa*'. This seems to me to be a mistake because 'not-*fa*' in the sense in which it is inconsistent with 'for all *x, fx*', is not the contradictory of '*fa*', but equivalent to the conjunction of '*a* exists' with the contradictory of '*fa*'. All that follows, then, from the fact that 'not-*fa*' is inconsistent with 'for all *x, fx*', is not that the latter entails '*fa*', but, as I said before, that the latter, *together with* '*a* exists', entails '*fa*'.

The second objection is one which Mr Ramsey calls 'more serious', and he says that he has not space to give a full answer to it. He tries, instead, to retort to it with a *tu quoque*. In this retort, however, he makes a step, of which I, at least, should deny the validity. He supposes that if the objector admits (as I should admit) that numerical difference is a *necessary relation*, he is bound also to admit that, supposing *a, b, c* are not everything, but there is also another thing *d*, then that *d* is not identical with *a, b*, or *c* is a *necessary fact*. But I should hold that, though numerical difference is a necessary relation, yet, in the case supposed, that *d* is other than *a* is *not* a necessary fact. For numerical difference is a *necessary relation* only in the sense that, *if a* and *d* both exist, then *a* must be other than *d*. But to say that '*a* is other than *d*' is a necessary fact would entail besides that '*a* exists' is necessary, and that '*d* exists' is necessary, which I should deny.

IV

IS GOODNESS A QUALITY?

I do not think that these words 'Is Goodness a Quality?' have any clear meaning. But the question which I intend to raise is, I think, a perfectly definite one; and I can explain quite simply what it is. In his recent book, *Some Problems in Ethics*, Mr Joseph tells us, in one place (page 75), that he is going to 'defend the assertion that goodness is not a quality'. Accordingly, the question: 'Is what Mr Joseph, in this passage, means by the words "Goodness is not a quality" true or false?' is, it seems to me, a definite question. And that is the question which I intend to raise. Other people might, no doubt, understand the words 'Goodness is not a quality' in a very different sense from that in which Mr Joseph understands them; and perhaps with equal, or even greater, justification. But I don't want to discuss whether what other people might mean by 'Goodness is not a quality' is or is not true. I want merely to discuss whether what Mr Joseph means by this sentence is so. I am, therefore, understanding the words 'Is Goodness a Quality?' simply as short for 'Is what Mr Joseph, in this passage, means by "Goodness is not a quality" true or not?'

I think this question is a definite one; but it does not seem to me to be a question which we can discuss, without first discussing what Mr Joseph does mean by these words. For he does not seem to me to have succeeded in making at all clear what he does mean. There are two distinct points about both of which I, personally, am very much puzzled: namely, firstly, how he is using the word 'goodness', and secondly, how he is using the word 'quality'. I will try to explain clearly what my doubts are as to his usage of each word, in the hope that this may help him to explain to us clearly how he actually is using them.

To begin with 'goodness'.

We all of us very often both use and understand sentences in which the adjective 'good' occurs. But it seems to me very certain that in different sentences we both use and understand this word in a considerable number of different senses. In other words, the word 'good' is highly ambiguous: it is not only used, but correctly used, in a number of different senses. This is a point which Dr Ross, in his *The Right and the Good*, seems to me to have been right in emphasizing. 'A study of the meaning of "good" . . . should', he says (page 65), 'begin by recognizing that there is a wide diversity of senses in which the word is used.' He goes on to try to enumerate and distinguish some of the chief of these senses; and I should have thought that no one could read what he says without at least being convinced that the word 'good' *is* used in a considerable number of different senses. But, if so, and if (as I gather Mr Joseph does) we use the word 'goodness' simply as the noun corresponding to the adjective 'good', there will be as many different senses of 'goodness' as there are of 'good'. And hence when we come to ask how Mr Joseph is using 'goodness' in the words 'Goodness is not a quality', we are faced with the questions: Is he perhaps talking of *all* the different senses of 'goodness' and saying that *none* of them are qualities? Or is he perhaps talking, not of all, but of a few selected senses, and saying that none of *them* are qualities? Or has he perhaps in view one sense, and one only, and is merely saying of that one that *it* is not a quality? And, if either of the latter alternatives is the true one, *which* are the senses or sense of which he is saying that *they* are not qualities, or that *it* is not a quality?

To none of these questions can I find any certain answer. I do not even know whether Mr Joseph admits that the word 'good' is ambiguous. Perhaps he thinks that it is not, and that we always use it in exactly the same sense. If so, then, if it is in fact ambiguous, he would, of course, be implying that *none* of its senses are qualities; and perhaps, in any case, he does hold this. But even if he does, there is, I think, some reason to think that it is only with regard to a specially selected group of senses that he is mainly anxious to assert that they are not qualities. And I will try to explain as clearly as I can what I think these senses are.

Mr Joseph introduces this contention that 'goodness is not a quality' as part, but only part, of an argument designed to show something else, namely this: that '*if* there is any character common to right acts, in virtue of which it is that we think we ought to do them . . . [this character] is not one that can properly be called a *quality* of them' (page 73). In order to prove this latter proposition, he assumes that the character in question (if there is one) is either 'a form of goodness' or else the character of being 'instrumental to the being of what is intrinsically good' (page 75). And, granted this assumption, it is obvious that, in order to reach his conclusion, he only needs to prove two further things: namely (1) that the character of being 'instrumental to the being of what is intrinsically good' cannot properly be called a *quality*; and (2) that no 'form of goodness' can properly be called a *quality*. Accordingly, he argues first (pages 73–5) that the character of being 'instrumental to the being of what is intrinsically good' is not a quality: his main argument being apparently that, if a given event *a* is the cause of another particular event *b* (say, for instance, a particular explosion), then the character of 'being cause of the explosion *b*' is identical with the relation 'being cause of' and hence since the relation 'being cause of' is not a quality of the event *a*, therefore the character of 'being cause of the explosion *b*' is not a quality of *a*; but he adds, as a subsidiary argument, that even if the character of 'being cause of the explosion *b*' is *not* identical with the relation 'being cause of' (as one would have thought was obviously the case), yet it is not a quality, because 'there is a fundamental distinction between ποιόν and πρός τι'. Having thus, in his own opinion, satisfactorily disposed of the view that the character of being 'instrumental to the being of what is intrinsically good' can properly be called a *quality*, he only needs, in order to complete his argument, to show that no 'form of goodness' can properly be called a *quality*. And it is in order to show this that he tries to show that 'goodness is not a quality'. He assumes as a premiss that, if goodness is not a quality, then no sort of *'intrinsic* goodness' is a quality (page 75). And it seems clear that he uses the expression 'No *form* of goodness is a quality' to mean precisely the same as 'No *sort* of *intrinsic* goodness is a quality'. What he wants to show, then, is that 'No sort of intrinsic goodness is a quality'. And his argument to show this is of the following form. There is assumed as a premiss that from 'Goodness is not a quality' there follows 'No sort of intrinsic goodness is a quality'. There then follows what he regards as an argument to prove the conclusion 'Goodness is not a quality'. And from this conclusion, together with the assumed premiss, there will, of course, follow 'No sort of intrinsic goodness is a quality'.

It seems clear, then, that what Mr Joseph is mainly anxious to show is that what he calls 'forms' or 'sorts' or 'kinds' (he

uses all three expressions in different places) of 'intrinsic goodness'
are in no case 'qualities'. And this suggests that what he is mainly
concerned with are those senses of the word 'good' (if there are
several), in which 'good' stands for a character which is, in some
sense, 'intrinsic' to anything which is 'good' in the sense in question. From the fact (if it were a fact) that none of the 'intrinsic'
characters for which 'good' stands was a quality, it might, perhaps,
follow that no 'sorts' of *intrinsic* goodness were qualities. Whereas
if we took any sense of the word 'good' in which it does *not* stand
for an 'intrinsic' character, it is difficult to see how from the fact
(if it were a fact) that such a character was not a quality, it could
possibly follow that any 'sort' of *intrinsic* goodness was not a
quality. It seems clear then, that even if Mr Joseph does wish to
assert that none of the different 'characters' for which 'good'
stands in its various different usages are qualities, the only part
of that assertion which could be relevant to his argument here
would be that which asserts that none of the *intrinsic* characters
for which it stands are qualities; and hence there is reason to
think that when he says 'Goodness is not a quality', what he has
mainly in mind is that specially selected group among the usages
of the word 'good' in which this word stands for an *intrinsic*
character.

I think, therefore, Mr Joseph is mainly concerned with those
among the usages of the word 'good' (if there are several), or
that one among those usages (if there is only one), in which the
word stands for a character which is, in some sense, 'intrinsic'.
He certainly does maintain that there are one or more *intrinsic*
characters among the characters for which it stands, and it is
certainly one of his main objects to show that none of *these*
are 'qualities'. But even if we substitute the more definite assertion
'None among the *intrinsic* characters for which the word "good"
stands is a quality', for his original 'Goodness is not a quality',
I am afraid we are still not at an end of the discussion of what he
means. For in what sense is he using this word 'intrinsic'? What
does he mean by *'intrinsic* goodness'? I do not think that the
meaning of the phrase is at all clear. I think it may be, and is,
used in more senses than one. And, so far as I can see, Mr Joseph
has made no attempt to explain in which of these various senses
he is using it. But until we know what is meant by saying, of a
particular usage of the word 'good', that the character for which it

stands in that usage is an 'intrinsic' character, we are not in a position to know in which usages (if any) 'good' does stand for an 'intrinsic' character; nor, therefore, of which of the usages of 'good' it is that Mr Joseph is particularly anxious to maintain that the character for which it stands in those usages (or that usage) is *not* a quality.

This business of getting clear oneself, and explaining to others, how one uses the expressions '*intrinsic* value' or '*intrinsically* good' is one which still puzzles me extremely. I have written about it twice already. In my *Ethics* (page 65) I define '*x* is intrinsically good' as meaning 'it would be a good thing that *x* should exist, even if *x* existed *quite alone*, without any further accompaniments or effects whatever'. And I still think both that this is *one* of the ways in which the phrase 'intrinsically good' can properly be used, and that there are things which are intrinsically good in this sense. But to this usage of the phrase, the following objection might, and I think would, be made by some people. It might be said: 'When you say that by "*x* is intrinsically good" you mean "it would be a *good* thing that *x* should exist, even if it existed quite alone", you presumably mean the words "it would be a *good* thing that" to be understood in one of the senses in which they are commonly used. But, as a matter of fact, all the senses in which these words are used are such that to say of anything, *x*, "it would be good that *x* should exist quite alone" is self-contradictory. Your conception of intrinsic goodness, therefore, though a clear one enough, is a self-contradictory one; and it is, therefore, quite impossible that anything should be "intrinsically good" in your sense.' Now, I do not think this is true; but to show that it is not true is certainly not an easy matter. It is by no means obvious that to say of anything that it would be good that it should exist, even if it existed quite alone, is not self-contradictory. It is not easy, therefore, to show that any of the senses in which we actually use the word 'good' is one in which 'good' means the same as 'intrinsically good' in *this* sense. And a similar objection applies to another and different definition of 'intrinsic value', which I gave in *Philosophical Studies* (page 260). I there say: 'To say that a kind of value is "intrinsic" means merely that the question whether a thing possesses it, and in what degree it possesses it, depends solely on the intrinsic nature of the thing in question.' And here again I still think I am

right in supposing that one thing that may properly be meant by
'*x* is intrinsically good' or 'intrinsically valuable' is '*x* is good
(or valuable) in a sense, such that the question whether a thing is
good (or valuable) in that sense, and in what degree it is so,
depends solely on the intrinsic nature of *x*'; and right also that
some things are 'intrinsically good' in such senses. But here
again many people would say (and perhaps they are right) that
there are *no* senses in which we use the words 'good' or 'valuable',
which are such that the question whether a thing is 'good' or
'valuable' in that sense, and in what degree it is, does depend
only on its intrinsic nature, in the sense of 'dependence' explained.

Is there not another way of explaining how the phrase 'intrinsically good' is used, which is not liable to this kind of
objection? I think there is. An expression which is fairly commonly
used, and which is, I think, intelligible to everybody, is that
which we use when we say of an experience which we have had
that it 'was worth having for its own sake'. 'Worth having for its
own sake' does not mean the same as 'worth having'; since we
may say of an experience, e.g. 'That experience was *worth having*,
because it taught me a lesson', whereas to say 'That experience
was *worth having for its own sake*, because it taught me a lesson'
would be self-contradictory; though, of course, to say 'That
experience was worth having *both* for its own sake *and* because
it taught me a lesson' is not self-contradictory and may perfectly
well be true. We can, of course, say that 'That experience was
worth having' means the same as 'That experience was a good' in
one of the senses in which the phrase 'a good' is used; and that
'That experience was worth having for its own sake' means the
same as 'That experience was a good', in *another* of the senses
in which the phrase 'a good' is used. And we can also say that
'That experience of mine was worth having' means the same as
'It was a good thing that I had that experience', in *one* of the
senses of 'It was a good thing that . . . '; and that 'That experience
of mine was worth having for its own sake' means the same as
'It was a good thing that I had that experience' in *another* of the
senses of 'It was a good thing that . . . ' Now suppose we say:
I use the phrase 'intrinsically good' to mean precisely the same
as 'worth having for its own sake'; and I use the expression
' "Good", in this usage, stands for an intrinsic character' to
mean precisely the same as ' "Good", in this usage, means the

same as "worth having for its own sake" '. It seems to me that, if we say this, we have given a clear explanation of how we use 'intrinsically good', and also of how we use ' "Good", in this usage, stands for an intrinsic character'; and that many people do actually use the expressions in this way. And, if we confine ourselves to saying that we use 'intrinsically good' in this way, it cannot be objected that what we express by these words is a self-contradictory character, or one which applies to nothing; for 'worth having for its own sake' certainly means something, and something not self-contradictory, and certainly many experiences may be worth having for their own sakes. I think that how this way of explaining a use of 'intrinsically good' is related to the other two, is as follows. It may be held, and I should be inclined to hold, that 'That experience was worth having for its own sake' means precisely the same as 'That experience would have been worth having, even if it had existed quite alone': but if you thus say that the two expressions do mean the same, you are saying something which may be questioned and is perhaps not true. Similarly, I am inclined to hold that the character which we express by 'worth having for its own sake' is, in fact, a character such that whether a given experience possesses it, and the degree in which it possesses it, depends solely on the intrinsic nature of that experience: but that it is is something doubtful, and which may and would be disputed. So long as I merely say that I use 'intrinsically good' to mean the same as 'worth having for its own sake', I think I am explaining fairly clearly how I use the term, and that without committing myself to either of these doubtful assertions.

It will be noticed that if we do use 'intrinsically good' in this sense, we are using it in a sense in which nothing but an experience *can* be 'intrinsically good', since nothing but an experience can be 'had' in the sense in which an experience is 'had': nothing but my experiences can be 'mine' in the same sense of 'mine' in which they are 'mine'. And this fact might seem to show that this cannot be the only sense in which Mr Joseph uses the expression 'intrinsically good'; since from his instances on pages 78–9, it would appear that he is using 'intrinsically good' both in such a sense that to say of a man that he is a good man is the same thing as to say that he is 'intrinsically good', and also in such a sense that to say of a poem that it is a good poem is the same

thing as to say that it is 'intrinsically good'. It seems to me quite
certain that these two senses of the word 'good' are different
both from one another and from that in which we use it when we
use it to mean the same as 'worth having for its own sake'. But
though this sense of 'intrinsically good' is perhaps not the *only*
one in which Mr Joseph uses that phrase, I think it is *one* of
those in which he uses it, and *the* one in which he is using it in
connection with his main problem about right action. When
he says that right actions are sometimes 'intrinsically good', I
think he is using the term 'right action' in such a sense that a
'right action' always consists at least partly (perhaps wholly?)
in the having of some experience; and I should agree with him
that part, at least, of the experience in the having of which it
consists is often worth having for its own sake. At all events, part
at least of what he means by 'Goodness is not a quality' must,
I think, be that the character which we attribute to an experience
when we say that it was 'worth having for its own sake' is not a
quality; and this proposition, if only we could discover how he is
using the word 'quality', would, I think, be definite enough to be
discussed.

How, then, is he using the term 'quality'?

This, I think, is an even more puzzling question than the
question how he is using the word 'goodness'. All that I can do
is to try to pick up some hints which he has dropped in the course
of his 'defence' of the assertion that 'Goodness is not a quality'.

In what does this 'defence' consist?

It begins with the statement 'That goodness is not a quality
is the burden of Aristotle's argument in the *Nicomachean Ethics*,
I, vi, though equally the teaching of Plato in the *Republic*'.
And the first of these references certainly ought to throw some
light on what Mr Joseph means by 'Goodness is not a quality',
if only one could discover what the burden of that very obscure
chapter is. To me, I admit, Aristotle's meaning is too obscure
to throw any light on Mr Joseph's; and I cannot help doubting
whether there is any single proposition which can properly be
called *the* burden of his argument. As for the reference to Plato,
that must be useless for purposes of elucidating until Mr Joseph
tells us *which* of the thousand things which Plato teaches in the
Republic is *the* one which he identifies with his proposition.

There next follows a page and a half of quotations from my

Principia Ethica, intended to show that I have 'failed to appreciate, or at least to express myself as if I appreciated' that 'Goodness is not a quality'; and ending up with the statement '*All* this, if I may say so, seems to me error'. Just *one* item among the 'all' is a quotation in which I say that ' "good" denotes a simple and indefinable quality'. And what *I* meant by saying that 'good' denoted a *quality*, I think I can say quite simply. I meant merely that the character of being worth having for its own sake *was* a character and was *not* a relational property: that and nothing more. But this can hardly be all that Mr Joseph means to deny when he says 'Goodness is not a quality'. For, if it were, why make all the other quotations, which have nothing to do with this simple point?

So far I fail to find any 'defence' of the assertion that 'Goodness is not a quality' nor anything which helps to explain how Mr Joseph is using the word 'quality'.

For hints as to his usage we must look to the next two pages of the 'defence' (pages 78–9); and here I find the following:

(1) Mr Joseph tells us that the goodness of God 'cannot be thought of as a quality, *which he might get or lose*'. This suggests that part of what he means by saying that the character of being worth having for its own sake 'is not a quality', is simply that it can't be 'got or lost'. And so far as this is what he means, I completely agree with him.

(2) He says 'What is peculiar about good is that, if you could define *the* good or what has goodness (which Professor Moore says can be defined), you would thereby define its good or goodness (which he says is indefinable). That holds for any subject which *is* good . . . It is true of the goodness of a poem, which is really identical with the poem . . . If the poet in turn is good, his goodness is identical with him, as this spiritual being . . . ' And later on (page 79) 'Suppose there can be a perfectly good poem . . . *Its* goodness could not be apprehended or learnt by reading a different poem, nor without reading this; and the only definition of its goodness is really the poem itself'.

These passages hint, I think, at what is really the most important part of what Mr Joseph means by saying of any character, which is among those which the word 'good' is sometimes used to express, that it 'is not a quality'—at that part of his meaning on which he is really most anxious to insist. But they also hint that some-

D

thing else—something, I think, comparatively unimportant—is also a part of his meaning; and I will mention this comparatively unimportant thing first, to get it out of the way.

(a) Both the first and the last sentences quoted assert that some 'goodness' or other is definable—has a definition. And the fact that Mr Joseph thinks it worth while to assert this in his 'defence', suggests that part of what he means by saying of any character which the word 'good' expresses that it 'is not a quality', is simply that it is definable. Thus if we take the particular character of 'being worth having for its own sake', part of what he means by saying that this character 'is not a quality', would seem to be simply that it is definable. And if this is part of what he means, I would say at once that, so far as this part is concerned, I think he is very likely right. In *Principia* I asserted and proposed to prove that 'good' (and I think I sometimes, though perhaps not always, was using this word to mean the same as 'worth having for its own sake') was indefinable. But all the supposed proofs were certainly fallacious; they entirely failed to prove that 'worth having for its own sake' is indefinable. And I think perhaps it is definable: I do not know. But I also still think that very likely it *is* indefinable. And I entirely fail to see that Mr Joseph has brought forward any good reason for his view that it is definable. The only reason which I can find him alleging is that which I am going on now to consider; and I shall give my reasons for thinking that this is *not* a good one.

(b) What other hints do these passages contain as to what may be part of Mr Joseph's meaning? It will be noticed that the first of them insists that what is good is *identical* with '*its* goodness': a good poem *is identical with* '*its* goodness'; a good man *is identical with* '*his* goodness'. And, similarly, if we were to take that particular sense of 'good' in which 'good' means 'worth having for its own sake', I suppose Mr Joseph would insist that any one particular experience which was 'good' in this sense was identical with *its* goodness, and any other, different from the first, identical in its turn with *its*. But this expression 'its goodness', whatever particular sense of 'good' we take, is always ambiguous: it may mean either of two entirely different things. Suppose, for instance, that we take that sense of 'good' in which we use the word when we say that a poem is good. Then the statement, with regard to a particular poem, that it is identical with *its* goodness may mean either of two entirely different things. (1) We may be using 'its goodness' in such a way that we can substitute for those words the words 'the character which we are rightly attributing to this poem when we say that it is good'. If we use it in this way 'This poem is identical with its goodness' will mean 'This poem is identical with the character which we rightly attribute to it when we say that it is good'. And it will follow that the character which we rightly attribute to one poem when we say that it is good cannot possibly be identical with that which we rightly attribute to another when we say that *it* is good: that, in short, when we say of one poem that it is good, we are never using 'good' in the same sense as when we say of another that it is good: that on the contrary, when we say of one 'This poem is good' we are merely enunciating the tautology 'This poem is this poem', and when we say of another that *it* is good we are merely enunciating the different tautology '*This* poem is this poem'. (2) But we may be using 'its goodness' in an entirely different way. We may be so using it that for the words 'its goodness' we can substitute the words 'the special complex of characters which justify us in calling it a good poem'. 'This poem is identical with its goodness' will then mean 'This poem is identical with the special complex of characters which justify us in calling it good'. This, it seems to me, is how Mr Joseph is using the phrase 'its goodness' when on page 79 he says: 'Suppose there can be a perfectly good poem . . . *its* goodness could not be apprehended or learnt by reading a different poem, or without reading this'; and the fact that what he there says strikes us as true, shows, I think, that the phrase 'its goodness' can be naturally used in this way. 'Its goodness' may, then, mean either of two entirely different things, when we are using 'good' in the sense in which we apply it to a poem. And there is exactly the same ambiguity when we use it in the sense in which it means the same as 'worth having for its own sake'. The statement, with regard to a particular complex experience, 'This experience is identical with its goodness' *may* mean either (1) 'This experience is identical with the character which we rightly attribute to it when we say that it is worth having for its own sake', in which case it would follow that when we say of two different experiences that they are worth having for their own sake, we are never using the words 'worth having for its own sake' in the same sense in both cases; or (2) 'This experience is identical with the special complex of characters which justifies us in saying that it is worth having for its own sake'.

It seems to me that part of what Mr Joseph means by the statement that the character of being worth having for its own sake 'is not a quality' must be one or other or both of the statements —(a) that in the case of every experience which is worth having for its own sake (1) can truly be said, or (b) that in the case of every such experience (2) can truly be said. Which of the two, (a) or (b), is it that he is asserting, or is it both? I think both; and that he has confused the two. That he is asserting (a) is shown by three things. It is shown by the fact that he asserts in the first sentence that I have declared 'its good or goodness' to be indefinable: for he must have known that what I had asserted to be indefinable was only 'its goodness' in the sense of 'the character which we rightly attribute to it when we say that it is good', *not* in the sense of 'the complex of characters which justify us in calling it good'. It is shown further by the fact that it is only from (a), and not from (b), that it would follow that the character which we attribute to an experience when we say that it is worth having for its own sake is indefinable. And it is shown further, I think, by the fact that on page 83 he expressly asserts the self-contradictory proposition that 'in some examples of what is good, the goodness is at once (a) identical with what is good . . . ; and also (b) distinguishable from what is good'.

But, so far as he is asserting (a) it seems to me that he is quite certainly wrong. It seems to me quite certain that when I assert of two different experiences that they are both worth having for their own sakes, the character which I am attributing to the one is precisely the same as that which I am attributing to the other, and that hence this character cannot possibly be identical with either of the two experiences.

And in so far as he is asserting (b) also, I think he is also wrong. I think that the peculiar complex of characters which justifies us in saying that an experience is worth having for its own sake is *never* identical with the experience in question; for the simple reason that it is always possible that there should be *another* experience having exactly the same complex of characters. I think, perhaps, Mr Joseph may have been misled as to this by considering 'goodness' in the sense in which it belongs to a poem. In that case I think it may, perhaps, be true that a perfectly good poem really would be identical with the peculiar complex of characters which would justify us in calling it good. For there cannot be two different poems exactly like one another: the supposition is nonsensical. Whereas it is certainly not nonsensical to suppose that there may have been two different experiences exactly like one another.

V

IMAGINARY OBJECTS

Both Mr Ryle and Mr Braithwaite seem to me to raise so many different points in their papers that it is impossible to discuss them all; and I have not succeeded in getting any clear view as to which are the most important among these points. All I can hope to do, therefore, is to state clearly, and discuss, *some* of the points they seem to me to raise, without any confidence that I shall not omit others which are more important than those I touch on, and with a certainty that I shall not have arranged these points in the manner best calculated to throw light on their mutual connections.

I propose to confine myself to discussing the first of the three classes of propositions, which Mr Ryle distinguishes under the head of 'propositions which seem to be about Mr Pickwick'—namely the class which he describes as 'those which Dickens makes in *Pickwick Papers*'. And in dealing with this class I propose to do three things. First, I shall try to state as clearly as I can what class of propositions it is to which I take Mr Ryle to be referring by these words; secondly, I shall ask what are the main things which Mr Ryle seems to wish to say about propositions of this class, and whether those things are true; and thirdly, I shall ask what are the main things which Mr Braithwaite seems to wish to say about them, and whether the things he says about them are true.

(1) First, then: What exactly is the class of propositions which Mr Ryle describes as 'Propositions, seeming to be about Mr Pickwick, which Dickens makes in *Pickwick Papers*'?

I will give an example. In Chapter XII of *Pickwick Papers* we find the words: 'Mrs Bardell had fainted in Mr Pickwick's arms.' And the proposition which Dickens was making when he wrote these words is undoubtedly, I take it, an example of the class of propositions which Mr Ryle means. Of course the *words* 'Mrs Bardell had fainted in Mr Pickwick's arms' cannot be identified with the *proposition* which Dickens was making when he wrote them. If he had written the words, without attaching any meaning to them, he would not have been making any proposition at all, and would not therefore have been making the proposition that Mrs Bardell had fainted in Mr Pickwick's arms—which is the proposition he *was* making. And, on the other hand, he might quite easily have made this very same proposition, without using the words 'Mrs Bardell had fainted in Mr Pickwick's arms' at all: he would have done so, if he had written instead the very different words 'Mrs Bardell *s'était évanouie dans les bras de* Mr Pickwick'. The fact, therefore, that Dickens wrote the words 'Mrs Bardell had fainted, etc.' is a totally different fact from the fact that he made the proposition that Mrs Bardell had fainted in Mr Pickwick's arms. I take it that it is the proposition he made and not the words he used in making it which is a member of Mr Ryle's class of propositions; and I will speak of this proposition as the proposition which Dickens *expressed by the sentence* 'Mrs Bardell had fainted, etc.'

What other propositions besides the one expressed by this sentence belong to Mr Ryle's class? I think we can say at once: Obviously all the propositions which resemble this one, in the respect that they are propositions which Dickens expressed in *Pickwick Papers* by sentences in which the words 'Mr Pickwick' occur. But are these the only members of the class? I think not; I think Mr Ryle would include also propositions expressed by many sentences in *Pickwick Papers* in which the words 'Mr Pickwick' do *not* occur, provided there occurs in them *some* word, e.g. 'he' or 'him', such that the words 'Mr Pickwick' could be substituted for the word in question without altering the meaning of the sentence. So far as I can see, this will give us a sufficiently clear definition of the class Mr Ryle means.

(2) Assuming that this is the class of proposition meant, what are the main things which Mr Ryle wishes to tell us about propositions of this class, and are these things he tells us true?

(*a*) The point about them to which he seems to give most prominence is something which he expresses by saying that they are not 'about anyone' and are not 'about Mr Pickwick'. Is what he means by this true?

Consider the sentence 'Mrs Bardell had fainted, etc.' Mr Ryle says that the proposition which Dickens expressed by this sentence was not 'about anyone' and was not 'about Mr Pickwick'. And I think that *part* of what he means by this is as follows. I think he means that there never has existed any human being such that, if somebody had pointed at that human being and had said 'That is the person whom Dickens meant by "Mr Pickwick" in that sentence', the person who said so would have been speaking the truth. And so far as he does mean this, of course I agree with him. This is a characteristic which really does distinguish Dickens's use of the name Mr Pickwick in that sentence from Mr Ryle's use of the name 'Mr Baldwin', when, in the early part of his paper, he wrote 'Mr Baldwin is an English statesman'. There *has* existed a human being at which somebody could have pointed and said with truth 'That is the person Mr Ryle meant by the name "Mr Baldwin" when he wrote that sentence'.

But so far as Mr Ryle means this, as to which I agree, I think he is saying something which no philosopher would ever have disputed. No doubt what he says would have been disputed by any naïve person (if there has been such a person) who took *Pickwick Papers* for a true story. Such a person would have said: There has existed a person, at whom one might have pointed and said truly 'That is the person whom the writer of this story meant by "Mr Pickwick" '. His belief that this was so would have been part of his belief that *Pickwick Papers* was a true story—it would have been identical with that part of this belief which consisted in believing that Mr Pickwick was a real person. But I see no reason to believe that any philosopher has ever believed that *Pickwick Papers* was a true story; and, even if one had, that belief would have formed no part of his philosophical opinions. Mr Ryle seems to think that in saying that the proposition which Dickens expressed by 'Mrs Bardell had fainted, etc.' is *not about Mr Pickwick*, he is expressing a view which is inconsistent with *the philosophical views* of some philosopher. I conclude, therefore, that, though this proposition which nobody but a believer in the historicity of Mr Pickwick would dispute, is *part* of what he means, it cannot be the whole. What else does he mean? and is *that* true too?

I think another part of what he means is something with which I also agree, but which I cannot take space to explain fully. I think he means that, when Dickens wrote that sentence, he was not using 'Mr Pickwick' as what Mr Braithwaite calls 'a logically proper name'. This, I think, is something which some philosophers really have disputed as part of their philosophical opinions.

That Dickens was using 'Mr Pickwick' as a 'logically proper name' is, I think, part at least of what is meant by those who would insist that though Mr Pickwick never *existed* and, therefore, was of course not a real person, nevertheless Mr Pickwick 'has being' or 'does subsist'. So far as Mr Ryle means to deny this view of these philosophers, I, of course, agree with him. But it seems to me that in many parts of his paper, particularly in what he says about the meaning of 'being real', he utterly confuses this proposition that Dickens was not using 'Mr Pickwick' as a 'logically proper name', with the totally different proposition that he was not using 'Mr Pickwick' as a proper name (in the ordinary sense) *for anyone*. This, of course, involves a confusion between two corresponding senses of 'about'. So far as by 'Dickens's proposition was not *about* anyone' Mr Ryle means 'Dickens was not using "Mr Pickwick" as a logically proper name', he is using 'about' in one sense, and is saying something inconsistent with a philosophical view which has been held. So far as he means only 'There never existed anyone at whom one could have pointed and said truly' 'That is the person Dickens meant by 'Mr Pickwick' " ', he is using 'about' in a totally different sense, and is saying something that is of no interest for philosophy. But he seems to me to have been quite unaware of the difference between the two.

However, I agree that two things, both of which I think he means, are true. I have now to mention a third thing, which I think he also means, and which seems to me to be false. I think he really is thinking that there is *no* natural sense of the word 'about', such that the words 'That proposition of Dickens was about Mr Pickwick' express a true proposition. With this I simply cannot agree. It seems to me that these words are perfectly good natural English for something which *is* true. In suggesting, as I think he does, that there is *no* sense they might naturally bear, in which they express a truth, I think Mr Ryle is simply failing to do justice to the richness in ambiguity of the English language. Instead of describing the propositions we are concerned with as propositions 'which seem to be about Mr Pickwick' he might, in my opinion, have described them, far more naturally, and certainly quite correctly, as propositions which *are* about Mr Pickwick, and he might have done so in spite of the fact that, in the case of those of them which Dickens expresses by a sentence

D*

in which the words 'Mr Pickwick' occur, Dickens was neither using 'Mr Pickwick' as a proper name for any real person nor (which is an entirely different thing) using it as a 'logically proper name'.

(*b*) Another thing which Mr Ryle seems to me to tell us about the proposition which Dickens expressed by 'Mrs Bardell had fainted in Mr Pickwick's arms' is something about its analysis. He tells us this rather indirectly, and by way of implication; but I think he implies it very clearly. We have seen that he insists that this proposition is *not* 'about' Mr Pickwick. Now he devotes a whole section of his paper to trying to tell us what would be meant by saying that it *was* 'about' Mr Pickwick. In this section he takes as an example the proposition 'Mont Blanc is snow-capped', instead of our proposition; but if we apply his doctrine about 'Mont Blanc is snow-capped' to our proposition, we get the following result. To say 'Dickens's proposition *was* about Mr Pickwick' would mean '(1) Dickens's proposition says that one man and one man only was called "Mr Pickwick" and that Mrs Bardell had fainted in that man's arms; and (2) there *was* one man and one only called "Mr Pickwick" '. Evidently, then, Mr Ryle's own proposition 'Dickens's proposition was *not* about Mr Pickwick', means, in his opinion, '(1) Dickens's proposition says that one man and one man only was called "Mr Pickwick" and that Mrs Bardell had fainted in that man's arms; and (2) it is *not* the case that one man and one man only was called "Mr Pick-wick" '. Now since Mr Ryle believes that Dickens's proposition was *not* about Mr Pickwick, and that the other sentence expresses the very thing which he believes, it is to be presumed that he believes what this other sentence expresses. He believes, therefore, that Dickens's proposition says, as *part* of its meaning, that one man and only one was called 'Mr Pickwick': that is to say he tells us, about the analysis of the proposition which Dickens expressed by 'Mrs Bardell had fainted in Mr Pickwick's arms', that *part* of what it says is 'One man and only one was called "Pickwick" '.

Is this thing which Mr Ryle tells us about this proposition true?

It seems to me to be utterly and hopelessly false. I am as certain that it is false as I am that when I now say 'Mr Ryle is a Student of Christ Church' I am *not* saying that only one man is called 'Mr Ryle'; and that when I say 'Mont Blanc is snow-capped' I am *not* saying that only one mountain is called 'Mont Blanc'. The thing is perfectly ridiculous, as soon as you look at it. If, when I say 'Mr Ryle is a Student of Christ Church', I were saying 'Only one man is called "Mr Ryle"', you would only need to produce a pair of men, both of whose names were 'Ryle', in order to be entitled to say: 'Ha! you see you were wrong, your proposition is false; part of what you asserted in it was that only one man is called "Mr Ryle", and here, you see, are two both so-called; so, after all, Mr Ryle is *not* a Student of Christ Church.' And similarly my proposition that Mont Blanc is snow-capped (which I seriously make) would be refuted by the discovery that there was a small mountain in the Pyrenees called 'Mont Blanc' by the local inhabitants. Now it would certainly not be so refuted. For all I know, there may be only one mountain called 'Mont Blanc'; but when I say 'Mont Blanc is snow-capped' I am certainly not committing myself to the assertion that there is only one; and, if there happen to be two or more, that fact would be in no way inconsistent with the *complete* truth of the proposition I express by 'Mont Blanc is snow-capped'.

Mr Ryle seems to me here to have fallen into the extraordinarily simple-minded view, which, if only it were true, would render the whole doctrine of the use of proper names so delightfully easy, that whenever we use a proper name 'N' in a sentence, we could, without altering the meaning of the sentence, substitute for 'N' the phrase 'the only thing called "N"' or 'the only person called "N"'. Mr Braithwaite has avoided the extreme error of this view by allowing that *sometimes* we use proper names in other ways; but he says something almost as bad, when he asserts that he *usually* means by 'Jane Austen' the same as is meant by 'the person called "Jane Austen"'. So far from its being true that he usually means this, I would venture confidently to assert that never once has he used 'Jane Austen' with such a meaning: never once, in uttering a sentence in which 'Jane Austen' occurred, has he committed himself to the view that only one person has ever been called 'Jane Austen'. I think, however, that perhaps he did not here mean what he says; and that his saying it is only due to laxity of language. For, a little lower down, when he uses the phrase 'there was one and only one thing referred to as "Jane Austen"' he adds in a bracket '(among, of course, a certain set of people)'. Perhaps, therefore, he meant us to understand this bracket here; and, if so, his real view as to what he usually means by 'Jane Austen' is a totally different one from that which he says he holds: it is only that he usually means the same as is meant by *some* phrase of the form 'the person called "Jane Austen" by *x*' or even, perhaps, some phrase of the form 'the person *most often* called "Jane Austen" by *x*', or some similar variation. If this is what he means, I do not think he is right, since I think that when he uses the name 'Jane Austen' he is hardly ever saying anything whatever *about* this name itself, as he would be doing if he meant by it anything of this kind; but at least his view would not be absurd, as is the view which he *says* he holds. Perhaps, also, when he says lower down that 'one of the properties described in *Pickwick Papers* is to be *the* man called "Pickwick" ' he means us to understand his bracket again. If not, he is committing himself to the view, which seems to me certainly false, that somewhere in *Pickwick Papers* Dickens says or implies that only one man was ever called 'Pickwick'.

I think, therefore, Mr Ryle implies something monstrously false about our proposition, when he implies that part of what it says is that only one man was ever called 'Pickwick'. And I think the error is a double one, because I think that a less extreme view, which is entailed by this one, is also false. I mean the view that part of what Dickens was saying, when he said 'Mrs Bardell fainted in Mr Pickwick's arms', was at least '*Someone* was called "Pickwick" '. I do not believe that even this forms any part of what he was saying: I think he was not talking *about* the name 'Pickwick' at all, as he must have been doing if this was part of what he was saying, but simply *using* it. I think he was no more talking *about* it than, when I say 'McTaggart used to wear a red tie', I am talking *about* the word 'red'. Sometimes, of course, when we use proper names, we *are* talking *about* them. If I introduce my friend, Mr Smith, to a person who has never either met him or heard of him before, by saying 'This is my friend, Smith', part of what I am saying *is* 'This person's name is "Smith" '. But if I point out Mr Baldwin at a public meeting to a person who does not know him by sight but who, I know, has often heard of him, and say 'Look, that's Mr Baldwin', no part of what I am saying is 'That person is called "Mr Baldwin" ': I am simply *using* the name and not talking *about* it. It seems to me that in the immense majority of cases in which proper names are used, both in common life, in history, and in fiction, nothing whatever is being said *about* the name used: it is *only* being used. That is to say, the proposition which is expressed by the sentence in which the name 'N' occurs, neither says nor entails the proposition 'Somebody is called "N"'. Of course, by using the name, we *imply* that somebody is called 'N', but not in the sense that the proposition which we express *entails* this proposition. Mr Ryle evidently thinks otherwise. He thinks that if I say now 'Mr Baldwin is rather a short man' this sentence entails (he even says 'means') what is meant by 'Somebody who is called "Mr Baldwin" is rather a short man'. But I cannot help thinking that this is a complete mistake.

(*c*) I am not quite sure whether Mr Ryle would say about the sentence 'Mrs Bardell had fainted in Mr Pickwick's arms', as used by Dickens, one thing which he makes a great point of with regard to the sentence 'Mr Pickwick is an imaginary object', namely something which he expresses by saying that in it 'Mr Pickwick' is 'a concealed predicative expression' or 'is really signifying an attribute'. But I think, from many indications, that this must be his view; and, if so, that, when he wrote these words, Dickens was using 'Mr Pickwick' as 'a concealed predicative expression', would certainly be one of the things he would be most anxious to insist on with regard to the analysis of the proposition Dickens was expressing by them. Supposing this is his view, is it true?

With regard to this question, I have to confess that I cannot get any reasonably clear idea as to what Mr Ryle means by saying of a given expression that it is 'a predicative expression' (concealed or unconcealed), except in so far as he means that the expression in question is not a 'logically proper name'. I think this is certainly part at least of what he means, though it may not be the whole; and, so far as this point is concerned, I have already said that I agree with him.

But, if this is what he means, I think he makes a great mistake when he goes on to infer that, for that reason, Dickens's proposition cannot be 'about' a Mr. Pickwick in the way in which 'Christ Church is a big college' is 'about' Christ Church. For it seems to me that 'Christ Church' is certainly no more a 'logically proper name' than 'Pickwick' is, and I should have thought also must be 'a concealed predicative expression' in any extra sense (if any) which Mr Ryle may attach to those words. If so, the fact that 'Pickwick' is so, cannot possibly be a reason for saying that Dickens's proposition is not 'about' Pickwick; for, if it were, the fact that 'Christ Church' is so too, would also be a reason for saying that 'Christ Church is a big college' is not 'about' Christ Church. Indeed, in making this inference, Mr Ryle seems to me to contradict a true thing which he himself has said elsewhere. He holds, if I understand him rightly, that sentences of the form 'x is real' and 'x is imaginary' are precisely on a level in respect of the fact that in both cases any word that is substituted for x must be a 'concealed predicative expression'. If so, 'Christ Church' must certainly be a 'concealed predicative expression'; since 'Christ Church is a real college' certainly has meaning. Whether 'Pickwick' and 'Christ Church' are 'concealed predicative expressions' or not, is simply a question as to the *meaning* of these expressions; and from an answer to this question, however you answer it, nothing can possibly follow as to the question of *fact* whether 'Mrs Bardell fainted in Mr Pickwick's arms' is (in Mr Ryle's sense) 'about' Mr Pickwick.

(3) What does Mr Braithwaite tell us about the proposition which Dickens expressed by 'Mrs Bardell had fainted in Mr Pickwick's arms'? And is what he tells us true?

Mr Braithwaite has something to say about it which is very intriguing, and, in part (to me, at least), very difficult to understand.

He says that, when Dickens wrote the sentence 'Mrs Bardell had fainted etc.', he was using the words 'Mr Pickwick' (and, of course, the words 'Mrs Bardell' also) 'in two incompatible ways which prevent the sentence as a whole having any meaning'. It must be noted that by this he does not mean that Dickens was attaching to 'Mr Pickwick' two incompatible *meanings*; if this were what he meant, he would be merely saying that Dickens was expressing a self-contradictory proposition; and he would then only need to tell us what were the two incompatible meanings which, in his view, Dickens was attaching to this symbol, for us to understand his view perfectly and discuss whether it is true or not. But what he means is that Dickens was using the symbol, not with two incompatible *meanings*, but, as he says, with 'two incompatible *sorts* of meaning'; and what this means becomes plainer, if we consider what, according to him, the two *sorts* of meaning in question are. He says that Dickens was using 'Mr Pickwick' both (1) as a variable and (2) as a constant—maintaining that, in the latter case, he was using it to mean the same as is meant by 'the thing called by the name "Pickwick" ' or 'the man called "Pickwick" '. And he tells us that 'if a symbol is used as a variable, it cannot at the same time be used as a constant'. When, therefore, he says that Dickens, when he wrote the sentence, was using 'Mr Pickwick' 'in two incompatible ways', he means, apparently, that he was using it in both of two ways, in which it *cannot* be used at the same time. It looks, therefore, at first sight, as if Mr Braithwaite's own proposition is self-contradictory: as if he were asserting that Dickens was actually doing something which at the same time he asserts cannot be done! Perhaps it was a feeling that this was a self-contradictory proposition, which made him say just before, *not* that Dickens *was* doing this apparently impossible thing, but only that he 'was trying to do it'. But I think we must admit that Mr Braithwaite's proposition is not self-contradictory. During the short time in which he was writing the sentence in question there was, no doubt, time for Dickens to attach both meanings *successively* to 'Mr. Pickwick'. What cannot, I think, strictly be justified is Mr Braithwaite's assertion that the fact that Dickens was doing this (if it be a fact) 'prevents the sentence as a whole from having any meaning' and 'reduces it to nonsense'. I think all that would follow is that the sentence as a whole has both of two incompatible meanings: that there is no proposition which is *the* proposition which Dickens expressed by it.

But what does Mr Braithwaite mean by saying that Dickens was using 'Mr Pickwick' as a variable? This is a question which has puzzled me dreadfully. But I think I can see something which he may possibly have meant, and which fits in with other things he says. Suppose I begin a story by 'There was a boy, called "Jack", who was a very naughty boy. Once, when he was sent out to sell his mother's cow, he exchanged it for a bag of beans. His mother threw the beans into the garden, and next morning there had grown from one of them a beanstalk which reached into the clouds. Jack climbed up the beanstalk, and etc. etc.' Suppose also two other things, namely (1) that by 'There was a boy, called "Jack" ' I mean only what Mr Russell has often told us such a phrase does mean, viz. 'There was *at least* one boy, called

"Jack" '; and (2) that nowhere in the story do I introduce any statement which means or implies that Jack was the *only* boy of whom so and so was true. Then it is quite plain that all that I am saying by the story, from beginning to end, is only that there was *at least* one boy who *both* was called 'Jack', *also* was naughty, *also* exchanged his mother's cow, etc. etc.: nowhere am I saying that there was *only* one boy of whom all these things were true, nor am I mentioning anything which might be true of a boy, with regard to which I am saying, that there was *only* one boy of whom both that thing and all the other things were true. And it is also quite plain that none of the sentences in the story have a meaning independent of what precedes: they are all governed by the original 'There was at least one boy who . . . '. For instance, the sentence 'Jack climbed up the beanstalk' tells us, and can tell us, no more than: 'There was *at least* one boy who *both* was called "Jack", *and* was naughty, *and* . . . , *and* . . . etc., *and* climbed up the beanstalk'. I suggest that Mr Braithwaite would express the fact that my story fulfilled these conditions by saying that 'Jack', on all occasions after the first, where it means the name 'Jack', is *used as a variable*: the essential points being (1) that none of the sentences in which it occurs have a meaning independent of what precedes but are all governed by the original 'There was *at least* one boy who', (2) that the possibility that everything which is said of 'Jack' may have been true of several boys called 'Jack' is not excluded.

So much for what Mr Braithwaite means, so far as I can see, by saying that in our sentence Dickens was using 'Mr Pickwick' as a variable. As for what he means by saying that he was also using it as equivalent to 'the man called "Pickwick" ', I have already said that I cannot tell whether he means what he says, or whether he means only that Dickens used it as equivalent to *some* phrase of the form 'the man called "Pickwick" by *x*' or of some similar form. Is Mr Braithwaite right in supposing that Dickens, in that sentence, was using 'Mr Pickwick' in both of these two ways?

I don't believe he is right. On the contrary, so far from its being true that Dickens was using it in *both*, I believe he was using it in *neither*. As regards the contention that he was using it as a variable, I think the mistake lies in the assumption that, where Dickens first introduces Mr Pickwick, he does so by a statement equivalent to 'There was *at least* one man who was called "Pickwick" and who etc. etc.' I think that what he meant and what we all understand is: 'There was *only* one man of whom it's true *both* that *I'm going to tell you about him and* that he was called "Pickwick" *and* that, etc. etc.' In other words, he is saying, from the beginning, that he has one and only one real man in his mind's eye, about whom he is going to tell you a story. That he has, is, of course, false; it is part of the fiction. But it is this which gives unique reference to all subsequent uses of 'Mr Pickwick'. And it is for this reason that Mr Ryle's view that, if, by coincidence, there happened to have been a real man of whom everything related of Mr Pickwick in the novel was true, then 'we could say that Dickens's propositions were true of somebody', is to be rejected. For Dickens's propositions are all of the form 'There was only one man of whom it's true both that *I'm telling you of him and* that, etc. etc.' And *ex hypothesi no* proposition of this form would be true about the man in question, since *Dickens was not telling us of him*: that is what is meant by saying that it is only 'by coincidence' that there happened to be such a man. So, too, we *could* say, with perfect truth: 'Oh, he is not identical with the hero of the story'; for to say that he was would be to say that Dickens *was* telling us of him: and Dickens was *not*. Again we should still be entitled to say 'Mr Pickwick was not a real person', since all we mean by this is 'Dickens didn't mean anybody by "Mr Pickwick"' or (which is equivalent to this) 'In sentences in which "Mr Pickwick" occurs Dickens wasn't telling us about any real man, to whom he was referring by that name'; and all this would still remain true, in spite of the existence of what Mr Ryle calls 'the real Mr Pickwick'.

As for Mr Braithwaite's contention that Dickens meant by 'Mr Pickwick' what is meant by 'the man called "Pickwick"', the reason why I think this false is because, as I have said, I do not believe that, when Dickens wrote that sentence, he was making a proposition about the name 'Pickwick' at all. I think Mr Braithwaite is right in thinking that 'Mr Pickwick' has unique reference, in the sense that it is logically impossible that *all* that Dickens is stating to be true of *somebody* by that sentence, should have been true of more than one real man; but I think he tries to get the unique reference in the wrong way. By the time that Dickens had got as far as that in the novel I don't believe for a moment that

VI

IS EXISTENCE A PREDICATE?

I am not at all clear as to the meaning of this question. Mr Kneale says that existence is not a predicate. But what does he mean by the words 'Existence is not a predicate'?

In his second paragraph, he says that the word 'predicate' has two different senses, a logical sense and a grammatical one. If so, it would follow that the words 'Existence is not a predicate' may have two different meanings, according as the person who uses them is using 'predicate' in the logical or the grammatical sense. And I think it is clear that he means us to understand that when *he* says 'Existence is not a predicate', he is using 'predicate' in the logical sense, and not in the grammatical one. I think his view is that if anyone were to say 'Existence is a predicate', using 'predicate' in the grammatical sense, such a person would be perfectly right: I think he holds that existence really is a predicate in the grammatical sense. But, whether he holds this or not, I think it is clear that he does not wish to discuss the question whether it is or is not a predicate in the grammatical sense, but solely the question whether it is so in the logical one.

Now I think it is worth noticing that if we assert 'Existence is a predicate', using 'predicate' in the grammatical sense, our proposition is a proposition about certain *words*, to the effect that they are often used in a certain way; but not, curiously enough, about the word 'existence' itself. It is a proposition to the effect that the word 'exists' and other finite parts of the verb 'to exist', such as 'existed', 'will exist' or 'exist' (in the plural) are often the predicates (in some grammatical sense) of sentences in which they occur; but nobody means to say that the word 'existence' itself is often the predicate of sentences in which it occurs. And I think Mr Kneale implies that, similarly, the proposition which anyone would express, if he asserted 'Existence is a predicate', using 'predicate' in the logical sense, is again equivalent to a proposition, *not* about the word 'existence' itself, but about the word 'exists' and other finite parts of the verb 'to exist'. He implies that 'Existence is a predicate', with this use of 'predicate', is equivalent

to the proposition that the word 'exists', and other finite parts
of the verb, often do '*stand for* a predicate in the logical sense'.
It would appear, therefore, that one difference between the two
different meanings of 'Existence is a predicate' is as follows:
namely that, if a person who says these words is using 'predicate'
in the grammatical sense, he is *not* saying that the words, 'exists',
etc., ever '*stand for* a predicate in the logical sense'; whereas,
if he is using 'predicate' in the logical sense, he is saying that they
do (often, at least) '*stand for* a predicate in the logical sense'.
What Mr Kneale himself means by 'Existence is not a predicate'
is apparently some proposition which he would express by saying:
'The words, "exists", etc., never *stand for* a predicate in the
logical sense'.

What I am not clear about is as to what is meant by saying of a
particular word (or particular phrase) in a particular sentence that
it 'stands for a predicate in the logical sense'; nor, therefore, as
to what is meant by saying of another particular word in another
particular sentence that it does *not* 'stand for a predicate in the
logical sense'. Mr Kneale does, indeed, tell us that a 'predicate
in the logical sense' is the same as 'an attribute'; but, though
I think that the meaning of the word 'attribute' is perhaps a little
clearer than that of the phrase 'predicate in the logical sense',
it still seems to me far from clear; I do not clearly understand
what he would mean by saying that 'exists', etc., do not 'stand
for attributes'. But, from examples which he gives, it is, I think,
clear that he would say that in the sentence 'This is red' the
word 'red', or the phrase 'is red' (I am not clear which), does
'stand for an attribute'; and also that in the sentence 'Tame tigers
growl', 'growl' so stands, and in the sentence 'Rajah growls',
'growls' does. It is, therefore, presumably some difference between
the way in which 'exists', etc., are used in sentences in which they
occur, and the way in which 'is red' (or 'red') and 'growl' and
'growls' are used in these sentences, that he wishes to express
by saying that, whereas 'exists', etc., do *not* 'stand for attributes',
these words in these sentences do. And if we can find what
differences there are between the use of finite parts of the verb
'to exist', and the use of 'is red', 'growl' and 'growls', we may
perhaps find what the difference is which he expresses in this way.

I. It will, I think, be best to begin with one particular use of 'exist'—the one, namely, which Mr Kneale illustrates by the example 'Tame tigers exist'. He clearly thinks that there is some very important difference between the way in which 'exist' is used here, and the way in which 'growl' is used in 'Tame tigers growl'; and that it is a difference which does not hold, e.g. between the use of 'scratch' in 'Tame tigers scratch' and the use of 'growl' in 'Tame tigers growl'. He would say that 'scratch' and 'growl' both 'stand for attributes', whereas 'exist' does not; and he would also say that 'Tame tigers exist' is a proposition of a different *form* from 'Tame tigers growl', whereas I think he would say that 'Tame tigers growl' and 'Tame tigers scratch' are *of the same form*. What difference between 'Tame tigers exist' and 'Tame tigers growl' can be the one he has in mind?

(1) That there is a difference between the way in which we use 'exist' in the former sentence and 'growl' in the latter, of a different kind from the difference between our usages of 'scratch' and 'growl' in the two sentences 'Tame tigers scratch' and 'Tame tigers growl', can, I think, be brought out in the following way.

The sentence 'Tame tigers growl' seems to me to be ambiguous. So far as I can see, it might mean 'All tame tigers growl', or it might mean merely 'Most tame tigers growl', or it might mean merely 'Some tame tigers growl'. Each of these three sentences has a clear meaning, and the meaning of each is clearly different from that of either of the two others. Of each of them, however, it is true that the proposition which it expresses is one which cannot possibly be true, unless some tame tigers do growl. And hence I think we can say of 'Tame tigers growl' that, whichever sense it is used in, it means something which cannot possibly be true unless some tame tigers do growl. Similarly I think it is clear that 'Tame tigers exist' means something which cannot possibly be true unless some tame tigers do exist. But I do not think that there is any ambiguity in 'Tame tigers exist' corresponding to that which I have pointed out in 'Tame tigers growl'. So far as I can see 'Tame tigers exist' and 'Some tame tigers exist' are merely two different ways of expressing exactly the same proposition. That is to say, it is not true that 'Tame tigers exist' might mean 'All tame tigers exist', or 'Most tame tigers exist', instead of merely 'Some tame tigers exist'. It always means just 'Some tame tigers exist', and nothing else whatever. I have said it is never used to mean 'All tame tigers exist', or 'Most tame tigers exist'; but I hope it will strike everyone that there is something queer about this proposition. It seems to imply that 'All tame tigers exist' and 'Most tame tigers exist' have a clear meaning, just as have 'All tame tigers growl' and 'Most tame tigers growl'; and that it is just an accident that we do not happen ever to use 'Tame tigers exist' to express either of those two meanings instead of the meaning 'Some tame tigers exist', whereas we do sometimes use 'Tame tigers growl' to mean 'All tame tigers growl' or 'Most tame tigers growl', instead of merely 'Some tame tigers growl'. But is this in fact the case? Have 'All tame tigers exist' and 'Most tame tigers exist' any meaning at all? Certainly they have not a clear meaning, as have 'All tame tigers growl' and 'Most tame tigers growl'. They are puzzling expressions, which certainly do not carry their meaning, if they have any, on the face of them. That this is so indicates, I think, that there is some important difference between the usage of 'exist' with which we are concerned, and the usage of such words as 'growl' or 'scratch'; but it does not make clear just what the difference is.

I think this can be made clear by comparing the expressions 'Some tame tigers don't growl' and 'Some tame tigers don't exist'. The former, whether true or false, has a perfectly clear meaning— a meaning just as clear as that of 'Some tame tigers do growl'; and it is perfectly clear that both propositions might be true together. But with 'Some tame tigers don't exist' the case is different. 'Some tame tigers exist' has a perfectly clear meaning: it just means 'There are some tame tigers'. But the meaning of 'Some tame tigers don't exist', if any, is certainly not equally clear. It is another queer and puzzling expression. Has it any meaning at all? and, if so, what meaning? If it has any, it would appear that it must mean the same as: 'There are some tame tigers, which don't exist.' But has *this* any meaning? And if so, what? Is it possible that there should be any tame tigers which don't exist? I think the answer is that, if in the sentence 'Some tame tigers don't exist' you are using 'exist' with the same meaning as in 'Some tame tigers exist', then the former sentence as a whole has no meaning at all—it is pure nonsense. *A* meaning can, of course, be given to 'Some tame tigers don't exist'; but this can only be done if 'exist' is used in a different way from that in which it is used in 'Some tame tigers exist'. And, if this is so, it will follow that 'All tame tigers exist' and 'Most tame tigers exist', also have no meaning at all, if you are using 'exist' in the sense with which we are concerned. For 'All tame tigers growl' is equivalent to the conjunction 'Some tame tigers growl, and there is no tame tiger which does not growl'; and this has a meaning, because 'There is at least one tame tiger which does not growl' has one. If, therefore, 'There is at least one tame tiger which does not exist' has no meaning, it will follow that 'All tame tigers exist' also has none; because 'There is no tame tiger which does not exist' will have none, if 'There is a tame tiger which does not exist' has none. Similarly 'Most tame tigers growl' is equivalent to the conjunction 'Some tame tigers growl, and the number of those (if any) which do not growl is smaller than that of those which do'—a statement which has a meaning only because 'There are tame tigers which do not growl' has one. If, therefore, 'There are tame tigers which don't exist' has no meaning, it will follow that 'Most tame tigers exist' will also have none. I think, therefore, we can say that one important difference between the use of 'growl' in 'Some tame tigers growl' and the use of 'exist' in 'Some tame tigers exist', is that if in the former case we insert 'do not' before 'growl', without changing the meaning of 'growl', we get a sentence which is significant, whereas if, in the latter, we insert 'do not' before 'exist' without changing the meaning of 'exist', we get a sentence which has no meaning whatever; and I think we can also say that this fact explains why, with the given meaning of 'growl', 'All tame tigers growl' and 'Most tame tigers growl' are both significant, whereas, with the given meaning of 'exist', 'All tame tigers exist' and 'Most tame tigers exist' are utterly meaningless. And if by the statement that 'growl', in this usage, 'stands for an attribute', whereas 'exist', in this usage, does not, part of what is meant is that there is this difference between them, then I should agree that 'exist', in this usage, does not 'stand for an attribute'.

But is it really true that if, in the sentence 'Some tame tigers exist', we insert 'do not' before 'exist', without changing the meaning of 'exist', we get a sentence which has no meaning whatever? I have admitted that a meaning *can* be given to 'Some tame tigers do not exist'; and it may, perhaps, be contended by some people that the meaning which 'exist' has in this sentence, where it is significant, *is* precisely the same as that which it has in

'Some tame tigers exist'. I cannot show the contrary as clearly as I should like to be able to do; but I will do my best.

The meaning which such an expression as 'Some tame tigers do not exist' sometimes does have, is that which it has when it is used to mean the same as 'Some tame tigers are imaginary' or 'Some tame tigers are not real tigers'. That 'Some tame tigers are imaginary' may really express a proposition, whether true or false, cannot I think be denied. If, for instance, two different stories have been written, each of which is about a different imaginary tame tiger, it will follow that there are at least two imaginary tame tigers; and it cannot be denied that the sentence 'Two different tame tigers occur in fiction' is significant, though I have not the least idea whether what it means is true or false. I know that at least one unicorn occurs in fiction, because one occurs in 'Alice Through the Looking Glass'; and it follows that there is at least one imaginary unicorn, and therefore (in a sense) at least one unicorn which does not exist and never did. Again, if it should happen that at the present moment two different people are each having an hallucination of a different tame tiger, it will follow that there are at the present moment two different imaginary tame tigers; and the statement that two such hallucinations are occurring now is certainly significant, though it may very likely be false. The sentence 'There are some tame tigers which do not exist' is, therefore, certainly significant, if it means only that there are some imaginary tigers, in either of the two senses which I have tried to point out. But what it means is that either some real people have written stories about imaginary tigers, or are having or have recently had hallucinations of tame tigers, or, perhaps, are dreaming or have dreamed of particular tame tigers. If nothing of this sort has happened or is happening to anybody, then there are no imaginary tame tigers. But if 'Some tame tigers do not exist' means all this, is it not clear that 'exist' has not, in this sentence, the same comparatively simple meaning as it has in 'Some tame tigers exist' or in 'No tame tigers exist'? Is it not clear that 'Some tame tigers do not exist', if it means all this, is not related to 'Some tame tigers exist', in the same simple way in which 'Some tame tigers do not growl' is related to 'Some tame tigers growl'?

(2) There is, I think, also another important difference be-

tween this use of 'exist' and the use of 'growl', which may be brought out as follows.

Mr Russell has said[1] 'When we say "some men are Greeks", that means that the propositional function "*x* is **a** man and a Greek" is sometimes true'; and has explained **just** previously that by 'sometimes true' he means 'true in at least one instance'. With this explanation of what he means by 'sometimes true', I do not think that his statement as to the meaning of 'Some men are Greeks' is strictly correct; since I think that the use of the plural implies that '*x* is a man and a Greek' is true in *more* than one instance, that is to say, in at least two instances. Let us suppose that he would accept this correction and say that what 'Some men are Greeks' means is not, strictly, that '*x* is a man and a Greek' is true in at least one instance, but that it is true in at least two. He has further implied (page 158) that to say of a propositional function that it is true in at least two instances is the same thing as to say that at least two 'values' of it are true; and he has told us (page 156) that the 'values' of propositional functions are propositions. With these explanations, his view would appear to be that what 'Some men are Greeks' means is that at least two propositions, related to the propositional function '*x* is a man and a Greek' in some way which he expresses by saying that they are 'values' of that function, are true. Now I cannot imagine what sort of propositions would be 'values' of '*x* is a man and a Greek', except propositions of the following sort. There are propositions which we express by pointing at (or indicating in some other way) an object which we are seeing (or perceiving in some other way) and uttering the words 'This is a so and so' (or equivalent words in some other language). Let us suppose that the kind of propositions which would be 'values' of '*x* is a man and a Greek' would be propositions of this sort, where the words used were '*This* is a man and a Greek'. Mr Russell's doctrine would then be that 'Some men are Greeks' means that at least two different *true* propositions of this sort could be made: that there must have been at least two different objects at which a man might have pointed and said truly 'This is a man and a Greek'. And, if this is his doctrine, it seems to me to be true. Surely 'Some men are Greeks' cannot possibly be true,

[1] *Introduction to Mathematical Philosophy* (Allen & Unwin, London 1919), p. 159.

unless there are at least two different objects, in the case of each of which a man might have seen it, pointed at it, and said with truth 'This is a man and a Greek'?

On this view 'Some tame tigers growl' means that at least two values of 'x is a tame tiger and growls' are true; and this means that there are at least two objects, in the case of each of which a man might have seen it, pointed at it, and said with truth 'This is a tame tiger and growls'. Now in this sentence 'This is a tame tiger and growls' it is clear that, except for the difference consisting in the fact that 'growls' is in the singular and 'growl' in the plural, the word 'growls' has the same meaning as has the word 'growl' in 'Some tame tigers growl'. We can say, then, that one feature about our use of 'growl' is that, if we consider a 'value' of the propositional function which is such that 'Some tame tigers growl' means that at least two values of it are true, then the singular of 'growl' can be used, with the same meaning, in the expression of such a value. And perhaps this may be part of what is meant by saying that 'growl' 'stands for an attribute'. It may perhaps be meant that to point at an object which you are seeing, and utter the words 'This object growls', is significant—that the words and gesture together with the object pointed at do really express a proposition, true or false.

But now consider 'Some tame tigers exist': is the same true of 'exist' in this sentence? Mr Russell says[1] 'We say that "men exist" or "a man exists" if the propositional function "x is human" is sometimes true'. And he goes on to protest that though the proposition 'Socrates is a man' is '*equivalent*' to 'Socrates is human', it 'is not the very same proposition'. For my part I doubt whether we ever do use 'is human' in such a way that 'Socrates is human' is equivalent to 'Socrates is a man'. I think Mr Russell is using 'is human' in a very special sense, in which nobody but he has ever used it, and that the only way of explaining how he is using it is to say that he is using it to mean precisely that which we ordinarily express by 'is a human being'. If this is so, and if we are allowed to distinguish, as I think we ought, between 'men exist' and 'a man exists', and to say that 'men exist' means, *not* ' "x is a human being" is true in at least one instance', but ' "x is a human being" is true in at least two instances', then I think his doctrine is true; provided, again, that

[1] *Introduction to Mathematical Philosophy*, pp. 171-2.

we are allowed to regard the sort of propositions which we express, e.g. by pointing at an object which we are seeing, and saying the words 'This is a human being', as being those which are values of 'x is a human being'. Surely 'Human beings exist' can be true if, and only if, there are at least two objects, such that, if a man were to see and point to either of them and utter the words 'This is a human being', he would be expressing a true proposition by what he did?

Now, if this is right, we see at once that the use of 'growl' in 'Some tame tigers growl' differs from that of 'exist' in 'Some tame tigers exist', in the respect that, while the first asserts that more than one value of 'x is a tame tiger *and growls*' is true, the second asserts, *not* that more than one value of 'x is a tame tiger *and exists*' is true, but merely that more than one value of 'x is a tame tiger' is true. Owing to this view of his that 'Some tame tigers exist' means the same as 'Some values of the propositional function "x is a tame tiger" are true', Mr Russell has been led to say[1]: 'Existence is essentially a property of a propositional function' and (page 196) 'It is of propositional functions that you can assert or deny existence' and (page 197) that it is a fallacy to transfer 'to the individual that satisfies a propositional function a predicate which only applies to a propositional function'; so that, according to him, existence is, after all, in this usage, a 'property' or 'predicate', though not a property of individuals, but only of propositional functions! I think this is a mistake on his part. Even if it is true that 'Some tame tigers exist' means the same as 'Some values of "x is a tame tiger" are true' it does not follow, I think, that we can say that 'exist' means the same as 'is sometimes true', and 'some tame tigers' the same as 'x is a tame tiger': indeed, I think it is clear that we cannot say this; for certainly ' "x is a tame tiger" exists' would not mean the same as 'Some tame tigers exist'. But what I think does follow from this interpretation of 'Some tame tigers exist' is another thing which Mr Russell himself holds, namely, that if a proposition which you express by pointing at something which you see and saying 'This is a tame tiger', is a 'value' of 'x is a tame tiger', then if, pointing at the same thing, you were to say the words 'This exists', and, if you were using 'exists' merely as the singular of 'exist' in the sense in which it is used in 'Some tame tigers exist', what you did would not express a proposition at all, but would be

[1] *Monist*, April 1919, p. 195.

absolutely meaningless. That is to say, there is between 'Some tame tigers growl' and 'Some tame tigers exist', not only the difference that, whereas the first asserts that some values of 'x is a tame tiger *and growls*' are true, the second asserts only that some values of 'x is a tame tiger' are true; there is also the further and more important difference that, why the second asserts only that some values of 'x is a tame tiger' are true, is not because we happen to use 'This is a tame tiger' to mean the same as 'This is a tame tiger *and exists*', but because by pointing and saying 'This *exists*' we should express *no proposition at all*, so long as we were using 'exists' as the singular of the use of 'exist' with which we are concerned; whereas by pointing and saying 'This growls' we certainly should be expressing a proposition, even though we were using 'growls' merely as the singular of 'growl' with the meaning it has in 'Some tame tigers growl'. 'This is a tame tiger, *and exists*' would be not tautologous but meaningless.

This, I think, gives us a second true thing, which may perhaps be sometimes part of what is meant by saying that 'exist', in this usage, 'does not stand for an attribute'.

II. So far I have been solely concerned with the use of 'exist' in such sentences as 'Some tame tigers exist', and have tried to point out two differences between its use here and the use of 'growl' in 'Some tame tigers growl', which may perhaps be part of what is meant by saying that 'exist', in this usage, does not 'stand for an attribute', whereas 'growl' does. But I cannot help thinking that there are other significant uses of 'exists'; and I want, in particular, to try to point out two such, and to consider what, if anything, true can be meant by saying that in these usages also 'exists' does not 'stand for an attribute'.

(1) I have just said that to point at a thing which you see and say 'This exists' seems to me to be meaningless, if 'exists' is the singular of 'exist' in the sense in which it is used in 'Tame tigers exist'; but I cannot help thinking that in the case of anything to point at which and say 'This is a tame tiger' is significant, it is also significant to point at it and say 'This exists', *in some sense or other*. My reason for thinking this is that it seems to me that you can clearly say *with truth* of any such object 'This *might* not have existed', 'It is *logically possible* that this should not have existed'; and I do not see how it is possible that 'This might not have

existed' should be true, unless 'This does in fact exist' is also true, and therefore the words 'This exists' significant. If the sentence (a) 'It is logically possible that this should not have existed' expresses a true proposition, it seems to follow that the sentence (b) 'This does not exist', where 'this' refers to the same object to which it refers in (a), must express a proposition, though a false one; and, if so, the sentence 'This exists', which expresses its contradictory, must also be significant, and the proposition it expresses true. Now I cannot help thinking that in every case in which I point at an object which I am perceiving and say significantly 'This is a tame tiger', 'This is a book', etc., my proposition is in fact a proposition about some sense-datum, or some set of sense-data, which I am perceiving; and that part of what I am saying is that this sense-datum (or these sense-data) is 'of' a physical object. That is to say, I am saying of some sense-datum that it is 'of' a physical object in the sense in which it is true to say of an after-image which I see with my eyes shut that it is *not* 'of' a physical object. And I think that part, at least, of what we mean by 'This exists', where we are using 'this' in the same way as when we point and say 'This is a book', is 'This sense-datum is *of* a physical object', which seems to me to be certainly significant. If 'of' here stood for a relation, we might say that 'This is a book' was short for 'The thing which this sense-datum is "of" is a book', and therefore 'This exists' short for 'The thing which this sense-datum is "of" exists'; in which case the use of 'exists' in question would be that which in *Principia Mathematica* is symbolized by 'E!' and there would be the same sort of reason for saying that it does not 'stand for an attribute' as in the case of the 'exist' which occurs in 'Some tame tigers exist'. I do not believe, however, that 'of' here does stand for a relation, nor therefore that 'This' in 'This is a book' can be said to be short for the sort of phrase which Russell has called 'a definite description'; and, this being so, I am not at all clear as to what that is true could be meant by saying that 'exists', in this usage, 'does not stand for an attribute'. The only suggestion I can make is this. It seems to me that 'This exists' (in this usage) always forms part of what is asserted by 'This is a book', 'This is red', etc. etc., where 'this' is used in the manner with which we are now concerned; and possibly part of what is meant by saying that 'is a book', 'is red', etc., 'stand for attributes', is that *part but not the whole* of what is asserted by any 'value' of '*x* is a book', '*x* is red', etc., is 'This exists'. In that case 'exists' in 'This exists' would not 'stand for an attribute', solely because the whole of what it asserts, and not merely a part, is 'This exists'.

(2) Another reason why 'This exists', where 'this' is used as it is in 'This is a book', seems to me to be significant, is because it seems to me not only significant to say of a given sense-datum 'This *is* of a physical object' or 'This is *not* of a physical object', but also to say of the sense-datum itself 'This exists'. If this is so, we have to do with a new sense of 'exists', since certainly no part of the meaning of such an assertion with regard to a sense-datum is that it, or any other sense-datum, is 'of' a physical object. But my reason for holding that it is significant for me to say, for instance, of an after-image which I am seeing with my eyes shut, 'This exists', is similar to that which I gave in the last case: namely that it seems to me that in the case of every sense-datum which anyone ever perceives, the person in question could always say with truth of the sense-datum in question 'This might not have existed'; and I cannot see how this could be true, unless the proposition 'This does in fact exist' is also true, and therefore the words 'This exists' significant. That 'This exists' has any meaning in such cases, where, as Mr Russell would say, though falsely, we are using 'this' as a 'proper name' for something with which we are 'acquainted', is, I know, disputed; my view that it has, involves, I am bound to admit, the curious consequence that 'This exists', when used in this way, is always true, and 'This does not exist' always false; and I have little to say in its favour except that it seems to me so plainly true that, in the case of every sense-datum I have, it is logically possible that the sense-datum in question should not have existed—that there should simply have been no such thing. If, for instance, I am seeing a bright after-image with my eyes shut, it seems to me quite plainly conceivable that I should have had instead, at that moment, a uniform black field, such as I often have with my eyes shut; and, if I had had such a field, then that particular bright after-image simply would not have existed.

But, supposing 'This exists', in this usage, has a meaning, why should we not say that 'exists' here 'stands for an attribute'? I can suggest no reason why we should not, except the same which I suggested in the last case.

VII

PROOF OF AN EXTERNAL WORLD

In the preface to the second edition of Kant's *Critique of Pure Reason* some words occur, which, in Professor Kemp Smith's translation, are rendered as follows:

> It still remains a scandal to philosophy . . . that the existence of things outside of us . . . must be accepted merely on *faith*, and that, if anyone thinks good to doubt their existence, we are unable to counter his doubts by any satisfactory proof.[1]

It seems clear from these words that Kant thought it a matter of some importance to give a proof of 'the existence of things outside of us' or perhaps rather (for it seems to me possible that the force of the German words is better rendered in this way) of 'the existence of *the* things outside of us'; for had he not thought it important that a proof should be given, he would scarcely have called it a 'scandal' that no proof had been given. And it seems clear also that he thought that the giving of such a proof was a task which fell properly within the province of philosophy; for, if it did not, the fact that no proof had been given could not possibly be a scandal to *philosophy*.

Now, even if Kant was mistaken in both of these two opinions, there seems to me to be no doubt whatever that it is a matter of some importance and also a matter which falls properly within the province of philosophy, to discuss the question what sort of proof, if any, can be given of 'the existence of things outside of us'. And to discuss this question was my object when I began to write the present lecture. But I may say at once that, as you will find, I have only, at most, succeeded in saying a very small part of what ought to be said about it.

The words 'it . . . remains a scandal to philosophy . . . that we

[1] B xxxix, note: Kemp Smith, p. 34. The German words are 'so bleibt es immer ein Skandal der Philosophie . . . , das Dasein der Dinge ausser uns . . . bloss auf *Glauben* annehmen zu müssen, und wenn es jemand einfällt es zu bezweifeln, ihm keinen genugtuenden Beweis entgegenstellen zu können'.

are unable . . .' would, taken strictly, imply that, at the moment at which he wrote them, Kant himself was unable to produce a satisfactory proof of the point in question. But I think it is unquestionable that Kant himself did not think that he personally was at the time unable to produce such a proof. On the contrary, in the immediately preceding sentence, he has declared that he has, in the second edition of his *Critique*, to which he is now writing the Preface, given a 'rigorous proof' of this very thing; and has added that he believes this proof of his to be 'the only possible proof'. It is true that in this preceding sentence he does not describe the proof which he has given as a proof of 'the existence of things outside of us' or of 'the existence of the things outside of us', but describes it instead as a proof of 'the objective reality of outer intuition'. But the context leaves no doubt that he is using these two phrases, 'the objective reality of outer intuition' and 'the existence of things (*or* 'the things') outside of us', in such a way that whatever is a proof of the first is also necessarily a proof of the second. We must, therefore, suppose that when he speaks as if *we* are unable to give a satisfactory proof, he does not mean to say that he himself, as well as others, is *at the moment* unable; but rather that, until he discovered the proof which he has given, both he himself and everybody else *were* unable. Of course, if he is right in thinking that he has given a satisfactory proof, the state of things which he describes came to an end as soon as his proof was published. As soon as that happened, anyone who read it was able to give a satisfactory proof by simply repeating that which Kant had given, and the 'scandal' to philosophy had been removed once for all.

If, therefore, it were certain that the proof of the point in question given by Kant in the second edition is a satisfactory proof, it would be certain that at least one satisfactory proof can be given; and all that would remain of the question which I said I proposed to discuss would be, firstly, the question as to what *sort* of a proof this of Kant's is, and secondly the question whether (contrary to Kant's own opinion) there may not perhaps be other proofs, of the same or of a different sort, which are also satisfactory. But I think it is by no means certain that Kant's proof is satisfactory. I think it is by no means certain that he did succeed in removing once for all the state of affairs which he considered to be a scandal to philosophy. And I think, therefore, that the question whether it is possible to give *any* satisfactory proof of the point in question still deserves discussion.

But what is the point in question? I think it must be owned that the expression 'things outside of us' is rather an odd expression, and an expression the meaning of which is certainly not perfectly clear. It would have sounded less odd if, instead of 'things outside of us' I had said 'external things', and perhaps also the meaning of this expression would have seemed to be clearer; and I think we make the meaning of 'external things' clearer still if we explain that this phrase has been regularly used by philosophers as short for 'things external to *our minds*'. The fact is that there has been a long philosophical tradition, in accordance with which the three expressions 'external things', 'things external to *us*', and 'things external to *our minds*' have been used as equivalent to one another, and have, each of them, been used as if they needed no explanation. The origin of this usage I do not know. It occurs already in Descartes; and since he uses the expressions as if they needed no explanation, they had presumably been used with the same meaning before. Of the three, it seems to me that the expression 'external to *our minds*' is the clearest, since it at least makes clear that what is meant is not 'external to *our bodies*'; whereas both the other expressions might be taken to mean this: and indeed there has been a good deal of confusion, even among philosophers, as to the relation of the two conceptions 'external things' and 'things external to *our bodies*'. But even the expression 'things external to our minds' seems to me to be far from perfectly clear; and if I am to make really clear what I mean by 'proof of the existence of things outside of us', I cannot do it by merely saying that by 'outside of us' I mean 'external to our minds'.

There is a passage (*K.d.r.V.*, A 373) in which Kant himself says that the expression 'outside of us' 'carries with it an unavoidable ambiguity'. He says that 'sometimes it means something which exists *as a thing in itself* distinct from us, and sometimes something which merely belongs to external *appearance*'; he calls things which are 'outside of us' in the first of these two senses 'objects which might be called external in the transcendental sense', and things which are so in the second '*empirically external* objects'; and he says finally that, in order to remove all uncertainty as to the latter conception, he will distinguish empirically

E

external objects from objects which might be called 'external' in the transcendental sense, 'by calling them outright things which are *to be met with in space*'.

I think that this last phrase of Kant's 'things which are to be met with in space', does indicate fairly clearly what sort of things it is with regard to which I wish to inquire what sort of proof, if any, can be given that there are any things of that sort. My body, the bodies of other men, the bodies of animals, plants of all sorts, stones, mountains, the sun, the moon, stars, and planets, houses and other buildings, manufactured articles of all sorts—chairs, tables, pieces of paper, etc., are all of them 'things which are to be met with in space'. In short, all things of the sort that philosophers have been used to call 'physical objects', 'material things', or 'bodies' obviously come under this head. But the phrase 'things that are to be met with in space' can be naturally understood as applying also in cases where the names 'physical object', 'material thing', or 'body' can hardly be applied. For instance, shadows are sometimes to be met with in space, although they could hardly be properly called 'physical objects', 'material things', or 'bodies'; and although in one usage of the term 'thing' it would not be proper to call a shadow a 'thing', yet the phrase 'things which are to be met with in space' can be naturally understood as synonymous with 'whatever can be met with in space', and this is an expression which can quite properly be understood to include shadows. I wish the phrase 'things which are to be met with in space' to be understood in this wide sense; so that if a proof can be found that there ever have been as many as two different shadows it will follow at once that there have been at least two 'things which were to be met with in space', and this proof will be as good a proof of the point in question as would be a proof that there have been at least two 'physical objects' of no matter what sort.

The phrase 'things which are to be met with in space' can, therefore, be naturally understood as having a very wide meaning— a meaning even wider than that of 'physical object' or 'body', wide as is the meaning of these latter expressions. But wide as is its meaning, it is not, in one respect, so wide as that of another phrase which Kant uses as if it were equivalent to this one; and a comparison between the two will, I think, serve to make still clearer what sort of things it is with regard to which I wish to ask what proof, if any, can be given that there are such things.

The other phrase which Kant uses as if it were equivalent to 'things which are to be met with in space' is used by him in the sentence immediately preceding that previously quoted in which he declares that the expression 'things outside of us' 'carries with it an unavoidable ambiguity' (A 373). In this preceding sentence he says that an 'empirical object' 'is called *external*, if it is presented (*vorgestellt*) *in space*'. He treats, therefore, the phrase 'presented in space' as if it were equivalent to 'to be met with in space'. But it is easy to find examples of 'things', of which it can hardly be denied that they are 'presented in space', but of which it could, quite naturally, be emphatically denied that they are 'to be met with in space'. Consider, for instance, the following description of one set of circumstances under which what some psychologists have called a 'negative after-image' and others a 'negative after-sensation' can be obtained. 'If, after looking steadfastly at a white patch on a black ground, the eye be turned to a white ground, a grey patch is seen for some little time.' (Foster's *Text-book of Physiology*, IV, iii, 3, page 1266; quoted in Stout's *Manual of Psychology*, 3rd edition, page 280.) Upon reading these words recently, I took the trouble to cut out of a piece of white paper a four-pointed star, to place it on a black ground, to 'look steadfastly' at it, and then to turn my eyes to a white sheet of paper: and I did find that I saw a grey patch for some little time—I not only saw a grey patch, but I saw it *on* the white ground, and also this grey patch was of roughly the same shape as the white four-pointed star at which I had 'looked steadfastly' just before—it also was a four-pointed star. I repeated this simple experiment successfully several times. Now each of those grey four-pointed stars, one of which I saw in each experiment, was what is called an 'after-image' or 'after-sensation'; and can anybody deny that each of these after-images can be quite properly said to have been 'presented in space'? I saw each of them on a real white background, and, if so, each of them was 'presented' on a real white background. But though they were 'presented in space' everybody, I think, would feel that it was gravely misleading to say that they were 'to be met with in space'. The white star at which I 'looked steadfastly', the black ground on which I saw it, and the white ground on which I saw the after-images, were, of course, 'to be met with in space': they were, in fact, 'physical objects' or surfaces of physical objects. But one important difference between them, on the one hand, and the grey after-images, on the other, can be quite naturally expressed by saying that the latter were *not* 'to be met with in space'. And one reason why this is so is, I think, plain. To say that so and so was at a given time 'to be met with in space' naturally suggests that there are conditions such that *any one* who fulfilled them might, conceivably, have 'perceived' the 'thing' in question— might have seen it, if it was a visible object, have felt it, if it was a tangible one, have heard it, if it was a sound, have smelt it, if it was a smell. When I say that the white four-pointed paper star, at which I looked steadfastly, was a 'physical object' and was 'to be met with in space', I am implying that *anyone*, who had been in the room at the time, and who had normal eyesight and a normal sense of touch, might have seen and felt it. But, in the case of those grey after-images which I saw, it is not conceivable that anyone besides myself should have seen any one of them. It is, of course, quite conceivable that other people, if they had been in the room with me at the time, and had carried out the same experiment which I carried out, would have seen grey after-images *very like* one of those which I saw: there is no absurdity in supposing even that they might have seen after-images *exactly* like one of those which I saw. But there is an absurdity in supposing that any one of the after-images which I saw could also have been seen by anyone else: in supposing that two different people can ever see the *very same* after-image. One reason, then, why we should say that none of those grey after-images which I saw was 'to be met with in space', although each of them was certainly 'presented in space' to me, is simply that none of them could conceivably have been seen by anyone else. It is natural so to understand the phrase 'to be met with in space', that to say of anything which a man perceived that it was to be met with in space is to say that it might have been perceived by *others* as well as by the man in question.

Negative after-images of the kind described are, therefore, one example of 'things' which, though they must be allowed to be 'presented in space', are nevertheless *not* 'to be met with in space', and are *not* 'external to our minds' in the sense with which we shall be concerned. And two other important examples may be given.

The first is this. It is well known that people sometimes see things double, an occurrence which has also been described by psychologists by saying that they have a 'double image', or two 'images', of some object at which they are looking. In such cases it would certainly be quite natural to say that each of the two 'images' is 'presented in space': they are seen, one in one place, and the other in another, in just the same sense in which each of those grey after-images which I saw was seen at a particular place on the white background at which I was looking. But it would be utterly unnatural to say that, when I have a double image, each of the two images is 'to be met with in space'. On the contrary it is quite certain that *both* of them are not 'to be met with in space'. If both were, it would follow that somebody else might see the *very same* two images which I see; and, though there is no absurdity in supposing that another person might see a pair of images exactly similar to a pair which I see, there is an absurdity in supposing that anyone else might see the *same identical pair*. In every case, then, in which anyone sees anything double, we have an example of at least one 'thing' which, though 'presented in space' is certainly not 'to be met with in space'.

And the second important example is this. Bodily pains can, in general, be quite properly said to be 'presented in space'. When I have a toothache, I feel it *in* a particular region of my jaw or *in* a particular tooth; when I make a cut on my finger smart by putting iodine on it, I feel the pain in a particular place in my finger; and a man whose leg has been amputated may feel a pain *in* a place where his foot might have been if he had not lost it. It is certainly perfectly natural to understand the phrase 'presented in space' in such a way that if, in the sense illustrated, a pain is felt *in* a particular place, that pain is 'presented in space'. And yet of pains it would be quite unnatural to say that they are 'to be met with in space', for the same reason as in the case of after-images or double images. It is quite conceivable that another person should feel a pain exactly like one which I feel, but there is an absurdity in supposing that he could feel *numerically the same* pain which I feel. And pains are in fact a typical example of the sort of 'things' of which philosophers say that they are *not* 'external' to our minds, but 'within' them. Of any pain which *I* feel they would say that it is necessarily *not* external to my mind but *in* it.

And finally it is, I think, worth while to mention one other

class of 'things', which are certainly not 'external' objects and
certainly not 'to be met with in space', in the sense with which
I am concerned, but which yet some philosophers would be
inclined to say are 'presented in space', though they are not
'presented in space' in quite the same sense in which pains,
double images, and negative after-images of the sort I described
are so. If you look at an electric light and then close your eyes,
it sometimes happens that you see, for some little time, against
the dark background which you usually see when your eyes are
shut, a bright patch similar in shape to the light at which you
have just been looking. Such a bright patch, if you see one, is
another example of what some psychologists have called 'after-
images' and others 'after-sensations'; but, unlike the negative
after-images of which I spoke before, it is seen when your eyes
are shut. Of such an after-image, seen with closed eyes, some
philosophers might be inclined to say that this image too was
'presented in space', although it is certainly not 'to be met with in
space'. They would be inclined to say that it is 'presented in
space', because it certainly is presented as at some little distance
from the person who is seeing it: and how can a thing be presented
as at some little distance from me, without being 'presented in
space'? Yet there is an important difference between such after-
images, seen with closed eyes, and after-images of the sort I
previously described—a difference which might lead other philosophers to deny that these after-images, seen with closed eyes, are
'presented in space' at all. It is a difference which can be expressed
by saying that when your eyes are shut, you are not seeing any
part of *physical* space at all—of the space which is referred to
when we talk of 'things which are to be met with in *space*'. An
after-image seen with closed eyes certainly is presented in *a*
space, but it may be questioned whether it is proper to say that it is
presented in *space*.

It is clear, then, I think, that by no means everything which
can naturally be said to be 'presented in space' can also be naturally
said to be 'a thing which is to be met with in space'. Some of the
'things', which are presented in space, are very emphatically
not to be met with in space: or, to use another phrase, which may
be used to convey the same notion, they are emphatically *not*
'physical realities' at all. The conception 'presented in space' is
therefore, in one respect, much wider than the conception 'to

be met with in space': many 'things' fall under the first conception which do not fall under the second—many after-images, one at least of the pair of 'images' seen whenever anyone sees double, and most bodily pains, are 'presented in space', though none of them are to be met with in space. From the fact that a 'thing' is presented in space, it by no means follows that it is to be met with in space. But just as the first conception is, in one respect, wider than the second, so, in another, the second is wider than the first. For there are many 'things' to be met with in space, of which it is not true that they are presented in space. From the fact that a 'thing' is to be met with in space, it by no means follows that it is presented in space. I have taken 'to be met with in space' to imply, as I think it naturally may, that a 'thing' *might be* perceived; but from the fact that a thing *might be* perceived, it does not follow that it *is* perceived; and if it is not actually perceived, then it will not be presented in space. It is characteristic of the sorts of 'things', including shadows, which I have described as 'to be met with in space', that there is no absurdity in supposing with regard to any one of them which *is*, at a given time, perceived, both (1) that it might have existed at that very time, without being perceived; (2) that it might have existed at another time, without being perceived at that other time; and (3) that during the whole period of its existence, it need not have been perceived at any time at all. There is, therefore, no absurdity in supposing that many things, which were at one time to be met with in space, never were 'presented' at any time at all, and that many things which *are* to be met with in space now, are not now 'presented' and also never were and never will be. To use a Kantian phrase, the conception of 'things which are to be met with in space' embraces not only objects of actual experience, but also objects of *possible* experience; and from the fact that a thing is or was an object of *possible* experience, it by no means follows that it either was or is or will be 'presented' at all.

I hope that what I have now said may have served to make clear enough what sorts of 'things' I was originally referring to as 'things outside us' or 'things external to our minds'. I said that I thought that Kant's phrase 'things that are to be met with in space' indicated fairly clearly the sorts of 'things' in question; and I have tried to make the range clearer still, by pointing out that this phrase only serves the purpose, if (a) you understand it in a sense, in which many 'things', e.g. after-images, double images, bodily pains, which might be said to be 'presented in space', are nevertheless *not* to be reckoned as 'things that are to be met with in space', and (*b*) you realize clearly that there is no contradiction in supposing that there have been and are 'to be met with in space' things which never have been, are not now, and never will be perceived, nor in supposing that among those of them which have at some time been perceived many existed at times at which they were not being perceived. I think it will now be clear to everyone that, since I do not reckon as 'external things' after-images, double images, and bodily pains, I also should not reckon as 'external things', any of the 'images' which we often 'see with the mind's eye' when we are awake, nor any of those which we see when we are asleep and dreaming; and also that I was so using the expression 'external' that from the fact that a man was at a given time having a visual hallucination, it will follow that he was seeing at that time something which was *not* 'external' to his mind, and from the fact that he was at a given time having an auditory hallucination, it will follow that he was at the time hearing a sound which was *not* 'external' to his mind. But I certainly have not made my use of these phrases, 'external to our minds' and 'to be met with in space', so clear that in the case of every kind of 'thing' which might be suggested, you would be able to tell at once whether I should or should not reckon it as 'external to our minds' and 'to be met with in space'. For instance, I have said nothing which makes it quite clear whether a reflection which I see in a looking-glass is or is not to be regarded as 'a thing that is to be met with in space' and 'external to our minds', nor have I said anything which makes it quite clear whether the sky is or is not to be so regarded. In the case of the sky, everyone, I think, would feel that it was quite inappropriate to talk of it as 'a thing that is to be met with in space'; and most people, I think, would feel a strong reluctance to affirm, without qualification, that reflections which people see in looking-glasses are 'to be met with in space'. And yet neither the sky nor reflections seen in mirrors are in the same position as bodily pains or after-images in the respect which I have emphasized as a reason for saying of these latter that they are *not* to be met with in space— namely that there is an absurdity in supposing that *the very same* pain which I feel could be felt by someone else or that *the very same* after-image which I see could be seen by someone else. In the case of reflections in mirrors we should quite naturally, in certain circumstances, use language which implies that another person may see the same reflection which we see. We might quite naturally say to a friend: 'Do you see that reddish reflection in the water there? I can't make out what it's a reflection of', just as we might say, pointing to a distant hill-side: 'Do you see that white speck on the hill over there? I can't make out what it is.' And in the case of the sky, it is quite obviously *not* absurd to say that other people see it as well as I.

It must, therefore, be admitted that I have not made my use of the phrase 'things to be met with in space', nor therefore that of 'external to our minds', which the former was used to explain, so clear that in the case of every kind of 'thing' which may be mentioned, there will be no doubt whatever as to whether things of that kind are or are not 'to be met with in space' or 'external to our minds'. But this lack of a clear-cut definition of the expression 'things that are to be met with in space', does not, so far as I can see, matter for my present purpose. For my present purpose it is, I think, sufficient if I make clear, in the case of many kinds of things, that I am so using the phrase 'things that are to be met with in space', that, in the case of each of these kinds, from the proposition that there are things of that kind it *follows* that there are things to be met with in space. And I have, in fact, given a list (though by no means an exhaustive one) of kinds of things which are related to my use of the expression 'things that are to be met with in space' in this way. I mentioned among others the bodies of men and of animals, plants, stars, houses, chairs, and shadows; and I want now to emphasize that I am so using 'things to be met with in space' that, in the case of each of these kinds of 'things', from the proposition that there are 'things' of that kind it *follows* that there are things to be met with in space: e.g. from the proposition that there are plants or that plants exist it *follows* that there are things to be met with in space, from the proposition that shadows exist, it *follows* that there are things to be met with in space, and so on, in the case of all the kinds of 'things' which I mentioned in my first list. That this should be clear is sufficient for my purpose, because, if it is clear, then it will also be clear that, as I implied before, if you have proved that two plants exist, or that a plant and a dog exist,

E*

or that a dog and a shadow exist, etc. etc., you will *ipso facto* have proved that there are things to be met with in space: you will not require *also* to give a separate proof that from the proposition that there are plants it *does* follow that there are things to be met with in space.

Now with regard to the expression 'things that are to be met with in space' I think it will readily be believed that I may be using it in a sense such that no proof is required that from 'plants exist' there follows 'there are things to be met with in space'; but with regard to the phrase 'things external to our minds' I think the case is different. People may be inclined to say: 'I can see quite clearly that from the proposition "At least two dogs exist at the present moment" there *follows* the proposition "At least two things are to be met with in space at the present moment", so that if you can prove that there are two dogs in existence at the present moment you will *ipso facto* have proved that two things at least are to be met with in space at the present moment. I can see that you do not also require a separate proof that from "Two dogs exist" "Two things are to be met with in space" *does* follow; it is quite obvious that there couldn't be a dog which wasn't to be met with in space. But it is not by any means so clear to me that if you can prove that there are two dogs or two shadows, you will *ipso facto* have proved that there are two things *external to our minds*. Isn't it possible that a dog, though it certainly must be "to be met with in space", might *not* be an external object—an object external to our minds? Isn't a separate proof required that anything that is to be met with in space must be external to our minds? Of course, if you are using "external" as a mere synonym for "to be met with in space", no proof will be required that dogs are external objects: in that case, if you can prove that two dogs exist, you will *ipso facto* have proved that there are some external things. But I find it difficult to believe that you, or anybody else, do really use "external" as a mere synonym for "to be met with in space"; and if you don't, isn't some proof required that whatever is to be met with in space must be external to our minds?'

Now Kant, as we saw, asserts that the phrases 'outside of us' or 'external' are in fact used in two very different senses; and with regard to one of these two senses, that which he calls the 'transcendental' sense, and which he tries to explain by saying that it is a sense in which 'external' means 'existing *as a thing in itself* distinct from us', it is notorious that he himself held that things which are to be met with in space are *not* 'external' in that sense. There is, therefore, according to him, *a* sense of 'external', a sense in which the word has been commonly used by philosophers—such that, if 'external' be used in that sense, then from the proposition 'Two dogs exist' it will *not* follow that there are some external things. What this supposed sense is I do not think that Kant himself ever succeeded in explaining clearly; nor do I know of any reason for supposing that philosophers ever have used 'external' in a sense, such that in *that* sense things that are to be met with in space are *not* external. But how about the other sense, in which, according to Kant, the word 'external' has been commonly used—that which he calls 'empirically external'? How is this conception related to the conception 'to be met with in space'? It may be noticed that, in the passages which I quoted (A 373), Kant himself does not tell us at all clearly what he takes to be the proper answer to this question. He only makes the rather odd statement that, in order to remove all uncertainty as to the conception 'empirically external', he will distinguish objects to which it applies from those which might be called 'external' in the transcendental sense, by 'calling them outright things which are *to be met with in space*'. These odd words certainly suggest, as one possible interpretation of them, that in Kant's opinion the conception 'empirically external' is *identical* with the conception 'to be met with in space'—that he does think that 'external', when used in this second sense, is a mere synonym for 'to be met with in space'. But, if this is his meaning, I do find it very difficult to believe that he is right. Have philosophers, in fact, ever used 'external' as a mere synonym for 'to be met with in space'? Does he himself do so?

I do not think they have, nor that he does himself; and, in order to explain how they have used it, and how the two conceptions 'external to our minds' and 'to be met with in space' are related to one another, I think it is important expressly to call attention to a fact which hitherto I have only referred to incidentally: namely the fact that those who talk of certain things as 'external to' our minds, do, in general, as we should naturally expect, talk of other 'things', with which they wish to contrast the first, as 'in' our minds. It has, of course, been often pointed out that when 'in' is thus used, followed by 'my mind', 'your mind', 'his mind', etc., 'in' is being used metaphorically. And there are some metaphorical uses of 'in', followed by such expressions, which occur in common speech, and which we all understand quite well. For instance, we all understand such expressions as 'I had you in mind, when I made that arrangement' or 'I had you in mind, when I said that there are some people who can't bear to touch a spider'. In these cases 'I was thinking of you' can be used to mean the same as 'I had you in mind'. But it is quite certain that this particular metaphorical use of 'in' is not the one in which philosophers are using it when they contrast what is 'in' my mind with what is 'external' to it. On the contrary, in their use of 'external', you will be external to my mind even at a moment when I have you in mind. If we want to discover what this peculiar metaphorical use of *in* my mind' is, which is such that nothing, which is, in the sense we are now concerned with, 'external' to my mind, can ever be 'in' it, we need, I think, to consider instances of the sort of 'things' which they would say are 'in' my mind in this special sense. I have already mentioned three such instances, which are, I think, sufficient for my present purpose: any bodily pain which I feel, any after-image which I see with my eyes shut, and any image which I 'see' when I am asleep and dreaming, are typical examples of the sort of 'thing' of which philosophers have spoken as *in* my mind'. And there is no doubt, I think, that when they have spoken of such things as my body, a sheet of paper, a star—in short 'physical objects' generally—as 'external', they have meant to emphasize some important difference which they feel to exist between such things as these and such 'things' as a pain, an after-image seen with closed eyes, and a dream-image. But *what* difference? What difference do they feel to exist between a bodily pain which I feel or an after-image which I see with closed eyes, on the one hand, and my body itself, on the other—what difference which leads them to say that whereas the bodily pain and the after-image are 'in' my mind, my body itself is *not* 'in' my mind—not even when I am feeling it and seeing it or thinking of it? I have already said that one difference which there is between the two, is that my body is to be met with in space, whereas the bodily pain and the after-image are not. But I think it would be quite wrong to say that this is *the* difference which has led philosophers to speak of the two latter as 'in' my mind, and of my body as *not* 'in' my mind.

The question what the difference is which has led them to speak in this way, is not, I think, at all an easy question to answer; but I am going to try to give, in brief outline, what I *think* is a right answer.

It should, I think, be noted, first of all, that the use of the word 'mind', which is being adopted when it is said that any bodily pains which I feel are 'in my mind', is one which is not quite in accordance with any usage common in ordinary speech, although we are very familiar with it in philosophy. Nobody, I think, would say that bodily pains which I feel are 'in my mind', unless he was also prepared to say that it is *with* my mind that I feel bodily pains; and to say this latter is, I think, not quite in accordance with common non-philosophic usage. It is natural enough to say that it is with my mind that I remember, and think, and imagine, and feel *mental* pains—e.g. disappointment, but not, I think, quite so natural to say that it is with my mind that I feel *bodily* pains, e.g. a severe headache; and perhaps even less natural to say that it is with my mind that I see and hear and smell and taste. There is, however, a well-established philosophical usage according to which seeing, hearing, smelling, tasting, and having a bodily pain are just as much *mental* occurrences or processes as are remembering, or thinking, or imagining. This usage was, I think, adopted by philosophers, because they saw a real resemblance between such statements as 'I saw a cat', 'I heard a clap of thunder', 'I smelt a strong smell of onions', 'My finger smarted horribly', on the one hand, and such statements as 'I remembered having seen him', 'I was thinking out a plan of action', 'I pictured the scene to myself', 'I felt bitterly disappointed', on the other—a resemblance which puts all these statements in one class together, as contrasted with other statements in which 'I' or 'my' is used, such as, e.g., 'I was less than four feet high', 'I was lying on my back', 'My hair was very long'. What is the resemblance in question? It is a resemblance which might be expressed by saying that all the first eight statements are the sort of statements which furnish data for psychology, while the three latter are not. It is also a resemblance which may be expressed, in a way now common among philosophers, by saying that in the case of all the first eight statements, if we make the statement more specific by adding a date, we get a statement such that, if it is true, then it *follows* that I was 'having an experience' at the date in question, whereas this does not hold for the three last statements. For instance, if it is true that I saw a cat between 12 noon and 5 minutes past, today, it *follows* that I was 'having some experience' between 12 noon and 5 minutes past, today; whereas from the proposition that I was less than four feet high in December 1877, it does not *follow* that I had any experiences in December 1877. But this philosophic use of 'having an experience' is one which itself needs explanation, since it is not identical with any use of the expression that is established in common speech. An explanation, however, which is, I think, adequate for the purpose, can be given by saying that a philosopher, who was following this usage, would say that I was at a given time 'having an experience' if and only if either (1) I was conscious at the time or (2) I was dreaming at the time or (3) something else was true of me at the time, which resembled what is true of me when I am conscious and when I am dreaming, in a certain very obvious respect in which what is true of me when I am dreaming resembles what is true of me when I am conscious, and in which what would be true of me, if at any time, for instance, I had a vision, would resemble both. This explanation is, of course, in some degree vague; but I think it is clear enough for our purpose. It amounts to saying that, in this philosophic usage of 'having an experience', it would be said of me that I was, at a given time, having *no* experience, if I was at the time neither conscious nor dreaming nor having a vision nor *anything else of the sort*; and, of course, this is vague in so far as it has not been specified what else would be *of the sort*: this is left to be gathered from the instances given. But I think this is sufficient: often at night when I am asleep, I am neither conscious nor dreaming nor having a vision nor *anything else of the sort*—that is to say, I am having no experiences. If this explanation of this philosophic usage of 'having an experience' is clear enough, then I think that what has been meant by saying that any pain which I feel or any after-image which I see with my eyes closed is '*in* my mind', can be explained by saying that what is meant is neither more nor less than that there would be a contradiction in supposing *that very same pain* or *that very same after-image* to have existed at a time at which I was having no experience; or, in other words, that from the proposition, with regard to any time, that *that* pain or *that* after-image existed at that time, it *follows* that I was having some experience at the time in question. And if so, then we can say that the felt difference between bodily pains which I feel and after-images which I see, on the one hand, and my body on the other, which has led philosophers to say that any such pain or after-image is '*in* my mind', whereas my body *never* is but is always 'outside of' or 'external to' my mind, is just this, that whereas there is a contradiction in supposing a pain which I feel or an after-image which I see to exist at a time when I am having no experience, there is no contradiction in supposing my body to exist at a time when I am having no experience; and we can even say, I think, that just this and nothing more is what they have meant by these puzzling and misleading phrases 'in my mind' and 'external to my mind'.

But now, if to say of anything, e.g. my body, that it is external to *my* mind, means merely that from a proposition to the effect that it existed at a specified time, there in no case follows the further proposition that *I* was having an experience at the time in question, then to say of anything that it is external to *our* minds, will mean similarly that from a proposition to the effect that it existed at a specified time, it in no case follows that any of *us* were having experiences at the time in question. And if by *our* minds be meant, as is, I think, usually meant, the minds of human beings living on the earth, then it will follow that any pains which animals may feel, any after-images they may see, any experiences they may have, though not external to *their* minds, yet are external to *ours*. And this at once makes plain how different is the conception 'external to our minds' from the conception 'to be met with in space'; for, of course, pains which animals feel or after-images which they see are no more to be met with in space than are pains which *we* feel or after-images which *we* see. From the proposition that there are external objects —objects that are not in any of *our* minds, it does *not* follow that there are things to be met with in space; and hence 'external to our minds' is not a mere synonym for 'to be met with in space': that is to say, 'external to our minds' and 'to be met with in space' are two different conceptions. And the true relation between these conceptions seems to me to be this. We have already seen that there are ever so many kinds of 'things', such that, in the

case of each of these kinds, from the proposition that there is at
least one thing of that kind there *follows* the proposition that there
is at least one thing to be met with in space: e.g. this follows
from 'There is at least one star', from 'There is at least one
human body', from 'There is at least one shadow', etc. And I
think we can say that of every kind of thing of which this is true,
it is also true that from the proposition that there is at least one
'thing' of that kind there *follows* the proposition that there is
at least one thing external to our minds: e.g. from 'There is at
least one star' there follows not only 'There is at least one thing
to be met with in space' but also 'There is at least one external
thing', and similarly in all other cases. My reason for saying this is
as follows. Consider any kind of thing, such that anything of that
kind, if there is anything of it, must be 'to be met with in space':
e.g. consider the kind 'soap-bubble'. If I say of anything which I
am perceiving, 'That is a soap-bubble', I am, it seems to me,
certainly implying that there would be no contradiction in
asserting that it existed before I perceived it and that it will
continue to exist, even if I cease to perceive it. This seems to me
to be part of what is meant by saying that it is a real soap-bubble,
as distinguished, for instance, from an hallucination of a soap-
bubble. Of course, it by no means follows, that if it really is a
soap-bubble, it did in fact exist before I perceived it or will
continue to exist after I cease to perceive it: soap-bubbles are an
example of a kind of 'physical object' and 'thing to be met with in
space', in the case of which it is notorious that particular specimens
of the kind often do exist only so long as they are perceived
by a particular person. But a thing which I perceive would not be a
soap-bubble unless its existence at any given time were *logically
independent* of my perception of it at that time; unless that is to
say, from the proposition, with regard to a particular time, that it
existed at that time, it *never* follows that I perceived it at that
time. But, if it is true that it would not be a soap-bubble, unless it
could have existed at any given time without being perceived by
me at that time, it is certainly also true that it would not be
a soap-bubble, unless it *could* have existed at any given time,
without its being true that I was having any experience of any
kind at the time in question: it would not be a soap-bubble,
unless, whatever time you take, from the proposition that it
existed at that time it does *not* follow that I was having any ex-

perience at that time. That is to say, from the proposition with regard to anything which I am perceiving that it is a soap-bubble, there *follows* the proposition that it is external to *my* mind. But if, when I say that anything which I perceive is a soap-bubble, I am implying that it is external to *my* mind, I am, I think, certainly also implying that it is also external to all other minds: I am implying that it is not a thing of a sort such that things of that sort *can* only exist at a time when somebody is having an experience. I think, therefore, that from any proposition of the form 'There's a soap-bubble!' there does really *follow* the proposition 'There's an external object!' 'There's an object external to *all* our minds!' And, if this is true of the kind 'soap-bubble', it is certainly also true of any other kind (including the kind 'unicorn') which is such that, if there are any things of that kind, it follows that there are *some* things to be met with in space.

I think, therefore, that in the case of all kinds of 'things', which are such that if there is a pair of things, both of which are of one of these kinds, or a pair of things one of which is of one of them and one of them of another, then it will follow at once that there are some things to be met with in space, it is true also that if I can prove that there are a pair of things, one of which is of one of these kinds and another of another, or a pair both of which are of one of them, then I shall have proved *ipso facto* that there are at least two 'things outside of us'. That is to say, if I can prove that there exist now both a sheet of paper and a human hand, I shall have proved that there are now 'things outside of us'; if I can prove that there exist now both a shoe and sock, I shall have proved that there are now 'things outside of us'; etc.; and similarly I shall have proved it, if I can prove that there exist now two sheets of paper, or two human hands, or two shoes, or two socks, etc. Obviously, then, there are thousands of different things such that, if, at any time, I can prove any one of them, I shall have proved the existence of things outside of us. Cannot I prove any of these things?

It seems to me that, so far from its being true, as Kant declares to be his opinion, that there is only one possible proof of the existence of things outside of us, namely the one which he has given, I can now give a large number of different proofs, each of which is a perfectly rigorous proof; and that at many other times I have been in a position to give many others. I can prove now,

for instance, that two human hands exist. How? By holding up
my two hands, and saying, as I make a certain gesture with the
right hand, 'Here is one hand', and adding, as I make a certain
gesture with the left, 'and here is another'. And if, by doing this,
I have proved *ipso facto* the existence of external things, you
will all see that I can also do it now in numbers of other ways:
there is no need to multiply examples.

But did I prove just now that two human hands were then
in existence? I do want to insist that I did; that the proof which
I gave was a perfectly rigorous one; and that it is perhaps impossible to give a better or more rigorous proof of anything
whatever. Of course, it would not have been a proof unless three
conditions were satisfied; namely (1) unless the premiss which I
adduced as proof of the conclusion was different from the conclusion I adduced it to prove; (2) unless the premiss which I
adduced was something which I *knew* to be the case, and not
merely something which I believed but which was by no means
certain, or something which, though in fact true, I did not know to
be so; and (3) unless the conclusion did really follow from the
premiss. But all these three conditions were in fact satisfied by
my proof. (1) The premiss which I adduced in proof was quite
certainly different from the conclusion, for the conclusion was
merely 'Two human hands exist at this moment'; but the premiss
was something far more specific than this—something which I
expressed by showing you my hands, making certain gestures,
and saying the words 'Here is one hand, and here is another'.
It is quite obvious that the two were different, because it is quite
obvious that the conclusion might have been true, even if the
premiss had been false. In asserting the premiss I was asserting
much more than I was asserting in asserting the conclusion.
(2) I certainly did at the moment *know* that which I expressed
by the combination of certain gestures with saying the words
'There is one hand and here is another'. I *knew* that there was one
hand in the place indicated by combining a certain gesture with
my first utterance of 'here' and that there was another in the
different place indicated by combining a certain gesture with
my second utterance of 'here'. How absurd it would be to suggest
that I did not know it, but only believed it, and that perhaps it
was not the case! You might as well suggest that I do not know
that I am now standing up and talking—that perhaps after all

I'm not, and that it's not quite certain that I am! And finally (3) it is quite certain that the conclusion did follow from the premiss. This is as certain as it is that if there is one hand here and another here *now*, then it follows that there are two hands in existence *now*.

My proof, then, of the existence of things outside of us did satisfy three of the conditions necessary for a rigorous proof. Are there any other conditions necessary for a rigorous proof, such that perhaps it did not satisfy one of them? Perhaps there may be; I do not know; but I do want to emphasize that, so far as I can see, we all of us do constantly take proofs of this sort as absolutely conclusive proofs of certain conclusions—as finally settling certain questions, as to which we were previously in doubt. Suppose, for instance, it were a question whether there were as many as three misprints on a certain page in a certain book. A says there are, B is inclined to doubt it. How could A prove that he is right? Surely he *could* prove it by taking the book, turning to the page, and pointing to three separate places on it, saying 'There's one misprint here, another here, and another here': surely that is a method by which it *might* be proved! Of course, A would not have proved, by doing this, that there were at least three misprints on the page in question, unless it was certain that there was a misprint in each of the places to which he pointed. But to say that he *might* prove it in this way, is to say that it *might* be certain that there was. And if such a thing as that could ever be certain, then assuredly it was certain just now that there was one hand in one of the two places I indicated and another in the other.

I did, then, just now, give a proof that there were *then* external objects; and obviously, if I did, I could *then* have given many other proofs of the same sort that there were external objects *then*, and could now give many proofs of the same sort that there are external objects *now*.

But, if what I am asked to do is to prove that external objects have existed *in the past*, then I can give many different proofs of this also, but proofs which are in important respects of a different *sort* from those just given. And I want to emphasize that, when Kant says it is a scandal not to be able to give a proof of the existence of external objects, a proof of their existence in the past would certainly *help* to remove the scandal of which he is speaking. He says that, if it occurs to anyone to question their existence, we ought to be able to confront him with a satisfactory proof. But by a person who questions their existence, he certainly means not merely a person who questions whether any exist at the moment of speaking, but a person who questions whether any have *ever* existed; and a proof that some have existed in the past would certainly therefore be relevant to *part* of what such a person is questioning. How then can I prove that there have been external objects in the past? Here is one proof. I can say: 'I held up two hands above this desk not very long ago; therefore two hands existed not very long ago; therefore at least two external objects have existed at some time in the past, Q.E.D.' This is a perfectly good proof, provided I *know* what is asserted in the premiss. But I *do* know that I held up two hands above this desk not very long ago. As a matter of fact, in this case you all know it too. There's no doubt whatever that I did. Therefore I have given a perfectly conclusive proof that external objects have existed in the past; and you will all see at once that, if this is a conclusive proof, I could have given many others of the same sort, and could now give many others. But it is also quite obvious that this sort of proof differs in important respects from the sort of proof I gave just now that there were two hands existing *then*.

I have, then, given two conclusive proofs of the existence of external objects. The first was a proof that two human hands existed at the time when I gave the proof; the second was a proof that two human hands had existed at a time previous to that at which I gave the proof. These proofs were of a different sort in important respects. And I pointed out that I could have given, then, many other conclusive proofs of both sorts. It is also obvious that I could give many others of both sorts now. So that, if these are the sort of proof that is wanted, nothing is easier than to prove the existence of external objects.

But now I am perfectly well aware that, in spite of all that I have said, many philosophers will still feel that I have not given any satisfactory proof of the point in question. And I want briefly, in conclusion, to say something as to why this dissatisfaction with my proofs should be felt.

One reason why, is, I think, this. Some people understand 'proof of an external world' as including a proof of things which I haven't attempted to prove and haven't proved. It is not quite easy to say *what* it is that they want proved—*what* it is that is such that unless they got a proof of it, they would not say that they had a proof of the existence of external things; but I can make an approach to explaining what they want by saying that if I had proved the propositions which I used as *premisses* in my two proofs, then they would perhaps admit that I had proved the existence of external things, but, in the absence of such a proof (which, of course, I have neither given nor attempted to give), they will say that I have not given what they mean by a proof of the existence of external things. In other words, they want a proof of what I assert *now* when I hold up my hands and say 'Here's one hand and here's another'; and, in the other case, they want a proof of what I assert *now* when I say 'I did hold up two hands above this desk just now'. Of course, what they really want is not merely a proof of these two propositions, but something like a general statement as to how *any* propositions of this sort may be proved. This, of course, I haven't given; and I do not believe it can be given: if this is what is meant by proof of the existence of external things, I do not believe that any proof of the existence of external things is possible. Of course, in some cases what might be called a proof of propositions which seem like these can be got. If one of you suspected that one of my hands was artificial he might be said to get a proof of my proposition 'Here's one hand, and here's another', by coming up and examining the suspected hand close up, perhaps touching and pressing it, and so establishing that it really was a human hand. But I do not believe that any proof is possible in nearly all cases. How am I to prove now that 'Here's one hand, and here's another'? I do not believe I can do it. In order to do it, I should need to prove for one thing, as Descartes pointed out, that I am not now dreaming. But how can I prove that I am not? I have, no doubt, conclusive reasons for asserting that I am not now dreaming; I have conclusive evidence that I am awake: but that is a very different thing from being able to prove it. I could not tell you what all my evidence is; and I should require to do this at least, in order to give you a proof.

But another reason why some people would feel dissatisfied with my proofs is, I think, not merely that they want a proof of something which I haven't proved, but that they think that, if I cannot give such extra proofs, then the proofs that I have given

VIII

RUSSELL'S 'THEORY OF DESCRIPTIONS'

F. P. Ramsey, in one of his posthumously published writings, used the phrase 'that paradigm of philosophy, Russell's theory of descriptions.'[1] What statement or statements of Russell's was Ramsey calling 'Russell's theory of descriptions'? And what reasons are there for regarding this statement, or these statements, as a 'paradigm of philosophy'?

I think there is no doubt that when Ramsey spoke of 'Russell's theory of descriptions' he was using the word 'descriptions' in one or other of two different technical senses, in each of which Russell has, in different places, used the word. One of these two technical senses is that in which it is used in *Principia Mathematica*, where the word occurs as a title in three separate places;[2] and this sense is one which the authors, where they first introduce the word,[3] try to explain by saying: 'By a "description" we mean a phrase of the form "the so and so" or of some equivalent form.' The other is a sense in which Russell has used the word in two later writings, his *Introduction to Mathematical Philosophy* and his lectures on 'The Philosophy of Logical Atomism'.[4] And what this other sense is is partly explained by the following sentences from the former, 'A "description"', says Russell,[5] 'may be of two sorts, definite and indefinite (or ambiguous). An indefinite description is a phrase of the form "a so-and-so", and a definite description is a phrase of the form "the so-and-so" (in the singular).' It is clear, I think, that 'description' is here being used in a much wider sense than that in which it was used in *Principia*. In *Principia* it was so used that no phrase would be a 'description' unless it were what Russell is now calling a 'definite description'; in fact, in *Principia* 'description' was used as a perfect synonym

---

[1] *The Foundations of Mathematics and other Logical Essays* (Kegan Paul, London, 1931), p. 263, n.

[2] *Principia Mathematica*, I² (Cambridge, 1910, 2nd edition 1925) p. 30; p. 66; p. 173. (My references throughout are to the paging of the second edition, which is unfortunately slightly different from that of the first: I indicate this by writing I².)

[3] *Ibid.*, p. 30.   [4] *The Monist*, xxix, 2 (April 1919), pp. 206 ff.

[5] *Introduction to Mathematical Philosophy* (Allen & Unwin, London, 1919), p. 167.

for the new expression 'definite description', in the sense which
Russell is now giving to that expression. But here, quite plainly,
it is being used in such a sense that immense numbers of phrases
which are *not* 'definite descriptions' are nevertheless 'descriptions'. We may say that here 'descriptions' is being used as a
name for a genus of which 'descriptions', in the *Principia* sense,
are only one species, the other species being what Russell is now
calling 'indefinite' or 'ambiguous' descriptions.

In which of these two senses, the wider or the narrower one,
was Ramsey using the word when he spoke of 'Russell's theory
of descriptions'? If he were using it in the narrower one, the one
in which it is used in *Principia*, he would be saying that some of
the statements which Russell has made about phrases of the sort
which, later on, he called 'definite descriptions', are by themselves
sufficient to constitute a 'paradigm of philosophy'. But, if he were
using it in the wider one (the sense in which 'indefinite descriptions' are just as truly 'descriptions' as 'definite' ones), he would
not be committing himself to this assertion. On the contrary,
it might be his view that, in order to get a 'paradigm of philosophy',
we have to take into account not only statements which Russell
has made about 'definite descriptions', but also statements
which he has made about 'indefinite' ones. Now I think it is
pretty certain that, of these two alternatives, the former is the
true one. I think Ramsey was using 'descriptions' in the narrower
of the two technical senses, *not* in the wider one; and that he
did consider that statements which Russell has made about
'definite descriptions' are by themselves sufficient to constitute
a 'paradigm of philosophy', without taking into account any of the
statements which he has made about 'indefinite' ones. And that
he was using 'descriptions' in the narrower sense—the sense of
Principia—I think we have *some* evidence (though not conclusive
evidence) in another passage, in which he also speaks of 'Russell's
theory of descriptions'. In this other passage,[1] he says, 'A theory
of descriptions which contented itself with observing that "The
King of France is wise" could be regarded as asserting a possibly
complex multiple relation between kingship, France and wisdom,
would be miserably inferior to Mr Russell's theory, which explains exactly what that relation is'. This looks as if he regarded
Russell's theory as a theory about phrases which resemble the

[1] *Foundations of Mathematics*, p. 142.

phrase 'The King of France' in a respect in which the phrase 'A King of France' does not resemble it. But whether or not (as I am pretty certain he did) Ramsey meant by 'Russell's theory of descriptions' Russell's theory of *definite* descriptions, I am going to confine myself exclusively to statements which Russell makes about *definite* descriptions. Which of these could Ramsey have regarded as constituting his 'theory of descriptions'? And why should he have thought them a 'paradigm of philosophy'?

Now if we read the three different passages in *Principia* which are headed with the title 'Descriptions';[1] if we then read pages 172–80 of the chapter entitled 'Descriptions' in the *Introduction to Mathematical Philosophy*; and if, finally, we read pages 209–22 in *The Monist* for April 1919, we shall find that in all those passages, taken together, quite a large number of different statements are made. Which among all those different statements are statements about 'definite descriptions'? And which among those which are can be regarded as forming part of 'Russell's theory of descriptions'? I propose to begin with one which is a statement about a 'definite description'; which nevertheless cannot, I think, be regarded as itself forming part of Russell's theory of descriptions; but which is such that, by reference to it, two of the most fundamental propositions which do, I think, form a part of that theory, can be explained.

The statement I mean is one which is made by Russell on page 177 of the *Introduction to Mathematical Philosophy*. He there writes out in a list the three following propositions:

(1) At least one person wrote *Waverley*.
(2) At most one person wrote *Waverley*.
(3) Whoever wrote *Waverley* was Scotch.

and then proceeds to make about these three propositions the following statement:

All these three are implied by 'the author of *Waverley* was Scotch'. Conversely, the three together (but no two of them) imply that the author of *Waverley* was Scotch. Hence the three together may be taken as defining what is meant by the proposition, 'the author of *Waverley* was Scotch'.

Now it is quite clear that, in making this statement, Russell

[1] *P.M.*, p. 12, pp. 30–1; pp. 66–7; pp. 73–186.

has made a considerable number of different assertions. But it seems to me that the language which he has used in making them is, in some respects, such as not to make it quite clear just what he is asserting. I will mention in order the chief respects in which this seems to me to be the case.

It will be seen that he has expressed the proposition numbered (3) by the words 'whoever wrote *Waverley* was Scotch'. Now it seems to me that the most natural way, and even, so far as I can see, the *only* natural way of understanding these words, is as expressing a proposition which cannot be true unless somebody did write *Waverley*: i.e. is such that the proposition 'whoever wrote *Waverley* was Scotch, but nobody did write *Waverley*' is self-contradictory. But, if Russell had been using the words in such a sense as this, then clearly his statement that though (1), (2) and (3) together imply that the author of *Waverley* was Scotch, yet *no two of them* do imply this, would be false: for (3) would imply (1), and hence (3) and (2) by themselves would imply everything that is implied by (1), (2), and (3) together. It is certain, I think, not only from this fact but from other things, that he was using these words in a sense such that the proposition expressed by them does not imply (1). And I think that the proposition which he was using them to express is one which can be expressed more clearly by the words, 'There never was a person who wrote *Waverley* but was not Scotch'. In the case of this proposition, which I will call (4), it is, I think, quite clear that it does not imply (1), but is quite consistent with the falsehood of (1); for it is quite clear that if (1) were false, (4) would necessarily be true: if nobody ever did write *Waverley*, it would follow that there never was a person who did write *Waverley* but was not Scotch. I shall assume that (4) is the proposition which Russell was intending to express (improperly, as I think) by the words 'whoever wrote *Waverley* was Scotch'. And I shall assume that he was intending to assert of (1), (2), and (4) all the things which he actually asserts of (1), (2), and (3).

The next point as to which there might, I think, be some doubt, is as to how he is using the word 'implies'. I shall assume that he is so using it that one proposition p can only be said, with truth, to 'imply' another q, if it can also be said with truth that q follows from p, and that the assertion that p was true but q false would be not merely false but *self-contradictory*. It follows that the meaning with which 'implies' is being used here is not what the authors of *Principia* describe[1] as 'the special meaning which we have given to implication', and which they say[2] they will sometimes express by the compound expression 'material implication'. For this 'special meaning' is such that, provided it is false that p is true and q false, then it follows that it can be said with truth that p implies q. It is clear, I think, that Russell was not here using 'implies' with this special meaning; for, if he had been, his assertion that no two of the propositions (1), (2), and (3) imply that the author of *Waverley* was Scotch, would have been obviously false. For, in fact, it is true that the author of *Waverley* was Scotch, and consequently, if 'implies' be used in the special sense adopted in *Principia*, it follows that not merely any *two*, but any *one* of the three propositions, (1), (2), and (3) implies that the author of *Waverley* was Scotch; it follows, in fact, that any other proposition whatever, true or false, implies it—for instance, the proposition that the moon is made of green cheese. I feel no doubt that Russell was here using 'implies', not in this 'special' sense, but in one of the senses which the word can properly bear in English; nor yet that he was using it in that one among its common senses, in which p cannot be truly said to imply q, unless the proposition that q is false is inconsistent or incompatible with the proposition that p is true; unless it is *impossible* that p should be true and q false; unless, if p is true, q *must* be true too—is *necessarily* true too. In other words, 'implies' is being used in such a sense that a *necessary* condition for its being true that p implies q is that it shall be *self-contradictory* to assert that p is true but q is false. But I do not think it is being used in such a sense that the fact that it would be self-contradictory to assert that p is true but q false is a *sufficient* condition for its being true that p implies q. I doubt if there is any common sense of 'implies' such that this is a *sufficient* condition. For, of course, the assertion that p is true but q false will necessarily be self-contradictory, if the assertion that p is true is by itself self-contradictory, or the assertion that q is false is by itself self-contradictory. But I do not think that in ordinary language 'implies' is ever so used that in all cases where this is so, it would be true to say that p implies q.

Owing to the ambiguity of the word 'implies', I think it is

often desirable where, as here, we are concerned with what it expresses when used with that particular one among its common meanings which I have tried to describe (though, of course, I have not attempted to define it), to use another word instead, as a synonym for 'implies' when used in this particular way. And I shall do that now. I shall use the word 'entails'. I shall express the proposition which (I take it) Russell is here expressing by saying that the proposition 'the author of *Waverley* was Scotch' both implies and is implied by the proposition which is the conjunction of (1), (2) and (4) by saying that each of these two propositions *entails* the other, or that they are 'logically equivalent'.

The third point which seems to call for some explanation is Russell's use of the phrase 'may be taken as defining what is meant by'. I take it that he is here using the expression 'may be taken as defining', in what, I think, is its most natural sense, namely as meaning 'may, *without error*, be taken as defining': in other words, he is asserting that any person who should 'take it' that (1), (2) and (4) do define what is meant by the proposition 'the author of *Waverley* was Scotch', would not be in error—would not be making a *mistake*—in 'taking it' that this was the case. But, if he is asserting this, then his whole assertion is logically equivalent to the assertion that (1), (2) and (4) *do* define what is meant by the proposition in question: if a person would not be in error in 'taking it' that *p* is the case, it follows that *p* is the case; and if *p* is the case, it follows that a person would not be in error in taking it that *p* is the case. Russell is therefore implying that the conjunction if (1), (2) and (4) *does* 'define what is meant by' the proposition in question. But what can be meant by saying that one proposition 'defines what is meant by' another? To define, in the commonest sense in which that word is used, is to 'give a definition of' in a sense in which a *person* may give a definition (true or false) but in which a *proposition* cannot possibly do any such thing. If we talk of a proposition 'defining what is meant by' something else, we must be using 'define' in some sense which can be defined in terms of that other sense of 'define' in which persons sometimes define but propositions never do. And I think it is plain enough what the sense is in which a proposition may be said 'to define'. To say that the conjunction of (1), (2) and (4) defines what is meant by the sentence S means neither more nor less than that anyone who were to assert 'The sentence S means neither more nor less than the conjunction of (1), (2) and (4)' would be giving a *correct* definition of what is meant by the sentence S. But if we say that anyone who were to assert that the sentence S means neither more nor less than the conjunction of (1), (2) and (4) would be giving a *correct* definition of what is meant by S, we are saying two distinct things about any such person: we are saying (a) that *what* he asserts is true, i.e. that the sentence S *does* mean neither more nor less than the conjunction of (1), (2) and (4), and we are saying also (b) that what he asserts is of such a nature that he can properly be said to be *giving a definition* of S (or of the meaning of S) by asserting it. These two things are certainly distinct, because by no means every true assertion of the form 'The sentence S means neither more nor less than *p*', is such that it can properly be called a *definition* of *p*. The assertion 'The sentence '*au moins une personne a écrit* WAVERLEY' means neither more nor less than that at least one person wrote *Waverley*' is (I believe) true; but a person who asserts it is certainly not *giving a definition* of the French sentence named. And the assertion, 'The sentence, "The sun is larger than the moon" means neither more nor less than that the moon is smaller than the sun' is certainly true, and yet anybody who asserted it would certainly not be *giving a definition* of the English sentence named. To give one last example: The assertion, 'The sentence "George VI is a male sibling" means neither more nor less than that George VI is a brother' is true but is certainly not a definition of the sentence 'George VI is a male sibling'; whereas, on the other hand, the assertion 'The sentence "George VI is a brother" means neither more nor less than that George VI is a male sibling', which again is true, is also such that anybody who were to assert it could be correctly said to be *giving a definition* of one correct use of the sentence 'George VI is a brother'. On the question what conditions a statement of the form '*s* means neither more nor less than *p*' must satisfy if it is properly to be called a *definition* of the meaning of *s*, it will be necessary to say something later. For the present I only wish to make clear that I shall assume that, when Russell says 'The conjunction of (1), (2) and (4) may be taken as defining what is meant by the proposition "the author of *Waverley* was Scotch" ', he is committing himself to the two assertions, (a) that the proposition 'the author of *Waverley* was Scotch' means neither more nor less than the

conjunction of (1), (2) and (4), and (*b*) that anybody who asserts
(*a*) can be correctly said to be 'giving a definition', and (since
(*a*) is true) a *correct* definition of the meaning of the proposition
named.

But now we come to one final point. What Russell actually
says is that (1), (2) and (4) may be taken as defining what is
meant by the *proposition* 'the author of *Waverley* was Scotch';
he does not say that they may be taken as defining what is meant
by the *sentence* 'the author of *Waverley* was Scotch'. If, therefore,
I am right in what I said in the last paragraph, he is committing
himself to the assertion that the *proposition* 'the author of *Waverley*
was Scotch' means neither more nor less than the conjunction of
(1), (2) and (4); but he is also committing himself to the assertion
that the *sentence* 'the author of *Waverley* was Scotch' means
neither more nor less than the conjunction of (1), (2) and (4).
It is quite certain, I think, that an expression which consists of the
words 'the proposition' followed by a given sentence in inverted
commas, *can* be properly used in such a way that it has *not* the
same meaning as the expression which consists of the words
'the sentence' followed by the same sentence in inverted commas;
and I am inclined to think that it can *not* be properly used in
such a way that it *has* the same meaning. The *proposition* 'The
sun is larger than the moon' is the *same* proposition as the *proposition* '*Le soleil est plus grand que la lune*', and one would be misusing
the word 'proposition', if one used it in such a sense that they were
not the same; but the *sentence*, 'The sun is larger than the moon'
is *not* the same sentence as the *sentence* '*Le soleil est plus grand
que la lune*', and one would be misusing the word 'sentence'
if one used it in such a sense that they were the same. If we write
the words 'the sentence' before a sentence in inverted commas,
we shall be misusing language unless we are using the sentence
in inverted commas *merely* as a name for itself and in no other
way; but if we write the words 'the proposition' before the very
same sentence in inverted commas, we shall certainly not be
misusing language if we are *not* using the sentence in inverted
commas merely as a name for itself, and I think we *shall* be
misusing language if we *are* using it merely as a name for itself.
If we had to translate into French the sentence 'The proposition
"the person who wrote *Waverley* was Scotch" implies that at
least one person wrote *Waverley*', we should certainly not be

giving an incorrect translation, if for the English sentence 'the person who wrote *Waverley* was Scotch', we substituted the French sentence '*la personne qui a écrit* WAVERLEY *était une personne écossaise*', and wrote '*La proposition "la personne qui a écrit* WAVERLEY *était une personne écossaise" implique qu'au moins une personne a écrit* WAVERLEY', and I *think* we should be giving a definitely incorrect translation, unless we *did* substitute the French sentence for the English one; but if we had to translate, 'The sentence "the person who wrote *Waverley* was Scotch" means neither more nor less than the conjunction of (1), (2) and (4)' our translation would be definitely incorrect if we did substitute a French sentence for the English sentence 'the person who wrote *Waverley* was Scotch'. It appears, then, that if Russell had written 'The proposition "the author of *Waverley* was Scotch" means neither more nor less than the conjunction of (1), (2) and (4)', he would not have been using language incorrectly, if the assertion which he was making by the use of these words had been precisely the same as he might have made quite correctly by substituting for the English sentence 'the author of *Waverley* was Scotch' a French sentence which was a correct translation of it. But suppose he had used such a French sentence, instead of the English one: would he, in that case, have been committing himself to any statement at all about the meaning of the English one? It seems to me to be quite certain that from the proposition or assertion or statement 'The *proposition "l'auteur de* WAVERLEY *était une personne écossaise"* means neither more nor less than the conjunction of (1), (2) and (4)' *by itself* nothing whatever follows about the English *sentence* 'the author of *Waverley* was Scotch'; although perhaps from the conjunction of this statement with the statement 'The sentence "the author of *Waverley* was Scotch" is a correct translation of the sentence *"l'auteur de* WAVERLEY *était une personne écossaise"* ', it will follow that the *sentence* 'the author of *Waverley* was Scotch' means neither more nor less than the conjunction of (1), (2) and (4).[1] And I think, therefore, that a person who were to assert 'The pro-

---

[1] In his copy of the Schilpp volume on Russell, in which this article originally appeared, Moore crossed out the lines beginning with the word 'although', and wrote in the margin 'No', adding that there is also required another conjunct, viz. 'The sentence "*l'auteur de* WAVERLEY *était une personne écossaise*" means the proposition "*l'auteur de* WAVERLEY *était une personne écossaise*" '.—C. L.

position "the author of *Waverley* was Scotch" means neither more nor less than the conjunction of (1), (2) and (4)' would perhaps, if he were using the expression 'the proposition "the author of *Waverley* was Scotch" ' correctly, *not* be committing himself to the assertion that the *sentence* 'the author of *Waverley* was Scotch' means neither more nor less than the conjunction of (1), (2) and (4). But I feel no doubt that when Russell said 'the conjunction of (1), (2) and (4) may be taken as defining what is meant by the *proposition* "the author of *Waverley* was Scotch" ', he was (whether correctly or incorrectly) using the expression 'the proposition "the author of *Waverley* was Scotch" ' in such a way that he was committing himself to the assertion that the *sentence* 'the author of *Waverley* was Scotch' means neither more nor less than the conjunction of (1), (2) and (4); and I shall assume that this was so.

But now, assuming that in all these four respects I am right in my interpretation of Russell's words, it follows that among the various assertions which he was making in the statement quoted, two are as follows:

(*a*) The proposition that the author of *Waverley* was Scotch both entails and is entailed by the proposition that (1), (2) and (4) are all of them true; or, in other words, these two propositions are logically equivalent.

(*b*) The *sentence* 'the author of *Waverley* was Scotch' means neither more nor less than the conjunction of (1), (2) and (4); and anyone who says that it does, will, by so saying, be giving a definition of its meaning.

Are these two assertions, (*a*) and (*b*), true?

It is, I think, worth noticing that neither can be true, unless the expression 'is the author of' can properly be used in such a sense that a person who is not male can be correctly said to have been 'the author' of a given work; unless, for instance, Jane Austen can be properly said to have been 'the author' of *Pride and Prejudice*. For it is quite certain that the conjunction of (1), (2) and (4) implies nothing whatever as to the sex of the person who wrote *Waverley*. Consequently, if nobody who is not male can properly be called an author, (*b*) cannot possibly be true, since there would then be no sense in which the sentence 'the author of *Waverley* was Scotch' can properly be used, in which *all* that it means is the conjunction of (1), (2) and (4): that sentence

would in any proper use mean *also* that some *male* person composed *Waverley*. And for the same reason the assertion of (*a*)
that the conjunction of (1), (2) and (4) entails that the author of
Waverley was Scotch would be false. For if the only proper use of
'author' were such that nobody could have been the author of
Waverley except a male, then (1), (2) and (4) would be quite
consistent with the proposition that *nobody* was the author of
Waverley, and therefore also with the proposition that it is not
the case that the author of *Waverley* was Scotch, which would
necessarily be true if nobody was the author of *Waverley*. It is,
therefore, only if Jane Austen can be properly said to have been
the author of her novels, that (*a*) and (*b*) can be true. But I think
it does not follow from this that (*a*) and (*b*) are false, since I think
it is questionable whether 'author' cannot be properly thus used,
without any implication of male sex.

But I think that (*a*) and (*b*) are both of them unquestionably
false for another reason. The reason is that there is no proper
use of the word 'author', which is such that the statement that
a given person did not write a given literary composition is
inconsistent with the statement that he was its author. Scott might
perfectly well have been the author of *Waverley* without having
written it. And my reason for saying this is not the obvious fact
that he certainly might have been the author, even if he had
dictated every word of it to an amanuensis and not written a word
himself. I think this would have been a bad reason, because, so
far as I can see, we have so extended the meaning of the word
'write' that a person who has only dictated an original composition
of his own may quite properly be said to have 'written' it; perhaps
he may be so said even if he only dictated it to a dictaphone.
But it is surely unquestionable that a poet who, before the invention of writing, composed a poem or a story which was never
written down, can *not* be properly said to have 'written' it and
yet may undoubtedly have been its *author*. There is no legitimate
sense of the word 'author' in which he will not have been its
author, provided that he invented or composed it without the
collaboration of any other person, and provided also that no other
person or set of persons invented or composed the same poem
or story independently. I think this shows clearly that there is no
legitimate sense of the word 'author' such that the proposition
that a given person was the author of a given work is inconsistent

F

with the proposition that the work in question was never written at all. It might have been true at the same time both that Scott was the author of *Waverley* and also that *Waverley* was never written at all: there is no *contradiction* in supposing this to have been the case. He certainly would have been its author if he had composed or invented the whole of it by himself, without collaboration, and if also no other person or set of collaborators had invented it independently; and it is certainly *logically possible* that this should have happened, without *Waverley's* having ever been written. I think, therefore, that it is a sheer mistake on Russell's part to say that 'the author of *Waverley* was Scotch' implies 'at least one person wrote *Waverley*'. It does *not* imply this: the proposition 'the author of *Waverley* was Scotch, but it is not the case that at least one person wrote *Waverley*' is not self-contradictory. (*a*), therefore, I think, is certainly false. And (*b*) is false too, for the same reason. There is no legitimate use of the sentence 'the author of *Waverley* was Scotch' which is such that this sentence means neither more nor less than the conjunction of (1), (2) and (4). In its only legitimate use it means *less* than this conjunction. It does mean (if 'author' can be properly used without implying male sex) neither more nor less than that at least one person invented *Waverley*, at most one person invented *Waverley*, and there never was a person who invented *Waverley* but was not Scotch. But to assert this conjunction is to assert *less* than to assert the conjunction (1), (2) and (4); since to assert that at least one person *wrote Waverley* is to assert that at least one person *invented* it, *and* something *more* as well.

Russell's statements (*a*) and (*b*) are, then, certainly false; but the fact that they are so makes nothing against his 'theory of descriptions', since they form no part of that theory. And, though they are false, they will, I think, serve just as well as if they were true to explain the nature of two statements, which do, as far as I can see, form part of that theory and which, I think, are true.

I. The first of these two statements is a statement with regard to a class of propositions of which (*a*) is a member. And what it asserts with regard to this class is *only* that enormous numbers of propositions which are members of it are true. It does not assert, with regard to any particular member of the class, that that particular member is true, nor does it assert that *all* of its members are true.

What is the class of propositions with regard to which it makes this assertion?

I think it can be defined by first defining a certain class of English *sentences*, which I will call 'class C'. Once we have defined this class of *sentences*, C, we can define the class of *propositions*, with regard to which I. makes the assertion that enormous numbers of them are true, by reference to this class of sentences.

What then is the class of sentences which I am proposing to call 'Class C'?

It is a class of which the following sentence, which I will call 'S', is a member, viz. 'The proposition "the author of *Waverley* was Scotch" both entails and is entailed by the proposition "at least one person wrote *Waverley*, at most one person wrote *Waverley*, and there never was a person who wrote *Waverley* but was not Scotch" ', and the rest of the members of class C are those sentences, and those only, which resemble S in certain respects which have now to be defined.

(This sentence, S, it will be seen, is merely another way of expressing that very same proposition of Russell's which I called (*a*), but which I then expressed by a different sentence.)

(1) In order to be a sentence which resembles S in the respects in question, a sentence must first of all resemble it in the following respects: it must begin with the words 'the proposition'; these words must be immediately followed by an English sentence enclosed between inverted commas; this sentence must be immediately followed by the words 'both entails and is entailed by the proposition'; these words again must be immediately followed by another English sentence enclosed between inverted commas—a sentence which is not identical with the earlier one enclosed between inverted commas; and this second sentence in inverted commas must complete the whole sentence. It is obviously very easy to tell whether a sentence does fulfil these conditions or not; and it is obvious that S does fulfil them.

(2) But, in order that a sentence, other than S, should belong to the class C, it is by no means sufficient that it should resemble S in the respects just mentioned under (1). It must also resemble S in other respects; and these other respects concern the two sentences in inverted commas which it must contain. These two sentences must resemble the two in inverted commas which

S contains in the following respects: (α) the first of them must, like the first in S, begin with the word 'the' followed by a noun in the *singular*, though it need not be *immediately* followed by such a noun—there may be an adjective in between: e.g. 'the male inhabitant of London' or 'the first President of the United States' will be just as good beginnings as 'the author of *Waverley*'; (β) the second of them must, like the second in S, consist of three separate sentences, the last two of which are joined by the word 'and'; and of these three sentences (again as in S) the first must begin with the words 'at least one', the second with the words 'at most one', and the third with the words 'there never was' or with 'there is not' or with 'there will not be', while also there must be one identical phrase which occurs in all three of them, just as 'wrote *Waverley*' occurs in all three of those which occur in the second in S. And finally (γ) the second of the two sentences in inverted commas must end with the same word or phrase as the first, just as, in S, they both end with the word 'Scotch', though here, perhaps, it should be added that this will be only true if 'stinks' is counted as the same word as 'stink', and 'limps' as 'limp', etc. etc.

Here again, I think, there is no difficulty whatever in seeing whether a sentence, which does satisfy the conditions mentioned in (1), also satisfies these further conditions or not. S obviously does satisfy them; and they will also obviously be satisfied by each of the four sentences, satisfying the conditions of (1), in which the first and second sentences within inverted commas are the following pairs: 'the chop in that cupboard stinks' and 'at least one among all the things which exist at present is a chop in that cupboard, at most one among all the things which exist at present is a chop in that cupboard, and there is not any among all the things which exist at present which is a chop in that cupboard and which does not stink'; 'the male inhabitant of London limps' and 'at least one person is a male inhabitant of London, at most one person is a male inhabitant of London, and there is not any person who is a male inhabitant of London and who does not limp'; 'the first President of the United States was called "Jefferson"' and 'at least one person was President of the United States before anyone else was, at most one person was President of the United States before anyone else was, and there never was a person who was President of the United States

before anyone else was and who was not called "Jefferson" ';
'the next book I shall read will be a French one' and 'at least one
book will be read by me before I read any other, at most one book
will be read by me before I read any other, and there will not be
any book which will be read by me before any other and which
will not be a French one'.

There is, therefore, no difficulty in understanding what class of
sentences I am proposing to call 'class C'; and a class of *propositions*,
which I will call 'Class Γ', can be defined by reference to C as
follows: A proposition will be a member of class Γ if and only if
some sentence belonging to class C will, if the word 'entails'
is used in the way I have explained, and if the rest of the sentence
is used in accordance with correct English usage, express that
proposition.

Now of the propositions which belong to class Γ enormous
numbers are false. Russell, as we have seen, happened to hit
upon a false one, namely (*a*), which he declared to be true. But,
though enormous numbers are false, I think it is also the case
that enormous numbers are true; and I think there is no doubt that
one proposition or statement which forms a part of Russell's
'theory of descriptions' is this true statement that

> *Enormous numbers of propositions which are members of Class* Γ
> *are true.*

That this is true seems to me to be quite certain. Consider,
for example, the C-sentence 'The proposition "the King of
France is wise" both entails and is entailed by the proposition
"at least one person is a King of France, at most one person is
a King of France, and there is nobody who is a King of France and
is not wise" '—a sentence in which the first sentence enclosed in
inverted commas is the very sentence which Ramsey used in the
statement about the theory of descriptions which I quoted above.[1]
To anyone who understands English a very little reflection is,
I think, sufficient to make it obvious that if, in this sentence,
the word 'entails' is being used in the way I explained, and if
the rest of the sentence is being used in accordance with correct
English usage, then the proposition which it expresses, which is,
in that case, a Γ-proposition, is true. And, once this is seen,
it is surely also obvious that it would be possible to go on

[1] See p. 152 above.

indefinitely producing other examples of Γ-propositions which are true. That this is so, is, I think, obvious as soon as it is pointed out. But had anyone before Russell pointed it out? I do not know. But it seems to me that, in philosophy, it is often a great achievement to notice something which is perfectly obvious as soon as it is noticed, but which had not been noticed before. And I am inclined to think that it was a great achievement on Russell's part to notice the obvious fact that enormous numbers of Γ-propositions are true.

II. A second statement which seems to me to form part of the theory of descriptions is, like this last, a statement with regard to a certain class of propositions, to the effect that enormous numbers of propositions of that class are true. The class in question is a class of which the false proposition of Russell's which I have called (*b*) is a member, and I propose to call this class 'class Δ'. The statement which the theory of descriptions makes about Δ-propositions is only that enormous numbers of them are true: it does not state that all are, nor does it state with regard to any particular Δ-proposition that that one is true.

This class of propositions, Δ, can be defined by reference to a particular class of English *sentences* which I propose to call 'D'. A proposition will belong to Δ, if and only if it can be properly expressed in English by a D-sentence; but, of course, the same proposition may also be capable of being properly expressed by sentences which are not D-sentences. Sentences which are exact translations of a D-sentence in a foreign language will also properly express Δ-propositions, and there may be English sentences which are not D-sentences, but which may be properly used to express the same proposition which a D-sentence expresses.

What class of sentences it is that I am proposing to call 'D-sentences' can, I think, be most easily explained by reference to the class of C-sentences. A sentence will be a D-sentence, if and only if there is some C-sentence from which it differs and which it resembles in the following respects. Take any C-sentence you like: you will obtain the D-sentence which corresponds to it as follows. Substitute for the words 'the proposition' with which the C-sentence begins the words 'the sentence'; write down next, within inverted commas, the very same sentence which comes next in the C-sentence within inverted commas; then substitute for the words 'both entails and is entailed by the proposition', which come next in the C-sentence, the words 'means neither more nor less than that'; then write after those words, but *without putting it in inverted commas*, the very same sentence which is the second sentence in inverted commas in the C-sentence; and finally add at the end the words 'and anyone who says that it does will be giving a definition of its meaning'. Thus, if we take the C-sentence which I have called 'S', the corresponding D-sentence will be 'The sentence "The author of *Waverley* was Scotch" means neither more nor less than that at least one person wrote *Waverley*, at most one person wrote *Waverley*, and there never was any person who wrote *Waverley* but was not Scotch; and anyone who says that it does will, by so saying, be giving a definition of its meaning'. It will be seen that this particular D-sentence is merely another correct way of expressing the very same false proposition of Russell's which I called '(*b*)' above, but which I then expressed by a different sentence; and that therefore this proposition (*b*) *is* a member of the class of propositions which I am calling 'Δ', since it *can* be properly expressed by a D-sentence.

Now it is certain that enormous numbers of Δ-propositions are false; but what this statement II of the theory of descriptions asserts is only that enormous numbers are true. And this, I believe, is a true statement.

So far as I can see, the only way of seeing that it is true, is to see, in the case of some one particular Δ-proposition, that *it* is true, and then to see that an indefinite number of others could be found which are certainly also true, if this one is.

Now the following Δ-proposition seems to me to be true: namely 'The sentence "The King of France is wise" means neither more nor less than that at least one person is a King of France, at most one person is a King of France, and there is not anybody who is a King of France and is not wise; and anyone who says that it does, will, by so saying, be giving a definition of its meaning'.

Is this proposition true?

We have to consider two points; namely (α) whether the sentence 'The King of France is wise', a sentence which I will now call 'T', does mean neither more nor less than what this Δ-proposition says it does, and (β) whether anybody who says it does, will, by so

doing, be 'giving a definition' of the meaning of T. I will consider
(β) first.

(β) I have already pointed out[1] that a person who makes
an assertion of the form 'the sentence *s* means neither more nor
less than the proposition *p*' can by no means always be properly
said to be giving a definition of the meaning of *s* by so doing.
And the question whether he is giving a definition or not seems
to me to depend on whether or not the *sentence* which he is using
to express *p* is or is not related in one or other of certain ways
to the *sentence s*. Now, in stating above the Δ-proposition about
T, which I said I believed to be true, the sentence which I used
to state the proposition about which that proposition asserted that
T meant neither more nor less than it, was the sentence 'at least
one person is a King of France, at most one person is a King of
France, and there is not anybody who is a King of France and is
not wise',—a sentence which I will now call 'U'. Now U has to
T the following relation: it contains words or phrases which
mention separately a greater number of distinct conceptions or
'objects' than are mentioned separately in T. Thus we can say
that T and U both mention separately the conceptions of kingship
and wisdom and the 'object' France; but U mentions separately
in addition the conception expressed by 'at least one . . .', that
expressed by 'at most one . . .', that expressed by 'there is . . .',
and the conception of negation; and even if we can say that T
mentions separately some conception or conceptions, besides
kingship and wisdom, it certainly does not mention separately as
many more as U does. That the sentence which expresses the
definiens in a definition does thus, as a rule, *mention separately*
a greater number of conceptions than are mentioned by the
sentence which is or expresses the *definitum*, is, I think, the reason
why the authors of *Principia* were able to say[2] that some of their
definitions 'contain an analysis of a common idea'. But I do not
think that the mere fact that, in making a statement of the form
'*s* means neither more nor less than *p*', the sentence used to express
p mentions separately a larger total number of conceptions or
objects than *s* does, is by itself a sufficient reason for saying that the
person who makes such a statement is giving a definition of *s*.
Consider the two following statements. 'The sentence "the sun is
larger than the moon" means neither more nor less than that

[1] See p. 157 above.   [2] *P.M.*, I[2], p. 12.

anyone who were to believe that the sun is larger than the **moon** would not be in error in so believing'. 'The sentence "the sun is larger than the moon" means neither more nor less than that it is false that it is false that the sun is larger than the moon.' In both these cases the second sentence used certainly mentions separately a greater total number of conceptions and objects than the sentence in inverted commas; and yet I do not think that a person who were to assert either of those things, could be properly said to be giving a definition, either correct or incorrect, of the meaning of the sentence in inverted commas. But both these cases obviously differ from the case of T and U, in the respect that the second sentence used *contains as a part* the very same sentence with regard to the meaning of which an assertion is being made; whereas U does not contain T as a part of itself. And I think that this is a sufficient reason for saying that a person who were to make either of these two assertions would not, by making them, be giving a definition at all. It may, perhaps, be suggested that he might be giving a definition, but that, if he were, it would be a circular one. But I think it is not incorrect to say that a circular definition is not a definition at all. One may, of course, commit a *circulus in definiendo*—that is to say, one may commit a circle in *trying* to define; but I think it is not incorrect to say that, if one does, then one has not succeeded in defining at all, either correctly or incorrectly. However that may be, it is, so far as I can see, a sufficient condition for saying that, in making an assertion of the form '*s* means neither more nor less than *p*', one has *given a definition* (correct or incorrect) of *s*, that the sentence used to express *p* should (1) mention separately a greater total number of conceptions and objects than *s* does and (2) should also not contain as a part of itself either *s* or any other sentence which has the same meaning as *s*. If this is so it follows that a person who uses U to say what T means, will, by so doing, be giving a *definition* (though, perhaps not a correct one) of the meaning of T. But though this, which I have stated, seems to me a *sufficient* condition for saying that a person who makes an assertion of the form '*s* means neither more nor less than *p*' is, by so doing, giving a definition, correct or incorrect, of the meaning of *s*, I do not think that it is a *necessary* condition. For it seems to me that a person who were to say 'The sentence "It is true that the sun is larger than the moon" means neither more nor less than that the sun is larger than the

F*

moon' might be correctly said to be giving a definition of the meaning of the sentence 'It is true that . . . etc.'; and here condition (1) is certainly not fulfilled. But, so far as I can see, it is only where, as in this case, the sentence used to express the *definiens*, or some sentence which has the same meaning, forms a part of the sentence which is the *definitum*, that one can be properly said to be giving a definition in spite of the fact that (1) is not fulfilled.

I think, therefore, there is no doubt that any person who says 'The sentence T means neither more nor less than that at least one person is a King of France, at most one person is a King of France, and there is not anybody who is a King of France but is not wise' can be properly said to be giving a definition of the meaning of the sentence T. But will he be giving a *correct* one? He will be doing so only if this assertion which he makes is true; i.e. if the sentence T *does* mean neither more nor less than what he says it means. But does it?

This is the question which I called (α) above (page 167).

(α) Let us call the assertion, with regard to which we are here asking whether it is true, 'P'. If we want to consider whether or not P is true, it is, I think, very important to distinguish P clearly from another proposition with which it is liable to be confused. In stating P, I have, as I pointed out in discussing (β), made use of the sentence U, that is to say, the compound sentence 'at least one person is a King of France, at most one person is a King of France, and there is not anybody who is a King of France and is not wise'. But I was not, in stating P, using U merely as a name for itself, whereas I was using T merely as a name for itself. That I was not so using U is clearly shown by the fact that it was preceded by the words 'means neither more nor less than *that*'. Wherever a sentence is preceded by a 'that', used in this particular way, not as a demonstrative but as a conjunction, it is, I think, a sign that the sentence in question is not being used *merely* as a name for itself, but in the way in which sentences are most often used—a way which can, I think, be not incorrectly described by saying that they are used to express propositions. It is true that I could have expressed P, not incorrectly, in another way; namely, instead of writing U preceded by 'that' and *not* putting inverted commas round it, I might have written, instead of 'that', the words 'the proposition', and followed these words by U *in inverted commas*. The fact that U, in inverted commas, was preceded by the words 'the proposition' would again have been a sign that U was not being used *merely* as a name for itself. What I could not have done, if I wanted to express P correctly, is to write instead of the word 'that' the words 'the sentence', and to follow these words by U in inverted commas. For the fact that U, in inverted commas, was preceded by the words 'the sentence' or 'the words' would have been a sign that U was being used *merely* as a name for itself; and hence this would not have been a correct way of expressing P. Yet I am afraid it is not uncommon among philosophers to make, in similar cases, a confusion, which, if they made it in this case, would consist in supposing that P is identical with the proposition 'T means neither more nor less than U'. In the sentence which I have just used to express this latter proposition, the words 'means neither more nor less than' are, of course, used (quite correctly) as short for 'means neither more nor less than *is meant by*'. But in the sentence which I used to express P, the same words 'means neither more nor less than' are not short for 'means neither more nor less than *is meant by*', because the words which follow (i.e. the sentence U) are not being used merely as a name for themselves: 'means' is being used in an equally correct and a more primitive way. It would be strange, would it not, if 'means' were *always* used to mean 'means what is meant by'. Yet I am afraid it is not uncommon to suppose that when we give a definition by saying, e.g. 'the expression "is a triangle" *means* "is a plane rectilineal figure, having three sides" ', the statement we are making is identical with the statement 'the expression "is a triangle" *means what is meant by* the expression "is a plane rectilineal figure, having three sides" '. Mr W. E. Johnson, in his *Logic*, seems to suppose this; but he also makes a true remark, which shows quite clearly that he was wrong in so supposing. His true remark is that, when we give a definition, a hearer or reader will not understand our definition unless he understands the expression which we use to express our *definiens*. I think this is obviously true; but if it is true, it follows that we are never giving a definition, if we merely say of one expression that it means what is meant by another. For, if this is all we are saying, a hearer or reader can understand us perfectly without needing to understand *either* of the expressions in question. I might, for instance, point to two sentences in a book, written in a language I do not understand at all, and say (pointing at the first) this sentence means what is meant by that (pointing at the second). And I might, by accident, or because somebody who knew the language had told me so, be right! The first sentence might really mean what is meant by the second, and the second might really be so related to the first that it could be *used* to give a definition of the first. Suppose this were so: then a person who saw the sentences and understood the English words 'means what is meant by' would be able to understand my assertion perfectly, without understanding either of the two sentences any better than I did! Since, therefore, it is *not* necessary, in order to understand such a statement, that either sentence be understood, it follows that such a statement is *never* a definition. Now P *is* a definition: that is to say, anyone who asserts P can be properly said to be giving a definition of the meaning of T. It follows that P is *not* the same proposition as 'T means neither more nor less than is meant by U'; since this latter proposition could be understood perfectly by a person who did not understand either T or U. The important point is that, when I *use* U in stating P, I am not using U merely as a name for itself; whereas if I say 'T means neither more nor less than U', I *may* be using U merely as a name for itself, and, if so, am not asserting P.

Let us call the proposition 'T means neither more nor less than is meant by U' 'Q'. Even if it be admitted that, as I have argued, Q is *not* the same proposition as P, though liable to be confused with it, there is, I think, still a great temptation to suppose that P follows from Q, and Q from P, i.e. that P and Q mutually entail one another. But this, I think, is a mistake. From P, *by itself*, Q does not follow: it is only from P, *together with another premiss*, that Q follows; and why there is a temptation to think that P, *by itself*, entails Q, is because this other premiss is so obviously true that people assume it without noticing that they are doing so. And similarly from Q, *by itself*, P does not follow: it is only from Q, *together with another premiss*, that P follows; but here again the other premiss is so obviously true, that we are tempted to think that Q, by itself, entails P. What is the other premiss which must be conjoined with P in order that we may be entitled to infer Q? I have already pointed out, in another instance, that, in order to express P, it is not necessary to use the sentence U *at all*; whereas, in order to express Q, it is absolutely necessary to use U *as a name for itself*, but in no other way. We can express P by using, instead of U, any sentence which is a correct translation of U in a foreign language; e.g. if my French is correct (which perhaps it isn't), we can express P by '*Les mots* "The King of France is wise" *veulent dire qu'une personne au moins est un roi de France, qu'une personne au plus est un roi de France, et qu'il n'y a aucune personne qui soit un roi de France et qui ne soit pas sage, et ces mots ne veulent dire ni plus ni moins que cela*'. And it seems obvious that some other premiss, in addition to this proposition P, is required in order to entitle us to infer that the English sentence T means neither more nor less than what is meant by the English sentence U. *What* other premiss is required? So far as I can see, the additional premiss required is merely that the sentence U (which is, we remember, the sentence 'at least one person is a King of France, at most one person is a King of France, and there is not anybody who is a King of France and is not wise') means neither more nor less than that at least one person is a King of France, at most one person is a King of France, and there is not anybody who is a King of France and is not wise. Let us call this premiss 'R'. From P and R *together* Q obviously does follow; since P asserts of T that it means neither more nor less than the very same proposition with regard to which R asserts that U means neither more nor less than that very proposition: and, if T and U both mean neither more nor less than this particular proposition, it follows that T means neither more nor less than is meant by U—a consequence which is the proposition Q. But now R is a proposition which seems to be quite obviously true; and there is a great temptation to think that it is a mere tautology; and if it were, then any proposition which followed from the conjunction of it with P, would follow from P alone; and since Q does follow from the conjunction of P and R, and R seems to be a tautology, people are naturally led to suppose that Q follows from P alone. But I think it is a mistake to suppose that R is a tautology: it *is* obviously true, but that is not because it is a tautology, but because we who understand English, know so well what the sentence U does mean. The question at issue can be more conveniently discussed in the case of a shorter sentence than U. If R is a tautology, then the proposition which I will call 'W', namely 'The sentence "At least one person is a King of France" means that at least one person is a King of France',

is also a tautology; and if R is *not* a tautology, then W is also *not*
a tautology. Is W a tautology? There is certainly a great temptation to think so; but the following reasons lead me to think that it
is a mistake to think so. (1) W is the same proposition as '*Les mots*
"At least one person is a King of France" *veulent dire qu'une
personne au moins est un roi de France*'. But I think it is quite
obvious that this proposition is not a tautology; and since it is the
same proposition as W, it would follow that W is not either. It is
true, of course, that the English sentence which I originally used to
express W differs from this French sentence in a notable way.
In the English sentence the expression 'At least one person is a
King of France', an expression which I will call 'Z', occurs twice
over, once, in inverted commas, *merely* as a name for itself—
once, without inverted commas, *not* merely as a name for itself
but to express a proposition; whereas, in the French sentence, Z
occurs once only, *merely* as a name for itself. And owing to this
difference, if one wanted to assert W, it would always be quite
useless to use the English sentence in order to do so, since nobody
could possibly understand the English sentence unless he already
knew what Z did mean. But from this fact that it will be useless
to assert W by means of the English sentence, it does not follow
that W is a tautology. I suggest that one reason why we are
tempted to think that the proposition 'The sentence "At least one
person is a King of France" means that at least one person is a
King of France' is a tautology is for the irrelevant reason that
we all see at once that we could not possibly convey any information to anybody by saying these words. (2) I think it is also
obvious, on reflection, that the sentence Z *might*, quite easily,
not have meant that at least one person is a King of France.
To say that it does mean this is to say something about the
correct English use of the words which occur in Z and of the
syntax of Z. But it might easily not have been the case that those
words and that syntax ever were used in that way: that they are
so used is merely an empirical fact, which might not have been the
case. There is, therefore, no *contradiction* in the supposition that
Z does *not* mean that at least one person is a King of France:
it *might* have been the case that it did not. Of course, if Z had not
meant this, the words 'Z does not mean that at least one person is a
King of France' would not have been a correct way of expressing
the fact that Z had not this meaning. Anybody who, in that case,

had used these words to say this, would, of course, have been
saying something that was true, but would have been expressing
this true proposition incorrectly; since he would have been
using Z, in the second place in which he used it, to mean something which it does now in fact mean, but which, in the case
supposed, it would not have meant. But though no person, in the
case supposed, could have expressed correctly the proposition
which would in that case have been true by saying 'Z does not
mean that at least one person is a King of France', we can express
correctly this proposition, which would then have been true,
by saying it would then have been true that Z did not mean that at
least one person was King of France. In short, it seems that, in the
case supposed, the very same proposition would have been true,
which, as things *are* (considering, that is, how these words and their
syntax are actually used), would be correctly expressed by 'Z
does not mean that at least one person is King of France', but
which is, as things are, false. But if this proposition would have
been true, provided that a supposition which is certainly not self-
contradictory had been the case, it cannot be self-contradictory.
It seems, then, that the proposition 'Z does *not* mean that at least
one person is a King of France' is *not* self-contradictory, and
therefore that the proposition 'Z means that at least one person
is a King of France' is not a tautology. But it must be owned
that though the first of these two propositions, though false,
seems not to be self-contradictory, yet there is a special absurdity
in expressing it by the words I have just used. The absurdity I
mean arises from the fact that when we use expressions to make an
assertion, we *imply* by the mere fact of using them, that we are
using them in accordance with established usage. Hence if we
were to assert 'Z does *not* mean that at least one person is a King of
France' we should imply that Z *can* be properly used to mean what,
on the second occasion on which we are using it, we are using it
to mean. And this which we *imply* is, of course, the contradictory
of what we are asserting. We *imply* it, by using this language to
make our assertion, though we do not assert it, nor is it implied
(i.e. entailed) by what we do assert. To make our assertion by
the use of this language is consequently absurd for the same reason
for which it is absurd to say such a thing as 'I believe he has
gone out, but he has not'. This, though absurd, is not self-
contradictory; for it may quite well be true. But it is absurd,

because, by saying 'he has not gone out' we *imply* that we do *not* believe that he has gone out, though we neither assert this, nor does it follow from anything we do assert. That we *imply* it means only, I think, something which results from the fact that people, in general, do not make a positive assertion, unless they do not believe that the opposite is true: people, in general, would not assert positively 'he has not gone out', if they believed that he had gone out. And it results from this general truth, that a hearer who hears me say 'he has not gone out', will, in general, assume that I don't believe that he has gone out, although I have neither asserted that I don't, nor does it follow, from what I have asserted, that I don't. Since people will, in general, assume this, I may be said to *imply* it by saying 'he has not gone out', since the effect of my saying so will, in general, be to make people believe it, and since I know quite well that my saying it will have this effect. Similarly, if I use the words 'at least one person is a King of France' not merely as a name for themselves, but to express a proposition, people will, in general, assume that I am using the words in their ordinary sense, and hence I may be said to *imply* that I am, though I am not asserting that I am, nor does it follow that I am from anything which I am asserting. Now suppose I *am* using them in their ordinary sense when I say 'Z does not mean that at least one person is a King of France'. What I am asserting is then the false proposition that Z, if used in its ordinary sense, does *not* mean the very thing which, using it in its ordinary sense, I am using it to mean. But, by the mere fact of using it, I imply, though I do not assert, that, if used in its ordinary sense, it does mean what I am using it to mean. I am, therefore, *implying* a proposition which is the contradictory of what I am asserting, but which is not being asserted by me and is not entailed by what I assert. Owing to this peculiar absurdity which attaches to the asserting that Z does not mean that at least one person is a King of France, *by the use of those words*, we are tempted to think that that proposition is itself self-contradictory, when, in fact, it is not, but is only obviously false; and this, I think, is another reason why we are tempted to think that its negation, the proposition W, the proposition 'The sentence "At least one person is a King of France" means that at least one person is a King of France' is a mere tautology, when in fact it is not, but only obviously true.

But if W is not a tautology, then neither is R a tautology; and I am right in saying that Q does not follow from P by itself, but only from the conjunction of P and R. R is an extra premiss required to be added to P in order to entitle us to infer Q. And the same extra premiss, R, has also to be added to Q, in order to entitle us to infer P. P and Q, therefore, are not only different propositions; it is also true that neither entails the other. And it was important to bring this out, because the particular objection to P, which I want to consider, would be invalid if P were identical with Q.

The objection is this:

P is the proposition that the sentence T, i.e. the sentence 'The King of France is wise', means neither more nor less than that at least one person is a King of France, at most one person is a King of France and there is nobody who is a King of France and is not wise. But (1) it is quite certainly true that T means neither more nor less than that the King of France is wise. (2) If, therefore, P is true, we shall be expressing a true proposition both by the use of the sentence I have used to express P, and also by saying 'T means neither more nor less than that the King of France is wise'. But (3) if we are using 'means neither more nor less than' correctly, then it cannot be said with truth both that T means neither more nor less than that at least one person is a King of France, at most one person is a King of France, and there is not anybody who is a King of France and is not wise, and also that T means neither more nor less than that the King of France is wise, unless it can also be said with truth that the proposition 'at least one person is a King of France, at most one person is a King of France, and there is nobody who is a King of France and is not wise' is *the same proposition* as 'The King of France is wise'. But (4) if this last can be said with truth, it will follow that it can also be said with truth that P is *the same proposition* as the proposition (which I will call 'X') that T means neither more nor less than that the King of France is wise. But (5) P is certainly *not* the same proposition as X; and hence (6) it cannot be said with truth that 'The King of France is wise' is *the same proposition* as 'at least one person is a King of France, at most one person is a King of France, and there is nobody who is a King of France and is not wise', and hence (7) since (1) is true, P cannot be true.

And a similar argument can be used against the proposition Q, i.e. the proposition that T means neither more nor less than is meant by U. This argument would be as follows. (1) T means neither more nor less than that the King of France is wise, and (this is the proposition which I previously called 'R') U means neither more nor less than that at least one person is a King of France, at most one person is a King of France, and there is nobody who is a King of France and is not wise. But (2), from the conjunction of (1) with Q, it follows that the proposition 'The King of France is wise' *is the same proposition as* the proposition 'at least one person is a King of France, at most one person is a King of France, and there is nobody who is a King of France and is not wise'. But (3) if this is so, it follows that the proposition 'The proposition "The King of France is wise" both entails and is entailed by the proposition "at least one person is a King of France, at most one person is a King of France, and there is nobody who is a King of France and is not wise" ', *is the same proposition as* 'The proposition "The King of France is wise" both entails and is entailed by the proposition "The King of France is wise" '. But (4) the conclusion of (3) is certainly false. Therefore (5) the conclusion of (2) is also false; and (6), since (1) is true, Q must be false.

Now, as regards these two arguments, it seems to me unquestionable that, in the case of the first, (1), (2) and (3) are all true, and, in the case of the second, both (1) and (2) are true; and also unquestionable that, in the case of the first, (5) is true, and, in the case of the second, (4). If, therefore, we are to avoid the conclusion that P and Q are both false, we must, in the case of the first argument, dispute (4), and, in the case of the second, dispute (3). And I think it is pretty certain that both the assertion which the first argument makes in (4), and the assertion which the second makes in (3) are false. But I don't think it's at all easy to see why they are false. Both are certainly very plausible.

To begin with, it must, I think, be admitted to those who may be inclined to say that 'The King of France is wise' is *not* the same proposition as 'at least one person is a King of France, at most one person, etc.,' that our use of 'is the same proposition as' is such, that, even if it is correct to say that these two are the same proposition, it is *also* not incorrect to say that they are *not*. That this is so is implicit in the very language I have just used; for how could it be correct to say that *these two* are the same proposition, unless it were correct to say that 'The King of France is wise' is *one* proposition and 'at least one person is a King of France, etc.' is *another*? It is, indeed, not by any means always the case that where we can say with truth 'the proposition "——" is the same proposition as the proposition "——" ', a different *sentence* being enclosed within the first inverted commas from that which is enclosed within the second, we can also substitute, with truth, the words 'is *not* the same proposition as' for the words '*is* the same proposition'. For instance, if one of the two sentences is an exact translation in a foreign language of the other, the proposition obtained by this substitution would, I think, be definitely false. '*Le roi de France est chauve*' is the same proposition as 'The King of France is bald', and it would be definitely incorrect to say that it is a different proposition, or *not* the same. A person who were to use the first sentence, in its ordinary sense at a given time, to make an assertion, would definitely be making the *same* assertion or statement or proposition as a person who at the same time used the second sentence, in its ordinary sense, to make an assertion; and it would be definitely *wrong* to say that the one was making a *different* proposition or statement from that which the other was making, in spite of the fact that they were using different sentences. But the same would not hold, if one of them said 'The King of France is bald' and the other said '*Une personne au moins est un roi de France, une personne au plus est un roi de France, et il n'y a aucune personne qui soit un roi de France et qui ne soit pas chauve*'. Here even if we could (as I think we can) correctly say that they were making the same assertion or statement or proposition by the use of different sentences, on the ground that the information they were giving, if their statements were true, was exactly the same; yet it would also not be incorrect to say that the one was making a *different* proposition from that which the other was making. Anyone who offered the French sentence as a translation of the English one, would be definitely giving an *incorrect* translation of it; and I think that wherever we can say that one sentence is *not* a correct translation of another, it is also not incorrect to say that it expresses a *different* proposition from that which the other expresses, though it may also be quite correct to say that it expresses the same proposition. Again, whenever, using two different sentences in the two different places enclosed by inverted commas, we can make, with truth, a proposition of the form 'The proposition "——" both entails and is entailed by the proposition "——" ', we can, I think, also make with truth the corresponding proposition of the form 'The proposition "——" is a different proposition from the proposition "——" '. If we were to say 'The proposition "The King of France is bald" both entails and is entailed by the proposition "*Le roi de France est chauve*" ', we should be definitely misusing the expression 'both entails and is entailed by'; it is definitely incorrect to say that 'The King of France is bald' is a different proposition from '*Le roi de France est chauve*', and therefore also definitely incorrect to say that we have here an instance of *two* propositions, which are logically equivalent—of *two* propositions, each of which entails the other. But if we say 'The proposition "The King of France is bald" both entails and is entailed by "*Une personne au moins est un roi de France, une personne au plus est un roi de France, et il n'y a aucune personne qui soit un roi de France et qui ne soit pas chauve*" ', we are using 'both entails and is entailed by' perfectly correctly, because it is also correct to say that we have here an instance of *two* different propositions, each of which entails *the other*. This ambiguity which attaches to the expression 'is the same proposition as', and is such that, in hosts of cases, where, writing one sentence in inverted commas after the words 'the proposition' the first time they occur and a different sentence after the same words the second time they occur, we can say, with truth 'the proposition "——" is the same proposition as the proposition "——" ', we can *also* say, with truth, 'the proposition "——" is *not* the same proposition as the proposition "——" ', also, it seems to me, attaches to two other expressions which are frequently used. In hosts of cases where it is not incorrect to say of one sentence that it 'means the same as' another, it is also not incorrect to say of the same two sentences that the one does *not* 'mean the same as' the other. And in hosts of cases where it is not incorrect to say of a given sentence that it is 'merely another way of saying' that so-and-so is the case, it is also not incorrect to say of the very same sentence that it is *not merely* another way of saying that so-and-so is the case, in spite of the fact that in both cases the sentence used to express the 'so-and-so' in question is exactly the same. And, in all three cases, I doubt if any precise rules can be laid down as to what distinguishes the cases where it is correct to say both of the two apparently contradictory things from those in which it is not correct to say both. Certainly, if we are to say of two different sentences, which we *can* say express two different propositions, that they also express the *same* proposition, a *necessary* condition for our saying so with truth, is that we should also be able to say with truth that each proposition *entails* the other; but I doubt whether this is a *sufficient* condition for saying so. In cases where, having two different *sentences* before us, we can rightly say that we have *two* propositions before us, we certainly cannot rightly say that those two propositions are the *same* proposition, unless conditions which are necessary and sufficient for the truth of the one are precisely the same as those which are necessary and sufficient for the truth of the other; and in many cases where this condition is fulfilled, we can, I think, rightly say that they are the same proposition: but I doubt whether we can in all. On the other hand, where we have two sentences, like T and U, of which we can (as I think) rightly say that they express the same proposition or have the same meaning, a *sufficient* condition for its being also correct to say that they express different propositions or have *not* the same meaning, is, I think, that we should be able to say that, for those who understand the language or languages involved, the hearing or reading of the one sentence brings before the mind of the hearer or reader ideas which the other does not bring before his mind. It can, I think, hardly be denied that to those who understand English, the hearing or reading of U will, in general, bring before the mind ideas which the hearing or reading of T will not in general bring before the mind, for the very reason which makes it right to say that you can *give a definition* of T by means of U, i.e. that U mentions separately a greater total number of conceptions and objects than T does; and this, I think, is a sufficient justification for saying that *in a sense* U does *not* 'mean the same' as T, and does *not* 'express the same proposition'. This, I think, is the element of truth contained in the argument, often used, that two given sentences do *not* 'mean the same', because, when we understand the one, 'what we are thinking' is not the same as what we are thinking when we understand the other. But what those who use this argument often overlook is that even where we can rightly say, for this reason, that two sentences do *not* 'mean the same', it may also be perfectly right to say that, in another, and perhaps more important sense, they *do* mean the same. Though, however, the fact that one sentence will, in general, bring before the mind of those who understand it ideas which a different sentence, though in one sense it has the same meaning, will not bring before the mind is, I think, *sufficient* to make it correct to say that the proposition expressed by the one is a different proposition from that expressed by the other, I doubt if this is *necessary* to make it correct to say so. Consider the two sentences 'The sun is larger than the moon' and 'The moon is smaller than the sun'. It is certainly not incorrect to say that these two sentences are different ways of expressing the same proposition, and that they have the same meaning. Yet I doubt whether it is incorrect to say that the proposition 'the sun is larger than the moon' is one proposition, and the proposition 'the moon is smaller than the sun' is *another* proposition. It is worth noticing that if we had to translate '*Le soleil est plus grand que la lune*' into English, it would be definitely incorrect to translate it by the second of these two sentences instead of by the first. And it is also, I think, not incorrect to say: 'The proposition that the sun is larger than the moon both entails and is entailed by the proposition that the moon is smaller than the sun: these *two* propositions are logically equivalent.' Whereas it would be definitely incorrect to say 'The proposition "*Le soleil est plus grand que la lune*" both entails and is entailed by the proposition "The sun is larger than the moon" ', or to say that we have here *two* propositions which are logically equivalent. And yet I do not think we can say that the sentence 'The sun is larger than the moon' brings before the mind any ideas which are not brought before it by the sentence 'The moon is smaller than the sun', nor yet that the latter brings before the mind any ideas which are not brought before it by the former.

I think, therefore, it must be admitted to those who may be inclined to say that P and Q are false, that, so far as they are saying only that it is not incorrect to say that the proposition expressed by U is *not* the same as that expressed by T, and not incorrect to say that T and U do not have the same meaning, they are right. But the arguments which I gave, as arguments which might be used to show that P and Q are false, would seem to show more than this. For, when, in the first argument, (5) asserts that P and X are certainly not the same proposition, it seems that this is unquestionably true not merely in the sense that it is not incorrect to say that they are not the same, but in the sense that it is definitely *incorrect* to say that they *are* the same—that there is no sense whatever in which they can be correctly said to be the same. And similarly, in the second argument when (4) asserts that 'the proposition "The King of France is wise" both entails and is entailed by "At least one person is a King of France, at most, etc." ' is *not* the same proposition as ' "The King of France is wise" both entails and is entailed by "The King of France is wise" ', it seems that this is unquestionably true not merely in the sense that it is not incorrect to say so, but in the sense that it would be definitely incorrect to say that they *are* the same. And in both cases it is not at all easy to see how it can be definitely incorrect to say that the propositions in question are the same, if it is not incorrect to say that 'The King of France is wise' is the same proposition as 'At least one person is a King of France, at most one, etc.' The question is: If it is definitely *incorrect* to say that P and X are the same, and that the propositions which (4), in the second argument, declares to be *not* the same, are the same, can it possibly be correct to say that 'The King of France is wise' is the same proposition as 'At least one person is a King of France, etc.'? I am convinced that it can and is, but I must confess that I am unable to see *how* it can be, and *why* it is. I must, therefore, confess that I am unable to point out where the fallacy lies in these arguments to show that what P and Q say is definitely incorrect.

But that there is some fallacy in the arguments is, I think, evident from the fact that, if there were not, then, so far as I can see, *no* definition would ever be correct. Consider, for instance, the following definition of 'is a widow': 'is a widow' means neither more nor less than 'was at one time wife to a man who is now dead, and is not now wife to anyone'. This is, I think, clearly a correct definition of at least one way in which the expression 'is a widow' can be properly used in English. And it is clearly correct to say: The sentence 'Queen Victoria was a widow in 1870' means neither more nor less than that, in 1870, Queen Victoria had been wife to a man who was then dead, and was not then wife to anyone. And yet this proposition which I have just written down can certainly *not* be correctly said to be the same proposition as: The sentence 'Queen Victoria was a widow in

1870' means neither more nor less than that Queen Victoria was a widow in 1870. And it can certainly not be correctly said either that the proposition 'The proposition that Queen Victoria was a widow in 1870 both entails and is entailed by the proposition that, in 1870, Queen Victoria had been wife to a man who was then dead, and was not then wife to anyone' is the same proposition as 'The proposition that Queen Victoria was a widow in 1870 both entails and is entailed by the proposition that Queen Victoria was a widow in 1870'. But the fact that neither of these two things can be correctly said is, I think, clearly not inconsistent with the proposition that the proposition 'Queen Victoria was a widow in 1870' can be correctly said to be the same proposition as 'In 1870, Queen Victoria had been wife to a man who was then dead, and was not then wife to anyone', though I cannot explain *why* they are not inconsistent with this proposition.

I think, then, that what I have described as Prop. II of Russell's theory of descriptions, namely, the statement that immence numbers of propositions, which resemble, in the respects I specified, the proposition 'The sentence "The King of France is wise" means neither more nor less than that at least one person is a King of France, at most one person is a King of France, and there is not anybody who is a King of France and is not wise; and anyone who were to assert that this is so would be giving a definition of the meaning of the sentence "The King of France is wise" ' are true, is certainly true.

And I think it must have been this statement made by the theory of descriptions, which led Ramsey to mention, as a merit of that theory, that it explains *exactly what* multiple relation between kingship, France and wisdom is asserted by 'The King of France is wise'. I think that if we are told that the sentence 'The King of France is wise' means neither more nor less than that at least one person is a King of France, at most one person is a King of France, and there is nobody who is a King of France and is not wise, this statement, if true (as I have argued that it is), can be fairly said to explain exactly what multiple relation we should be asserting to hold between kingship, France and wisdom, if we were to assert that the King of France is wise. And I think it is a great merit in Russell's theory of descriptions that it should have pointed out (for the first time, so far as I know) that, in the case of enormous numbers of sentences, similar in certain respects to

'The King of France is wise', an explanation, similar *mutatis mutandis* to this one, of what we are asserting if we use them to make an assertion, can be given.

But it should be emphasized, I think, that from this statement, which I am calling Prop. II of the theory of descriptions, it does not *follow* that 'The King of France is wise' means neither more nor less than that at least one person is a King of France, at most one person is a King of France, and there is nobody who is a King of France and is not wise. Prop. II only says that enormous numbers of Δ-propositions are true; and from this it will not follow, in the case of any particular Δ-proposition whatever, that *that* one is true. It would have been quite a different matter if Russell, or Whitehead and Russell, had somewhere, in what they say about 'descriptions', presented us with a true *universal* proposition to the effect that *all* Δ-propositions, which satisfy certain specified conditions, are true. The conditions specified might have been such that from this universal proposition it *followed* that the Δ-proposition 'The sentence "The King of France is wise" means neither more nor less than that at least one person is a King of France, at most one, etc.' is true, and similarly in the case of every other true Δ-proposition. But I cannot see that we have anywhere been presented with a true universal proposition of this kind. In order to find such a universal proposition, it would be necessary, so far as I can see, to do two things. Δ-propositions, as I have defined them, are propositions which make about some sentence beginning with the word 'the' followed (with or without an intervening adjective) by a noun in the singular, a statement, similar in respects which I specified, to the statement made about the sentence 'The King of France is wise' by the Δ-proposition which I have just mentioned. And, so far as I can see, there are many sentences beginning with 'the' followed by a noun in the singular, about which *no* true Δ-proposition can be made. Take, for instance, these: 'The heart pumps blood into the arteries', 'The right hand is apt to be better developed than the left', 'The triangle is a figure to which Euclid devoted a great deal of attention', 'The lion is the king of beasts', or (to borrow an example from Professor Stebbing) 'The whale is a mammal'. It is obvious that no part of the meaning of any one of these sentences is (respectively) 'at most one object is a heart', 'at most one object is a right hand', 'at most one object is a triangle', 'at most one object is a lion', 'at most one object is a whale'. And even if (which I doubt) there could, in each case, be constructed in some complicated way a Δ-proposition which was true of that sentence, I think it is obvious that they are examples of uses of (to use Russell's phrase) '*the* in the singular', very different from those which he had in mind in what he says about 'definite descriptions'. He has, it seems to me, given a true, and most important, account of at least one use of '*the* in the singular', and perhaps this use is far the commonest; but there are other quite common uses to which his account does not apply. And, if I am right in thinking that there are many sentences beginning with '*the* in the singular', about which *no* Δ-proposition is true, then, in order to get a true *universal* proposition to the effect that all Δ-propositions *of a certain kind* are true, we should need to find some characteristic which distinguishes those sentences beginning with '*the* in the singular' about which some Δ-proposition is true, from those about which none is true—some characteristic, that is to say, *other* than the mere fact that some Δ-proposition is true of each of the sentences in question. If we could find such a characteristic, say Φ, we should be able to make the true universal proposition: Of *all* sentences beginning with '*the* in the singular' which have the characteristic Φ, some Δ-proposition is true; and Φ might be such that from this universal proposition it could be deduced that of the sentence 'The King of France is wise' *some* Δ-proposition is true. But I doubt whether any such characteristic can be found; and even if one could, I do not think that Russell, or *Principia*, have anywhere mentioned such a characteristic. But, even if this could be done, something more would plainly be required, if we wanted to find a universal proposition from which it followed that the sentence 'The King of France is wise' means neither more nor less than that at least one person *is a King of France*, at most one person *is a King of France*, and there is not anybody who is *a King of France*, and is not wise; and from which, similarly, every other true Δ-proposition also followed. We should need, in fact, a universal rule, which would tell us, in the case of each different phrase of the form 'the so-and-so' such that *some* Δ-proposition was true of any sentence beginning with that phrase, *what* phrase must follow the words 'at least one', 'at most one', and 'there is not', in order to get a sentence which expressed a true Δ-proposition. That it is easy to make a mistake as to this is shown by the fact that Russell himself thought, falsely, as I have tried to show, that the statement 'The sentence "The author of *Waverley* was Scotch" means neither more nor less than that at least one person *wrote Waverley*, at most one person *wrote Waverley*, and there never was anybody who *wrote Waverley* and was not Scotch' was a true Δ-proposition. In order to get a sentence which does express a true Δ-proposition, in this case, we certainly need to substitute some other word for 'wrote'. It is, I think, clearly quite impossible to give any general rule whatever, which would ensure us against making mistakes of this kind. And hence I do not believe that it is possible to find any *universal* proposition to the effect that *all* Δ-propositions which are of a certain kind are true.

I think, therefore, that it is perhaps only by a stretch of language that the theory of descriptions can be said to explain exactly what relation we are asserting to hold between kingship, France and wisdom, if we assert that the King of France is wise. The theory of descriptions, I should say, consists only of *general* propositions. But general propositions may be of two kinds, which we may call *universal* propositions and *existential* propositions. I do not think that it contains, or could contain, any *universal* proposition from which it would follow, in the case of any Δ-proposition whatever which *is* true, that that proposition is true. And from the existential proposition that enormous numbers of Δ-propositions are true, it plainly will not follow, in the case of any particular one, that *that* one is true. But even if, as I think, the theory of descriptions only gives us a statement of the form 'Enormous numbers of Δ-propositions are true' and does not give us any universal proposition of the form 'All Δ-propositions, which have the characteristic Φ, are true', it is, I think, just as useful and important, as if it had given us such a universal proposition. The statement that enormous numbers are true is sufficient to suggest that, where we find a sentence beginning with '*the* in the singular', it will be wise to consider whether it is not one of which some Δ-proposition is true, and whether, therefore, the consequences which follow from its being one are not true of it. When once this question is suggested by the theory of descriptions, it is, I think, easy to see in particular cases, both that a given sentence is one of which *some* Δ-proposition is true, and *what* Δ-proposition is true of it. It is, I think, only in this sense that this theory of descriptions can be said to tell us that 'The King of France is wise' means neither more nor less than that at least one person is a King of France, at most one person is a King of France, and there is nobody who is a King of France and is not wise.

III. Is there any other statement, forming a part of the 'theory of descriptions', which is both true and important? I think there is at least one. But the subject which I am now going to discuss seems to me to be one about which it is very difficult to see clearly what is true, and about which I may easily be wrong.

Prop. II has told us that, in enormous numbers of cases where we have a sentence beginning with 'the' followed (with or without an intervening adjective) by a noun in the singular, some Δ-proposition is true of that sentence. Now suppose we have found such a sentence, of which some Δ-proposition is true, and have also found some Δ-proposition which is true of it. We then have a correct answer to the question: What is the meaning of that sentence? Thus, e.g., a correct answer to the question: What does the sentence 'The King of France is wise' mean? is 'It means that at least one person is a King of France, at most one, etc.' But having got a correct answer to the question: What is the meaning of this sentence as a whole? We may want to raise another question, namely: What is the meaning of that part of it which consists in the words 'The King of France'? This is a question which has obviously interested Russell, and about which he has said a good deal. There is no doubt, that if some Δ-proposition is true of the sentence 'The King of France is wise', then the words or phrase 'The King of France' are what he would call a 'definite description'. And the corresponding words in any sentence of which a Δ-proposition is true would also be called by him a 'definite description'. For example, in the sentence 'The first President of the United States who was called "Roosevelt" hunted big game', the words 'The first President of the United States who was called "Roosevelt" ' would be a 'definite description', provided that some Δ-proposition is true of that sentence, as I think is obviously the case. One thing which is, I think, not clear about his use of the phrase 'definite description' (or, in *Principia*, 'description') is whether or not a phrase, which, when used in the way in which it is used in a sentence of which a Δ-proposition is true, is a 'definite description', is also to be called a 'definite description' if (supposing that were possible) in another sentence it is used in a different way. Does to say that a phrase is 'a definite description' mean only that it is *sometimes* used in a particular way, so that any phrase, which is *ever* so used, will be a 'definite description', even when it is not so used? or can the very same phrase be a 'definite description' when used in one way, and *not* a 'definite description' when used in another? However that may be, Russell is certainly interested in the question what meaning such phrases have *when* used in sentences about which some Δ-proposition is true.

And his theory of descriptions is certainly supposed by him to give an answer to this question different, in important respects, from what he himself and other philosophers had formerly held to be a correct answer to it. This appears very plainly from the first of his writings in which he put forward the views which he subsequently expressed under the heading 'Descriptions'. In this early article in *Mind*, entitled 'On Denoting',[1] he uses the name 'denoting phrases' as a synonym for 'Descriptions' in the wider of the two senses in which, as I have pointed out, he subsequently used 'Descriptions', i.e. to include both what he subsequently called 'definite descriptions' and what he subsequently called 'indefinite' or 'ambiguous' descriptions; but he says (page 481) that 'phrases containing "the" are by far the most interesting and difficult of denoting phrases' and he is chiefly concerned with these. He points out difficulties which he finds in the views about such phrases put forward by Meinong and Frege, and says[2] that the theory which he himself formerly advocated in the *Principles of Mathematics* was very nearly the same as Frege's, and quite different from that which he is now advocating.

Now I think it is quite clear that this change of view arose from his having noticed that, e.g., 'The King of France is wise' entails and is entailed by 'at least one person is a King of France, at most one person is a King of France, and there is nobody who is a King of France and is not wise'; and having further thought that this fact must be relevant to the question what 'the King of France' means, or (as it is put in *Principia*) that 'in seeking to define the use' of such a symbol 'it is important to observe the import of propositions in which it occurs'.[3] Apparently when he wrote the *Principles* it had not occurred to him that the fact that

[1] *Mind*, N.S., xiv, p. 479.   [2] *Ibid*., p. 480, n. 1.   [3] *P.M.*, p. 12, p. 67.

such a proposition as 'The King of France is wise' cannot be true unless at least one man and at most one man is a King of France, must be relevant to the question what 'the King of France' means; nor, so far as I know, had it ever occurred to any other philosopher. That the noticing that it was relevant was, at least in part, the origin of the new view, first expressed in 'On Denoting', and embodied in *Principia*, is, I think, quite clear. But what *is* the new view? and how does it differ from the old?

One novelty in the new view is one which the authors of *Principia* try to express by saying that such a phrase as 'The King of France' is not supposed to have any meaning in isolation, but is only defined in certain contexts'[1] and later by saying that 'we must not attempt to define' such a phrase itself, but instead 'must define the propositions', in 'the expression' of which it occurs. They propose[2] to use the new technical term 'is an incomplete symbol' as a short way of saying that this is true of a given phrase; and accordingly declare that 'descriptions' are 'incomplete symbols'.

Now when they say that we 'must not attempt to define' such a phrase as 'The King of France', as used in the sentence 'The King of France is wise', I suppose their reason for saying so must be that they think that, if we did attempt to define it, we should necessarily fail to get a *correct* definition of it. If it were possible to get a correct definition of it, there would seem to be no reason why we shouldn't attempt to get one. I think, therefore, their meaning must be that it is *impossible* to give a correct definition of this phrase *by itself*; and when they say that we must define 'propositions' in the 'expression' of which it occurs, I think what they mean might have been equally well expressed by saying that we must define *sentences* in which it occurs.

But why does Russell hold that though we can define such a sentence as 'The King of France is wise' we can *not* define that part of this sentence which consists in the words 'The King of France'? By introducing a new technical term for those phrases, occurring as parts of sentences, which can't themselves be defined although the sentences of which they are parts can be, he implies, of course, that there are other phrases which are parts of sentences, in the case of which we can not only define the whole sentence, but *also* define the phrase which is a part of it. And this

[1] *P.M.*, p. 66.   [2] *Ibid.*, p. 67.

certainly seems to be the case. To use an illustration which I gave above: we can define the sentence 'Mrs Smith is a widow' by saying that it means 'Mrs Smith was formerly wife to somebody who is now dead, and is not now wife to anybody'. And we can also say that *any* sentence of the form '*x* is a widow' means that the person in question was formerly wife to somebody who is now dead and is not now wife to anybody. But in this case it seems also perfectly correct to take the phrase 'is a widow' by itself, and to say 'is a widow' means 'was formerly wife to somebody who is now dead, and is not now wife to anybody'. In this case, as in hosts of others, it seems that we can both define sentences in which a given phrase occurs, and *also* define the phrase by itself. This, which seems to be possible in so many cases, Russell seems to be declaring to be *impossible* in the case of phrases like 'The King of France'. *Why* does he declare it to be impossible? If we can define 'is a widow' *as well as* sentences in which it occurs, why should we be unable to define 'The King of France' *as well as* sentences in which it occurs?

I think there *is* a good reason for making this distinction between 'The King of France' as used in the sentence 'The King of France is wise', and 'is a widow' as used in 'Mrs Smith is a widow'; but this, which I am going to give, is the only good reason I can see.

Let us consider a *different* definition of the sentence 'The King of France is wise' from that which we have hitherto considered. Instead of considering the proposition 'The sentence "The King of France is wise" means neither more nor less than that at least one person is a King of France, at most one person is a King of France, and there is nobody who is a King of France and is not wise', let us consider the proposition 'The sentence "The King of France is wise" means neither more nor less than that there is somebody or other of whom the following three things are all true, viz. (1) that he is a King of France, (2) that nobody other than he is a King of France, and (3) that he is wise'. This latter proposition is just as good a definition of the sentence in question as the former; and indeed, instead of saying that it is a *different* definition, but just as good a one, we can say, if we please, equally correctly, that it is *the same definition* differently expressed. For a very little reflection is sufficient to make it evident that the proposition 'at least one person is a King of France, at most one person is a King of France, and there is nobody who is a King of France and is not wise' both entails and is entailed by 'there is somebody or other of whom it is true that he is a King of France, that nobody else is a King of France, and that he is wise': if the first is true, the second *must* be true too, and if the second is true, the first *must* be true too. And I think this is obviously a case, such as I spoke of before, in which it is equally correct to say either of the two apparently contradictory things: This is the same proposition as that; and: These *two* propositions are logically equivalent; and also equally correct to say of the two *sentences* each of the two apparently contradictory things: This sentence means the same as that, they are merely two different ways of saying the same thing; and: These two sentences have *not* quite the same meaning, they are *not* merely two different ways of saying the same thing. In support of the assertion that the two sentences have *not* the same meaning, and therefore do not express the same proposition, it may, for instance, be pointed out that the first proposition is a conjunction of three *independent* propositions, whereas the second is not: how could the *same* proposition be both?

Let us, then, consider the proposition (which is a definition): The sentence ' "The King of France is wise" means neither more nor less than that there is somebody or other of whom it is true that he is a King of France, that nobody other than he is a King of France and that he is wise'. If this be true (as it is) it follows that we can correctly say: The sentence 'The King of France is wise' means the same as the sentence 'There is somebody or other of whom it is true that he is a King of France, that nobody else is so, and that he is wise'. But now it appears that we can also correctly say that in these two sentences the words 'is wise' mean the same. But since the whole sentences mean the same, and one part of each means the same as a part of the other, it seems natural to conclude that the part of the one which is left over when 'is wise' is subtracted from it *must* mean the same as the part of the other which is left over when 'is wise' is subtracted from it: i.e. that 'The King of France' means the same as 'There is somebody or other of whom it is true that he is a King of France, that nobody else is, and that he . . .' But do those two phrases mean the same? I think we must answer: No; they certainly don't. For some reason or other, we can't do in the case of these two sentences what we could do in the case of 'Mrs Smith is a widow' and 'Mrs Smith was formerly wife to somebody who is now dead and is not now wife to anyone'. There we could subtract 'Mrs Smith' from both sentences, and say correctly that what was left of the one meant the same as what was left of the other. Here we can't say correctly that what is left of the one sentence when 'is wise' is subtracted from it means the same as what is left of the other when 'is wise' is subtracted from it; and this in spite of the fact that the two whole sentences certainly do mean the same!

Now, so far as I can see, if you take any sentence whatever which can be used to express the *definiens* in a correct definition of 'The King of France is wise', provided that the definition in question is not a definition of the sentence *only* because it yields a definition of 'is wise' or of 'king' or of 'France', it will always be found that the part of the sentence which is left over when 'is wise', or that part of it which has the same meaning as 'is wise', is subtracted from it, can *not* be said to have the same meaning as the phrase 'The King of France'. And this, I think, is a good reason for saying, as I have supposed Whitehead and Russell intended to say, that you can't define 'The King of France' (in this usage), though you can define sentences in which that phrase occurs. If this is what they mean by saying that 'The King of France', in this usage, is an 'incomplete symbol', then I think it must be admitted that it *is* an incomplete symbol.

In support of my contention that we cannot possibly say that the phrase 'The King of France', in this sentence means the same as the phrase 'There is somebody or other of whom it is true (1) that he is a King of France (2) that nobody other than he is so and (3) that he', I should like to call attention to the following point. There is no doubt that the expression 'The King of France' can be properly called, as Russell once called it, a 'denoting phrase', if we agree that a phrase can be properly called a 'denoting phrase', provided it is the *sort* of phrase which *could* have a denotation as well as a meaning, even if it actually has no denotation. If a person were to assert *now* that the King of France is wise by the use of the sentence 'The King of France is wise', it would be correct to say that 'The King of France', as used by him, though a 'denoting phrase', 'does not denote anything' or has no denotation because at present there is not a King of France; but, if an Englishman in 1700 had used that sentence to say that the King of France was wise, it would have been quite correct

G

to say that 'The King of France' as used by him, did 'denote' Louis XIV, or, if we had been in the presence of Louis, it would have been correct to point at Louis and say 'The phrase "The King of France" denotes that person'. It appears from Russell's article 'On Denoting' that one of the things which had puzzled him before he arrived at the theory explained in that article (that is to say, his 'theory of descriptions') was that it seemed to him that, in such a case as that of an Englishman saying in 1700 'The King of France is wise', the Englishman's proposition would certainly have been 'about' the *denotation* of the phrase 'The King of France', i.e. about Louis, and *not* about the *meaning* of the phrase; and he was unable to see how the meaning was related to the denotation, when such a proposition was made. This puzzle his 'theory of descriptions' seemed to him to solve. But the point I wish now to make is this: In the case of such an Englishman in 1700, it would certainly have been correct to say that his phrase 'The King of France' *denoted* Louis XIV; but if he had said instead 'There is somebody or other of whom it is true that he is a King of France, that nobody other than he is, and that he', would it have been correct to say that *this* phrase 'denoted' Louis? I think nobody could possibly say so: and this seems to me a good reason for saying that his phrase 'The King of France' would *not* have 'meant the same' as this other phrase. And yet his whole sentence 'The King of France is wise' would certainly have 'meant the same' as the sentence 'There is somebody or other of whom it is true that he is a King of France, that nobody else is, and that he is wise', if used at that time.

But, though in the case of sentences which resemble 'The King of France is wise' in the respect that a true Δ-proposition can be made about them, there is, I think, good reason for saying that we can't define the phrase of the form 'the so-and-so', with which they begin, though we can define the sentences in which the phrase occurs, it does not seem to me at all so clear that we cannot define such phrases when used in certain sentences in which they do not begin the sentence. Contrast, for instance, with 'The King of France is wise', the sentence 'There is a person who is the King of France', or the sentence 'That person is the King of France', as it might have been used by an Englishman pointing at Louis XIV in 1700. Here, I think, we can certainly say that 'is the King of France' does 'mean the same' as 'is a person of whom it is true both that he is a King of France and that no one other than he is'. If so, we must, I think, say that, in this usage, 'The King of France' is *not* an incomplete symbol, though, where it begins a sentence about which a true Δ-proposition can be made, it *is* an incomplete symbol. It seems to me by no means paradoxical to say that the two usages are different; and even to say that, in this usage, 'The King of France' never has denoted anyone, though in the other it has.

However that may be, there does seem to me to be good reason for saying that in the case of sentences about which some Δ-proposition is true, the phrase of the form 'the so-and-so' with which such sentences begin, never can be defined, although the sentences in which it occurs can. And the statement that this is so should, I think, be reckoned as a third important part of 'Russell's theory of descriptions'.

Perhaps there are other statements, deserving to be called a part of that theory, which are also important, or perhaps even *as* important, as these three I have distinguished. But it seems to me that these three, viz.:

I. Enormous numbers of Γ-propositions are true.
II. Enormous numbers of Δ-propositions are true.
III. In the case of every sentence about which some Δ-proposition is true, the phrase, of the form 'the so-and-so', with which it begins, cannot be defined *by itself*, although the sentences in which it occurs can be,

statements, none of which, so far as I know, had ever been made before by any philosopher, are by themselves sufficient to justify Ramsey's high praise of the theory.

IX

FOUR FORMS OF SCEPTICISM

My object in this lecture is to discuss four different philosophical views, each of which may, I think, be properly called a form of Scepticism. Each of these views consists in holding, with regard to one particular *sort* of thing, that no human being ever knows with complete certainty anything whatever of that sort; and they differ from one another only in respect of the sort of thing with regard to which each of them holds this.

I hope that nobody will be misled by my use of the word 'thing' in the above statement. I was not using it in the sense in which this pencil is one 'thing' and this piece of paper another. I was using it in the sense in which it is used, for instance, if one says: 'I know very little about American history, but there are two *things* I do know about it, namely that Washington was the first President of the United States, and that Lincoln was President at the time of the Civil War'. This use of 'thing' seems to me to be perfectly good and idiomatic English, and I intend to continue to use the word in this way; but obviously it is quite a different use of the word from that in which chairs or tables are 'things': nobody would say that '*that* Washington was the first President of the United States' is a 'thing' in the same sense in which this pencil is a thing.

At first sight it may seem as if, in this use, 'thing' is a mere synonym for 'fact', and as if, therefore, instead of speaking of four sorts of 'things', I might just as well have spoken of four sorts of *facts*. That Washington was the first President of the United States is a fact; and there is nothing strange in this use of the word 'fact'. But the use of 'thing' with which I am concerned is not only one in which it makes sense to say, e.g. 'That the sun is larger than the moon is a thing which I know for certain', but also one in which it makes sense to say 'That the sun is larger than the moon is a thing which *nobody knows for certain*'. Indeed, as we shall see, one of the four forms of scepticism with which I am concerned holds that the latter proposition is true; and though perhaps this is nonsense in the sense that it is obviously untrue, it is not nonsense in the peculiar sense in which, if we substituted the word 'fact' for the word 'thing' in this sentence, we should get a nonsensical statement. Consider the form of words 'That the sun is larger than the moon is a *fact* which nobody knows for certain'. Here the proposition 'That the sun is larger than the moon is a fact' is logically equivalent to the proposition 'The sun is larger than the moon'. But the proposition 'Nobody knows for certain that the sun is larger than the moon' is logically equivalent to the proposition 'It is possible that the sun is not larger than the moon'. Hence the combination of the two gives us 'The sun is larger than the moon, but it's possible that it's not' or 'That the sun is larger than the moon is a fact, but possibly it's not a fact'. And these are a peculiar kind of nonsense like 'I am at present sitting down, but possibly I'm not' or like 'I'm at present sitting down, but I don't believe I am'. But the person who says 'That the sun is larger than the moon is a *thing* which nobody knows for certain', though he may be talking nonsense, is certainly not talking *this sort* of nonsense. And hence it follows that this is a sentence in which 'thing' is not a mere synonym for 'fact'—a sentence in which the word 'fact' cannot be substituted for the word 'thing', without changing the meaning of the sentence.

Once it is realized that the word 'thing' in this usage is not a synonym for 'fact', it is natural to suggest that perhaps it is a synonym for 'proposition'. But this also, I think, will not do, for the following reason. 'I don't know that the sun is larger than the moon' certainly is logically equivalent to 'I don't know that the proposition that the sun is larger than the moon *is true*'; but it seems to me that it is not good English to use the expression 'I don't know the proposition that the sun is larger than the moon' to mean the same as the latter or to mean anything which is logically equivalent to the latter. This is a respect in which our use of the word 'know' differs from our use of the word 'believe'. Whenever a man believes a given proposition p, we can also rightly say that he believes that p is true; but from the fact that a boy *knows* the fifth proposition of Euclid, it by no means follows that he knows that that proposition is *true*. Hence for the expression 'That the sun is larger than the moon is a *thing* which I know' we cannot rightly substitute 'That the sun is larger than the moon is a *proposition* which I know'; since the former is logically equivalent to ' . . . is a proposition which I know *to be true*', while the latter is not. I may 'know' a given proposition in the sense of being perfectly familiar with it, and yet *not* know it to be true. We can, I think, say that the usage of 'thing' with which we are concerned is one in which the expression 'That the sun is larger than the moon is a *thing* which nobody knows for certain' is short for ' . . . is a proposition which nobody knows for certain *to be true*'; but we cannot always, in the case of this usage, simply substitute the word 'proposition' for the word 'thing', since it is not good English to use an expression of the form 'I know the proposition *p*' as short for the corresponding expression of the form 'I know that the proposition *p* is true'.

Assuming then, that my use of the word 'thing' is understood, we can say that I am so using the term 'scepticism' that anybody who *denies* that we ever know for certain 'things' of a certain sort can be said to be 'sceptical' about our *knowledge* of 'things' of that sort. And I think that this is *one* correct usage of the words 'scepticism' and 'sceptical'. But it is worth noting that, if it is so, then to say that a man is sceptical about certain sorts of things, or holds certain forms of scepticism, does not necessarily imply that he is *in doubt* about anything whatever. I think this is worth noting because people seem very commonly to assume that doubt is essential to any form of scepticism. But, if I am right in my use of the word, it is obvious that this is a mistake. For a man who *denies* that we ever know for certain things of a certain sort, obviously need not feel any doubt about that which he asserts —namely, that no human being ever does know for certain a thing of the sort in question; and in fact many who have made this sort of denial seem to have felt no doubt at all that they were right: they have been as dogmatic about it as any dogmatist. And also, curiously enough, a man who denies that we ever know for certain things of a certain sort, need not necessarily feel any doubt whatever about *particular* things of the sort in question. A man who, like Bertrand Russell, believes with the utmost confidence that he never knows for certain such a thing as that he is sitting down, may nevertheless feel perfectly sure, without a shadow of doubt, on thousands of occasions, that he is sitting down. And yet his view that we never do know for certain things of that sort can, I think, be obviously quite rightly called a form of scepticism—scepticism about our knowledge of things of that sort.

In the case of all the four forms of scepticism with which I shall be concerned, it is, I think, the case that those who have held them have constantly felt no doubt at all about particular things of the very sort with regard to which they have held that nobody knows for certain things of that sort. Even if, on a particular occasion, such a man remembers his philosophical view that such things are never known for certain, and accordingly says quite sincerely e.g. 'I don't know for certain that I am at present sitting down', it by no means follows that he doubts in the least degree that he is sitting down. It is true that if he really believes that he doesn't know for certain that he is, he can also be truly said to believe that *it is doubtful* whether he is. But from the fact that he sincerely believes that it is doubtful whether he is, it certainly does not follow that he *doubts* whether he is. I think that the con.mon opinion that doubt is essential to scepticism arises from the mistaken opinion that if a man sincerely believes that a thing is doubtful he must doubt it. In the case of sincere philosophical opinions this seems to me to be certainly not the case. Accordingly I think that all that is *necessary* for a man to be properly called a sceptic with regard to our knowledge of certain kinds of things is that he should sincerely hold the view that things of that kind are always doubtful; and that this is a thing which he may do both without having any doubt at all that such things always are doubtful and also without ever doubting any particular thing of the sort. There is, therefore, a sort of scepticism which is *compatible* with a complete absence of doubt on any subject whatever. But, of course, though it is compatible with a complete absence of doubt, it is also quite compatible with doubt. A man who sincerely holds that certain kinds of things are always doubtful *may* nevertheless doubt whether he is right in this opinion: he need not necessarily be dogmatic about it: and also he *may* sometimes be in actual doubt about particular things of the sort. All that I think is true is that he *need* not have any doubt of either of those kinds: from the fact that he does hold that all things of a certain kind are doubtful it does not logically follow that he has any doubts at all. At all events, whether or not I am right as to this, I wish it to be clearly understood that I am so using the term 'scepticism' that all that is necessary for a man to be a sceptic in this sense with regard to our knowledge of certain kinds of things is that he should hold the view (whether doubtfully or not) that no human being

ever knows for certain a thing of the sort in question. It is only
with scepticism in this sense that I shall be concerned.

All four of the sceptical views with which I shall be concerned
have, I believe, been held in the past, and still are held, by a good
many philosophers. But I am going to illustrate them exclusively
by reference to two books of Russell's—his *Analysis of Matter*[1]
and the book which in the English edition was called *An Outline of Philosophy*, and in the American edition *Philosophy*.
When he wrote these books, Russell held, so far as I can make
out, with regard to each of the four kinds of 'things' which I shall
describe, that no human being has ever known for certain anything of that kind, and I shall give you quotations from these
books to show why I think that this was his view. Now I can't
help thinking that I myself have often known for certain things
of all the four kinds, with regard to which Russell declares that
no human being has ever known any such thing for certain;
and when he says that no human being has ever known such
things, I think he implies that I haven't, and that therefore I
am wrong in thinking that I have. And the question I want to
discuss is simply this: Was he right in thinking that I haven't,
or am I right in thinking that I have? Of course, if I am right in
thinking that *I* have, I think it is quite certain that other people,
including Russell himself, often have too—that all of you, for
instance, have very, very often known for certain things of each
of these sorts with regard to which he asserts that no human
being has ever known for certain anything whatever of that sort.
But I don't want to discuss whether other people have, nor yet
the very interesting question *why* it's certain that, if I have, other
people have too. The question I want to raise is merely whether
I am right in thinking that *I* have, or Russell is right in thinking
that I never have.

I will now try to state what these four sorts of things are with
regard to which Russell implies that I have never known for
certain anything whatever of any of these sorts, whereas I can't
help thinking that I have often known for certain things of all four
sorts.

(1) The first sort is this. I have, according to him, never known
with complete certainty anything whatever about *myself*. I do not,

[1] Bertrand Russell: *Analysis of Matter* and *An Outline of Philosophy*;
Allen & Unwin, London, 1927.

according to him, know now with certainty even that I am 'having a white percept',[1] and I never have known any such thing. This is a view which is implied by him in two different passages in the *Outline*. The first is where (on page 171), having raised the question whether Dr Watson or Descartes is right as to 'the region of *minimum* doubtfulness', he goes on to say: 'What, from his own point of view, [Descartes] should profess to know is not "*I* think" but "there is thinking" . . . To translate this into "*I* think" is to assume a great deal that a previous exercise in scepticism ought to have taught him to call in question.' That is to say, Russell is saying: 'Your proposition "*I* am having a white visual percept" is not so certainly true as the proposition "There is a white visual percept"; it is not a proposition of *minimum* doubtfulness'. From which, of course, it will follow that 'I am having a white percept' is not a thing which I know with complete certainty. And the same is implied in a later passage (page 214) where he says that the difference between two such propositions as '*There's a triangle!*' and 'I see a triangle' is only 'as to surroundings *of which we are not certain*'. All that is *quite* certain, he says, is something common to both, namely, something which could be properly expressed by 'There is a visual triangle', where 'There is' means the same as '*Es gibt*' (page 216), not, as in the second expression, the same as '*Da ist*'. That is to say, '*I* am seeing a white percept' includes, according to him, besides something which is quite certain, something else which is not.

(2) The second class of things with regard to which he seems to imply that I have never known with certainty any such things is a class to which he refers as if it embraced all those things, and those things only, which I have at some time remembered. That is to say, he implies that, when I seem to remember, at a given time, e.g. that there was 'a white visual percept' a little while

---

[1] It should be noted that in the *Outline* Russell uses the word 'percept' in such a sense that by no means everything which would commonly be said to be 'perceived' is a 'percept'. I have, e.g., perceived each instance of the word 'the' which I have written on this paper; but no instance of the word 'the', though it is 'perceived', is a 'percept' in Russell's sense. It is a physical object, and no physical object is identical with what he means by a 'percept'. He uses the word 'percept' in the same sense in which others have used the word 'sense-datum', except that the word 'sense-datum' of course implies that sense-data are given, whereas his view seems to be that 'percepts' are not 'given', or at least that it's not certain that they are—two very different views, which he seems, in this case, not very clearly to distinguish from one another.

G*

ago, I never know with complete certainty that there was. Thus, according to him I do not even know with certainty now that a sound like 'ago' existed a little while ago; still less, of course (because that involves the first point also), that *I* heard such a sound; and still less (because that involves a third point also) that I have been uttering words for some time past.

This view seems to me to be implied by him in the following passages.

Take first a passage in the *Analysis of Matter* (page 26). He there says: 'The inference from a recollection (which occurs now) to what is recollected (which occurred at a former time) appears to me to be essentially similar to the inferences in physics. The grounds for the trustworthiness of memory seem to be of the same kind as those for the trustworthiness of perception.'

Now he has repeatedly insisted that inferences in physics cannot give complete certainty; and I think, therefore, that when he wrote this he must have meant to accept the implication that I cannot be completely certain now even of such a thing as that there was a white visual percept a little while ago.

But a much stronger and clearer statement of this view is to be found in the *Outline*. The passage in which he gives this strong statement occurs in the place before mentioned (page 171), where he is considering whether Descartes or Dr Watson is right as to the 'region of *minimum* doubtfulness'. He here (page 174) uses these words: 'In dreams we often remember things that never happened; at best therefore we *can be sure* of our present momentary experience, *not of anything that happened even half a minute ago.*[1] And before we can so fix our momentary experience as to make it the basis of a philosophy, it will be past, *and therefore uncertain.* When Descartes said "I think", he may have had certainty; but by the time he said "therefore I am", he was relying on memory, and *may have been deceived.*'

(3) The third kind of thing about which he implies that I can never know anything of that kind with certainty, is the sort of thing which I might express on a particular occasion by pointing at a particular person and saying 'That person is seeing something', 'That person is hearing something': or 'That person saw something just now' or 'That person heard something just now'; or, more definitely, 'That person is seeing now, or saw just now,

[1] My italics.

a white visual percept'; or 'That person is hearing, or heard just now, the sound "that" '.

There can, I think, be no doubt whatever that Russell holds the view that I never do know for certain anything of this sort. I may refer first to a passage in the *Analysis*, in the chapter on what he calls 'The Causal Theory of Perception', where he is expressly dealing with the question: 'What grounds have we for inferring that our percepts and what we recollect do not constitute the entire universe?' (page 200). He here says: 'Someone says "There's Jones", and you look round and see Jones. It would seem odd to suppose that the words you heard were not caused by a perception analogous to what you had when you looked round. Or your friend says, "Listen", and after he has said it you hear distant thunder. Such experiences lead irresistibly to the conclusion that the percepts *you call other people*[1] are associated with percepts which you do not have, but which are like those you would have if you were in their place.' And it is obvious, I think, that the imaginary instances to which he refers in the first three sentences, are instances in which you might be either believing or knowing things of just the sort to which I have referred. In the first case, if, at the time when you saw Jones, you were seeing also the person who had just said 'There's Jones', you would either be believing or knowing something which might be naturally expressed by pointing at the person who said it and saying 'That person saw just now a visual percept resembling this one'—where this one is the one you are now having in seeing Jones. And in the second case, if at the time when you heard the distant thunder you are also seeing your friend who has just said 'Listen'; you would similarly be *either* believing or knowing what would be expressed by pointing at your friend and saying 'That person heard just now a rumbling sound like this'. And if, in these cases, Russell would say, as we shall see he would, that you would not, under *any* circumstances, be knowing *for certain* that that person did see a visual percept like this or that this one did hear a rumbling sound like this, we may, I think, safely conclude that he would say that nothing of *any* of the kinds of which I have given instances is ever known for certain by any of us.

But in the case of Russell's last sentence, there is an important ambiguity to which I wish to call attention. He says that

[1] My italics.

such experiences 'lead irresistibly' to a certain 'conclusion'; the conclusion, namely, 'that the percepts you call other people are associated with percepts which you do not have, but which are like what you would have if you were in their place'. And it is quite impossible to infer from this language whether what he means is that each such experience leads irresistibly to a conclusion different in each case and a conclusion which belongs to our class of things, namely the first to the conclusion 'That person saw just now a visual percept like this', the second to the conclusion 'That person heard just now a rumbling sound like the this', and so on. Or whether what he means is that a number of such experiences *taken together* lead irresistibly to the *general conclusion*: *Sometimes* other people have percepts which I don't have. Of course, neither of these things is what he actually says. In what he says he is implying, what seems to me certainly false, that it is *percepts of your own* which you call 'other people', i.e. that if I say now, pointing at Professor Stace, 'That person heard just now the sound "Stace" ', it is a *percept* of my own which I am calling 'that person'—that it is of a visual percept of mine that I am saying that *it had* an auditory percept of the kind 'Stace'. Surely this is absurd; and it is perhaps because Russell himself felt it to be absurd that he uses the queer expression 'other people are *associated with* percepts which you don't have', where what he seems to mean is merely 'other people *have* percepts which you don't have'. There is no absurdity in saying that a visual percept is *associated with* an auditory percept, nor in saying that another person *has* an auditory percept; but there is an absurdity in saying that a visual percept *has* an auditory percept; and these facts perhaps make it clear that it is certainly false that we ever 'call' a percept another person.

But this mistake which Russell makes, and his queer use of 'is associated with' to mean 'has', do not affect my present point. My present point is to call attention to the difference between the *general* conclusion 'Other people sometimes have percepts which I don't have but which are similar to percepts which I have had', and *particular* conclusions of the form 'This person had just now a percept which I did not have, but which was similar to that one which I did have'. I want to call attention to this difference, partly because the question whether we ever know for certain the *general* conclusion is, I think, easily confused with the question whether we ever know for certain any *particular* conclusion of the sort indicated; and I want to make it quite clear that in my view I often know for certain not merely the general conclusion, but particular conclusions of the sort 'This person had just now a percept of this sort'. And I call attention to it also partly because I gather from what immediately follows in Russell, that his view is that the *general* conclusion is *more* certain than *any* particular conclusion of the form in question ever is; from which it would, of course, follow that in his view I never do know with complete certainty any particular thing of the kind we are now concerned with, since the degree of certainty with which I know such a thing is always, according to him, less than some degree of certainty with which I know the general conclusion.

But that Russell does hold that I never do know with complete certainty any particular thing of this sort is, I think, directly drawn from many things he says. He says, for instance, immediately after (page 205): 'We *may* be mistaken in any given instance'. And here, I think, clearly the force of 'may' is, what it often is, i.e. he is saying: In *no* particular instance do I *know for certain* that I am not mistaken. Moreover, he has just said that 'the argument is not demonstrative' in any of these cases; and it is clear that what he means by 'not demonstrative', is what he has expressed on page 200 by saying that 'it has not the type of cogency that we should demand in pure mathematics'; and he then says that what he means by saying that an argument has not this type of cogency is that its conclusion is *only* probable.

But here are three passages from the *Outline*, which seem to make it clear that this is his view.

The first is on pages 8–10, where he says:

'I ask a policeman the way, and he says: "Fourth to the right, third to the left". That is to say, I hear these sounds, and perhaps I see what I interpret as his lips moving. I assume that he has a mind more or less like my own, and has uttered these sounds with the same intention as I should have had if I had uttered them, namely to convey information. In ordinary life, all this is not, in any proper sense, an inference; it is a belief which arises in us on the appropriate occasion. But, if we are challenged, we have to substitute inference for spontaneous belief, and the more the inference is examined the more shaky it looks.' He concludes on page 10 with the words 'The inference to the policeman's mind certainly *may* be wrong'.

In these concluding words I think he certainly means by 'may' the same as before; i.e. he is saying that in no such case does anyone ever know for certain that the policeman was conscious.

The second passage in the *Outline* to which I wish to call attention is on page 157, where he says:

'For the present, I shall take it for granted that we may accept testimony, with due precautions. In other words, I shall assume that what we hear, when, as we believe, others are speaking to us, does in fact have "meaning" to the speaker and not only to us; with a corresponding assumption as regards writing. This assumption will be examined at a later stage. For the present, I will merely emphasise that it *is* an assumption, and that it may possibly be false, since people seem to speak to us in dreams, and yet, on waking, we become persuaded that we invented the dream. It is impossible to prove by a demonstrative argument, that we are not dreaming; the best we can hope is a proof that this is improbable.'

In this passage, it seems to me, Russell clearly means to say *both* that when in any particular case I either believe or think I know 'That person meant this', I *may* be wrong, i.e. that I never know for certain 'That person did mean this', *and also* that I never know for certain even the general proposition 'Sometimes other people have meant something'. And when he says I cannot *prove* this proposition to be more than probable, he means, I think, as usual, that, *since* I cannot prove it to be more than probable, it follows that I do not *know for certain* that it is true; since it is a kind of thing which, according to him, cannot be *known for certain* unless it can be proved by a demonstrative argument.

Finally I will quote a passage from the chapter on 'The Validity of Inference', to which I think he must have been referring when he said on page 157 'This assumption will be examined at a later stage', since I cannot find any other place in which he does seem to examine the assumption in question.

He here says (page 278):

'The belief in external objects is a learned reaction acquired in the first months of life, and it is the duty of the philosopher to treat it as an inference whose validity must be tested. A very little consideration shows that, logically, the inference cannot be demonstrative, but must be at best probable. It is not *logically impossible* that my life may be one long dream, in which I merely imagine all the objects that I believe to be external to me. If we are to reject this view, we must do so on the basis of an inductive or analogical argument, which cannot give *complete certainty*. We perceive other people behaving in a manner analogous to that in which we behave, and we assume that they have had similar stimuli. We may hear a whole crowd say "Oh" at the moment when we see a rocket burst, and it is natural to suppose that the crowd saw it too.' And he concludes with the words 'It remains possible . . . that there is no crowd watching the rocket; my percepts *may* be all that is happening in such cases'; where, I think, he clearly means that I never do know for certain in such a case 'There were other percepts, not mine, like those of mine', far less, therefore, such a thing as '*That* person had just now a percept like this of mine'.

I think, therefore, it is pretty clear that Russell did hold, when he wrote both books, not only that I never know for certain any things of the sort I have stated, but also that I never know for certain even the general proposition that some people have had percepts which I have not had, but like mine, or even that there have been percepts other than mine.

(4) The fourth class of things of which I think I have often known for certain particular specimens, whereas Russell seems to have thought that no human being had ever known for certain anything whatever of the kind, is as follows. It consists of such things as that this is a pencil; that this is a piece of paper, that this pencil is much longer than it's thick; that this piece of paper is longer than it's broad, and that its thickness is very much less than either its length or its breadth; that this pencil is now nearer to this piece of paper than it is to my left hand; and that now, again, it is moving towards this piece of paper, etc. etc. All these things that I have mentioned I think I knew with certainty at the time when I mentioned them; and though Russell does not talk very much *expressly* about things of this sort, there can, I think, be no doubt he did hold that no human being has ever known for certain anything whatever of the sort.

I will give references only from the *Outline*, where he comes nearest to expressly mentioning things of the sort in question. We have already seen that he raises the question whether Descartes or Dr Watson is right as to 'the region of *minimum* doubtfulness'; and it is precisely in things of this sort (though Russell does not *expressly* say so) that Dr Watson, according to him, finds the region of minimum doubtfulness. Russell gives as an example of the kind of thing which Dr Watson takes to be particularly certain, what he calls 'the movements of rats in mazes', and says that a lover of paradox might sum up Watson's philosophy by saying that, whereas Descartes said 'I think, therefore I am', Dr Watson says 'There are rats in mazes, therefore I don't think' (page 176). And here is a passage (page 140) in which he expressly deals, quite seriously, with Watson's view about rats in mazes. 'Even', he says, 'when we assume the truth of physics, what we know most indubitably through perception is not the movements of matter, but certain events in ourselves which are connected, in a manner not quite invariable, with the movements of matter. To be specific, when Dr Watson watches rats in mazes, what he knows, apart from difficult inferences, are certain events in himself. The behaviour of the rats can only be inferred by the help of physics, and is by no means to be accepted as something accurately knowable by direct observation.' What interests us here is that the kind of thing which Watson (according to Russell) takes himself to know with certainty when he watches rats in mazes is obviously (though Russell does not expressly say so) just the kind of thing I have illustrated: it is, e.g., 'This rat is now running down that passage' (which includes, of course, 'This is a rat' and 'That is a passage'), etc. etc. And we see Russell here says that such things are *never* what Watson is knowing most *indubitably*; *never* therefore things he is quite certain of, because there are other things of which he is more certain. And he says also that these things are things which can only be inferred *by difficult inferences*; the inferences meant being obviously of the kind we have seen he has already so often referred to, and which he says at best yield probability and not certainty. I think this leaves no doubt at all that he does hold that *nothing* of the kind I have mentioned is ever known by me *with certainty*.

But I will give one other example. On page 156, he tells us: 'When my boy was three years old, I showed him Jupiter and told him that Jupiter was larger than the earth. He insisted that I must be speaking of some other Jupiter, because, as he patiently explained, the one he was seeing was obviously quite small. After some efforts, I had to give it up and leave him unconvinced.' Now here what Russell said to his son must have been just one of the things with which I am now concerned: he must have pointed at the planet and said 'That is Jupiter', just as I now point at this pencil and say 'This is a pencil'. And while he is telling this story Russell speaks, you see, as if he himself entertained no doubt whatever that we sometimes do know for certain things of this sort as well as of all the other three *sorts* which we have found he really thinks no human being ever does know for certain. He speaks as if there were no doubt whatever that he *did* point out Jupiter to his son; that is to say as if at the moment when he said 'That is Jupiter', he knew for certain 'That is Jupiter'. He speaks, again, as if, when telling the story, he knew for certain that an incident of the kind he describes really did occur in the past, i.e. knew for certain something which he then remembered. He speaks, again, as if he knew for certain things about himself— that *he* did in the past see Jupiter, say the words 'That is Jupiter', etc. etc. And finally, as if, at the time of the incident in question, he knew for certain 'This boy is seeing Jupiter', 'This boy is having a very small percept', etc. etc. Yet we have seen that, as regards the two latter points at all events, he certainly holds that he *cannot* have known for certain any such thing. If, therefore, in telling the story he had been concerned to relate only what he thought he really knew, he would have had to have said: *It is highly probable* that, when my boy was three years old, I showed him Jupiter and told him that it was larger than the earth; but *perhaps* I didn't. It is highly probable that he insisted that I must be speaking of some other Jupiter; but *perhaps* he didn't. It is highly probable that after some efforts I had to give it up; but *perhaps* I never made such efforts. And we have now to see that he holds similarly that, if he ever did say in the past to his boy 'That is Jupiter', he did not know for certain that it was Jupiter. For he goes on to say, in the next sentence: 'In the case of the heavenly bodies, adults have got used to the idea that what is really there can only be *inferred* from what they see; but where rats in mazes are concerned, they still tend to think that they are seeing what is happening in the physical world. The difference, however, is only one of degree.' He holds, that is to say, that if he ever did say 'That is Jupiter', what he thereby expressed was only something which he had *inferred*, and *inferred* by the same kind of process by which Dr Watson infers 'That is a rat, and that is a passage in a maze, and that rat is running down that passage'—a kind of information which we have seen he clearly holds can only give *probability*, not certainty. He holds, therefore, that he did not know for certain 'That is Jupiter', when (if ever) he said 'That is Jupiter'. And the same appears, I think, very clearly from what he says two pages later, viz.:

'A lamp at the top of a tall building might produce the same visual stimulus as Jupiter, or at any rate one practically indistinguishable from that produced by Jupiter. A blow on the nose might make us "see stars". Theoretically, it should be possible to apply a stimulus to the optic nerve, which should give us a visual sensation. Thus when we think we see Jupiter, we may be mistaken. We are less likely to be mistaken if we say that the surface of the eye is being stimulated in a certain way, and still less likely to be mistaken if we say that the optic nerve is being stimulated in a certain way. We do not eliminate the risk of error completely unless we confine ourselves to saying that an event of a certain sort is happening in the brain: this statement may still be true if we see Jupiter in a dream' (page 138). Here, I think, he clearly means: *Always*, when we think we see Jupiter, we *may* be mistaken; and by this again: In no case do we know for certain that we are not mistaken; from whence it will follow: In no case does any human being know *for certain* 'That is Jupiter'. We have seen, then, that Russell implies that I have never at any time known for certain any things of any of the following four classes: viz. (1) anything whatever about *myself*, i.e. anything whatever which I could properly express by the use of the words 'I' or 'me'; (2) anything whatever which I remember; (3) any such thing as 'That person has or had a visual percept or an auditory percept of this kind'; nor even the truth of the *general* proposition: 'Some people have had percepts which I have not had but which were like what I have had'; and (4) any such thing as 'This is a pencil', 'This is a sheet of paper', 'This pencil is moving towards this sheet of paper', etc. etc.

Now I cannot help thinking that I have often known *with complete certainty* things of all these four sorts. And I want to **raise** the question: Is Russell right with regard to this, or am I?

Obviously it is a logical possibility that he should be right with regard to some of these four classes of things, and I with regard to others. And it seems to me that, in respect of the arguments which he brings forward for his position, there is an important difference between those which he brings forward for saying that he is right as to the first two classes, and those which he brings forward for saying that he is right as to the last two. I propose, therefore, first to consider the first two classes separately.

To begin with the first. Russell says that I do not know with complete certainty now even that I am having a white percept; *only* that there *is* a white percept. And the only argument I can discover which he brings forward in favour of this position is the one already mentioned: 'the meaning of the word "I" evidently depends on memory and expectation' (page 215). If this premiss is to yield the desired result that I do not know for certain now that I am having a white percept, what it must mean is that in asserting that I have a white percept I am asserting something both with regard to the past and with regard to the future; and the argument must be: Since I don't know with certainty anything with regard to the past or with regard to the future it follows that a *part* of what I am asserting in asserting that I have a white percept is something that I don't know with certainty. Russell is therefore assuming two distinct things both with regard to the past and with regard to the future. With regard to the past he is assuming: (1) In asserting 'I have a white percept now' you are asserting something or other with regard to the past, and (2) You don't know for certain *that* (whatever it is) which you are asserting with regard to the past. And even if we grant, what I must confess seems to me by no means so evident as Russell thinks it is, that I *am* asserting something with regard to the past; I should maintain that there is no reason whatever why what I am asserting with regard to the past shouldn't be something which I do know with certainty. Russell's reasons for saying that it is not, must be those which he has for saying that I don't know for certain anything which I remember; so that so far as the past is concerned, the validity of his argument for saying that I don't know with certainty anything about myself entirely depends on the validity of his argument for saying that I don't know with certainty anything which I remember—to which I shall presently come. The only independent argument here offered is, therefore, that with regard to the future: and here again he is making two assumptions. He is assuming (1) that part of what I assert in asserting 'I am now having a white visual percept' is a proposition with regard to the future and (2) that *that* (whatever it is) which I am asserting with regard to the future is something which I do not know with certainty to be true. Now here, if it were true that in asserting 'I am now having a white visual percept', I were asserting anything whatever with regard to the future, I should be inclined to agree with him that that part of what I assert must be something that I do not know for certain: since it does seem to me very certain that I know little, if anything, with certainty with regard to the future. But Russell's first assumption that in asserting that I am seeing a white percept I *am* asserting anything whatever with regard to the future, seems to me a purely preposterous assumption, for which there is nothing whatever to be said. I now assert 'I am now having a white visual percept'. The moment at which I asserted that is already past, but it seems to me quite evident that the whole of what I then asserted is something which might quite well have been true, *whatever* happened subsequently to it, and even if nothing happened subsequently at all: even if that had been the last moment of the Universe. I cannot conceive any good reason for asserting the contrary.

The only argument, independent of the question whether I ever know with certainty what I remember, which Russell brings forward in favour of the view that I never know with certainty anything about myself, seems to me, therefore, to be extremely weak. But there is another argument, which he might have used, and which he hints at in the *Analysis of Mind*, though so far as I know he has not expressly mentioned it in either of these two books; and I want just to mention it, because it raises a question, about which there really seems to me some doubt, and which is of great importance in philosophy. You all know, probably, that there is a certain type of philosophers, who are fond of insisting that myself includes my body as well as my mind; that I am a sort of union of the two—a 'psycho-physical organism'. And if we were to take this view strictly, it would follow that *part* of what I am asserting whenever I assert anything about myself, is something about my body. It would follow, therefore, again that I cannot know for certain anything about myself, with-

out knowing for certain something about my body; and hence
that I cannot know for certain anything about myself, unless
I can know for certain some things of my fourth class. For of
course the propositions 'This is a body', 'This body has eyes',
etc. etc., are just as much propositions of my fourth class, as
the proposition 'That is a human body'. If this were so, then
Russell's arguments to prove that I cannot know with certainty
anything of my fourth class would, if they proved this, also prove
that I cannot know with certainty anything of this first one—
anything about myself. This, of course, does not seem to me to
prove that I don't know with certainty anything about myself,
since as I have said I think I do know with certainty things of
my fourth class. But it seems to me important to point out that
the two questions are possibly connected in this way: that, *if*
the dogma that I am a psycho-physical organism were true, then
I could not know for certain anything about myself, without
knowing for certain things of my fourth class, and that hence any
arguments which appear to show that I can't know for certain
things of this class would be relevant to the question whether
I can know for certain anything about myself. For my part I feel
extremely doubtful of the proposition that when I assert 'I am
now seeing a white visual percept', I am asserting anything at all
about my body. Those who take this view seem to me to have
overlooked one consequence of it, which constitutes a very strong
argument against it. So far as I can see, if this view were true,
then it would follow that the proposition 'This body is *my* body'
was a tautology: and it seems to me that it is not a tautology.
But nevertheless I don't feel perfectly confident that their view
may not possibly be true.

However, so far as the arguments actually brought forward
by Russell in the *Outline* are concerned, it seems to me he has
no good reason whatever for the view that I do not know with
certainty anything whatever about myself, *unless* he has good
reasons for his second proposition that I do not know with
certainty anything whatever that I remember.

Let us then now turn to consider this.

When I first described this second form of Scepticism (page 201),
I said that the class of things which it denies that I have ever
known for certain is one to which Russell refers as if it embraced
all those things, and those things only, which I have at some

time remembered; and I have since myself adopted his way of expressing this second sceptical view: I have spoken of it as if it really were the view that I have never known for certain anything whatever that I remembered. But I think that, in fact, this is a very incorrect way of expressing the view which Russell really holds and which constitutes this second form of Scepticism. For if, in the sentence 'We never know for certain anything that we remember', the word 'remember' were being used in accordance with ordinary English usage, the proposition expressed by this sentence would, I think, be a self-contradictory one. We ordinarily so use the word 'remember' that *part* of what is asserted by expressions of the form 'I remember that *p*' is 'I know for certain that *p*'; so that anybody who were to say, e.g., 'I remembered that I had promised to dine with you on Tuesday, but I didn't know for certain that I had' would be asserting the self-contradictory proposition 'I knew for certain that I had promised, but I didn't know for certain that I had'. Suppose you were to ask a friend who had failed to keep an engagement 'Didn't you remember that you had promised to come?', and he were to answer, 'Oh yes, I remembered all right that I had promised to come, but I didn't know for certain that I had promised', what would you think of such an answer? I think you would be entitled to say: 'What on earth do you mean? What an absurd thing to say! If you did remember that you had promised, of course you knew for certain that you had; and if you didn't know for certain that you had, you can't possibly have *remembered* that you had, though you may possibly have *thought* you remembered it'. I think, therefore, that if the word 'remember' were being correctly used, the sentence 'We never know for certain what we remember' would express a self-contradictory proposition. But I have no doubt that the view which Russell intended to express was not a self-contradictory one. It follows, therefore, if I am right as to the correct use of 'remember', that he was not expressing his view correctly.

It is also worth notice that, although towards the beginning of the *Outline* (page 16) Russell says truly that the word 'memory' has a variety of meanings, he never, so far as I can discover, even tries to tell us to which of these various meanings his sceptical view is supposed by him to apply. I think, however, that there is one well-understood sense in which the word is used, which is the one in which he is using it in stating his sceptical view. It is a use which we can perhaps call 'personal memory', and which can be defined as that meaning in which nobody can be properly said to 'remember' that so-and-so was the case, unless he (or she) himself (or herself) either witnessed or experienced that it was the case. That this is a different sense of the word from others which are in common use can be seen from the fact that I can properly be said to 'remember' that 7×9 *is* 63, which differs from the usage in question in respect of the fact that we cannot properly say that 7×9 *was* 63, or, to use an expression used by Russell, that 7×9 *is* 63 is not something which 'happened' in the past; and we can also quite properly say we 'remember' that the Battle of Hastings happened in 1066, yet, though the Battle of Hastings was a thing which 'happened', no living person can have either witnessed or experienced that it happened at that time; in other words, this is not a 'personal' memory of any living person.

But where Russell gives as a reason for his sceptical view, as he does in my second quotation, that, in a dream we often 'remember' what never happened; he is, it seems to me, merely making a mistake. For though, in relating a dream, it is perfectly correct to say that I (or he or she) 'remembered' a thing which never happened, it is, it seems to me, a mere mistake to think that we are here using 'remember' in the sense defined above. In relating a dream, it seems to me, we use 'remember' in a special sense, namely as short for I (or he or she) *dreamt* that I (or he or she) remembered, which is not identical with any sense in which we ordinarily use the word; just as, in relating a dream, it is correct to use, e.g., 'I saw John' as short for 'I dreamt that I saw John'. And there is no difficulty in understanding why, in relating a dream, we should use 'remembered' in this special sense, since it is obvious that once we have made it quite plain that it is a dream which we are relating, it is unnecessary and would be tiresome to repeat with regard to every item in the dream the full phrase 'I (or he or she) *dreamt* that so-and-so was the case'. In place of this, it is natural to say 'I (or he or she) remembered' or 'saw John', etc. etc. It follows, if I am right, that the use we make of the word 'remember' in relating a dream, is one of that 'variety of meanings' in which Russell rightly declares that we use the word 'memory'. Yet this obvious possibility seems never to have occurred to him. He says that 'dreams would

have supplied a sufficient argument' for his sceptical view (page
172). But if it is true, as I think it is, that the use of 'remember',
in relating a dream, is different from any ordinary use, it is not
true that dreams would have supplied a sufficient argument, for
any ordinary use.

But even if, as I think, the reference to dreams as a proof
of his scepticism is a mistake on Russell's part, because when
we use 'remembered', in relating a dream, we are using 'remember' in a special sense, not identical with any ordinary sense,
it is nevertheless true, that even when they are using 'remember'
in the sense defined above, many people do (as Russell does
not fail to point out) think they remember what, in fact, never
happened. What is Russell's reason, based on this fact, for
holding his sceptical view that it is always only probable, never
quite certain, that what we think we remember to have happened
did in fact happen?

He seems to come nearest to suggesting a reason in a passage
in which he suggests that we can only know with certainty that
so-and-so is true, if the 'so-and-so' in question belongs to some
class of which it is true that no member of that class ever 'leads
us into error'. This seems to be the principle to which he is
appealing when he suggests that perhaps we can each be sure of
'our present momentary experience'; though he does not seem
quite sure that we can be certain even of this, since he goes on to
say only that 'there is no reason' to suppose that our present
momentary experience ever leads us into error. But is it true
that we can be certain of our present momentary experience and
of nothing else? Russell seems to suppose that his sceptical
conclusion follows *directly* from this principle. But does it? If
the principle is true at all, that it is true seems to require some
further argument, which Russell does not supply. To me it
seems certain that sometimes we do know with certainty things
of classes which, like the class of what we think we remember,
do sometimes lead us into error.

The truth seems to be that Russell has never noticed the
fact that, sometimes at least, we use the word 'remember' in
such a sense that if a thing did not actually happen we say that
any person who thinks he remembers that it happened *only*
thinks that he remembers its happening but does not in fact
remember it. In other words we so use the word that it is *logically*

impossible that what did not in fact occur should be remembered; since to say that it did not occur, but nevertheless is remembered, is to be guilty of a contradiction. This is certainly the case if we so use the word that in saying that a person remembers that so-and-so happened, we are not only saying something about that person's state of mind at the moment, but are also saying that the so-and-so in question did in fact happen in the past. Russell, on the contrary, expressly says that it is logically possible that 'acts of remembrance' should occur which are of things which never happened (*Outline*, page 7). This is certainly a mistake if, as I think, we often use the word 'remember' in such a sense that when we say that a person remembers that so-and-so was the case, part (but, of course, *only* a part) of what we are saying is something not concerned merely with what his state was at the moment, but also that the so-and-so which he thinks he remembers to have happened did actually occur in the past. If Russell was using 'remember' to include such cases, we must say that what he here calls 'acts of remembrance' are not 'acts of remembrance' at all, but only the sort of act which we perform when we *think* we remember that so-and-so was the case, but do not in fact remember that it was the case. He seems constantly to assume that whether a person 'remembers' what he thinks he remembers depends only on what his state was at the moment, never at all on whether what he thought he remembered actually occurred. And this assumption of his is, no doubt, partly responsible for his view that 'dreams would have supplied a sufficient argument' to prove his sceptical conclusion (*Outline*, page 172), a view which we have seen to be false, because, in relating a dream, it is correct to use 'I (or he or she) remembered' in the special sense 'I (or he or she) *dreamt that* I (or he or she) remembered'. So far as I can see, the only sense in which 'remember' can correctly be used (other than the special sense) whenever, as happens so often, the words 'remembers' or 'remembered' are followed by a clause beginning with 'that', is that sense in which, in saying that a person 'remembers' or 'remembered' so-and-so to have happened, we are not merely saying something about the person's state at the moment, but are also saying that what the person (I or he or she) 'remembers' or 'remembered' did in fact happen at some time previous to that at which the memory occurred. When, on the other hand, the word 'remember' is followed by a noun, as often happens, it seems not incorrect to speak of remembering 'correctly' or 'incorrectly'; but such cases, so far as I can see, can always be analysed into cases where the word 'remember' is followed by one or more that-clauses, the memory being 'correct', if *all* the that-clauses say what is true, i.e. are remembered, and 'incorrect' if some of them say what is false, i.e. say what the person in question *only* thought he remembered, but did not in fact 'remember'.

If, therefore, we are to discuss whether Russell is right in the view which he expresses by saying that I have never known for certain anything whatever which I remembered, we must try to find out what view he is expressing in this self-contradictory way: we must try to find out in *what* unusual way he is using the word 'remember'; and I do not think that this is quite an easy thing to do. The natural way of trying to express it is to say that his view is: When we *think* that we remember so-and-so, we never do in fact know for certain the so-and-so in question, i.e. we never do in fact remember it. But obviously this is inaccurate, since the immense majority of the cases he really wants to consider are cases where we don't really *think* we remember, but simply either do remember or else do something else which is just what has got to be defined.

The best way I can find of stating what he means to say is this. He is saying that: In cases in which, *if* the question happened to occur to us whether we are remembering or not that so-and-so happened, we should feel very sure that we are remembering, we are never really knowing for certain that the thing in question did happen. I intend to speak of all such cases as cases where we *feel just as if we were remembering* a thing, using this expression in such a way that whenever (if ever) we *are* remembering the thing in question it is always true that we feel as if we were, though we sometimes feel as if we were when in fact we are not. Using this language, then, if I am right as to the proper use of 'remember', we can say Russell's view is that when we feel as if we were remembering, we *never* are in fact remembering.

Assuming that this, or something like it, is what he means, what arguments does he give for his view? In the *Analysis* he does not profess, so far as I can see, to bring forward any arguments at all in favour of the view there put forward, which, as we saw, implies this view; and in the *Outline* I can find only one argument, and that a very short one, which seems to be definitely put forward as an argument for this view. But, though short, it is, I think, very important to consider it carefully; because it is, if I'm not mistaken, of the same nature as one of the chief arguments put forward by Russell in favour of his view that I never know for certain things of the two last classes, which we are presently to consider.

The argument occurs in the passage I quoted before. And it is this: 'In dreams we often remember things that never happened. At best, *therefore*, we can be sure of our present momentary experience, not of anything that happened even half a minute ago.' That is all. What precisely is the nature of this argument, and is it a good one? Russell says to me: 'You don't now know for certain that you heard the sound "Russell" a little while ago, not even that there *was* such a sound, *because* in dreams we often remember things that never happened.' In what way could the alleged reason, if true, be a reason for the conclusion? This alleged reason is, of course, according to me, badly expressed; since if the word 'remember' were being properly used, it would be self-contradictory. If a thing didn't happen, it follows that I can't remember it. But what Russell means is quite clearly not self-contradictory. What he means is roughly: In dreams we often feel as if we were remembering things which in fact never happened. And that we do sometimes, not only in dreams, but also in waking life, feel as if we remembered things which in fact never happened, I fully grant. That this is true I don't feel at all inclined to question. What I do feel inclined to question is that this fact is in any way *incompatible* with the proposition that I do now know for certain that I heard a sound like 'Russell' a little while ago. Suppose I have had experiences which resembled this one in the respect that I felt as if I remembered hearing a certain sound a little while before, while yet it is not true that a little while before I did hear the sound in question. Does that prove that I don't know for certain *now* that I did hear the sound 'Russell' just now? It seems to me that the idea that it does is a mere fallacy, resting partly at least on a confusion between two different uses of the words 'possible' or 'may'.

What really does follow from the premiss is this: That it is possible for an experience of a sort, of which my present experience is an example, i.e. one which resembles my present experience in a certain respect, *not* to have been preceded within a certain period by the sound 'Russell'. Whereas the conclusion alleged to follow is: It is possible that *this* experience was not preceded within that period by the sound 'Russell'. Now in the first of these sentences the meaning of 'possible' is such that the whole sentence means merely: Some experiences of feeling as if one remembered a certain sound are not preceded by the sound in question. But in the conclusion: It is possible that this experience was not preceded by the word 'Russell'; or This experience *may* not have been preceded by the word 'Russell'; 'possible' and 'may' are being used in an entirely different sense. Here the whole expression merely means the same as: '*It is not known* for certain that this experience was preceded by that sound.' And how from 'Some experiences of this kind were not preceded' can we possibly be justified in inferring 'It is not known that this one was preceded'? The argument seems to me to be precisely on a par with the following: It is possible for a human being to be of the female sex; (but) I am a human thing; *therefore* it is possible that I am of the female sex. The two premisses here are perfectly true, and yet obviously it does not follow from them that I do not know that I am not of the female sex. I do (in my view) happen to know this, in spite of the fact that the two premisses are both true; but whether I know it or not the two premisses certainly don't prove that I don't. The conclusion *seems* to follow from the premisses because the premiss 'It is possible for a human being to be of the female sex' or 'Human beings may be of the female sex' is so easily falsely taken to be of the same form as 'Human beings are mortal', i.e. to mean 'In the case of *every* human being, it is possible that the human being in question is of the female sex', or '*Every* human being *may* be of the female sex'. If, and only if, it did mean this, then, from the combination of this with the minor premiss 'I am a human being' would the conclusion follow: It is possible that I am of the female sex; or *I may* be of the female sex. But in fact the premiss 'Human beings *may* be of the female sex' does not mean 'Every human being *may* be', but only 'Some human beings *are*'. 'May' is being used in a totally different sense, from any in which you could possibly assert of a particular human being 'This human being *may* be so-and-so'. And so soon as this is realized, it is surely quite plain that from this, together with the premiss 'I am a human being', there does not follow 'I may be of the female sex'. There may perhaps be something more than this simple fallacy in the argument that because experiences of this sort are sometimes not preceded by the sound of which they feel as if they were a memory, and this is an experience of this sort, therefore this experience *may* not have been preceded by that sound, i.e. that I do not know for certain that it *was* so preceded. But I cannot see that there is anything more in it.

The only argument, therefore, which Russell seems to bring forward to persuade me that I don't know for certain that I heard the word 'Russell' just now, does not seem to me one to which it is reasonable to attach any weight whatever. I cannot, therefore, find in him any good reason for doubting that I do know for certain things of both my first two classes: that I do know for certain things about myself; and that I also know for certain things about the past—in short that I *do* remember things.

But let us now turn to consider my third and fourth class of things. I take them together, because, so far as I can see, his arguments in both cases are the same. What arguments has he in favour of the view that I never know for certain such things as 'That person is seeing', 'That person is hearing' etc.?

Now here I think it is extremely difficult to discover what his reasons are: and in trying to distinguish them I shall very likely omit some or make mistakes. There is no passage, so far as I can discover, in which he tells us quite clearly 'These are the arguments in favour of this view', and, so far as I can see, he uses in different places arguments of very different orders, without being conscious of the difference between them. All I can do is to try to distinguish and consider separately each of the arguments which seem to me to differ in an important way.

I will begin by quoting three from the *Analysis* (page 205) which are the ones which lead up to his conclusion before quoted that 'we may be mistaken in any given instance'. The thing to be proved, I may remind you, is that when you hear your friend say 'There's Jones' and look round and see Jones, you can never be *quite* certain that your friend did just before have a visual percept like the one you're now having. And these are the supposed proofs: 'A conjurer might make a waxwork man with a gramophone inside, and arrange a series of little mishaps of which the gramophone would give the audience warning. In dreams, people give evidence of being alive which is similar in kind to that which they give when they are awake; yet the people we see in dreams are supposed to have no external existence. Descartes's malicious dream is a logical possibility.' 'For these reasons', says Russell, 'we may be mistaken in any given instance.'

Each of these three arguments seems to me to differ from the other two in important respects. I will take each separately, and try to explain what the differences are; beginning with the second, because that seems to me of exactly the same nature as the argument just considered in the case of memory.

Russell is trying to persuade me that I don't know for certain now that that person there is conscious; and his argument is: In dreams you have evidence of the same kind for the proposition 'That person is conscious'; yet in that case the proposition is *supposed* not to be true. Now it seems to me quite certain that in dreams the proposition in question often *is* not true; and that nevertheless I have then evidence for it of the same kind *in certain respects* as what I now have for saying that person is. I admit, further, that sometimes when I am awake I have evidence of the same kind *in certain respects* for 'That person is conscious' when yet the proposition is not true. I have actually, at Mme Tussaud's, mistaken a waxwork for a human being. I admit, therefore, the proposition: This percept of mine is of a kind such that percepts of that kind are in fact sometimes (to use Russell's phrase) *not* associated with a percept that belongs to someone else. But from the general proposition 'Percepts of this kind *may* fail to be associated with a percept that belongs to someone else', which means merely 'Some percepts of this kind are in fact not so associated', I entirely deny that there follows the conclusion '*This* percept *may* not be so associated', which means 'It's not known for certain that it is associated'. It seems to me a pure fallacy to argue that it does; and I have nothing more to say about *that* argument, if that is all that is meant. I don't see any reason to abandon my view that I do know for certain (to use Russell's language) that this percept which I have in looking at Professor Stace *is* associated with a percept that is not mine; I suspect that Russell may be at least partly influenced by the same fallacious argument when he tells me (as he does tell me, *Outline*, page 157) that I *may* now be dreaming. I think I know for certain that I am not dreaming now. And the mere proposition, which I admit, that percepts of the same kind *in certain respects* do sometimes occur in dreams, is, I am quite certain, no good reason for saying: this percept *may* be one which is occurring in a dream.

I pass next to the argument beginning 'A conjurer *might* make a waxwork'. The important difference between this argument and the last, is that Russell does not here say that a conjurer now *has* made a waxwork of the kind supposed and fulfilled the other supposed conditions; he is not therefore saying: Percepts like this in a certain respect *may* fail to be associated, meaning 'are sometimes actually not associated'; but merely 'Percepts like this *might* fail to be associated'. In that respect this argument is like one that he uses in the *Outline* on page 173, in dealing with our fourth class of cases, when he says: 'It would be theoretically possible to stimulate the optic nerve artificially in just the way in which light coming from the moon stimulates it; in this case, we should have the same experience as when we "see the moon" but should be deceived as to its external source.' He does not say that such a percept ever *has* been produced in this way; but only that it is theoretically possible that it *might* be. And obviously he might have used the same argument here. He might have said: 'It would be theoretically possible to stimulate the optic nerve artificially in such a way as to produce a percept like this one of yours, which would then *not* be associated with a percept belonging to another person.' But it is, I think, quite obviously just as fallacious to argue directly from 'Percepts like this *might* not be associated with a percept of another form' to '*This* percept *may* not be so associated' meaning 'It is not known that it is so associated': as from 'Percepts like this sometimes are not associated' to the same conclusion.

We pass next to the argument: 'Descartes's malicious demon is a logical possibility.' This is obviously quite different from both the two preceding. Russell does not say that any percepts *are* produced by Descartes's malicious demon; nor does he mean that it is practically or theoretically possible for Descartes's malicious demon to produce in me percepts like this, in the sense in which it is (perhaps) practically possible that a conjurer should, and theoretically possible that a physiologist should by stimulating the optic nerve. He only says it is a *logical possibility*. But what exactly does this mean? It is, I think, an argument which introduces quite new considerations, of which I have said nothing so far, and which lead us to the root of the difference between Russell and me. I take it that Russell is here asserting that it is *logically possible* that this particular percept of mine, which I think I know to be associated with a percept belonging to someone else, was in fact produced in me by a malicious demon when there was no such associated percept: and that, therefore, I cannot know for certain what I think I know. It is, of course, being assumed that, *if* it was produced by a malicious demon, then it follows that it is not associated with a percept belonging to someone else, in the way in which I think I know it is: that is how the phrase 'was produced by a malicious demon' is being used. The questions we have to consider are, then, simply these three: What is meant by saying that it is *logically possible* that this percept was produced by a malicious demon? Is it *true* that this is logically possible? And: If it is true, does it follow that I don't know for certain that it was *not* produced by a malicious demon?

Now there are three different things which might be meant by saying that this proposition is logically possible. The first is that it is not a self-contradictory proposition. This I readily grant. But from the mere fact that it is not self-contradictory, it certainly does not follow that I don't know for certain that it is false. This Russell grants. He holds that I do know for certain to be false, propositions about my percepts which are not self-contradictory. He holds, for instance, that I do know for certain that there is a white visual percept now; and yet the proposition that there isn't is certainly not self-contradictory.

He must, therefore, in his argument, be using 'logically possible' in some other sense. And one sense in which it might naturally be used is this: Not logically incompatible with anything that I know. If, however, he were using it in this sense, he would be simply begging the question. For the very thing I am claiming to know is that this percept was *not* produced by a malicious demon: and of course the proposition that it was produced by a malicious demon *is* incompatible with the proposition that it was *not*.

There remains one sense, which is, I think, the sense in which he is actually using it. Namely he is saying: The proposition 'This percept was produced by a malicious demon' is *not* logically incompatible with anything you know *immediately*. And if this is what he means, I own that I think Russell is right. This is a matter about which I suppose many philosophers would disagree with us. There are people who suppose that I *do* know immediately, in certain cases, such things as: That person is conscious; at least, they use this language, though whether they mean exactly what I am here meaning by 'know immediately' may be doubted. I can, however, not help agreeing with Russell that I never do know *immediately* that that person is conscious, nor anything else that is *logically incompatible* with 'This percept was produced by a malicious demon'. Where, therefore, I differ from him is in supposing that I do know for certain things which I do not know immediately and which also do *not* follow logically from anything which I do know immediately.

This seems to me to be the fundamental question at issue in considering my classes (3) and (4) and what distinguishes them from cases (1) and (2). I think I do know *immediately* things about myself and such things as 'There was a sound like "Russell" a little while ago'—that is, I think that memory is *immediate* knowledge and that much of my knowledge about myself is immediate. But I cannot help agreeing with Russell that I never know immediately such a thing as 'That person is conscious' or 'This is a pencil', and that also the truth of such propositions never follows logically from anything which I do know immediately, and yet I think that I do know such things for certain. Has he any argument for his view that if their falsehood is *logically possible* (i.e. if I do not know *immediately* anything logically incompatible with their falsehood) then I do *not* know them for certain? This is a thing which he certainly constantly assumes; but I cannot find that he anywhere gives any distinct arguments for it.

So far as I can gather, his reasons for holding it are the two assumptions which he expresses when he says: 'If (I am to reject the view that my life is one long dream) I must do so on the basis of an analogical or inductive argument, which cannot give complete certainty' (*Outline*, page 218). That is to say he assumes: (1) My belief or knowledge that this is a pencil is, *if* I do not know it immediately, and if also the proposition does not follow logically from anything that I know immediately, in some sense 'based on' an analogical or inductive argument; and (2) What is 'based on' an analogical or inductive argument is never certain knowledge, but only more or less probable belief. And with regard to these assumptions, it seems to me that the first must be true in some sense or other, though it seems to me terribly difficult to say exactly what the sense is. What I am inclined to dispute, therefore, is the second: I am inclined to think that what is 'based on' an analogical or inductive argument, in the sense in which my knowledge or belief that this is a pencil is so, may nevertheless be certain knowledge and *not* merely more or less probable belief.

What I want, however, finally to emphasize is this: Russell's view that I do not know for certain that this is a pencil or that you are conscious rests, if I am right, on no less than four distinct assumptions: (1) That I don't know these things immediately; (2) That they don't follow logically from any thing or things that I do know immediately; (3) That, *if* (1) and (2) are true, my belief in or knowledge of them must be 'based on an analogical or inductive argument'; and (4) That what is so based cannot be *certain knowledge.* And what I can't help asking myself is this: Is it, in fact, as certain that all these four assumptions are true, as that I *do* know that this is a pencil and that you are conscious? I cannot help answering: It seems to me *more* certain that I *do* know that this is a pencil and that you are conscious, than that any single one of these four assumptions is true, let alone all four. That is to say, though, as I have said, I agree with Russell that (1), (2) and (3) *are* true; yet of no one even of these three do I feel *as* certain as that I do know for certain that this is a pencil. Nay more: I do not think it is *rational* to be as certain of any one of these four propositions, as of the proposition that I do know that this is a pencil. And how on earth is it to be decided which of the two things it is *rational* to be most certain of?

X

CERTAINTY

I am at present, as you can all see, in a room and not in the open air; I am standing up, and not either sitting or lying down; I have clothes on, and am not absolutely naked; I am speaking in a fairly loud voice, and am not either singing or whispering or keeping quite silent; I have in my hand some sheets of paper with writing on them; there are a good many other people in the same room in which I am; and there are windows in that wall and a door in this one.

Now I have here made a number of different assertions; and I have made these assertions quite positively, as if there were no doubt whatever that they were true. That is to say, though I did not expressly say, with regard to any of these different things which I asserted, that it was not only true but also *certain*, yet by asserting them in the way I did, I *implied*, though I did not say, that they were in fact certain—implied, that is, that I myself knew for certain, in each case, that what I asserted to be the case was, at the time when I asserted it, in fact the case. And I do not think that I can be justly accused of dogmatism or over-confidence for having asserted these things positively in the way that I did. In the case of some kinds of assertions, and under some circumstances, a man can be justly accused of dogmatism for asserting something positively. But in the case of assertions such as I made, made under the circumstances under which I made them, the charge would be absurd. On the contrary, I should have been guilty of absurdity if, under the circumstances, I had *not* spoken positively about these things, if I spoke of them at all. Suppose that now, instead of saying 'I am inside a building', I were to say 'I *think* I'm inside a building, but perhaps I'm not: it's not *certain* that I am', or instead of saying 'I have got some clothes on', I were to say 'I think I've got some clothes on, but it's just possible that I haven't'. Would it not sound rather ridiculous for me now, under these circumstances, to say 'I *think* I've got some clothes on' or even to say 'I not only think I have, I know that it is very likely indeed that I

have, but I can't be quite sure'? For some persons, under some
circumstances, it might not be at all absurd to express themselves
thus doubtfully. Suppose, for instance, there were a blind man,
suffering in addition from general anaesthesia, who knew, because
he had been told, that his doctors from time to time stripped
him naked and then put his clothes on again, although he himself
could neither see nor feel the difference: to such a man there might
well come an occasion on which he would really be describing
correctly the state of affairs by saying that he *thought* he'd got
some clothes on, or that he knew that it was very likely he had,
but was not quite sure. But for me, now, in full possession of my
senses, it would be quite ridiculous to express myself in this way,
because the circumstances are such as to make it quite obvious
that I don't merely think that I have, but know that I have. For me
now, it would be absurd to say that I *thought* I wasn't naked,
because by saying this I should imply that I didn't know that I
wasn't, whereas you can all see that I'm in a position to know
that I'm not. But if *now* I am not guilty of dogmatism in asserting
positively that I'm not naked, certainly I was not guilty of dogmatism when I asserted it positively in one of those sentences
with which I began this lecture. I knew then that I had clothes
on, just as I know now that I have.

Now those seven assertions with which I began were obviously,
in some respects, not all of quite the same kind. For instance:
while the first six were all of them (among other things) assertions
about myself, the seventh, namely that there were windows in that
wall, and a door in this one, was not about myself at all. And
even among those which were about myself there were obvious
differences. In the case of two of these—the assertions that I was
in a room, and the assertion that there were a good many other
people in the same room with me—it can quite naturally be said
that each gave a partial answer to the question what sort of
environment I was in at the time when I made them. And in the
case of three others—the assertions that I had clothes on, that I was
speaking in a fairly loud voice, and that I had in my hand some
sheets of paper—it can also be said, though less naturally, that
they each gave a partial answer to the same question. For, if I
had clothes on, if I was in a region in which fairly loud sounds
were audible, and if I had some sheets of paper in my hand,
it follows, in each case that the surroundings of my body were,

in at least one respect, different from what they would have been if that particular thing had not been true of me; and the term 'environment' is sometimes so used that any true statement from which it follows that the surroundings of my body were different, in any respect, from what they might have been is a statement which gives *some* information, however little, as to the kind of environment I was in. But though each of these five assertions can thus, in a sense, be said to have given, if true, *some* information as to the nature of my environment at the time when I made it, one of them, the assertion that I was speaking in a fairly loud voice, did not *only* do this: it also, if true, gave some information of a very different kind. For to say that I was speaking in a fairly loud voice was not only to say that there were audible in my neighbourhood fairly loud sounds, and sounds of which it was also true that they were words; it was also to say that some sounds of this sort were *being made by me*—a causal proposition. As for the sixth of the assertions which I made about myself—the assertion that I was standing up—that can hardly be said to have given any information as to the nature of my environment at the time when I made it: it would be naturally described as giving information only as to the posture of my body at the time in question. And as for the two assertions I made which were not about myself at all—the assertions that there were windows in that wall and a door in this one—though they were, in a sense, assertions about my environment, since the two walls about which I made them were, in fact, in my neighbourhood at the time; yet in making them I was not expressly asserting that they were in my neighbourhood (had I been doing so, they would have been assertions about myself) and what I expressly asserted was some-thing which might have been true, even if they had not been in my neighbourhood. In this respect they were unlike my assertion that I was in a room, which could not have been true, unless some walls had been in my neighbourhood. From the proposition that there is a door in that wall it does not follow that that wall is in my neighbourhood; whereas from the proposition that I am in a room, it does follow that a wall is in my neighbourhood.

But in spite of these, and other, differences between those seven or eight different assertions, there are several important respects in which they were all alike.

(1) In the first place: All of those seven or eight different

assertions, which I made at the beginning of this lecture, were alike in this respect, namely, that every one of them was an assertion, which, though it wasn't in fact false, yet *might have been false*. For instance, consider the time at which I asserted that I was standing up. It is certainly true that at that very time I *might* have been sitting down, though in fact I wasn't; and if I *had* been sitting down at that time, then my assertion that I was standing up would have been false. Since, therefore, I might have been sitting down at that very time, it follows that my assertion that I was standing up was an assertion which *might have been false*, though it wasn't. And the same is obviously true of all the other assertions I made. At the time when I said I was in a room, I might have been in the open air; at the time when I said I had clothes on, I might have been naked; and so on, in all the other cases.

But from the fact that a given assertion might have been false, it always follows that the negation or contradictory of the proposition asserted is not a self-contradictory proposition. For to say that a given proposition might have been false is equivalent to saying that its negation or contradictory might have been true; and from the fact that a given proposition might have been true, it always follows that the proposition in question is not self-contradictory, since, if it were, it could not possibly have been true. Accordingly all those things which I asserted at the beginning of this lecture were things of which the *contradictories were not self-contradictory*. If, for instance, when I said 'I am standing up' I had said instead 'It is not the case that I am standing up', which would have been the contradictory of what I did say, it would have been correct to say 'That is not a self-contradictory proposition, though it is a false one'; and the same is true in the case of all the other propositions that I asserted. As a short expression for the long expression 'proposition which is not self-contradictory and of which the contradictory is not self-contradictory' philosophers have often used the technical term 'contingent proposition'. Using the term 'contingent' in this sense, we can say, then, that one respect in which all those seven propositions which I asserted at the beginning of this lecture resembled one another was that *they were all of them contingent*.

And before I go on to mention some other respects in which they were all alike, I think I had better now at once say some things about the consequences of this first fact that they were all of them contingent—things which are very relevant to a proper understanding of the use of the word which forms the title of this lecture, the word 'Certainty'.

The first thing I want to say about the consequences of the fact that all those propositions were contingent is this: namely, that from the mere fact that they were all of them contingent, it does not follow that they were not all *known to be true*—nay more, it does not follow, in the case of any particular person whatever, that *that* person did not know them to be true. Some philosophers have in fact suggested that no contingent proposition is ever, as a matter of fact, known to be true. And I am not *now* disputing that suggestion, though I do in fact hold it to be false, and intend, in the course of this lecture to dispute it. All that I am asserting *now* is that, even if it is a fact that no contingent proposition is ever known to be true, yet in no case does this *follow* from the mere fact that it is contingent. For instance, that I am now standing up is a contingent proposition; but from the mere fact that it is so, from that fact *alone*, it certainly does not *follow* that I do not know that I am standing up. If it is to be shown—as many philosophers think they can show—that I do *not* know now that I am standing up, some other argument must be brought forward for this contention, over and above the mere fact that this proposition is contingent; for from this fact, by itself, it certainly does not *follow* that I don't know that I am standing up. I say that this is certain, and I do not know that any-one would dispute it. But if I were asked to defend my assertion, I do not know that I could give any better defence than merely to say that the conjunctive proposition 'I know that I am at present standing up, and yet the proposition that I am is contingent' is certainly not itself self-contradictory, even if it is false. Is it not obvious that if I say 'I know that I am at present standing up, although the proposition that I am is contingent', I am certainly not contradicting myself, even if I *am* saying something which is false?

The second thing I want to say about the consequences of the fact that all those seven propositions were contingent is something which follows from the first: namely that from the fact that they were contingent it does not follow, in the case of any single one among them, that it was *possible* that the proposi-

tion in question was false. To take, for instance, again, the
proposition that I was then standing up: from the fact that this
proposition was contingent, it does not follow that, if I had said
'It is possible that it is not the case that I am standing up', I
should have been saying something true. That this is so follows
from my former contention that the contingency of the proposition
in question does not entail that it was not known to be true,
because one, at least, of the ways in which we use expressions
of the form 'It is possible that p' is such that the statement in
question cannot be true if the person who makes it knows for
certain that p is false. We very, very often use expressions of the
form 'It is possible that p' in such a way that by using such an
expression we are making an assertion of our own ignorance on a
certain point—an assertion namely that we do not *know* that p
is false. This is certainly one of the very commonest uses of the
word 'possible'; it is a use in which what it expresses is often
expressed instead by the use of the word 'may'. For instance,
if I were to say 'It is possible that Hitler is dead at this moment'
this would naturally be understood to mean exactly the same as
if I said 'Hitler *may* be dead at this moment'. And is it not quite
plain that if I did assert that Hitler *may* be dead at this moment
part at least of what I was asserting would be that I personally
did not know for certain that he was not dead? Consequently if I
were to assert now 'It is possible that I am not standing up' I
should naturally be understood to be asserting that I do not
know for certain that I am. And hence, if I do know for certain
that I am, my assertion that it is possible that I'm not would be
false. Since therefore from the fact that 'I am standing up' is a
contingent proposition it does not follow that I do not know
that I am, it also does not follow from this fact that it is possible
that I am *not*. For if from the contingency of this proposition it did
follow that it is possible that I am not standing up, it would also
follow that I do not know that I *am* standing up: since from 'It
is possible that I am not standing up' there follows 'I do not know
that I am standing up'; and if p entails q, and q entails r, it *follows*
that p entails r. Since, therefore, our p ('the proposition "I am
standing up" is contingent') does not entail our r ('I do not know
that I am standing up'), and since our q ('It is possible that I am not
standing up') *does* entail our r, it follows that our p does not
entail our q: that is to say, the fact that the proposition 'I am

standing up' is contingent does not entail the consequence that it is possible that it is false that I am standing up. In no case whatever from the mere fact that a proposition p is contingent does it *follow* that it is *possible* that p is false. But this, of course, is not to deny that it may, *as a matter of fact*, be true of every contingent proposition that it is possible that it is false. This *will* be true, if no contingent proposition is ever known to be true. But even if this is so, it still remains true that from the mere fact that a proposition is contingent it never *follows* that it *may* be false; this remains true because from the mere fact that a proposition is contingent it never follows that it is not known to be true, and never follows, either, in the case of any particular person, that that person does not know it to be true.

In the above paragraph I confined myself to saying that there is at least one common use of expressions of the form 'It is possible that p', such that any person who makes such an assertion is asserting that he personally does not know that p is false; and hence the only conclusion to which I am so far entitled is that the mere fact that a given proposition p is contingent does not entail the consequence that what is expressed by 'it is possible that not-p' will be true, *when 'possible' is used in the way in question.* And it may be thought that there is another use of 'possible' such that from 'p is contingent' there does follow 'it is possible that p is false'. The fact is that the expression 'logically possible' has often been used by philosophers in such a way that many might be tempted to think that it is a mere synonym for 'not self-contradictory'. That it is not a mere synonym for this can, I think, be seen from the fact that the expression 'it is not self-contradictory that I am not standing up' is not English at all, whereas the expression 'It is logically possible that I am not standing up' certainly is English, though it may be doubted whether what it expresses is true. If, however, we consider the expression 'the proposition that I am not standing up is not self-contradictory' I think it would not be incorrect to say that the words 'logically possible' are so used that *in this expression* they could be substituted for 'not self-contradictory' without changing the meaning of the whole expression; and that the same is true whatever other proposition you might take instead of the proposition that I am not standing up. If this be so, then it follows that, in the case of any proposition whatever, from the proposition that

that proposition is not self-contradictory it will follow that the proposition in question is also logically possible (and *vice versa*); in other words, for any *p*, '*p* is not self-contradictory' entails '*p* is logically possible'. But this being so, it is very natural to think that it follows that you can also take a further step and say truly that, for any *p*, '*p* is not self-contradictory' entails 'It is logically possible that *p*'; for surely from '*p* is logically possible' it must follow that 'it is logically possible that *p*.' Certainly it is very natural to think this; but for all that, I think it is a mistake to think so. To think that '*p* is logically possible' must entail 'It is logically possible that *p*' is certainly a mere mistake which does not do justice to the subtlety of the differences there may be in the way we use language. And I think it is actually a mistake to say that '*p* is not self-contradictory' entails 'It is logically possible that *p*', even though it does entail '*p* is logically possible'. Consider the following facts. 'It is logically possible that I *should have been* sitting down now' certainly does entail 'The proposition that I am sitting down now is not self-contradictory'. But if this latter proposition did entail 'It is logically possible that I *am* sitting down now' then it would follow that 'It is logically possible that I *should have been* sitting down now' entails 'It is logically possible that I *am* sitting down now'. But does it? Certainly it would be quite unnatural for me, who know that I am standing up, to say the latter, whereas it would be quite natural for me to say the former; and I think perhaps we can go further and say that if I said the latter I should be saying something untrue, whereas if I said the former I should be saying something true; just as if I said 'I *might have been* sitting down now', I should be saying something true, whereas if I said 'I *may* be sitting down now', I should be saying something false. In short I think that even the expression 'It is *logically* possible that so-and-so *is* the case' retains the characteristic which we have seen to belong to one ordinary use of the expression 'It is possible that so-and-so *is* the case', namely that it can only be said *with truth* by a person who does not know that the so-and-so in question is *not* the case. If I were to say now 'It is logically possible that I am sitting down' I should be implying that I don't know that I'm not, and therefore implying something which, if I do know that I'm not, is false. I think that perhaps philosophers have not always paid sufficient attention to the possibility that from the mere fact that a given proposition, *p*, is not self-contradictory, it perhaps does not follow that any person whatever can say with truth 'It is logically possible that *p is* true'. In the case of a non-self-contradictory proposition such as the proposition that I am at present sitting down, if there be a person, for instance some friend of mine in England, who does not know that this proposition is false, then, in his case, from the *conjunction* of the fact that the proposition is not self-contradictory with the fact that he does not know it to be false, it does follow that he could say with truth 'It is logically possible that Moore is at present sitting down'; but if there be another person, myself for instance, who does know that the proposition is false, it is by no means clear that from the mere fact that the proposition is not self-contradictory—from that fact *alone*—it follows that *I* can truly say 'It is logically possible that I am at present sitting down'. From the conjunction of the fact that the proposition is logically possible with the fact that I know it to be false, it does follow that I can truly say 'It is logically possible that I *should have been* sitting down at this moment'; but from the fact that I can truly say this, it certainly does not follow that I can *also* truly say 'It is logically possible that I *am* sitting down'; and it is certain that in fact the two are incompatible: that, if I can truly say 'It is logically possible that I *should have been* sitting down now' then it follows that I *cannot* truly say 'It is logically possible that I *am* sitting down now'. Perhaps, however, our use of the expression 'It is logically possible that so-and-so *is* the case' is not clearly enough fixed to entitle us to say this. What is important is to insist that if 'It is logically possible that *p is* true' is used in such a way that it does follow from '*p* is not self-contradictory', *by itself*, then from 'It is logically possible that *p is* true', it does not follow that *p* is not known to be false. And if a philosopher does choose to use 'It is logically possible that *p* is true' in such an unnatural way as this, there will be a danger that he will sometimes forget that that is the way in which he has chosen to use it, and will fall into the fallacy of thinking that from 'It is logically possible that *p is* true' there *does* follow '*p* is not known to be false'.

The third thing which I wish to say about the consequences of the fact that those seven assertions with which I began this paper were assertions of contingent propositions, is this: that this fact is quite compatible with its being true that every one of those seven things that I asserted was not only true but *absolutely certain*. That this is so again follows from the fact that the mere contingency of a given proposition, *p*, never entails, in the case of any person whatever, that that person does not know *p* to be true. It follows from this fact, because if any person whatever does at a given time know that a given proposition *p* is true, then it follows that that person could say with truth at that time 'It is absolutely certain that *p*'. Thus if I do know now that I am standing up, it follows that I can say with truth 'It is absolutely certain that I am standing up'. Since, therefore, the fact that this proposition is contingent is compatible with its being true that I know that I am standing up, it follows that it must also be compatible with its being true that it is absolutely certain that I am standing up.

I think that possibly some people might be inclined to object to what I have just said on the following ground. I have just said that if a person can ever say with truth, with regard to any particular proposition *p*, 'I know that *p* is true', it follows that he can also truly say 'It is absolutely certain that *p* is true'. But an objector might perhaps say: 'I admit that if a person could ever truly say "I know *with absolute certainty* that *p* is true" then it would follow that he could also truly say "It *is* absolutely certain that *p* is true". But what you said was not "know with absolute certainty" but "know"; and surely there must be some difference between "knowing" and "knowing with absolute certainty", since, if there were not, we should never be tempted to use the latter expression. I doubt, therefore, whether a mere "I know that *p*" does entail "It is absolutely certain that *p*".' To this objection I should reply: I do not think that the only possible explanation of the fact that we sometimes say 'I know with absolute certainty that so-and-so' and sometimes merely 'I know that so-and-so' is that the latter can be properly used to express something which may be true even when what is expressed by the former is not true: I doubt therefore whether 'I know that *p*' does not always entail 'I know with absolute certainty that *p*'. But even if 'I know that *p*' can be sometimes properly used to express something from which 'I know with absolute certainty that *p*' does *not* follow, it is certainly also sometimes used in such a way that if I don't know with absolute certainty that *p*, then it follows that I don't know that *p*. And I have been and shall be only concerned with uses of 'know' of the latter kind, i.e. with such that 'I know that p' does entail 'I know with absolute certainty that p'. And similarly, even if there are proper uses of the word 'certain', such that a thing can be 'certain' without being 'absolutely certain', there are certainly others (or at least one other) such that if a thing is not absolutely certain it cannot be truly said to be certain; and I have been and shall be concerned only with uses of 'certain' of this latter kind.

Another comment which might be made upon what I have said is that, even if there is *one* use of 'absolutely certain' such that, as I said, it is never logically impossible that a contingent proposition should be absolutely certain, yet there is another use of 'absolutely certain' such that this *is* logically impossible—a sense of 'absolutely certain', that is to say, in which only propositions whose contradictories are self-contradictory can be absolutely certain. Propositions whose contradictories are self-contradictory have sometimes been called 'necessary truths', sometimes 'a priori propositions', sometimes 'tautologies'; and it is sometimes held that the sense in which such propositions can be 'certain', and therefore also the sense in which they can be 'known to be true', must be different from the sense (if any) in which contingent propositions are sometimes 'certain' and 'known to be true'. That this may be so, I do not wish to deny. So far as I can see, it may be the case that, if I say, 'I know that' or 'It is certain that' 'it is not the case that there are any triangular figures which are not tri-lateral', or 'I know that' or 'It is certain that' 'it is not the case that there are any human beings who are daughters and yet are not female', I am using 'know that' and 'it is certain that' in a different sense from that in which I use them if I say 'I know that' or 'It is certain that' 'I have some clothes on'; and it may be the case that only necessary truths can be known or be certain in the former sense. Accordingly, my statements that from the fact that a given proposition, p, is contingent it does not follow that p is not known and is not certain, should be understood to mean only that there is at least one sense in which 'known' and 'certain' can be properly used, such that this does not follow; just as all that I asserted positively before about the phrase 'It is possible that' was that there is at least one sense in which this phrase can be properly used, such that 'p is contingent' does not entail 'It is possible that p is false'.

Finally, there is one slightly puzzling point about our use of the phrases 'it is possible that' and 'it is certain that', which might lead some people to suspect that some of the things I have been saying about the consequences which follow from the fact that a given proposition is contingent are false, and which therefore I think I had better try to clear up at once.

There are four main types of expression in which the word 'certain' is commonly used. We may say 'I feel certain that . . .', or we may say 'I am certain that . . .', or we may say 'I know for certain that . . .', or finally we may say 'It *is* certain that . . .'. And if we compare the first of these expressions with the two last, it is, of course, very obvious, and has been pointed out again and again, that whereas 'I feel certain that p' may quite well be true in a case in which p is not true—in other words that from the mere fact that I feel certain that so-and-so is the case it never follows that so-and-so is in fact the case—there is at least one common use of 'I know for certain that p' and 'It is certain that p' such that these things can't be true unless p is true. This difference may be brought out by the fact that, e.g., 'I felt certain that he would come, but in fact he didn't' is quite clearly not self-contradictory; it is quite clearly logically possible that I should have felt certain that he would come and that yet he didn't; while, on the other hand, 'I knew for certain that he would come, but he didn't' or 'It was certain that he would come but he didn't' are, for at least one common use of those phrases, self-contradictory: the fact that he didn't come *proves* that I didn't *know* he would come, and that it wasn't certain that he would, whereas it does not prove that I didn't *feel* certain that he would. In other words, 'I feel certain that p' does not *entail* that p is true (although by saying that I feel certain that p, I do *imply* that p is true), but 'I know that p' and 'It is certain that p' do entail that p is true; they can't be true, unless it is. As for the fourth expression 'I *am* certain that . . .' or 'I am quite sure that . . .' (it is perhaps worth noting that in the expressions 'I feel certain that . . .' and 'I am certain that . . .' the word 'sure' or the words 'quite sure' can be substituted for the word 'certain' without change of meaning, whereas in the expressions 'I know for certain that . . .' or 'it is certain that . . .' this is not the case) these expressions are, I think, particularly liable to give rise to fallacious reasoning in philosophical discussions about certainty, because, so far as I can see, they are sometimes used to mean the same as 'I feel certain that . . .' and sometimes, on the contrary, to mean the same as 'I know for certain that'. For instance, the expression 'I was quite sure that he would come, but yet he didn't' *can*, it seems to me, be naturally used in such a way that it is not self-contradictory—which can only be the case if it is in that case merely another way of saying 'I felt quite sure that he would come . . .'; but if on the other hand a philosopher were to say to me now (as many would say) 'You can't be quite sure that you are standing up', he would certainly not be asserting that I can't *feel* certain that I am—a thing which he would not at all wish to dispute—and he certainly would be asserting that, even if I do feel certain that I am, I don't or can't *know for certain* that I am.

There is, therefore, a clear difference in meaning between 'I feel certain that . . .' on the one hand, and 'I know for certain that . . .' or 'It is certain that . . .' on the other. But the point with which I am at present concerned is whether there is not also a difference of importance between each of these expressions 'I feel certain that . . .', 'I am certain that . . .', and 'I know for certain that . . .', on the one hand, and 'It *is* certain that . . .' on the other. The first three expressions are obviously, in spite of the important difference I have just pointed out between the first and the last of them, alike in one important respect—a respect which may be expressed by saying that their meaning is relative to the person who uses them. They are alike in this respect, because they all contain the word 'I'. In the case of every sentence which contains this word, its meaning obviously depends on who it is that says that sentence; if I say 'I am hot', what I assert by saying this is obviously something different from what any other person would be asserting by saying exactly the same words; and it is obvious that what I assert by saying so may quite well be true even though what another person asserts by saying exactly the same words at exactly the same time is false. 'I am hot' said by me at a given time, does not contradict 'I am not hot' said by you at exactly the same time: both may perfectly well be true. And in the same way, if I say 'I feel certain that there are windows in that wall' or 'I know for certain that there are windows', I, by saying this, am making an assertion different from, and logically independent of, what another person would be asserting by saying exactly the same words at the same time: from the fact that I feel certain of or know for certain a given thing it *never* follows, in the case of any other person whatever, that he feels certain of or knows the thing in question, nor from the fact that he does does it ever follow that *I* do. But if we consider, by contrast, the expression 'It *is* certain that there are windows in that wall', it looks, at first sight, as if the meaning of this expression was *not* relative to the person who says it: as if it were a quite impersonal statement and should mean the same whoever says it, provided it is said at the same time and provided the wall referred to by the words 'that wall' is the same. It is, indeed, obvious, I think, that a thing can't be certain, unless it is *known*: this is one obvious point that distinguishes the use of the word 'certain' from that of the word 'true'; a thing that nobody knows may quite well be true, but cannot possibly be certain. We can, then, say that it is a necessary condition for the truth of 'It is certain that p' that somebody should know that p is true. But the meaning of 'Somebody knows that p is true' is certainly not relative to the person who says it: it is as completely impersonal as 'The sun is larger than the moon', and if two people say it at the same time, then, if the one by saying it is saying something true, so must the other be. If, therefore, 'It is certain that p' meant merely 'Somebody knows that p is true', then the meaning of 'It is certain that p' would *not* be relative to the person who says it, and there would then be an important difference between it, on the one hand, and 'I feel certain that p' or 'I know for certain that p' on the other, since the meaning of these two *is* relative to the person who says them. But though 'Somebody knows that p is true' is a necessary condition for the truth of 'It is certain that p', it can be easily seen that it is *not* a sufficient condition; for if it were, it would follow that in any case in which somebody did know that p was true, it would always be false for anybody to say 'It is not certain that p'. But in fact it is quite evident that if I say now 'It is not certain that Hitler is still alive', I am not thereby committing myself to the statement that nobody knows that Hitler is still alive: my statement is quite consistent with its being true that Hitler is still alive, and that he himself and other persons know that he is so. The fact is, then, that all that follows from 'Somebody knows that p is true' is that *somebody* could say with truth 'It is certain that p': it does not follow that more than one person could; nor does it follow that there are not some who could say with truth 'It is *not* certain that *p*'. Two different people, who say, at the same time about the same proposition, *p*, the one 'It is certain that *p* is true', the other 'It is not certain that *p* is true', may both be saying what is true and not contradicting one another. It follows, therefore, that, in spite of appearances, the meaning of 'It *is* certain that *p*' *is* relative to the person who says it. And this, I think, is because, as I have implied above, if anybody asserts 'It is certain that *p*' part of what he is asserting is that he himself knows that *p* is true; so that, even if many other people do know that *p* is true, yet his assertion will be false, if he himself does not know it. If, on the other hand, a person asserts 'It is *not* certain that *p*' his assertion will not necessarily be true merely because he personally does not know that *p* is true, though it will necessarily be false if he personally does know that *p* is true. If *I* say 'It is certain that *p*', that *I* should know that *p* is true is both a necessary and sufficient condition for the truth of my assertion. But if I say 'It is *not* certain that *p*', then that I should *not* know that *p* is true, though it is a necessary, is not a sufficient condition for the truth of my assertion. And similarly the expression 'It is possible that *p* is true' is, though it looks as if it were impersonal, really an expression whose meaning is relative to the person who uses it. If *I* say it, that I should not know that *p* is false, is a necessary, though not a sufficient, condition for the truth of my assertion; and hence if two people say it at the same time about the same proposition it is perfectly possible that what the one asserts should be true, and what the other asserts false: since, if one of the two knows that *p* is false, his assertion will necessarily be false; whereas, if the other does not know that *p* is false, his assertion may be, though it will not necessarily be, true. On the other hand, if it were right to use the expression 'It is *logically* possible that *p*' as equivalent to '*p* is not self-contradictory', then the meaning of 'It is *logically* possible that *p*' would *not* be relative to the person who says it.

To sum up this digression. What I have said about the consequences of the fact that all those seven propositions with which I opened this lecture were contingent, is firstly (1) that this fact does *not* entail the consequence that I did not, when I made them, know them to be true; (2) that it does *not* entail the consequence that I could then have said with truth about any of them 'It is possible that this is false'; and (3) that it does not entail the consequence that I could then have said with truth about any of them 'It is not absolutely certain that this is true'. It follows that by asserting that those seven propositions were contingent, I have not committed myself to the view that they were not known to be true or that it was not absolutely certain they were. But on the other hand, even if I am right in saying that these consequences do *not* follow from the mere fact that they were contingent, it, of course, does not follow from this that I *did* know them to be true, when I asserted them, or that they were absolutely certain. The questions whether, when I first said that I was standing up, I did know that I was, and whether, therefore, it was absolutely certain that I was, still remain completely open.

(2) A second respect, in addition to the fact that they were all of them contingent, in which all those seven propositions resembled one another, was this: In the case of every one of them part at least of what I was asserting, in asserting it, was something from which nothing whatever about the state or condition of my own mind followed—something from which no psychological proposition whatever about myself followed. Every one of them asserted something which might have been true, no matter what the condition of my mind had been either at that moment or in the past. For instance, that I was then inside a room is something which might have been true, even if at the time I had been asleep and in a dreamless sleep, and no matter what my character or disposition or mental abilities might have been: from that fact alone no psychological proposition whatever about myself followed. And the same is true of part at least of what I asserted in each of the other six propositions. I am going to refer to this common feature of all those seven propositions, by saying that they were all of them propositions which implied the existence of *an external world*—that is to say, of a world *external to my mind*. These phrases 'external world' and 'external to my mind' have often been used in philosophy; and I think that the way in which I am now proposing to use them is in harmony with the way in which they generally (though not always) have been used. It is indeed not obvious that my assertion that I was standing up implied the existence of anything external to *my*

body; but it has generally been clear that those who spoke of a world *external* to any given individual, meant by that a world external to that individual's *mind*, and that they were using the expression 'external to a mind' in some metaphorical sense such that my body *must* be external to my mind. Accordingly a proposition which implies the existence of my body does, for that reason alone, with this use of terminology, imply the existence of a world *external to my mind*; and I think that the reason why it is said to do so is because from the existence of my body at a given time nothing whatever logically follows as to the state or condition of my mind at that time. I think, therefore, that I am not saying anything that will be misleading to those familiar with philosophical terminology, if I say, for the reason given, that each of those seven assertions implied the existence of something external to my mind; and that hence, if I did know any one of them to be true, when I asserted it, the existence of an external world was at that time absolutely certain. If, on the other hand, as some philosophers have maintained, the existence of an external world is never absolutely certain, then it follows that I cannot have known any one of these seven propositions to be true.

(3) A third characteristic which was common to all those seven propositions was one which I am going to express by saying that I had for each of them, at the time when I made it, *the evidence of my senses*. I do not mean by this that the evidence of my senses was the *only* evidence I had for them: I do not think it was. What I mean is that, at the time when I made each, I was seeing or hearing or feeling things (or, if that will make my meaning clearer, 'having visual, auditory, tactile or organic sensations'), or a combination of these, such that to see or hear or feel those things *was* to have evidence (not necessarily *conclusive* evidence) for part at least of what I asserted when I asserted the proposition in question. In other words, in all seven cases, what I said was at least partly *based* on 'the then present evidence of my senses'.

(4) Fourth and finally, I think that all those seven assertions shared in common the following characteristic. Consider the class of all propositions which resemble them in the second respect I mentioned, namely, that they imply the existence of something external to the mind of the person who makes them. It has been and still is held by many philosophers that no proposi-

tion which has this peculiarity is ever known to be true—is ever quite certain. And what I think is true of those seven propositions with which I began this lecture is this: namely, that, if I did not know them to be true when I made them, then those philosophers are right. That is to say, if those propositions were not certain, then nothing of the kind is ever certain: if *they* were not certain, then no proposition which implies the existence of anything external to the mind of the person who makes it is ever certain. Take any one of the seven you like: the case for saying that I *knew* that one to be true when I made it is as strong as the case ever is for saying of any proposition which implies the existence of something external to the mind of the person who makes it, that *that* person knows it to be true.

This, it will be seen, is not a matter of logic. Obviously it is logically possible, for instance, that it should have been false then that I knew I was standing up and yet should be true now that I know I am standing up. And similarly in the other cases. But though this is logically possible—though the proposition 'I know that I am standing up now, but I did not know then that I was' is certainly not self-contradictory—yet it seems to me that it is certainly false. If I didn't know then that I was standing up, then certainly I know nothing of the sort now, and never have known anything of the sort; and, not only so, but nobody else ever has. And similarly, conversely (though this also is not a matter of logic), if I did know then that I was standing up then I certainly also know that I am standing up now, and have in the past constantly known things of the sort; and, not only so, but millions of other people have constantly known things of the sort: we all of us constantly do. In other words, those seven propositions of mine seem to be as good test-cases as could have been chosen (*as* good as, but also no better than thousands of others) for deciding between what seems to me to be the only real (though far from the only logically possible) alternatives— namely the alternative that none of us ever knows for certain of the existence of anything external to his own mind, and the alternative that all of us—millions of us—constantly do. And it was because they seemed to me to be as good test-cases as could be chosen for deciding this that I chose them.

But can we decide between these two alternatives?

I feel that the discussion of this question is frightfully difficult;

and I feel sure that better and more decisive things could be said about it than I shall be able to say. All that I can do is to discuss, and that very inadequately, just one of the types of argument which have sometimes been alleged to show that nobody ever has known for certain anything about a world external to his mind.

Suppose I say now: 'I know for certain that I am standing up; it is absolutely certain that I am; there is not the smallest chance that I am not.' Many philosophers would say: 'You are wrong: you do not know that you are standing up; it is *not* absolutely certain that you are; there is *some* chance, though perhaps only a very small one, that you are not.' And one argument which has been used as an argument in favour of saying this, is an argument in the course of which the philosopher who used it would assert: 'You do not know for certain that you are not dreaming; it is not absolutely certain that you are not; there is *some* chance, though perhaps only a very small one, that you are.' And from this, that I do not know for certain that I am not dreaming, it is supposed to follow that I do not know for certain that I am standing up. It is argued: If it is not certain that you are not dreaming, then it is not certain that you are standing up. And that *if* I don't know that I'm not dreaming, I also don't know that I'm not sitting down, I don't feel at all inclined to dispute. From the hypothesis that I am dreaming, it would, I think, certainly follow that I don't *know* that I am standing up; though I have never seen the matter argued, and though it is not at all clear to me how it is to be proved that it would follow. But, on the other hand, from the hypothesis that I am dreaming, it certainly would not follow that I am *not* standing up; for it is certainly logically possible that a man should be fast asleep and dreaming, while he is standing up and not lying down. It is therefore logically possible that I should both be standing up and also at the same time dreaming that I am; just as the story, about a well-known Duke of Devonshire, that he once dreamt that he was speaking in the House of Lords and, when he woke up, found that he *was* speaking in the House of Lords, is certainly logically possible. And if, as is commonly assumed, when I am dreaming that I am standing up it may also be correct to say that I am *thinking* that I am standing up, then it follows that the hypothesis that I am now dreaming is quite consistent with the hypothesis that I am both thinking that I am standing up and also actually standing up. And hence, if, as seems to me to be certainly the case and as this argument assumes, from the hypothesis that I am now dreaming it *would* follow that I don't know that I am standing up, there follows a point which is of great importance with regard to our use of the word 'knowledge', and therefore also of the word 'certainty'—a point which has been made quite conclusively more than once by Russell, namely that from the conjunction of the two facts that a man thinks that a given proposition *p* is true, and that *p* is in fact true, it does *not* follow that the man in question *knows* that *p* is true: in order that I may be justified in saying that I know that I am standing up, something more is required than the mere conjunction of the two facts that I both think I am and actually am—as Russell has expressed it, true belief is not identical with knowledge; and I think we may further add that even from the conjunction of the two facts that I feel certain that I am and that I actually am it would not follow that I know that I am, nor therefore that it *is* certain that I am. As regards the argument drawn from the fact that a man who dreams that he is standing up and happens at the moment actually to be standing up will nevertheless not *know* that he is standing up, it should indeed be noted that from the fact that a man is dreaming that he is standing up, it certainly does not *follow* that he *thinks* he is standing up; since it does sometimes happen in a dream that we *think* that it is a dream, and a man who thought this certainly might, although he was dreaming that he was standing up, yet *think* that he was not, although he could not *know* that he was not. It is not therefore the case, as might be hastily assumed, that, if I dream that I am standing up at a time when I am in fact lying down, I am necessarily *deceived*: I should be deceived only if I thought I was standing when I wasn't; and I may dream that I am, without thinking that I am. It certainly does, however, often happen that we do dream that so-and-so is the case, without at the time thinking that we are only dreaming; and in such cases, I think we may perhaps be said to *think* that what we dream is the case *is* the case, and to be deceived if it is not the case; and therefore also, in such cases, if what we dream to be the case happens also to *be* the case, we may be said to be thinking truly that it is the case, although we certainly do not *know* that it is.

I agree, therefore, with that part of this argument which asserts that if I don't know now that I'm not dreaming, it follows that I don't *know* that I am standing up, even if I both actually am and think that I am. But this first part of the argument is a consideration which cuts both ways. For, if it is true, it follows that it is also true that if I *do* know that I am standing up, then I do know that I am not dreaming. I can therefore just as well argue: since I do know that I'm standing up, it follows that I do know that I'm not dreaming; as my opponent can argue: since you don't know that you're not dreaming, it follows that you don't know that you're standing up. The one argument is just as good as the other, unless my opponent can give better reasons for asserting that I don't know that I'm not dreaming, than I can give for asserting that I do know that I am standing up.

What reasons can be given for saying that I don't know for certain that I'm not at this moment dreaming?

I do not think that I have ever seen clearly stated any argument which is supposed to show this. But I am going to try to state, as clearly as I can, the premisses and the reasonings from them, which I think have led so many philosophers to suppose that I really cannot now know for certain that I am not dreaming.

I said, you may remember, in talking of the seven assertions with which I opened this lecture, that I had 'the evidence of my senses' for them, though I also said that I didn't think this was the only evidence I had for them, nor that this by itself was necessarily conclusive evidence. Now if I had *then* 'the evidence of my senses' in favour of the proposition that I was standing up, I certainly have *now* the evidence of my senses in favour of the proposition that I *am* standing up, even though this may not be all the evidence that I have, and may not be conclusive. But have I, in fact, the evidence of my senses *at all* in favour of this proposition? One thing seems to me to be quite clear about our use of this phrase, namely, that, if a man at a given time is only dreaming that he is standing up, then it follows that he has *not* at that time the evidence of his senses in favour of that proposition: to say 'Jones last night was *only* dreaming that he was standing up, and yet all the time he had the evidence of his senses that he was' is to say something self-contradictory. But those philosophers who say it is possible that I am now dreaming, certainly mean to say also that it is possible that I am *only dreaming* that I am standing up; and this view, we now see, entails that it is possible that I have *not* the evidence of my senses that I am. If, therefore, they are right, it follows that it is not certain even that I have the evidence of my senses that I am; it follows that it is not certain that I have *the evidence of my senses* for anything at all. If, therefore, I were to say now, that I certainly have the evidence of my senses in favour of the proposition that I am standing up, even if it's not certain that I am standing up, I should be begging the very question now at issue. For if it is not certain that I am not dreaming, it is not certain that I even have the evidence of my senses that I am standing up.

But, now, even if it is not certain that I have at this moment the evidence of my senses for anything at all, it is quite certain that I *either* have the evidence of my senses that I am standing up *or* have an experience which is *very like* having the evidence of my senses that I am standing up. *If* I am dreaming, this experience consists in having dream-images which are at least very like the sensations I should be having if I were awake and had the sensations, the having of which would constitute 'having the evidence of my senses' that I am standing up. Let us use the expression 'sensory experience', in such a way that this experience which I certainly am having will be a 'sensory experience', whether or not it merely consists in the having of dream-images. If we use the expression 'sensory experience' in this way, we can say, I think, that, if it is not certain that I am not dreaming now, then it is not certain that *all* the sensory experiences I am now having are not mere dream-images.

What then are the premisses and the reasonings which would lead so many philosophers to think that all the sensory experiences I am having now *may* be mere dream-images—that I do not know for certain that they are not?

So far as I can see, one premiss which they would certainly use would be this: 'Some at least of the sensory experiences which you are having now are similar in important respects to dream-images which actually have occurred in dreams.' This seems a very harmless premiss, and I am quite willing to admit that it is true. But I think there is a very serious objection to the procedure of using it as a premiss in favour of the derived conclusion. For a philosopher who does use it as a premiss, is, I think, in fact *implying*, though he does not expressly say, that he himself knows it to be true. He is *implying* therefore that he himself knows that dreams have occurred. And, of course, I think he would be right. All the philosophers I have ever met or heard of certainly did know that dreams have occurred: we all know that dreams *have* occurred. But can he consistently combine this proposition that he knows that dreams have occurred, with his conclusion that he does not know that he is not dreaming? Can anybody possibly know that dreams have occurred, if, at the time, he does not himself know that he is not dreaming? If he *is* dreaming, it may be that he is only dreaming that dreams have occurred; and if he does not know that he is not dreaming, can he possibly know that he is *not* only dreaming that dreams have occurred? Can he possibly know therefore that dreams *have* occurred? I do not think that he can; and therefore I think that anyone who uses this premiss and also asserts the conclusion that nobody ever knows that he is not dreaming, is guilty of an inconsistency. By using this premiss he implies that he himself knows that dreams have occurred; while, if his conclusion is true, it follows that he himself does not know that he is not dreaming, and therefore does not know that he is not only dreaming that dreams have occurred.

However, I admit that the premiss is true. Let us now try to see by what sort of reasoning it might be thought that we could get from it to the conclusion.

I do not see how we can get forward in that direction at all, unless we first take the following huge step, unless we say, namely: since there have been dream-images similar in important respects to some of the sensory experiences I am now having, it is logically possible that there should be dream-images *exactly like all* the sensory experiences I am now having, and logically possible, therefore, that all the sensory experiences I am now having *are* mere dream-images. And it might be thought that the validity of this step could be supported to some extent by appeal to matters of fact, though only, of course, at the cost of the same sort of inconsistency which I have just pointed out. It might be said, for instance, that some people have had dream-images which were *exactly like* sensory experiences which they had when they were awake, and that therefore it must be logically possible to have a dream-image exactly like a sensory experience which is *not* a dream-image. And then it may be said: If it is logically possible for some dream-images to be exactly like sensory experiences which are not dream-images, surely it must be logically possible for *all* the dream-images occurring in a dream at a given time to be exactly like sensory experiences which are not dream-images, and logically possible also for all the sensory experiences which a man has at a given time when he is awake to be exactly like all the dream-images which he himself or another man had in a dream at another time.

Now I cannot see my way to deny that it is logically possible that all the sensory experiences I am having now should be mere dream-images. And if this is logically possible, and if further the sensory experiences I am having now were the only experiences I am having, I do not see how I could possibly know for certain that I am not dreaming.

But the conjunction of my memories of the immediate past with these sensory experiences *may* be sufficient to enable me to know that I am not dreaming. I say it *may* be. But what if our sceptical philosopher says: It is *not* sufficient; and offers as an argument to prove that it is not, this: It is logically possible *both* that you should be having all the sensory experiences you are having, and also that you should be remembering what you do remember, and *yet* should be dreaming. If this is logically possible, then I don't see how to deny that I cannot possibly know for certain that I am not dreaming: I do not see that I possibly could. But can any reason be given for saying that it *is* logically possible? So far as I know nobody ever has, and I don't know how anybody ever could. And so long as this is not done my argument, 'I know that I am standing up, and therefore I know that I am not dreaming', remains at least as good as his, 'You don't know that you are not dreaming, and therefore don't know that you are standing up'. And I don't think I've ever seen an argument expressly directed to show that it is not.

One final point should be made clear. It is certainly logically possible that I *should have* been dreaming now; I *might* have been dreaming now; and therefore the proposition that I *am* dreaming now is not self-contradictory. But what I am in doubt of is whether it is logically possible that I should *both* be having all the sensory experiences and the memories that I have and *yet* be dreaming. The conjunction of the proposition that I have these sense experiences and memories with the proposition that I am dreaming does seem to me to be very likely self-contradictory.[1]

[1] It should, I think, be mentioned that Moore was particularly dissatisfied with the last four paragraphs of this paper, and I believe that he was thinking primarily of these paragraphs when he wrote, in the Preface, that the paper contains bad mistakes.—C. L.

XI

WITTGENSTEIN'S LECTURES
IN 1930–33

I

In January 1929, Wittgenstein returned to Cambridge after an absence of more than fifteen years. He came with the intention of residing in Cambridge and pursuing there his researches into philosophical problems. Why he chose Cambridge for this latter purpose I do not know: perhaps it was for the sake of having the opportunity of frequent discussion with F. P. Ramsey. At all events he did in fact reside in Cambridge during all three Full Terms of 1929, and was working hard all the time at his researches.[1] He must, however, at some time during that year, have made up his mind that, besides researching, he would like to do a certain amount of lecturing, since on October 16th, in accordance with his wishes, the Faculty Board of Moral Science resolved that he should be invited to give a course of lectures to be included in their Lecture List for the Lent Term of 1930.

During this year, 1929, when he was researching and had not begun to lecture, he took the Ph.D. degree at Cambridge. Having been entered as an 'Advanced Student' during his previous period of residence in 1912 and 1913, he now found that he was entitled to submit a dissertation for the Ph.D. He submitted the *Tractatus* and Russell and I were appointed to examine him. We gave him an oral examination on June 6th, an occasion which I found both pleasant and amusing. We had, of course, no doubt whatever that his work deserved the degree: we so reported, and when our report had been approved by the necessary authorities, he received the degree in due course.

In the same month of June in which we examined him, the Council of Trinity College made him a grant to enable him to

[1] The statement in the Obituary notice in *The Times* for May 2, 1951, that he arrived in Cambridge in 1929 'for a short visit' is very far from the truth. Fortunately I kept a brief diary during the period in question and can therefore vouch for the truth of what I have stated above about his residence in 1929, though there is in fact other evidence.

continue his researches. (They followed this up in December 1930, by electing him to a Research Fellowship, tenable for five years, which they afterwards prolonged for a time.)

In the following July of 1929 he attended the Joint Session of the Mind Association and Aristotelian Society at Nottingham, presenting a short paper entitled 'Some Remarks on Logical Form'. This paper was the only piece of philosophical writing by him, other than the *Tractatus*, published during his life-time. Of this paper he spoke in a letter to *Mind* (July 1933) as 'weak'; and since 1945 he has spoken of it to me in a still more disparaging manner, saying something to the effect that, when he wrote it, he was getting new ideas about which he was still confused, and that he did not think it deserved any attention.

But what is most important about this year, 1929, is that in it he had frequent discussions with F. P. Ramsey—discussions which were, alas! brought to an end by Ramsey's premature death in January 1930.[1] Ramsey had written for *Mind* (October 1923, page 465) a long Critical Notice of the *Tractatus*; and subsequently, during the period when Wittgenstein was employed as a village schoolmaster in Austria, Ramsey had gone out to see him, in order to question him as to the meaning of certain statements in the *Tractatus*. He stayed in the village for a fortnight or more, having daily discussions with Wittgenstein. Of these discussions in Austria I only know that Ramsey told me that, in reply to his questions as to the meaning of certain statements, Wittgenstein answered more than once that he had forgotten what he had meant by the statement in question. But after the first half of the discussions at Cambridge in 1929, Ramsey wrote at my request the following letter in support of the proposal that

[1] In the Preface to his posthumously published *Philosophical Investigations*, where Wittgenstein acknowledges his obligations to Ramsey (p. x), Wittgenstein himself says that he had 'innumerable' discussions with Ramsey 'during the last two years of his life', which should mean both in 1928 and in 1929. But I think this must be a mistake. I imagine that Wittgenstein, trusting to memory alone, had magnified into a series of discussions continuing for two years, a series which in fact only continued for a single year. It will be noticed that in the letter from Ramsey himself which I am about to quote, and which is dated June 14, 1929, Ramsey states that he had been in close touch with Wittgenstein's work 'during the last two terms', i.e. during the Lent and May Terms of 1929, implying that he had not been in close touch with it in 1928. And though I do not know where Wittgenstein was in 1928, he certainly was not resident in Cambridge where Ramsey was resident, so that it is hardly possible that they can have had in that year such frequent discussions as they certainly had in 1929.

Trinity should make Wittgenstein a grant in order to enable him to continue his researches.

'In my opinion Mr Wittgenstein is a philosophic genius of a different order from anyone else I know. This is partly owing to his great gift for seeing what is essential in a problem and partly to his overwhelming intellectual vigour, to the intensity of thought with which he pursues a question to the bottom and never rests content with a mere possible hypothesis. From his work more than that of any other man I hope for a solution of the difficulties that perplex me both in philosophy generally and in the foundations of Mathematics in particular.

'It seems to me, therefore, peculiarly fortunate that he should have returned to research. During the last two terms I have been in close touch with his work and he seems to me to have made remarkable progress. He began with certain questions in the analysis of propositions which have now led him to problems about infinity which lie at the root of current controversies on the foundations of Mathematics. At first I was afraid that lack of mathematical knowledge and facility would prove a serious handicap to his working in this field. But the progress he has made has already convinced me that this is not so, and that here too he will probably do work of the first importance.

'He is now working very hard and, so far as I can judge, he is getting on well. For him to be interrupted by lack of money would, I think, be a great misfortune for philosophy.'

The only other thing I know about these discussions with Ramsey at Cambridge in 1929 is that Wittgenstein once told me that Ramsey had said to him 'I don't like your method of arguing'.

Wittgenstein began to lecture in January 1930, and from the first he adopted a plan to which he adhered, I believe, throughout his lectures at Cambridge.[1] His plan was only to lecture once a week in every week of Full Term, but on a later day in each week to hold a discussion class at which what he had said in that week's lecture could be discussed. At first both lecture and discussion class were held in an ordinary lecture-room in the

---

[1] Professor von Wright has subsequently informed me that I was mistaken in believing this: that in 1939, Wittgenstein lectured twice a week and held no discussion class; and that in the Easter Term of 1947, he both gave two lectures a week and also held a discussion class. I have also remembered that at one time (I do not know for how long) he gave, besides his ordinary lectures, a special set of lectures for mathematicians.

University Arts School; but very early in the first term Mr
R. E. Priestley (now Sir Raymond Priestley), who was then
Secretary General of the Faculties and who occupied a set of
Fellows' rooms in the new building of Clare, invited Wittgenstein
to hold his discussion classes in these rooms. Later on, I think,
both lectures and discussion classes were held in Priestley's rooms,
and this continued until, in October 1931, Wittgenstein, being
then a Fellow of Trinity, was able to obtain a set of rooms of his
own in Trinity which he really liked. These rooms were those
which Wittgenstein had occupied in the academic year 1912-13,
and which I had occupied the year before, and occupied again
from October 1913, when Wittgenstein left Cambridge and went
to Norway. Of the only two sets which are on the top floor of
the gate-way from Whewell's Courts into Sidney Street, they were
the set which looks westward over the larger Whewell's Court,
and, being so high up, they had a large view of sky and also of
Cambridge roofs, including the pinnacles of King's Chapel. Since
the rooms were not a Fellow's set, their sitting-room was not
large, and for the purpose of his lectures and classes Wittgenstein
used to fill it with some twenty plain cane-bottomed chairs, which
at other times were stacked on the large landing outside. Nearly
from the beginning the discussion classes were liable to last at
least two hours, and from the time when the lectures ceased to
be given in the Arts School they also commonly lasted at least as
long. Wittgenstein always had a blackboard at both lectures and
classes and made plenty of use of it.

I attended both lectures and discussion classes in all three
terms of 1930 and in the first two terms of 1931. In the Michaelmas
Term of 1931 and the Lent Term of 1932 I ceased, for some
reason which I cannot now remember, to attend the lectures
though I still went to the discussion classes; but in May 1932,
I resumed the practice of attending the lectures as well, and
throughout the academic year 1932-33 I attended both. At
the lectures, though not at the discussion classes, I took what
I think were very full notes, scribbled in notebooks of which
I have six volumes nearly full. I remember Wittgenstein once
saying to me that he was glad I was taking notes, since, if anything
were to happen to him, they would contain some record of the
results of his thinking.

My lecture-notes may be naturally divided into three groups, to which I will refer as (I), (II) and (III). (I) contains the notes of his lectures in the Lent and May Terms of 1930; (II) those of his lectures in the academic year 1930–31; and (III) those of lectures which he gave in the May Term of 1932, after I had resumed attending, as well as those of all the lectures he gave in the academic year 1932–33. The distinction between the three groups is of some importance, since, as will be seen, he sometimes in later lectures corrected what he had said in earlier ones.

The chief topics with which he dealt fall, I think, under the following heads. First of all, in all three periods he dealt (A) with some very general questions about language, (B) with some special questions in the philosophy of Logic, and (C) with some special questions in the philosophy of Mathematics. Next, in (III) and in (III) alone, he dealt at great length, (D) with the difference between the proposition which is expressed by the words 'I have got toothache', and those which are expressed by the words 'You have got toothache' or 'He has got tooth-ache', in which connection he said something about Behaviourism, Solipsism, Idealism and Realism, and (E) with what he called 'the grammar of the word "God" and of ethical and aesthetic statements'. And he also dealt, more shortly, in (I) with (F) our use of the term 'primary colour'; in (III) with (G) some questions about Time; and in both (II) and (III) with (H) the kind of investigation in which he was himself engaged, and its difference from and relation to what has traditionally been called 'philosophy'.

I will try to give some account of the chief things he said under all these heads; but I cannot possibly mention nearly everything, and it is possible that some of the things I omit were really more important than those I mention. Also, though I tried to get down in my notes the actual words he used, it is possible that I may sometimes have substituted words of my own which misrepresent his meaning: I certainly did not understand a good many of the things he said. Moreover, I cannot possibly do justice to the extreme richness of illustration and comparison which he used: he was really succeeding in giving what he called a 'synoptic' view of things which we all know. Nor can I do justice to the intensity of conviction with which he said every-thing which he did say, nor to the extreme interest which he excited in his hearers. He, of course, never read his lectures:

he had not, in fact, written them out, although he always spent a great deal of time in thinking out what he proposed to say.

(A) He did discuss at very great length, especially in (II), certain very general questions about language; but he said, more than once, that he did not discuss these questions because he thought that language was the subject-matter of philosophy. He did not think that it was. He discussed it only because he thought that particular philosophical errors or 'troubles in our thought' were due to false analogies suggested by our actual use of expressions; and he emphasized that it was only necessary for him to discuss those points about language which, as he thought, led to these particular errors or 'troubles'.

The general things that he had to say about language fall naturally, I think, under two heads, namely (a) what he had to say about the meaning of single words, and (b) what he had to say about 'propositions'.

(a) About the meaning of single words, the positive points on which he seemed most anxious to insist were, I think, two, namely (α) something which he expressed by saying that the meaning of any single word in a language is 'defined', 'constituted', 'determined' or 'fixed' (he used all four expressions in different places) by the 'grammatical rules' with which it is used in that language, and (β) something which he expressed by saying that every significant word or symbol must essentially belong to a 'system', and (metaphorically) by saying that the meaning of a word is its 'place' in a 'grammatical system'.

But he said in (III) that the sense of 'meaning' of which he held these things to be true, and which was the only sense in which he intended to use the word, was only one of those in which we commonly use it: that there was another which he described as that in which it is used 'as a name for a process accompanying our use of a word and our hearing of a word'. By the latter he apparently meant that sense of 'meaning' in which 'to know the meaning' of a word means the same as to 'understand' the word; and I think he was not quite clear as to the relation between this sense of 'meaning' and that in which he intended to use it, since he seemed in two different places to suggest two different and incompatible views of this relation, saying in (II) that 'the rules applying to negation actually describe my experience

I

in using "not", i.e. describe my understanding of the word', and in one place in (III), on the other hand, saying, 'perhaps there is a causal connection between the rules and the feeling we have when we hear "not" '. On the former occasion he added that 'a logical investigation doesn't teach us anything about the meaning of negation: we can't get any clearer about its meaning. What's difficult is to make the rules explicit'.

Still later in (III) he made the rather queer statement that 'the idea of meaning is in a way obsolete, except in such phrases as "this means the same as that" or "this has no meaning" ', having previously said in (III) that 'the mere fact that we have the expression "the meaning" of a word is bound to lead us wrong: we are led to think that the rules are responsible to something not a rule, whereas they are only responsible to rules'.

As to (α) although he had said, at least once, that the meaning of a word was 'constituted' by the grammatical rules which applied to it, he explained later that he did not mean that the meaning of a word *was* a list of rules; and he said that though a word 'carried its meaning with it', it did not carry with it the grammatical rules which applied to it. He said that the student who had asked him whether he meant that the meaning of a word *was* a list of rules would not have been tempted to ask that question but for the false idea (which he held to be a common one) that in the case of a substantive like 'the meaning' you have to look for something at which you can point and say 'This is the meaning'. He seemed to think that Frege and Russell had been misled by the same idea, when they thought they were bound to give an answer to the question 'What *is* the number 2?' As for what he meant by saying that the meaning of a word is 'determined by' (this was the phrase which he seemed to prefer) the 'grammatical rules' in accordance with which it is used, I do not think he explained further what he meant by this phrase.

(β) As to what he meant by saying that, in order that a word or other sign should have meaning, it must belong to a 'system', I have not been able to arrive at any clear idea. One point on which he insisted several times in (II) was that if a word which I use is to have meaning, I must 'commit myself' by its use. And he explained what he meant by this by saying 'If I commit myself, that means that if I use, e.g., "green" in this case, I have to use it in others', adding 'If you commit yourself, there are consequences'. Similarly he said a little later, 'If a word is to have significance, we must commit ourselves', adding 'There is no use in correlating noises to facts, unless we commit ourselves to using the noise in a particular way again—unless the correlation has consequences', and going on to say that it must be possible to be 'led by a language'. And when he expressly raised, a little later, the question 'What is there in this talk of a "system" to which a symbol must belong?' he answered that we are concerned with the phenomenon of 'being guided by'. It looked, therefore, as if one use which he was making of the word 'system' was such that in order to say that a word or other sign 'belonged to a system', it was not only necessary but *sufficient* that it should be used in the same way on several different occasions. And certainly it would be natural to say that a man who habitually used a word in the same way was using it 'systematically'.

But he certainly also frequently used 'system' in such a sense that *different* words or other expressions could be said to belong to the *same* 'system'; and where, later on, he gave, as an illustration of what he meant by 'Every symbol must essentially belong to a system', the proposition 'A crotchet can only give information on what note to play in a system of crotchets', he seemed to imply that for a sign to have significance it is *not* sufficient that we should 'commit ourselves' by its use, but that it is also necessary that the sign in question should belong to the same 'system' with other signs. Perhaps, however, he only meant, not that for a sign to have *some* meaning, but that for *some* signs to have *the significance which they actually have in a given language*, it is necessary that they should belong to the same 'system' with other signs. This word 'system' was one which he used very very frequently, and I do not know what conditions he would have held must be satisfied by two different signs in order that they may properly be said to belong to the same 'system'. He said in one place in (II) that the 'system of projection' by which '2 + 3' can be projected into '5' is 'in no way inferior' to the 'system' by which '11 + 111' can be projected into '11111', and I think one can see, in this case, that '2 + 3 = 5' can be properly said to belong to the same 'system' as, e.g., '2 + 2 = 4', and also can properly be said to belong to a different 'system' from that to which '11 + 111 = 11111' and '11 + 11 = 1111' both belong, though I have no clear idea as to the sense in which these

things can properly be said. Nor do I know whether Wittgenstein
would have held, e.g., that in the case of *every* English word,
it could not have the significance which it actually has in English
unless it belonged to the same 'system' as other English words,
or whether he would have held that this is only true of *some*
English words, e.g. of the words 'five' and 'four', and of the
words 'red' and 'green'.

But besides these two positive things, (α) and (β), which he
seemed anxious to say about the meaning of words, he also
insisted on three negative things, i.e. that three views which have
sometimes been held are mistakes. The first of these mistakes
was (γ) the view that the meaning of a word was some image
which it calls up by association—a view to which he seemed to
refer as the 'causal' theory of meaning. He admitted that sometimes you cannot understand a word unless it calls up an image,
but insisted that, even where this is the case, the image is just
as much a 'symbol' as the word is. The second mistake was
(δ) the view that, where we can give an 'ostensive' definition of a
word, the object pointed at is the meaning of the word. Against
this view, he said, for one thing, that, in such a case 'the gesture
of pointing together with the object pointed at can be used
instead of the word', i.e. is itself something which has meaning
and has the same meaning as the word has. In this connection
he also pointed out that you may point at a red book, either to
show the meaning of 'book' or to show the meaning of 'red',
and that hence in 'This is a book' and 'This is the colour "red" ',
'this' has quite a different meaning; and he emphasized that,
in order to understand the ostensive definition 'This is "red" ',
the hearer must already understand what is meant by 'colour'.
And the third mistake was (ϵ) that a word is related to its meaning
in the same way in which a proper name is related to the 'bearer'
of that name. He gave as a reason for holding that this is false
that the bearer of a name can be ill or dead, whereas we cannot
possibly say that the meaning of the name is ill or dead. He said
more than once that the bearer of a name can be 'substituted'
for the name, whereas the meaning of a word can never be
substituted for that word. He sometimes spoke of this third mistake
as the view that words are 'representative' of their meanings, and
he held that in no case is a word 'representative' of its meaning,
although a proper name is 'representative' of its bearer (if it has

one). He added in one place: 'The meaning of a word is no longer for us an object corresponding to it.'

On the statement 'Words, except in propositions, have no meaning' he said that this 'is true or false, as you understand it'; and immediately went on to add that, in what he called 'language games', single words 'have meanings by themselves', and that they may have meaning by themselves even in our ordinary language 'if we have provided one'. In this connection he said, in (II), that he had made a mistake (I think he meant in the *Tractatus*) in supposing that a proposition must be complex. He said the truth was that we can replace a proposition by a simple sign, but that the simple sign must be 'part of a system'.

(*b*) About 'propositions', he said a great deal in many places as to answers which might be given to the question 'What is a proposition?'—a question which he said we do not understand clearly. But towards the end of (III) he had definitely reached the conclusion 'It is more or less arbitrary what we call a "proposition"', adding that 'therefore Logic plays a part different from what I and Russell and Frege supposed it to play'; and a little later he said that he could not give a general definition of 'proposition' any more than of 'game': that he could only give examples, and that any line he could draw would be 'arbitrary, in the sense that nobody would have decided whether to call so-and-so a "proposition" or not'. But he added that we are quite right to use the word 'game', so long as we don't pretend to have drawn a definite outline.

In (II), however, he had said that the word 'proposition', 'as generally understood', includes both 'what I call propositions', also 'hypotheses', and also mathematical propositions; that the distinction between these three 'kinds' is a 'logical distinction', and that therefore there must be some grammatical rules, in the case of each kind, which apply to that kind and not to the other two; but that the 'truth-function' rules apply to all three, and that that is why they are all called 'propositions'.

He went on to illustrate the difference between the first two kinds by saying that 'There seems to me to be a man here' is of the first kind, whereas 'There is a man here' is a 'hypothesis'; and said that one rule which applies to the first and not to the second is that I can't say 'There seems to me to seem to me to be a man here' whereas I can say 'There seems to me to be a man here'.

But, soon after, he said that the word 'proposition' is used in *two* different ways, a wider and a narrower, meaning by the wider that in which it included all three of the kinds just distinguished, and by the narrower, apparently, that in which it included the first two kinds, but not the third. For propositions in this narrower sense he seemed later very often to use the expression 'experiential propositions', and accordingly I will use this expression to include propositions of both the first two kinds. The things which he had to say about experiential propositions, thus understood, were extremely different from those which he had to say about the third kind; and I will therefore treat these two subjects separately.

(α) Of experiential propositions he said in (I) that they could be 'compared with reality' and either 'agreed or disagreed with it'. He pointed out very early something which he expressed by saying 'Much of language needs outside help', giving as an example your use of a specimen of a colour in order to explain what colour you want a wall painted; but he immediately went on to say (using 'language' in a different sense) that in such a case the specimen of a colour is 'a part of your language'. He also pointed out (as in the *Tractatus*) that you can assert a proposition or give an order without using any words or symbols (in the ordinary sense of 'symbol'). One of the most striking things about his use of the term 'proposition' was that he apparently so used it that in giving an order you are necessarily expressing a 'proposition', although, of course, an order can be neither true nor false, and can be 'compared with reality' only in the different sense that you can look to see whether it is carried out or not.

About propositions, understood in this sense, he made a distinction in (II) between what he called 'the sign' and what he called 'the symbol', saying that whatever was necessary to give a 'sign' significance was a part of 'the symbol', so that where, for instance, the 'sign' is a sentence, the 'symbol' is something which contains both the sign and also everything which is necessary to give that sentence sense. He said that a 'symbol', thus understood, *is* a 'proposition' and 'cannot be nonsensical, though it can be either true or false'. He illustrated this by saying that if a man says 'I am tired' his mouth is part of the symbol; and said that any explanation of a sign 'completes the symbol'.

Here, therefore, he seemed to be making a distinction between a proposition and a sentence, such that no sentence can be identical with any proposition, and that no proposition can be without sense. But I do not think that in his actual use of the term 'proposition' he adhered to this distinction. He seemed to me sometimes so to use 'proposition' that every significant sentence *was* a proposition, although, of course, a significant sentence does not contain everything which is necessary to give it significance. He said, for instance, that signs with different meanings must *be* different 'symbols'. And very often he seemed to me to follow the example of Russell in the Introduction to *Principia Mathematica* in so using the word 'proposition' that 'propositions', and not merely sentences, could be without sense; as, for instance, when he said at the beginning of (II) that his object was to give us some 'firm ground' such as 'If a proposition has a meaning, its negation must have a meaning'. And, towards the end of (III), in connection with the view at which he had then arrived that the words 'proposition', 'language' and 'sentence' are all 'vague', he expressly said that the answer to the question whether, when you say 'A unicorn looks like this' and point at a picture of a unicorn, the picture is or is not a part of the proposition you are making, was 'You can say which you please'. He was, therefore, now rejecting his earlier view that a proposition must contain everything which is necessary to make a sentence significant, and seemed to be implying that the use of 'proposition' to mean the same as 'sentence' was a perfectly correct one.

In connection with the *Tractatus* statement that propositions, in the 'narrower' sense with which we are now concerned, are 'pictures', he said he had not at that time noticed that the word 'picture' was vague; but he still, even towards the end of (III), said that he thought it 'useful to say "A proposition is a picture *or something like one*" ' although in (II) he had said he was willing to admit that to call a proposition a 'picture' was misleading; that propositions are not pictures 'in any ordinary sense'; and that to say that they are, 'merely stresses a certain aspect of the grammar of the word "proposition"—merely stresses that our uses of the words "proposition" and "picture" follow similar rules'.

In connection with this question of the similarity between experiential 'propositions' and pictures, he frequently used the words 'project' and 'projection'. Having pointed out that it is paradoxical to say that the words 'Leave the room' is a 'picture' of what a boy does if he obeys the order, and having asserted that it is, in fact, *not* a 'picture' of the boy's action 'in any ordinary sense', he nevertheless went on to say that it is 'as much' a picture of the boy's action as '2 + 3' is of '5', and that '2 + 3' really is a picture of '5' *'with reference to a particular system of projection'*, and that this system is 'in no way inferior' to the system in which '11 + 111' is projected into '11111', only that 'the method of projection is rather queer'. He had said previously that the musical signs '♯' and '♭' are obviously not pictures of anything you do on the keyboard of a piano; that they differ in this respect from

what, e.g. " ♯♯ " would be, if you had the rule that the second

crotchet is to stand for the white key on the piano that is next to the right of that for which the first crotchet stands, and similarly for the third and second crotchet; but nevertheless, he said, '♯' and '♭' 'work in exactly the same way' as these crotchets would work, and added that 'almost all our words work as they do'. He explained this by saying that a 'picture' must have been given by an explanation of how '♯' and '♭' are used, and that an explanation is always of the same kind as a definition, viz. 're-placing one symbol by another'. He went on to say that when a man reads on a piano from a score, he is 'led' or 'guided' by the position of the crotchets, and that this means that he is 'following a general rule', and that this rule, though not 'contained' in the score, nor in the result, nor in both together, must be 'contained' in his intention. But he said, that though the rule is 'contained' in the intention, the intention obviously does not 'contain' any *expression* of the rule, any more than, when I read aloud, I am conscious of the rules I follow in translating the printed signs into sounds. He said that what the piano player does is 'to see the rule in the score', and that, even if he is playing automatically, he is still 'guided by' the score, provided that he *would* use the general rule to judge whether he had made a mistake or not. He even said in one place that to say that a man is 'guided' by the score 'means' that he *would justify* what he played by reference to the score. He concluded by saying that, if he plays correctly, there is *a* 'similarity' between what he does on the piano and the score, 'though we usually confine "similarity" to projection according to certain rules only'; and that in the same sense there is *a* 'similarity' between automatic traffic signals and the movements of traffic which are guided by them. Later on he said that for any sign whatever there *could* be a method of projection such that it made sense, but that when he said of any particular expression 'That means nothing' or 'is nonsense', what he meant was '*With the common method of projection* that means nothing', giving as an instance that when he called the sentence 'It is due to human weakness that we can't write down all the cardinal numbers' 'meaningless', he meant that it is meaningless if the person who says it is using 'due to human weakness' as in 'It's due to human weakness that we can't write down a billion cardinal numbers'. Similarly, he said that surely Helmholtz must have been talking nonsense when he said that in happy moments he could imagine four-dimensional space, because *in the system he was using* those words make no sense, although 'I threw the chalk into four-dimentional space' would make sense, if we were not using the words on the analogy of throwing from one room into another, but merely meant 'It first disappeared and then appeared again'. He insisted more than once that we are apt to think that we are using a new system of projection which would give sense to our words, when in fact we are not using a new system at all: 'any expression' he said '*may* make sense, but you may think you are using it with sense, when in fact you are not'.

One chief view about propositions to which he was opposed was a view which he expressed as the view that a proposition is a sort of 'shadow' intermediate between the expression which we use in order to assert it and the fact (if any) which 'verifies' it. He attributed this view to W. E. Johnson, and he said of it that it was an attempt to make a distinction between a proposition and a sentence. (We have seen that he himself had in (II) made a different attempt to do this.) He said that it regarded the supposed 'shadow' as something 'similar' to the fact which verifies it, and in that way different from the expression which expresses it, which is not 'similar' to the fact in question; and he said that, even if there were such a 'shadow' it would not 'bring us any nearer to the fact', since 'it would be susceptible of different interpretations just as the expression is'. He said, 'You can't give any picture which can't be misinterpreted' and 'No interpolation between a sign and its fulfilment does away with a sign'. He added that the only description of an expectation

I*

'which is relevant for us' is 'the expression of it', and that 'the
expression of an expectation contains a description of the fact
that would fulfil it', pointing out that if I expect to *see a red patch*
my expectation is fulfilled if and only if I do *see a red patch*,
and saying that the words 'see a red patch' have the same meaning
in both expressions.

Near the beginning of (I) he made the famous statement, 'The
sense of a proposition is the way in which it is verified'; but
in (III) he said·this only meant 'You can determine the meaning
of a proposition by asking how it is verified' and went on to say,
'This is necessarily a mere rule of thumb, because "verification"
means different things, and because in some cases the question
"How is that verified?" makes no sense'. He gave as an example
of a case in which that question 'makes no sense' the proposition
'I've got toothache', of which he had already said that it makes
no sense to ask for a verification of it—to ask 'How do you know
that you have?' I think that he here meant what he said of 'I've
got toothache' to apply to all those propositions which he had
originally distinguished from 'hypotheses' as 'what I call propositions'; although in (II) he had distinguished the latter from
'hypotheses' by saying that they had 'a definite verification or
falsification'. It would seem, therefore, that in (III) he had
arrived at the conclusion that what he had said in (II) was wrong,
and that in the case of 'what he called propositions', so far from
their having 'a definite verification', it was senseless to say that
they had a verification at all. His 'rule of thumb', therefore, could
only apply, if at all, to what he called 'hypotheses'; and he went
on to say that, in many cases, it does not apply even to these,
saying that statements in the newspapers could verify the
'hypothesis' that Cambridge had won the boat-race, and that yet
these statements 'only go a very little way towards explaining
the meaning of "boat-race" '; and that similarly 'The pavement
is wet' may verify the proposition 'It has been raining', and that
yet 'it gives very little of the grammar of "It has been raining" '.
He went on to say 'Verification determines the meaning of a
proposition only where it gives the grammar of the proposition in
question'; and in answer to the question 'How far is giving a
verification of a proposition a grammatical statement about it?'
he said that, whereas 'When it rains the pavement gets wet' is not a
grammatical statement at all, if we say 'The fact that the pavement

is wet is a *symptom* that it has been raining' this statement is 'a matter of grammar'.

II

(β) The third kind of 'proposition' mentioned in Part I (page 261), of which at the very beginning of (I) Wittgenstein gave mathematical propositions as an example, saying that they are a 'very different sort of instrument' from, e.g. 'There is a piece of chalk here', and of which he sometimes said that they are not propositions at all, were those which have been traditionally called 'necessary', as opposed to 'contingent'. They are propositions of which the negation would be said to be, not merely false, but 'impossible', 'unimaginable', 'unthinkable' (expressions which he himself often used in speaking of them). They include not only the propositions of pure Mathematics, but also those of Deductive Logic, certain propositions which would usually be said to be propositions about colours, and an immense number of others.

Of these propositions he undoubtedly held that, unlike 'experiential' propositions, they cannot be 'compared with reality', and do not 'either agree or disagree' with it. But I think the most important thing he said about them, and certainly one of the most important things he said anywhere in these lectures, was an attempt to explain exactly how they differed from experiential propositions. And this attempt, so far as I can see, consisted in maintaining with regard to them two things, viz. (β') that the sentences, which would commonly be said to express them, do in fact, when used in this way, 'say nothing' or 'are without sense', and (β'') that this supposed fact that such sentences, when so used, are without sense, is due to the fact that they are related in a certain way to 'rules of grammar'. But *what*, precisely, was the relation to grammatical rules, which he held to be the reason why they had no sense? This question still puzzles me extremely.

For a time I thought (though I felt that this was doubtful) that he held so-called necessary propositions to be *identical* with certain grammatical rules—a view which would have yielded the conclusion that sentences, which would commonly be said to express necessary propositions, are in fact always merely expressing rules of grammar. And I think he did in fact hold that the very same expressions, which would commonly be said to express necessary propositions, can also be properly used in such a way that, when so used, they merely express rules of grammar. But I think he must have been aware (though I think he never expressly pointed this out) that, if so, then, *when* such expressions are being used merely to express rules of grammar they are being used in a very different way from that in which, on his view, they are being used when they would commonly be said to be expressing necessary propositions. For he certainly held, if I am not mistaken, of *all* expressions which would commonly be said to be expressing necessary propositions, what in the *Tractatus* he had asserted to be true of the particular case of 'tautologies', viz. both (1) that, when so used, they are 'without sense' and 'say nothing', and (2) that, nevertheless, they are, in a certain sense 'true', though he made plain, in these lectures, that he thought that the sense in which they are 'true' was very different from that in which experiential propositions may be 'true'. (As I have said (page 263), he seemed to me often to use the words 'proposition' and 'sentence' as if they meant the same, perhaps partly because the German word '*Satz*' may be properly used for either; and therefore often talked as if sentences could *be* 'true'). But of the same expressions, when used, as he thought they might be, merely to express rules, though he might perhaps have said that they 'say nothing', since he insisted strongly of one particular class of them, namely, those which express rules of deduction, that they are neither true nor false, he cannot, I think, have held that they are 'without sense'; indeed he said, at least once, of an expression which would commonly be said to express a necessary proposition, 'if it is to have any meaning, it must be a mere rule of a game'—thus implying that, if it is used to express a rule, it has a meaning. But in what sense was he using 'rules', when he insisted that his own 'rules of inference' were neither true nor false? I think this is an important question, because he seems to me to have used the expression 'rules of grammar' in two different senses, the difference between which he never expressly pointed out, and one of which is such that a grammatical rule, in that sense, will be true or false. He often spoke as if rules of grammar *allowed* you to use certain expressions and *forbade* you to use others, and he gave me the impression that, when so speaking, he was giving the name of 'rules' to actual statements that you are allowed or forbidden to use certain expressions—that, for instance, he would have called the statement, 'You can't say "Two men *was* working in that field" ' a rule of English grammar. This use of 'can't' is, indeed, one which is quite natural and familiar in the case of rules of games, to which he constantly compared rules of grammar; e.g. a chess-player might quite naturally say to an opponent, who was a beginner and was not yet familiar with the rules of chess, 'You can't do that' or 'You can't make that move', if the beginner moved a pawn, from its position at the beginning of the game, three squares forward instead of only two. But, if we so use 'rule' that the expression 'You can't do that', when thus used, is expressing a rule, then surely a rule *can* be true or false; for it is possible to be mistaken as to whether you can or can't make a certain move at chess, and 'You can't do that' will be true, if it is an *established* rule in chess not to make the kind of move in question, and will be false if there is no such established rule. But if we ask: What is the rule which *is* established in such a case? we come upon a very different sense of 'rule'; for the answer to this question will consist in describing or specifying a way in which somebody *might* act, whether anybody ever does so act or not; and with this sense of 'rule' it seems to me obvious that a rule cannot be true or false, and equally obvious that any expression which specifies it will have sense. In the case of rules of grammar, the possible action which such a rule specifies, will, of course, be a way of using words or forms of sentence in speaking or writing; and I think that the fact that 'rule' may be used in this sense, in which a 'rule' can obviously be neither true nor false, may have been partly responsible for Wittgenstein's assertion that his 'rules of inference' were neither true nor false. It is perhaps worth noting that the statement that such a rule is an *established* rule in a given language, (as is implied for English by, e.g., the statement, 'You can't say "Two men *was* working in that field" '), which really is true or false, is, of course, an experiential proposition about the way in which words or forms of sentence are actually used in the language in question; and that, therefore, if we suppose that the very same expression which is sometimes used to express a necessary proposition can also be used to express such an experiential proposition, then the ways in which it is used in these two cases must be very different; just as the ways in which the same expression is used, if used sometimes to express a necessary proposition and sometimes merely to specify a possible way of speaking or writing, must also be very different.

I think, therefore, that Wittgenstein cannot possibly have held that expressions which are being used in the way in which they would commonly be said to be expressing necessary propositions, are being used in the same way in which they are being used when used to express rules of grammar. But, if so, to *what* relation to rules of grammar did he hold it was due that expressions which are being used in the former way, have no sense? I am still extremely puzzled as to the answer to this question, for the following reason.

He seemed often to suggest that any sentence which is 'constructed in accordance with' (this is his own phrase) the rules of grammar of the language to which the sentence belongs, always has sense; e.g. that any English sentence which is constructed in accordance with the rules of English grammar, has sense. But, if so, since he held that, e.g. the sentences '2 + 2 = 4' or 'The proposition with regard to any two propositions that they are not both false follows logically from the proposition that they are both true', both of which would certainly be commonly said to express necessary propositions, are, when so used, without sense, he must have held that these two sentences, when so used, are not constructed in accordance with the rules of English grammar. Can he possibly have held that they are not? I think it is possible he did; but I do not know. But in the passage which I have already quoted (page 265) about Helmholtz's statement that he could imagine the fourth dimension, he seemed to be saying that if Helmholtz was 'projecting' the sentence 'I can imagine a piece of chalk being thrown into the fourth dimension' 'with the common method of projection', then he was talking nonsense, but that if he had been 'projecting' that sentence in an unusual way, so that it meant the same as 'I can imagine a piece of chalk first disappearing and then appearing again', then he would have been talking sense.

But is not 'projecting with the common method of projection' merely a metaphorical way of saying 'using in accordance with the established rules of grammar'? If so, then Wittgenstein was here saying that a sentence used in accordance with the established rules of grammar may nevertheless *not* make sense, and even implying that, in particular cases, the fact that it does not make sense is (partly) due to the fact that it *is* being used in accordance with the usual rules. I think, however, that possibly he intended to distinguish between 'projecting with the common method' and 'using in accordance with the usual rules', since he insisted strongly in at least one passage that any rule can be 'interpreted' in different ways, and also (if I have not misunderstood him) that it is impossible to add to any rule an unambiguous rule as to how it is to be interpreted. Possibly, therefore, he meant by 'projecting with the common method', *not* 'using in accordance with the usual rules', but '*interpreting* in the usual manner'—a distinction which would apparently allow him to hold that, when Helmholtz uttered his nonsensical sentence, he was *not* using that sentence in accordance with the usual rules, though he *was* interpreting in the usual manner the rules, whatever they may have been, in accordance with which he was using it. But I am very puzzled as to how this distinction could be used. Suppose, for instance, a person were to use 'I can imagine a piece of chalk being thrown into the fourth dimension' in such a way that it meant the same as 'I can imagine a piece of chalk first disappearing and then appearing again', how on earth could anyone (including the person in question) possibly decide whether in such a case the speaker or writer was doing what Wittgenstein called elsewhere 'changing his grammar', i.e. using the first expression *not* in accordance with the usual rules, but in accordance with rules such that it meant the same as the second means, or whether he was merely 'interpreting' in an unusual way the rules, whatever they may have been, in accordance with which he was using the first expression? I suspect, therefore, that when Wittgenstein said that Helmholtz must have been using the 'common method of projection', when he uttered his nonsensical sentence, he was not distinguishing this from using the sentence in accordance with the ordinary rules, and was therefore implying that a sentence constructed in accordance with the ordinary rules might nevertheless be without sense. But, if so, his view may have been that, e.g. '2 + 2 = 4', when used in the way in which it would commonly be said to express a necessary proposition, *is* used in accordance with the ordinary rules of grammar, and is nevertheless 'without sense', and is so partly *because* it *is* used in accordance with the ordinary rules; for he certainly would not have denied that that expression *might* be used in such a way that it had sense. But I do not know whether this was his view or not.

But finally there is still another reason why I am puzzled as to what his view was about sentences, which would commonly be said to express necessary propositions. His view was, if I am right, one which he expressed by the use of the expressions, (β′) 'without sense', as equivalent to which he often used the expressions 'nonsense', 'meaningless', and even 'useless' and (β″) 'rules of grammar'; and these two expressions were used by him constantly throughout these lectures. And my last puzzle is due to the fact that I think there is reason to suspect that he was not using either expression in any ordinary sense, and that I have not been able to form any clear idea as to how he was using them.

(β′) With regard to the expression 'without sense' I think there is no doubt that he was using it in the same way in which he used it in the *Tractatus*, 4.461, when he said that a 'tautology' is without sense (sinnlos). In that passage he gave as an example of the supposed fact that a 'tautology' is without sense the statement 'I know nothing about the weather, if I know that either it is raining or it is not'; and in these lectures he used a very similar example to show the same thing. Also in that passage of the *Tractatus* he said that a 'tautology' 'says nothing', and seemed to mean by this the same as what he meant by saying that it was 'without sense'; and this expression he also used in these lectures, and apparently in the same sense. And I think it is clearly true that we could say correctly of a man who only knew that either it was raining or it was not, that he knew nothing *about the present state of the weather*. But could we also say correctly of such a man that he knew *nothing at all*? I do not think we could; and yet, so far as I can see, it is only if we could say this correctly that we should be justified in saying that the sentence 'Either it is raining or it is not' 'says nothing' or is 'without sense'. I think, therefore, that Wittgenstein can only have been right in saying that 'tautologies' and other sentences, which would commonly be said to express necessary propositions, are 'without sense' and 'say nothing', if he was using these two expressions in some peculiar way, different from any in which they are ordinarily used. So far as

I can see, if we use 'make sense' in any way in which it is ordinarily used, 'Either it's raining or it's not' *does* make sense, since we should certainly say that the meaning of this sentence is different from that of 'Either it's snowing or it's not', thus implying that since they have different meanings, both of them have *some* meaning; and similarly, if 'say nothing' is used in any sense in which it is ordinarily used, Wittgenstein's proposition in *Tractatus* 5.43 that 'All the "Sätze" of Logic say the same, namely, nothing' seems to me to be certainly untrue. And that he was using these expressions in some peculiar way seems to me to be also suggested by the fact that in *Tractatus* 4.461, he seems to be saying that 'contradictions' are 'without sense' in the same sense in which 'tautologies' are, in spite of the fact that in the very same passage he asserts that the latter are 'unconditionally true', while the former are 'true under no condition'. But, if he was using these expressions (and also 'meaningless' and 'nonsense', which, as I have said, he often used as equivalent to them) in some peculiar sense, what was that sense? Later in (III) he expressly raised the questions 'What is meant by the decision that a sentence makes or does not make sense?' and 'What is the criterion of making sense?' having said that, in order to answer these questions, he must 'plunge into something terrible', and that he must do this in order to 'put straight' what he had just been saying, which, he said, he had not 'put correctly'. In trying to answer these questions or this question (for I think he was using the two expressions to mean the same) he said many things, including the statement that he had himself been 'misled' by the expression 'sense'; and he went on to say that his present view was that ' "sense" was correlative to "proposition" ' (meaning, apparently, here by 'proposition' what he had formerly called 'proposition in the narrower sense', i.e. 'experiential proposition', thus excluding, e.g., mathematical 'propositions') and that hence, if 'proposition' was not 'sharply bounded', 'sense' was not 'sharply bounded' either. He went on to say about 'proposition' the things which I have already quoted (pages 261-2); and then implied that where we say 'This makes no sense' we always mean 'This makes nonsense *in this particular game*'; and in answer to the question 'Why do we call it "nonsense"? what does it mean to call it so?' said that when we call a sentence 'nonsense', it is 'because of some similarity to sentences which have sense', and that 'nonsense always arises from forming symbols analogous to certain uses, where they have no use'. He concluded finally that ' "makes sense" is vague, and will have different senses in different cases', but that the expression 'makes sense' is useful just as 'game' is useful, although, like 'game', it 'alters its meaning as we go from proposition to proposition'; adding that, just as 'sense' is vague, so must be 'grammar', 'grammatical rule' and 'syntax'.

But all this, it seems to me, gives no explanation of how he was using the expression 'without sense' in the particular case of 'tautologies' and other sentences which would commonly be said to express necessary propositions: it only tells us that he might be using it in a different sense in that case from that in which he used it in other cases. The only explanation which, so far as I know, he did give as to how he was using it in the particular case of 'tautologies', was where he asked in (III), 'What does the statement that a tautology "says nothing" mean?' and gave as an answer, that to say that '$q \supset q$' 'says nothing' means that $p.(q \supset q) = p$; giving as an example that the logical product 'It's raining and I've either got grey hair or I've not' = 'It's raining'. If he did mean this, and if, as he seemed to be, he was using 'says nothing' to mean the same as 'is without sense', one important point would follow, namely, that he was not using 'without sense' in the same way in the case of 'tautologies' as in the case of 'contradictions', since he would certainly not have said that $p.(q.\sim q) = p$. But it gives us no further explanation of how he *was* using 'without sense' in the case of 'tautologies'. For if he was using that expression in any ordinary way, then I think he was wrong in saying that 'It's raining, and I've either got grey hair or I've not' = 'It's raining', since, in any ordinary usage, we should say that the 'sense' of 'either I've got grey hair or I've not' was different from that of, e.g., 'either I'm six feet high or I'm not', and should not say, as apparently he would, that both sentences say nothing, and therefore say the same.

In connection with his use of the phrase 'without sense', one other thing which he said or implied more than once should, I think, be mentioned, because it may give a partial explanation of why he thought that both 'contradictions' and 'tautologies' are without sense. He said in (I) that 'the linguistic expression' of 'This line can be bisected' is ' "This line *is* bisected" has sense', while at the same time insisting that 'the linguistic expression' of 'This line is infinitely divisible' is not ' "This line is infinitely divided" has sense' (he held that 'This line *is* infinitely divided' is senseless) but is 'an infinite possibility in language'. He held, therefore, that in many cases the 'linguistic expression' of 'It is possible that *p* should be true' or 'should have been true' is 'The sentence "*p*" has sense'. And I think there is no doubt that he here meant by 'possible' what is commonly called, and was called by him on a later occasion, 'logically possible'. But to say that a sentence '*p*' is the 'linguistic expression' of a *proposition* '*q*', would naturally mean that the sentence '*p*' and the *sentence* '*q*' have the same meaning, although for some reason or other '*p*' can be called a 'linguistic expression', though the sentence '*q*' cannot. And that he did hold that, if an expression '*p*' is 'the linguistic expression' of a *proposition* '*q*', then the expression '*p*' and the *expression* '*q*' have the same meaning was also suggested by a passage late in (III), where, having explained that by 'possible' he here meant 'logically possible', he asked the question 'Doesn't "I can't feel his toothache" mean that "I feel his toothache" has no sense?' obviously implying that the right answer to this question is 'Yes, it does'. And he also, in several other places, seemed to imply that '*p* can't be the case', where this means 'It is logically impossible that *p* should be the case' means the same as 'The sentence "*p*" has no sense'. I think that his view in the *Tractatus* that 'contradictions' are 'without sense' (sinnlos) may have been a deduction from this proposition. But why should he have held that 'tautologies' also are 'without sense'? I think that this view of his may have been, in part, a deduction from the conjunction of the proposition that 'It is logically impossible that *p*' means the same as 'The sentence "*p*" has no sense' with his principle, which I have already had occasion to mention (page 263), and which he said 'gave us some firm ground', that 'If a proposition has meaning, its negation also has meaning', where, as I pointed out, he seemed to be using 'proposition' to mean the same as 'sentence'. For it is logically impossible that the negation of a tautology should be true, and hence, if it is true that 'It is logically impossible that *p*' means the same as 'The sentence "*p*" has no sense', then it will follow from the conjunction of this proposition with his principle, that a 'tautology' (or should we say 'any sentence which expresses a tautology'?)

also has none. But why he thought (if he did) that 'It is logically impossible that p' means the same as 'The sentence "p" has no sense', I cannot explain. And it seems to me that if, as he certainly held, the former of these two propositions entails the latter, then the sentence 'It is logically impossible that p' must also have no sense; for can this sentence have any sense if the sentence 'p' has none? But, if 'It is logically impossible that p' has no sense, then, so far as I can see, it is quite impossible that it can mean the same as 'The sentence "p" has no sense', for this latter expression certainly has sense, if 'having sense' is being used in any ordinary way.

(β'') With regard to the expressions 'rules of grammar' or 'grammatical rules' he pointed out near the beginning of (I), where he first introduced the former expression, that when he said 'grammar should not allow me to say "greenish red" ', he was 'making things belong to grammar, which are not commonly supposed to belong to it'; and he immediately went on to say that the arrangement of colours in the colour octahedron 'is really a part of grammar, not of psychology'; that 'There is such a colour as a greenish blue' is 'grammar'; and that Euclidean Geometry is also 'a part of grammar'. In the interval between (II) and (III) I wrote a short paper for him in which I said that I did not understand how he was using the expression 'rule of grammar' and gave reasons for thinking that he was not using it in its ordinary sense; but he, though he expressed approval of my paper, insisted at that time that he was using the expression in its ordinary sense. Later, however, in (III), he said that 'any explanation of the use of language' was 'grammar', but that if I explained the meaning of 'flows' by pointing at a river 'we shouldn't naturally call this a rule of grammar'. This seems to suggest that by that time he was doubtful whether he was using 'rule of grammar' in quite its ordinary sense; and the same seems to be suggested by his saying, earlier in (III), that we should be using his 'jargon' if we said that whether a sentence made sense or not depended on 'whether or not it was constructed according to the rules of grammar'.

I still think that he was not using the expression 'rules of grammar' in any ordinary sense, and I am still unable to form any clear idea as to how he was using it. But, apart from his main contention (whatever that may have been) as to the connection between 'rules of grammar' (in his sense) and necessary propositions, there were two things upon which he seemed mainly anxious to insist about 'rules of grammar', namely (γ'), that they are all 'arbitrary' and (γ'') that they 'treat only of the symbolism'; and something ought certainly to be said about his treatment of these two points.

As for (γ') he often asserted without qualification that all 'rules of grammar' are arbitrary. But in (II) he expressly mentioned two senses of 'arbitrary' in which he held that some grammatical rules are *not* arbitrary, and in one place in (III) he said that the sense in which all were arbitrary was a 'peculiar' one. The two senses, of which he said in (II) that some grammatical rules were *not* arbitrary in those senses, were (1) a sense in which he said that rules about the use of single words were always 'in part' *not* arbitrary—a proposition which he thought followed from his proposition, which I have mentioned before (page 258), that all single words are significant only if 'we commit ourselves' by using them, and (2) a sense in which to say that a rule is an established rule in the language we are using is to say that it is not arbitrary: he gave, as an example, that if we followed a rule according to which 'hate' was an intransitive verb, this rule would be arbitrary, whereas 'if we use it in the sense in which we do use it', then the rule we are following is not arbitrary. But what, then, was the sense in which he held that all grammatical rules *are* arbitrary? This was a question to which he returned again and again in (II), trying to explain what the sense was, and to give reasons for thinking that in that sense they really are arbitrary. He first tried to express his view by saying that it is impossible to 'justify' any grammatical rule—a way of expressing it to which he also recurred later; but he also expressed it by saying that we can't 'give reasons' for grammatical rules, soon making clear that what he meant by this was that we can't give reasons for *following* any particular rule rather than a different one. And in trying to explain why we can't give reasons for following any particular rule, he laid very great stress on an argument, which he put differently in different places, and which I must confess I do not clearly understand. Two of the premisses of this argument are, I think, clear enough. One was (1) that any reason 'would have to be a description of reality': this he asserted in precisely those words. And the second was (2) that 'any

description of reality must be capable of truth and falsehood'
(these again were his own words), and it turned out, I think,
that part of what he meant by this was that any false description
must be significant. But to complete the argument he had to say
something like (what again he actually said in one place) 'and,
if it were false, it would have to be said in a language not using this
grammar'; and this is what I do not clearly understand. He gave as
an illustration of his meaning that it cannot be because of a
'quality in reality' that 'I use sweet' in such a way that 'sweeter'
has meaning, but 'identical' in such a way that 'more identical'
has none; giving as a reason 'If it were because of a "quality"
in reality, it must be possible to say that reality hasn't got this
quality, which grammar forbids'. And he had said previously
'I can't say what reality would have to be like, in order that
what makes nonsense should make sense, because in order to do so
I should have to use this new grammar'. But, though I cannot
put clearly the whole of his argument, I think one important point
results from what I have quoted—a point which he himself never
expressly pointed out. It results, namely, that he was using the
phrases 'description of reality' and 'quality in reality' in a restricted
sense—a sense, such that no statement to the effect that a certain
expression is actually used in a certain way is a 'description of
reality' or describes 'a quality in reality'. He was evidently so
using these terms that statements about the actual use of an
expression, although such statements are obviously experiential
propositions, are not to be called 'descriptions of reality'. He was
confining the term 'descriptions of reality' to expressions in which
no term is used as a name for itself. For if he were not, it is
obviously perfectly easy to say what reality would have to be like
in order that 'more identical', which is nonsense, should make
sense: we can say that if 'more identical' were used to mean what
we now mean by 'sweeter', then it would make sense; and the
proposition that 'more identical' is used in that way, even if it is a
false one (and I do not know for certain that the very words 'more
identical' are not used in that way in, e.g., some African language)
it is certainly not one which English grammar 'forbids' us to
make—it is certainly untrue that the sentence which expresses it
has no significance in English.

   It seems, therefore, that though in (II) he had said that what he
meant by saying that all 'grammatical rules' are 'arbitrary'

was that we cannot 'give reasons' for following any particular rule rather than a different one, what he meant was only that we cannot give reasons for so doing which are both (*a*) 'descriptions of reality' and (*b*) 'descriptions of reality' *of a particular sort*, viz. descriptions of reality which do not *mention*, or say anything *about*, any particular word or other expression, though of course they must *use* words or other expressions. And that this was his meaning is made, I think, plainer from a passage late in (III) in which he compared rules of deduction with 'the fixing of a unit of length' (or, as he said later, a 'standard' of length). He there said 'The reasons (if any) for fixing a unit of length do not make it "not arbitrary", in the sense in which a statement that so-and-so is the length of this object is not arbitrary', adding 'Rules of deduction are analogous to the fixing of a unit of length', and (taking '$3 + 3 = 6$' as an instance of a rule of deduction) ' "$3 + 3 = 6$" is a rule as to the way we are going to talk . . . it is a preparation for a description, just as fixing a unit of length is a preparation for measuring'. He seemed, therefore, here to be admitting that reasons *of a sort* can sometimes be given for following a particular 'grammatical rule', only not reasons of the special sort which a well-conducted operation of measurement may give (once the meaning of 'foot' has been fixed), for, e.g., the statement that a particular rod is less than four feet long. He did in fact mention in this connection that some 'grammatical rules' follow from others; in which case, of course, that they do so follow may be given as a reason for speaking in accordance with them. In this case, however, he would no doubt have said that the reason given is not a 'description of reality'. But it is obvious that reasons which are, in any ordinary sense, 'descriptions of reality' can also be given for following a particular rule; e.g. a particular person may give, as a reason for calling a particular length a 'foot', the 'description of reality' which consists in saying that that is how the word 'foot', when used for a unit of length, is generally used in English. And, in this case, of course, it may also be said that the reason why the word 'foot' was originally used, in English, as a name for the particular length which we do in fact so call, was that the length in question is not far from the length of those parts of a grown man's body which, in English, are called his 'feet'. In these cases, however, I think he might have urged with truth both (*a*) that the reason given, though a 'description of reality', is a description which 'mentions' or says something *about* the word 'foot' and does not merely *use* that word, and also (*b*) that it is not a reason for following the rule of calling that particular length a 'foot' in the same sense of the word 'reason' as that in which a well-conducted measurement may give a 'reason' for the statement that a particular rod is less than four feet long. It is surely obvious that a 'reason' for *acting* in a particular way, e.g. in this case, for using the word 'foot' for a particular length, cannot be a reason for so doing in the same sense of the word 'reason' as that in which a reason for thinking that so-and-so is the case may be a reason for so thinking. I think, therefore, if all these explanations are given, it becomes pretty clear in what sense Wittgenstein was using the word 'arbitrary' when he said that all grammatical rules were arbitrary.

But there remains one thing which he said in this connection which has puzzled me extremely. He actually introduced his comparison between rules of deduction and the fixing of a unit of length by saying: 'The statement that rules of deduction are neither true nor false is apt to give an uncomfortable feeling.' It appeared, therefore, as if he thought that this statement that they are neither true nor false followed from the statement that they are arbitrary, and that the comparison of them with the fixing of a unit of length would tend to remove this uncomfortable feeling, i.e. to make you see that they really are neither true nor false.

Now, in connection with his comparison between rules of deduction and the fixing of a unit of length, he gave (among other examples) as an example of a rule of deduction '3 + 3 = 6', and said a good deal about this example. And it certainly does give me a very uncomfortable feeling to be told that '3 + 3 = 6' is neither true nor false. But I think this uncomfortable feeling only arises because one thinks, if one is told this, that the *expression* '3 + 3 = 6' is being used in the way in which it most commonly is used, i.e. in the way in which it would commonly be said to be expressing a necessary proposition. And I think this uncomfortable feeling would completely vanish if it were clearly explained that the person who says this, is *not* using the expression '3 + 3 = 6' in this way, but in the very different way which I tried to distinguish above (page 269), i.e. the way in which it is merely used to specify a possible way of speaking and writing, which might or might not be actually adopted, although in this case the rule of speaking and writing in the way specified is, as a matter of fact, a well-established rule. I said that Wittgenstein never, so far as I knew, in these lectures expressly distinguished these two different ways of using the same expression (e.g. the expression '3 + 3 = 6'), but that I thought he did hold that, e.g., the expression '3 + 3 = 6' could be properly used in the second way as well as in the first, and that his thinking this might be partly responsible for his declaration that rules of deduction are neither true nor false (page 269). For it seemed to me quite obvious that, if the expression '3 + 3 = 6' is used in this second way, then it cannot possibly be either true or false. But I cannot help thinking that in this passage in (III) in which he compared rules of deduction with the fixing of a unit of length, he actually meant to say that even when used in the first way, i.e. in the way in which it would commonly be said to express a necessary proposition, it still expresses neither a true nor a false proposition.

In what he actually said about '3 + 3 = 6' in this passage, I think it is necessary to distinguish three different propositions which he made, of which the first two seem to me certainly true, but the third not to follow from the first two, and to be extremely doubtful. (1) He began by asking the question, 'Is "I've put 6 apples on the mantelpiece" the same as "I've put 3 there, and also another 3 there"?' and then, after pointing out that counting up to 3 in the case of each of two different groups, and arriving at the number '6' by counting *all* the apples, are 'three different experiences', he said 'You can imagine putting two groups of 3 there, and then finding only 5'. And the two propositions which seem to me certainly true are (*a*) that you can imagine this which he said you can imagine, and (*b*) (which he also said) that '3 + 3 = 6' does not 'prophesy' that, when you have had the two experiences of counting up to 3 in the case of each of two groups of apples which you certainly have put on the mantelpiece, you will also have the third experience of finding that there are 6 there, when you come to count *all* the apples that are there; or, in other words, he was saying that the proposition '3 + 3 = 6' is quite consistent with finding, by your third experience of counting, that there are only 5 there. This second proposition seems to me also true, because it seems to me clear that it is a

mere matter of experience, that when you have put two groups
of 3 apples on a mantelpiece, you will, under the circumstances
Wittgenstein was considering (e.g. that no apple has been taken
away) find that there are 6 there; or, in other words, it is a mere
matter of experience that apples don't simply vanish with no
apparent cause; and it surely should be obvious that '3 + 3 = 6'
certainly entails no more than that, *if* at any time there were in
any place two different groups, each numbering 3 apples, then
at that time there were 6 apples in the place in question: it entails
nothing about any future time. But (2) Wittgenstein went on to
add that if, on having put two groups of 3 on the mantelpiece,
and finding that there were only 5 there, you were to say (as you
certainly might under the circumstances he was considering)
'one must have vanished', this latter statement *only means* "If you
keep to the arithmetical rule '3 + 3 = 6' " you *have to say*
"One must have vanished" '. And it is this assertion of his
that, under the supposed circumstances, 'One must have vanished'
only means that, if you keep to a certain rule, you must *say so*,
which seems to me questionable and not to follow from the two
true propositions I have given under (1). (He had already said
something similar in (I) in connection with his very paradoxical
proposition that Euclidean Geometry is 'a part of grammar';
for he there said that what Euclid's proposition 'The three
angles of a triangle are equal to two right angles' asserts is 'If by
measurement you get any result for the sum of the three angles
other than 180°, you *are going to say* that you've made a mistake').

But I have been a good deal puzzled as to what he meant and
implied by this assertion that, under these circumstances the
words 'One must have vanished' *only mean* 'If you keep to the
arithmetical rule "3 + 3 = 6", you have to say so'. And, of
course, my view that it is very doubtful whether what he meant
and implied is true depends on my view as to what he did mean
and imply.

Of course, the circumstances under which he said that 'One
must have vanished' *only means* this, are extremely unusual:
possibly they never have happened and never will happen: but,
as I have said, I fully agree with him that they *might* happen—
that I can *imagine* their happening; and the question whether,
if they did, then the words 'One must have vanished' would *only
mean* what he says, seems to me to raise an extremely impor-

tant question, which does not only concern what would happen under these extremely unlikely circumstances, but concerns what is the case under circumstances which constantly do occur.

I will first try to state as accurately as I can what I take to be the circumstances he was supposing, and I will put them in the form of what he was supposing would be true of me, if I had been in those circumstances. He was supposing, I take it, (1) that I should know, because I had counted correctly, that I did put on the mantelpiece two groups of apples, each of which contained 3 apples and no more, (2) that I should know, by counting *at a subsequent time*, that there were *at that time* only 5 apples on the mantelpiece, (3) that I should also know, because I was watching all the time, that nothing had happened which would account in any normal way for the fact that, though I put 3 + 3 there, there are only 5 there now, e.g. I should know, in this way, that nobody had taken one away, that none had fallen off the mantelpiece, and that none had visibly flown away, and finally, (4) (and this, if I am not mistaken, was very essential to his point) that I should *not* know, by any operation of counting performed either by myself or by any other person who had told me his result, that I did put 6 apples on the mantelpiece, so that, if I asserted that I did put 6, this could only be a deduction from the proposition that I did put 3 + 3 there, which (1) asserts that I *have* found to be true by counting.

Under the circumstances stated in (1) and (3) I certainly should be very much surprised to find that what is stated in (2) was true, and I might quite naturally assert that one must have vanished, though I think I might equally naturally express my surprise by the use of words which contain no 'must', e.g. by saying 'Why! one has vanished!' And it is under these circumstances, if I am not mistaken, that Wittgenstein was asserting that if I did use the words 'One must have vanished' to make an assertion, these words would *'only mean'* 'If I keep to the arithmetical rule "3 + 3 = 6" I have to say that one must have vanished'.

And, first of all, I have felt some doubts on two separate points as to what he meant by the words 'you have to say so'. The first is this. I at first thought that he might be using the words 'say so', rather incorrectly, to mean 'say *the words* "One must have vanished" ' (or, of course, any equivalent words, e.g. in another language). But I now think there is no reason to suppose that he was not using the word 'say' quite correctly (i.e. as we usually do), to mean the same as 'assert', and there is some positive reason to suppose that he was doing so. One positive reason is that, among the circumstances which he was supposing was that which I have called (1), viz. that I should *know* that I did put $3 + 3$ apples on the mantelpiece; and I think he was certainly supposing that if I knew this, I should not merely say the words 'I put $3 + 3$ there', but should *assert* that I did—a proposition which does not seem to me certainly true, though, if I knew it, I should certainly be *willing* to assert it, unless I wanted to tell a lie. The second point is this: What did he mean by 'have to' in 'I should *have to* say so'? These words might naturally mean that I should be failing to keep to the rule '$3 + 3 = 6$' if I merely failed to assert that one must have vanished—if, for instance, I merely made no assertion. But I feel sure he did not mean to assert that I should be failing to keep to the rule (which I will in future call, for short, 'violating' the rule) if I merely omitted to say that one must have vanished. I think he certainly meant that I should be violating the rule only if I made some assertion the making of which was inconsistent with asserting that one must have vanished, e.g. if I asserted that none had vanished.

If I am right on these two points, his view as to what the words 'One must have vanished' would 'only mean' under the supposed circumstances, could be expressed more clearly as the view that these words would only mean 'If I assert that I put $3 + 3$ on the mantelpiece, I shall be keeping to the rule "$3 + 3 = 6$" if I also assert that one must have vanished, and shall be violating that rule, if I make any assertion the making of which is inconsistent with asserting that one must have vanished'. And I will, in future, assume that this was his view.

But now the question arises: Why should he have held that, under the supposed circumstances, the words 'One must have vanished' would 'only mean' a proposition which mentioned the arithmetical proposition '$3 + 3 = 6$'? How does '6' come in? I think the answer to this question is that he was assuming that among the propositions from which, under the supposed circumstances, the proposition that one had vanished would be a deduction (the 'must have', of course, indicates, as 'must' often does, that it would be a deduction from *some* propositions) would be not only the propositions given as known by me in (1), (2) and (3) of my description of the circumstances, but also the proposition 'I put 6 apples on the mantelpiece', which, according to (4) in my description is *not* known by me as a result of any operation of counting, but only, if at all, as a deduction from 'I put 3 + 3'. And I think his reason for asserting that, under the supposed circumstances 'One must have vanished' would 'only mean' what he said it would only mean, was that he was supposing that this sentence 'I put 6 on the mantelpiece' would *not*, under the circumstances described in (1) and (4), mean what it would mean if I had discovered, by counting *all* the apples I was putting on the mantelpiece, that I was putting 6, but, since I had not done this, would 'only mean' 'I shall be keeping to the rule "3 + 3 = 6", if I assert that I put 6, and shall be violating that rule if I make any assertion inconsistent with asserting that I put 6'—a proposition which to avoid clumsy repetitions, I will in future call 'B'. I think, therefore, he was implying that under the circumstances (1) and (4), the words 'I put 6 apples on the mantelpiece' would 'only mean' B. And I think the important question raised by his assertion as to what 'One must have vanished' would 'only mean' under circumstances (1), (2), (3) and (4), is this question as to whether, under circumstances (1) and (4), which might quite often occur, 'I put 6' would 'only mean' B—'only mean' being used, of course, in the same sense (whatever that may have been) in which he used it with regard to 'One must have vanished'.

But then the question arises: In what sense was he using the expression 'only mean'? If anyone tells us that, under the circumstances (1) and (4), the sentence 'I put 6 on the mantelpiece', if used to make an assertion, would 'only mean' B, I think the most natural interpretation of these words would be that anyone who, under circumstances (1) and (4), used this sentence to make an assertion would be using it to assert B. But I think it is quite incredible that anyone would ever actually use the expression 'I put 6' to assert B; and equally incredible that anyone would ever use the expression 'One must have vanished' to assert what Wittgenstein said would be their 'only meaning' under circumstances (1), (2), (3) and (4). In both cases the assertion which is said to be the 'only meaning' of a given expression is an assertion *about* the ordinary meaning of the expression in question, to the effect that you will be speaking in accordance with a certain rule if you use the expression in question to assert what it would be usually used to mean, and will be violating that rule if you make any assertion inconsistent with that ordinary meaning. And I think it is quite incredible that anybody would ever use a given expression to make such an assertion *about* the ordinary meaning of the expression in question; and, in both our cases, quite clear that anybody who did use the expression in question to make an assertion, would be using it to *make* the assertion which it would ordinarily mean, and not to make the assertion *about* its ordinary meaning which Wittgenstein said or implied would be its 'only meaning' under the circumstances described. And I do not think that he ever meant to make either of these incredible statements: he was not intending to say that the sentence 'One must have vanished' ever would be used, or could be properly used, to make the assertion which he says would be its 'only meaning' under the supposed circumstances. But, if so, how was he using the expression 'only mean'? I think he was using it, not in its most natural sense, but loosely, in a more or less natural sense, to say that the assertion which he said would be its 'only meaning' under the circumstances described, would be *the* true proposition which resembled most closely a proposition which he held to be false, but which he knew was commonly held to be true. In the case of 'I put 6', if he implied, as I think he did, that, under circumstances (1) and (4), 'I put 6' would 'only mean' B, the proposition which he held to be false was the proposition that if I put 3 + 3, it is *necessarily* also true that I put 6, and the proposition which he held to be *the* true proposition which most closely resembled this false proposition, and which might therefore have misled those who think to be true this proposition which he held to be false, was that, if 'I put 3 + 3' was true, then B would be true. I think, in fact, he was holding that the proposition that in putting 3 + 3 on the mantelpiece, I was *necessarily* putting 6 there, was false; that I can imagine that in putting 3 + 3 there, I was, e.g., only putting 5, and that, if there ever were 3 + 3 on the mantel-piece, nevertheless, if anybody had counted correctly how many there were altogether *at that very time*, he would possibly have found that there were only 5.

But whether or not he held, as I think he did, that in putting

3 + 3 apples on the mantelpiece, I was not necessarily putting 6, I think it is quite certain that he held another proposition, about the relation of which to this one I am not clear. He held, namely, that the expression '3 + 3 = 6' is *never* used in Arithmetic, not therefore even when it would commonly be held to express a necessary proposition, to express a proposition from which it follows that if I put 3 + 3, I necessarily put 6. And this view seems to me to follow from his two views (1) that (as is suggested by his phrase 'the arithmetical *rule* "3 + 3 = 6" ') the expression '3 + 3 = 6', as used in Arithmetic, *always* only expresses a 'rule of grammar', and (2) that rules of grammar 'treat only of the symbolism'. I shall shortly have to point out that there seems to me to be a serious difficulty in understanding exactly what he meant by saying that, e.g., '3 + 3 = 6' 'treats only of the symbolism'; but I think there is no doubt he meant at least this: that you will be speaking in accordance with that rule if, when you *assert* that you put 3 + 3, you also *assert* that you put 6, and violating it if, having *asserted* the former, you make any assertion the making of which is incompatible with asserting the latter, but that it by no means follows that, if you keep to the rule, what you assert will be *true*, nor yet that, if you violate it, what you assert will be *false*: in either case, he held, what you assert *may* be true, but also *may* be false. And I think his reason for this view of his can be made plainer by noticing that since (as he implies by his phrase 'the arithmetical rule "3 + 3 = 6" ') '3 + 3 = 6' is a well-established rule (if a rule of grammar at all), it will follow that, if you keep to that rule, you will be using language 'correctly' (or, with his use of 'grammar', speaking 'grammatically'), and that, if you violate it will be speaking 'incorrectly' (or, with his use of 'grammar', guilty of bad grammar); and that from the fact that you are using language correctly, in the sense of 'in accordance with an established rule', it by no means follows that what you assert, by this correct use of language, is 'correct' in the very different sense in which 'That is correct' = 'That is true', nor from the fact that you are using language incorrectly that what you assert by this incorrect use of language is 'incorrect' in the very different sense in which 'That is incorrect' = 'That is false'. It is obvious that you may be using language just as correctly when you use it to assert something false as when you use it to assert something true, and that when

you are using it incorrectly, you may just as easily be asserting something true by this incorrect use as something false. It by no means follows, for instance, from the fact that you are using the word 'foot' 'correctly', i.e. for the length for which it is usually used in English, that when you make such an assertion as 'This rod is less than four feet long', your assertion is true; and, if you were to use it 'incorrectly' for the length which is properly called in English an 'inch' or for that which is properly called a 'yard', it would by no means follow that any assertion you made by this incorrect use of the word 'foot' was false. I think Wittgenstein thought that similarly you will be using the phrase 'I put 6' correctly, if, when you assert that you put 3 + 3, you also assert that you put 6, and incorrectly if, when you assert that you put 3 + 3, you deny that you put 6, or even assert that it is possible that you did not put 6; and that this is *the* true proposition which has led people to assume, what he thought false, that the expression '3 + 3 = 6' is used in Arithmetic to express a proposition from which it follows that if I put 3 + 3, I necessarily put 6.

And I think this view of his also gives the chief explanation of what he meant by the puzzling assertion that 3 + 3 = 6 (and *all* rules of deduction, similarly) is neither true nor false. I think what he chiefly meant by saying this was not, as I suggested above (page 269) that 3 + 3 = 6 was a 'rule' in the sense in which rules can obviously be neither true nor false, but that he was using 'true' in a restricted sense, in which he would have said that 3 + 3 = 6 was only 'true' if it followed from it (as he denied to be the case) that if I put 3 + 3 on the mantelpiece, I necessarily put 6; in a sense, therefore, in which, even if, as I suggested (page 269), he sometimes used 'rule' in a sense in which the proposition 'You can't *say* that you put 3 + 3, and *deny* that you put 6'—a proposition which he held to be true in any ordinary sense, he would nevertheless have said that this proposition was not 'true', because it was a proposition about how words are actually used. I think he was using 'true' and 'false' in a restricted sense, just as he was using 'description of reality' in a restricted sense (above, page 279), i.e. in a sense in which no propositions about how words are used can be said to be 'true' or 'false'.

And the reason why I think it very doubtful whether he was right in holding (if he did hold) that it is not true that in putting 3 + 3 on the mantelpiece, I necessarily also put 6, is that I do not think I can imagine that in putting 3 + 3, I was not putting 6. I have already said (page 281) that I agree with him that I can imagine that, having put 3 + 3 there, I should find at *a subsequent time* that there were only 5 there, even under the circumstances described in (3) of my description of the circumstances he was supposing: I can imagine, I think, that one has really vanished. But it seems to be quite a different question whether I can imagine that, in putting 3 + 3, I was not putting 6, or that, if at any time there were 3 + 3 on the mantelpiece, there were *at that time* not 6 there. I admit, however, that the propositions that I was putting 6, or that there were 6 on the mantelpiece, do seem to me to entail that, *if* anybody had counted correctly, he would have found that there were 6; I am, therefore, implying that I cannot imagine these hypothetical propositions not to be true: but I do not think I can imagine this. And I also can see no reason to think that the expression '3 + 3 = 6' is never used in Arithmetic to express a proposition from which it follows that if I put 3 + 3, I put 6. I am not convinced that this expression, in Arithmetic, *always* only expresses a 'grammatical rule', i.e. a rule as to what language it will be correct to use, even if it sometimes does. Wittgenstein has not succeeded in removing the 'uncomfortable feeling' which it gives me to be told that '3 + 3 = 6' and '($p \supset q . p$) entails q' are neither true nor false.

(γ'') As for the proposition that rules of grammar 'treat only of the symbolism', he never, at least while I was present, expressly pointed out that such an expression as '2 = 1 + 1' can be used to express at least three very different propositions. It can be used (1) in such a way that anybody could understand what proposition or rule it was being used to express, provided only he understood how the sign '=' was being used, and did not understand either the expression '2' or the expression '1 + 1' except as names for themselves (what has been called 'autonymously'). But it can be used (2) in such a way that nobody could understand what proposition or rule it was being used to express, unless he understood non-autonymously both the sign '=' and also the expression '1 + 1', but need not understand the expression '2' other than autonymously. Or (3) it can be used in such a way that nobody could understand what proposition or rule it was being used to express, unless he understood non-autonymously *both* the expression '2' and the expression '1 + 1', as well as the

K

expression '$=$'. But, though he did not expressly point out that, e.g., '$2 = 1 + 1$' could be used in each of these three very different ways, he said things which seem to me to imply the view that in Arithmetic it was *only* used in the first way. He said, for instance, in (II) 'To explain the meaning of a sign means only to substitute one sign for another', and again, later on, 'An explanation of a proposition is always of the same kind as a definition, i.e. replacing one symbol by another'. In making these statements, he seems to me to have been confusing the true proposition that you can only explain the meaning of one sign by *using* other signs, with the proposition, which seems to me obviously false, that, when you explain the meaning of one sign by *using* another, all you are asserting is that the two signs have the same meaning or can be substituted for one another: he seems in fact to have been asserting that propositions, which are in fact of form (2), are only of form (1). And this mistake seems to be responsible for the astounding statement which he actually made in (III) that Russell had been mistaken in thinking that '$=$ Def.' had a different meaning from '$=$'. It seems to me obvious that a statement can only be properly called a 'definition' or 'explanation' of the meaning of a sign, if, in order to understand what statement you are making by the words you use, it is necessary that the hearer or reader should understand the *definiens*, and not merely take it as a name for itself. When, for instance, *Principia Mathematica* defines the meaning of the symbol '$\supset$' by saying that '$p \supset q$' is to mean '$\sim p \vee q$', it is surely obvious that nobody can understand what statement is being made as to how '$\supset$' will be used, unless he understands the expression '$\sim p \vee q$', and does not take it merely as a name for itself; and that therefore the statement which is being made is not merely a statement of form (1), to the effect that the two different expressions '$p \supset q$' and '$\sim p \vee q$' have the same meaning or can be substituted for one another, but a statement of form (2), i.e. that the *definiens* '$\sim p \vee q$' is *not* being used autonymously, though the *definiendum* '$\supset$' *is* being used autonymously.

But the most serious difficulty in understanding what he meant by saying that, e.g., '$3 + 3 = 6$' 'treats only of the symbolism' seems to me to arise from a question with which he only dealt briefly at the end of (I), and with which he there dealt only in a way which I certainly do not at all completely understand; namely, the question: Of *what* symbols did he suppose that '3 + 3 = 6' was treating? He did indeed actually assert in (III) that the proposition 'red is a primary colour' was a proposition about the word 'red'; and, if he had seriously held this, he might have held similarly that the proposition or rule '3 + 3 = 6' was merely a proposition or rule about the particular expressions '3 + 3' and '6'. But he cannot have held seriously either of these two views, because the *same* proposition which is expressed by the words 'red is a primary colour' can be expressed in French or German by words which say nothing about the English word 'red'; and similarly the *same* proposition or rule which is expressed by '3 + 3 = 6' was undoubtedly expressed in Attic Greek and in Latin by words which say nothing about the Arabic numerals '3' and '6'. And this was a fact which he seemed to be admitting in the passage at the end of (I) to which I refer. In this passage, which he introduced by saying that he would answer objections to the view (which he held) that the arithmetical calculus 'is a game', he began by saying, very emphatically, that it is *not* a game 'with ink and paper'; by which he perhaps meant (but I do not know) that it is not a game with the Arabic numerals. He went on to say that Frege had concluded from the fact that Mathematics is not a game 'with ink and paper' that it dealt not with the symbols but with 'what is symbolized'—a view with which he apparently disagreed. And he went on to express his own alternative view by saying 'What is essential to the rules is the logical multiplicity which all the different possible symbols have in common'; and here, by speaking of 'all the different possible symbols', I take it he was admitting, what is obvious, that the *same* rules which are expressed by the use of the Arabic numerals may be expressed by ever so many different symbols. But if the rules 'treat only of the symbolism' how can two rules which treat of *different* symbols, e.g. of '3' and 'III', possibly be the *same* rule? I suppose he must have thought that we use the word 'same' in such a sense that two rules, which are obviously *not* the same, in that they treat of different symbols, are yet said to be the same, provided only that the rules for their use have the same 'logical multiplicity' (whatever that may mean). But he never, I think, at least while I was present, returned to this point, or tried to explain and defend his view.

He did, however, in this passage, compare the rules of Arithmetic to the rules of chess, and used of chess the phrase, 'What

is characteristic of chess is the logical multiplicity of its rules'
just as he used of Mathematics the phrase 'What is essential
to its rules is the logical multiplicity which all the different
possible symbols have in common'. I doubt, however, whether
he was right in what he meant by saying '*What* is characteristic
of chess is the logical multiplicity of its rules', which, of course,
implies that this is sufficient to characterize chess. He was
undoubtedly right in saying that the material and the shape of
which the different pieces are commonly made is irrelevant to
chess: chess could certainly be played with pieces of any material
and any shape, e.g. with pieces of paper which were all of the
same shape. But if by 'the rules of chess' he meant, as I think
he probably did, the rules which govern the moves which may
be made by pieces of different sorts, e.g. by pawns and bishops,
and was suggesting that the 'logical multiplicity' of the rules
which govern the possible moves of a pawn and a bishop is
sufficient to distinguish a pawn from a bishop, I think he was
wrong. The rule that a pawn can only make certain moves certainly, I think, does not mean that any piece the rules for the
moves of which have a certain 'logical multiplicity' (whatever
that may mean) may only make the moves in question, even if he
was right in holding that the rules for the moves of pawns have a
different 'logical multiplicity' from those for the moves of bishops;
and similarly in the case of all the other different kinds of pieces.
Though a pawn is certainly not necessarily distinguished from a
bishop or a knight by its shape, as it usually is, it seems to me
that it is necessarily distinguished by the positions which it may
occupy at the beginning of the game, so that a rule which states
that pawns can only make such and such moves, states that pieces
which occupy certain positions at the beginning of the game can
only make such and such moves; and similarly with all the other
different kinds of piece: they are all necessarily distinguished
from one another by the positions which they occupy at the
beginning of the game, where 'necessarily' means that it would
not be chess that you were playing, if the pieces to which different
kinds of move are allowed, did not occupy certain positions rela-
tively to one another at the beginning of the game. Of course,
if you did play chess with pieces of paper which were all of the
same shape, it would be necessary that the pieces should have
some mark to show what positions they had occupied at the

beginning of the game, as might be done, for instance, by writing 'pawn' on those pieces which had occupied certain positions, and, e.g. 'bishop' on those which had occupied others; and it would also be necessary to distinguish by some mark (what is usually done by a difference of colour) those pieces which belonged to one of the two players from those which belonged to the other, as could, e.g., be easily done by writing an 'O' on all the pieces which belonged to one player, and a '+' on all which belonged to the other. I think, therefore, he was probably wrong in holding, as he apparently did, that the rules of chess are completely analogous, in respect of their relation to 'logical multiplicity', to what he held to be true of the rules of Arithmetic.

There remains one other matter which should be mentioned in treating of his views about necessary propositions. He made a good deal of use, especially in (II) in discussing rules of deduction, of the expression 'internal relation', even asserting in one place 'What justifies inference is an internal relation'. He began the discussion in which he made this assertion by saying that 'following' is called a 'relation' as if it were like 'fatherhood'; but said that where, for example, it is said that a proposition of the form '$p \lor q$' 'follows' from the corresponding proposition of the form '$p \cdot q$', the so-called 'relation' is 'entirely determined by the two propositions in question', and that, this being so, the so-called 'relation' is 'entirely different from other relations'. But it soon became plain that, when he said this about 'following', it was only one of the proper uses of the word 'follow' in English, as between two propositions, of which he was speaking, namely, that use which is sometimes called 'follows logically': he did, in fact, constantly use the word 'inference' as if it meant the same as 'deductive inference'. How he made plain that what he was talking of as 'following' was only 'following logically', was that he immediately went on to say that the kind of 'following' of which he was speaking, and which he exemplified by the sense in which any proposition of the form '$p \lor q$' 'follows' from the corresponding proposition of the form '$p \cdot q$', was 'quite different' from what is meant when, e.g., we say that a wire of a certain material and diameter *can't* support a piece of iron of a certain weight—a proposition which he actually expressed in the next lecture (quite correctly according to English usage) as the proposi-

tion that 'it *follows* from the weight of the piece of iron and the
material and diameter of the wire, that the wire will break if you
try to support that piece of iron by it'. He went on to express the
difference between these two uses of 'follow', by saying that, in
the case of the wire and the piece of iron, both (*a*) 'it remains
thinkable that the wire will not break', and (*b*) that 'from the
weight of the piece of iron and the material and diameter of the
wire *alone*, I can't know that the wire will break', whereas in the
case of a proposition of the form '$p \vee q$' and the corresponding
proposition of the form '$p \cdot q$' 'following' is an 'internal relation',
which, he said, means 'roughly speaking' 'that it is *unthinkable*
that the relation should not hold between the terms'. And he
immediately went on to say that the *general* proposition '$p \vee q$
follows from $p \cdot q$' 'is not wanted'; that 'if you can't see', by looking
at two propositions of these forms that the one follows from the
other, 'the general proposition won't help you'; that, if I say of
a proposition of the form '$p \vee q$' that it follows from the corresponding proposition of the form '$p \cdot q$' 'everything here is
useless, except the two propositions themselves'; and that if
another proposition were needed to justify our statement that
the first follows from the second, 'we should need an infinite
series'. He finally concluded 'A rule of inference' (meaning
'deductive inference') 'never justifies an inference'.

In the next lecture, which he began, as he often did, by
repeating (sometimes in a slightly different form and, if necessary,
with added explanations and corrections) the main points which
he had intended to make at the end of the preceding one, he
said that to say of one proposition 'q' that it 'follows' from another
'p' '*seems* to say that there is a relation between them which
justifies passing from one to the other', but that 'what makes one
suspicious about this is that we perceive the relation by merely
looking at the propositions concerned—that it is "internal"
and not like the proposition that "This wire will break" follows
from the weight of the iron and the material and diameter of the
wire'; and here he immediately went on to add that the expression
'internal relation' is misleading, and that he used it 'only because
others had used it'; and he proceeded to give a slightly different
formulation of the way in which the expression had been used,
viz. 'A relation which holds if the terms are what they are, and
which cannot therefore be imagined not to hold'. He also, shortly

afterwards, gave some further explanation of what he had meant by saying that if a rule were needed to justify the statement that one proposition follows (logically) from another, we should need an infinite series. He said that if a rule r, were needed to justify an inference from p to q, q would follow from the conjunction of p and r, so that we should need a fresh rule to justify the inference from this conjunction to q, and so on *ad infinitum*. Hence, he said, 'an inference can only be justified by what we see', and added that 'this holds throughout Mathematics'. He then gave his truth-table notation for '$p \lor q$' and '$p \cdot q$', and said that the 'criterion' for the statement that the former follows from the latter was that 'to every T in the latter there corresponds a T in the former'. He said that, in saying this, he had stated 'a rule of inference', but that this rule was only a 'rule of grammar' and 'treated only of the symbolism'. A little later he said that the relation of 'following' can be 'represented' by 'tautologies' (in his special sense), but that the tautology '$(p \cdot q) \supset (p \lor q)$' does not *say* that $p \lor q$ follows from $p \cdot q$, because it says nothing, but that the fact that it is a tautology *shows* that $p \lor q$ follows from $p \cdot q$. And a little later still he said that the relation of following 'can be seen by looking at the *signs*', and seemed to identify this with saying that it is 'internal'; and the fact that he here said that it can be seen by looking at the *signs*, whereas he had previously said that it can be seen by looking at the *propositions*, seems to me to show that, as I said (page 263) seemed to be often the case, he was identifying 'sentences' with 'propositions'. Finally he introduced a new phrase, in explanation of his view that the expression 'internal relation' is misleading, saying that internal and external relations are 'categorically' different; and he used the expression 'belong to different categories' later on in (III), where he said that 'follows' and 'implies' (a word which he here used, as Russell had done, as if it meant the same as the *Principia* symbol '$\supset$') 'belong to different categories'; adding the important remark that whether one proposition 'follows' from another 'cannot depend at all upon their truth of falsehood', and saying that it only depends on 'an internal *or grammatical* relation'.

III

(B) In the case of Logic, there were two most important matters with regard to which he said that the views he had held when he wrote the *Tractatus* were definitely wrong.

(1) The first of these concerned what Russell called 'atomic' propositions and he himself in the *Tractatus* had called 'Elementarsätze'. He said in (II) that it was with regard to 'elementary' propositions and their connection with truth-functions or 'molecular' propositions that he had had to change his opinions most; and that this subject was connected with the use of the words 'thing' and 'name'. In (III) he began by pointing out that neither Russell nor he himself had produced any examples of 'atomic' propositions; and said that there was something wrong indicated by this fact, though it was difficult to say exactly what. He said that both he and Russell had the idea that non-atomic propositions could be 'analysed' into atomic ones, but that we did not yet know what the analysis was: that, e.g., such a proposition as 'It is raining' might, if we knew its analysis, turn out to be molecular, consisting, e.g., of a conjunction of 'atomic' propositions. He said that in the *Tractatus* he had objected to Russell's assumption that there certainly were atomic propositions which asserted two-termed relations—that he had refused to prophesy as to what would be the result of an analysis, if one were made, and that it might turn out that no atomic proposition asserted less than, e.g., a four-termed relation, so that we could not even talk of a two-termed relation. His present view was that it was senseless to talk of a 'final' analysis, and he said that he would now treat as atomic all propositions in the expression of which neither 'and', 'or', nor 'not' occurred, nor any expression of generality, provided we had not expressly given an exact definition, such as we might give of 'It's rotten weather', if we said we were going to use the expression 'rotten' to mean 'both cold and damp'.

In saying this he seemed to me to be overlooking both the fact that a man often says that he is going to use an expression in a certain definite way and then does not in fact so use it, and also the fact that many common words, e.g. father, mother, sister, brother, etc., are often so used that such a sentence as 'This is my father' undoubtedly expresses a molecular proposition, although a person who so uses it has never expressly stated that he will so use it. These two facts, however, of course, do not prove that he was wrong in thinking that it is senseless to talk of a 'final' or 'ultimate' analysis.

(2) The second important logical mistake which he thought he had made at the time when he wrote the *Tractatus* was introduced by him in (III) in connection with the subject of 'following' (by which he meant, as usual, *deductive* following or 'entailment'—a word which I think he actually used in this discussion) from a 'general' proposition to a particular instance and from a particular instance to a 'general' proposition. Using the notation of *Principia Mathematica*, he asked us to consider the two propositions '(x) . fx entails fa' and 'fa entails $(\exists x)$. fx'. He said that there was a temptation, to which he had yielded in the *Tractatus*, to say that (x) . fx is identical with the logical product 'fa . fb . fc . . .', and $(\exists x)$. fx identical with the logical sum 'fa v fb v fc . . .'; but that this was in both cases a mistake. In order to make clear exactly where the mistake lay, he first said that in the case of such a universal proposition as 'Everybody in this room has a hat' (which I will call 'A'), he had known and actually said in the *Tractatus*, that, even if Smith, Jones and Robinson are the only people in the room, the logical product 'Smith has a hat, Jones has a hat and Robinson has a hat' cannot possibly be identical with A, because in order to get a proposition which entails A, you obviously have to add 'and Smith, Jones and Robinson are the only people in the room'. But he went on to say that if we are talking of 'individuals' in Russell's sense (and he actually here mentioned atoms as well as colours, as if they were 'individuals' in this sense), the case is different, because, in that case, there is no proposition analogous to 'Smith, Jones and Robinson are the only people in the room'. The class of things in question, if we are talking of 'individuals', is, he said, in this case, determined not by a proposition but by our 'dictionary': it is 'defined by grammar'. For example, he said that the class 'primary colour' is 'defined by grammar', not by a proposition; that there is no such proposition as 'red is a primary colour', and that such a proposition as 'In this square there is one of the primary colours' really is identical with the logical sum 'In this square there is either red or green or blue or yellow'; whereas in the case of Smith, Jones and Robinson, there is such a proposition as 'Smith is in this room' and hence

K*

also such a proposition as 'Smith, Jones and Robinson are the
only people in this room'. He went on to say that one great
mistake which he made in the *Tractatus* was that of supposing
that in the case of *all* classes 'defined by grammar', general
propositions were identical either with logical products or with
logical sums (meaning by this logical products or sums of the
propositions which are values of *fx*) as, according to him, they
really are in the case of the class 'primary colours'. He said
that, when he wrote the *Tractatus*, he had supposed that *all* such
general propositions were 'truth-functions'; but he said now
that in supposing this he was committing a fallacy, which is
common in the case of Mathematics, e.g. the fallacy of supposing
that $1 + 1 + 1 \ldots$ is a sum, whereas it is only a *limit*, and that
$\dfrac{dx}{dy}$ is a quotient, whereas it also is only a *limit*. He said he had
been misled by the fact that $(x) . fx$ can be replaced by $fa . fb . fc \ldots$,
having failed to see that the latter expression is not always a
logical product: that it is only a logical product if the dots are
what he called 'the dots of laziness', as where we represent the
alphabet by 'A, B, C . . .', and therefore the whole expression
can be replaced by an enumeration; but that it is not a logical
product where, e.g., we represent the cardinal numbers by 1, 2,
3 . . ., where the dots are not the 'dots of laziness' and the whole
expression cannot be replaced by an enumeration. He said that,
when he wrote the *Tractatus*, he would have defended the mistaken
view which he then took by asking the question: How can $(x) . fx$
possibly entail fa, if $(x) . fx$ is not a logical product? And he said
that the answer to this question is that where $(x) . fx$ is not a
logical product, the proposition '$(x) . fx$ entails fa' is 'taken as a
primary proposition', whereas where it is a logical product this
proposition is deduced from other primary propositions.

The point which he here made in saying that where we talk
of the cardinal numbers we are not talking of a logical product
was a point which he had made earlier, in (I), though he did not
there point out that in the *Tractatus* he had made the mistake
of supposing that an infinite series was a logical product—that it
could be enumerated, though we were unable to enumerate it.
In this passage in (I) he began by saying that by the proposition
'there are an infinite number of shades of grey between black
and white' we 'mean something entirely different' from what

we mean by, e.g., 'I see three colours in this room', because, whereas the latter proposition can be verified by counting, the former cannot. He said that 'There are an infinite number' does not give an answer to the question 'How many are there?' whereas 'There are three' does give an answer to this question. He went on to discuss infinite divisibility in the case of space, and said (as I have already mentioned, pages 274-5), that the 'linguistic expression' of 'This line can be bisected' was 'The words "This line has been bisected" have sense', but that the 'linguistic expression' of 'This line can be infinitely divided' is certainly not 'The words "This line has been infinitely divided" have sense'. He said that if we express 'has been bisected', 'has been trisected' 'has been quadrisected', etc., by $f(1 + 1), f(1 + 1 + 1), f(1 + 1 + 1 + 1)$, etc., we see that an internal relation holds between successive members of this series and that the series has no end; and he concluded by saying that the 'linguistic expression' of an infinite possibility is an infinite possibility in language. He also pointed out that $\Sigma 1 + \frac{1}{2} + \frac{1}{4} \ldots$ approaches a limit, whereas a logical product does not approach any limit. And he said finally that the cases to which the *Principia* notations $(x) . \phi x$ and $(\exists x) . \phi x$ apply, i.e. cases in which the former can be regarded as a logical product and the latter as a logical sum of propositions of the form ϕa, ϕb, ϕc, etc., are comparatively rare; that oftener we have propositions, such as 'I met a man', which do not 'presuppose any totality'; that the cases to which the *Principia* notations apply are only those in which we could give proper names to the entities in question; and that giving proper names is only possible in very special cases.

Besides these two cardinal cases, in which he said that the views which he had held at the time when he wrote the *Tractatus* were certainly wrong, I think that the chief logical points which he made were as follows.

(3) One point which he made was that Russell was quite wrong in supposing that, if expressions of the form '$p \supset q$' are used with the meaning which is given to '$\supset$' in *Principia Mathematica*, then it follows that from a false proposition we *can infer* every other proposition, and that from a true one we *can infer* any other true one. He said that Russell's holding this false opinion was partly due to his supposing that '$p \supset q$' can be translated by 'If p, then q'. He said that we never use 'If p, then q' to mean

merely what is meant by '$p \supset q$'; and that Russell had admitted this, but still maintained that in the case of what he called 'formal implications', i.e. propositions of the form $(x) . \phi x \supset \psi x$, such a proposition can be properly translated by 'If . . ., then . . .'. Wittgenstein said that this also was a mistake, giving as a reason that if, e.g., we substitute 'is a man' for ϕ and 'is mortal' for ψ, then the mere fact that there were no men would verify (x). $\phi x \supset \psi x$, but that we never so use 'If . . ., then . . .' that the mere fact that there were no men would verify 'If anything is a man, then that thing is mortal'.

(4) He also, on more than one occasion, said something about Sheffer's 'stroke notation', and, on one occasion, about Tarski's[1] '3-valued' Logic.

About the former he said that it resembled what are called mathematical 'discoveries' in respect of the fact that Sheffer had no rule for discovering an answer to the question 'Is there only one logical constant?' whereas there is a rule for discovering, e.g., the answer to a multiplication sum. He said that, where there is no rule, it is misleading to use the word 'discovery', though this is constantly done. He said that Russell or Frege might quite well have used the expression 'p/q' as short for '$\sim p . \sim q$', and yet still maintained that they had two primitive ideas, 'and' and 'not', and not one only. Plainly, therefore, he thought that Sheffer, though he admitted that Sheffer had actually defined 'p/q' as meaning '$\sim p . \sim q$', had done something else. But what else? He said that Sheffer's 'discovery' consisted in finding a 'new aspect' of certain expressions. But I am sorry to say that I did not and do not understand what he meant by this.

On Tarski's 3-valued Logic he said that it was all right 'as a calculus'—that Tarski had really 'discovered' a new calculus. But he said that 'true' and 'false' could not have in it the meaning which they actually have; and he particularly emphasized that Tarski had made the mistake of supposing that his third value, which he called 'doubtful', was identical with what we ordinarily mean by 'doubtful'.

(C) Of problems which are specifically problems in the philosophy of Mathematics, I think that those which he most discussed are the three following. But in this case I should like to remind

[1] See the correction on p 324.

the reader of what I said in the first part of this article (page 256) that I cannot possibly mention nearly everything which he said, and that it is possible that some things which I omit were really more important than what I mention; and also to give the warning that in this case it is particularly likely that I may have mis-understood or may misrepresent him, since my own knowledge of Mathematics is very small. But I think that what I say will at least give some idea of the *kind* of questions which he was eager to discuss.

(1) In (I) he said that there were two very different kinds of proposition used in Mathematics, 'neither of them at all like what are usually called propositions'. These were (1) propositions proved by a chain of equations, in which you proceed from axioms to other equations, by means of axioms, and (2) proposi-tions proved by 'mathematical induction'. And he added in (III) that proofs of the second kind, which he there called 'recur-sive proofs', are not proofs in the same *sense* as are proofs of the first kind. He added that people constantly commit the fallacy of supposing that 'true', 'problem', 'looking for', 'proof' always mean the same, whereas in fact these words 'mean entirely different things' in different cases.

As an example of a proposition of the second kind he took the Associative Law for the addition of numbers, namely, '$a + (b + c) = (a + b) + c$'; and he discussed the proof of this proposition at considerable length on two separate occasions, first in (I) and then later in (III). On both occasions he discussed a proof of it given by Skolem, though in (I) he did not expressly say that the proof discussed was Skolem's. He said in (I) that the proof seemed to assume at one point the very proposition which it professed to prove, and he pointed out in (III) that in one of the steps of his proof Skolem did actually assume the Associative Law. He said that since Skolem professed to be giving a proof, one would have expected him to prove it from other formulae, but that in fact the proof begins in an entirely different way, namely with a definition—the definition '$a + (b + 1) = (a + b) + 1$'; and he maintained both in (I) and in (III) that it was quite unnecessary for Skolem to assume the Associative Law in one step of his proof, saying in (I) that the proof 'really rests entirely on the definition', and in (III) that you don't in fact use the Associative Law in the proof at all.

He wrote the proof 'in his own way' in order to show this, saying that if you write the definition in the form '$\phi 1 = \psi 1$', then all that is proved is the two formulae $(a)\phi(c + 1) = \phi c + 1$ and $(b)\psi(c + 1) = \psi c + 1$, and that to prove these two formulae is the same thing as what is called 'proving the Associative Law *for all numbers*'. He went on to say that the fact that this proof proves all we want 'shows that we are not dealing with an extension at all'; that instead of talking of a *finite part* of the series '1, 2, 3 . . .', on the one hand, and of the *whole* series on the other hand, we should talk of a bit of the series and of *the Law which generates it*; that proving the Associative Law 'for *all* numbers' can't mean the same sort of thing as proving it, e.g., for three numbers, since, in order to do this latter, you would have to give a separate proof for each of the three; and that what we have in the proof is a general *form* of proof for *any* number. Finally he said that the generality which is misleadingly expressed by saying that we have proved the Associative Law for '*all* cardinals', really comes in in the definition, which might have been written in the form of a series, viz. '$1 + (1 + 1) = (1 + 1) + 1$' '$1 + (2 + 1) = (1 + 2) + 1$' '$2 + (1 + 1) = (2 + 1) + 1$' *and so on*; and that this series is not a logical product of which the examples given are a part, but a *rule*, and that 'the examples are only there to explain the rule'.

(2) Another problem in the philosophy of Mathematics, which he discussed on no less than three separate occasions, was what we are to say of the apparent question 'Are there anywhere in the development of π three consecutive 7's?' (Sometimes he took the question 'Are there *five* consecutive 7's?' instead of 'Are there three?') He first dealt with this apparent question in (I), in connection with Brouwer's view that the Law of Excluded Middle does not apply to some mathematical propositions; i.e. that some mathematical propositions are neither true nor false; that there is an alternative to being either true or false, viz. being 'undecidable'. And on this occasion he said that the words 'There are three consecutive 7's in the development of π' are nonsense, and that hence not only the Law of Excluded Middle does not apply in this case, but that no laws of Logic apply in it; though he admitted that if someone developed π for ten years and actually found three consecutive 7's in the development, this would prove that there were three consecutive 7's *in a ten years' development*, and seemed to be admitting, therefore, that

·it is possible that there might be. The next time he discussed the question, early in (III), he said that if anyone actually found three consecutive 7's this would prove that there are, but that if no one found them that wouldn't prove that there are not; that, therefore, it is something for the truth of which we have provided a test, but for the falsehood of which we have provided none; and that therefore it must be a quite different sort of thing from cases in which a test for both truth and falsehood is provided. He went on to discuss the apparent question in a slightly new way. He said we seem to be able to define π' as the number which, if there are three consecutive 7's in the development of π, differs from π in that, in the place in which three consecutive 7's occur in π, there occur in it three consecutive 1's instead, but which, if there are not, does not differ from π at all; and that we seem to be able to say that π', so defined, either is identical with π or is not. But he said here that, since we have no way of finding out whether π' is identical with π or not, the question whether it is or not 'has no meaning'; and, so far as I can see, this entails the same view which he had expressed in (I), viz. that the words 'There are *not* three consecutive 7's anywhere in the development of π' have no meaning, since, if these words had a meaning, it would seem to follow that '$\pi' = \pi$' also has one, and that therefore the question 'Is π' identical with π?' also has one. In the second passage in (III) in which he discussed this apparent question he expressly said that though the words (1) 'There are five consecutive 7's in the first thousand digits of π' have sense, yet the words (2) 'There are five consecutive 7's *somewhere* in the development' have none, adding that 'we can't say that (2) makes sense because (2) follows from (1)'. But in the very next lecture he seemed to have changed his view on this point, since he there said 'We ought not to say "There are five 7's in the development" has no sense', having previously said 'It has whatever sense its grammar allows', and having emphasized that 'it has a very curious grammar' since 'it is compatible with there not being five consecutive 7's in any development you can give'. If it has sense, although a 'very curious' one, it does presumably express a proposition to which the Law of Excluded Middle and the other rules of Formal Logic do apply; but Wittgenstein said nothing upon this point. What he did say was that 'All big mathematical problems are of the nature of "Are there five consecutive 7's in the development of π?" ' and that 'they are therefore quite different from multiplication sums, and not comparable in respect of difficulty'.

He said many other things about this question, but I cannot give them all, and some of them I certainly did not and do not understand. But one puzzling thing which he seemed to say in (III) was that, if we express the proposition that there is, in the development of π, a number of digits which is immediately followed by five consecutive 7's, by '($\exists n$) . fn', then there are two conceivable ways of proving ($\exists n$) . fn, namely, (1) by *finding* such a number, and (2) by proving that $\sim$($\exists n$) . fn is self-contradictory; but that the ($\exists n$) . fn proved in the latter way could not be the same as that proved in the former. In this connection he said that there is no 'opposite' to the first method of proof. He said also that '$\exists n$' means something different where it is possible to 'look for' a number which proves it, from what it means where this is not possible; and, generally, that 'The proof of an existence theorem gives the meaning of "existence" in that theorem', whereas the meaning of 'There's a man in the next room' does not depend on the method of proof.

(3) This last problem is connected, and was connected by him, with a general point which he discussed more than once in connection with the question 'How can we look for a method of trisecting an angle by rule and compasses, if there is no such thing?' He said that a man who had spent his life in trying to trisect an angle by rule and compasses would be inclined to say 'If you understand both what is meant by "trisection" and what is meant by "bisection by rule and compasses", you must understand what is meant by "trisection by rule and compasses" ' but that this was a mistake; that we can't imagine trisecting an angle by rule and compasses, whereas we can imagine dividing an angle into eight equal parts by rule and compasses; that 'looking for' a trisection by rule and compasses is not like 'looking for' a unicorn, since 'There are unicorns' has sense, although in fact there are no unicorns, whereas 'There are animals which show on their foreheads a construction by rule and compasses of the trisection of an angle' is just nonsense like 'There are animals with three horns, but also with only one horn': it does not give a description of any possible animal. And Wittgenstein's

answer to the original question was that by proving that it is impossible to trisect an angle by rule and compasses 'we change a man's idea of trisection of an angle' but that we should say that what has been proved impossible is the very thing which he had been trying to do, because 'we are willingly led in this case to identify two different things'. He compared this case to the case of calling what he was doing 'philosophy', saying that it was not the same kind of thing as Plato or Berkeley had done, but that we may feel that what he was doing 'takes the place' of what Plato and Berkeley did, though it is really a different thing. He illustrated the same point in the case of the 'construction' of a regular pentagon, by saying that if it were proved to a man who had been trying to find such a construction that there isn't any such thing, he would say 'That's what I was trying to do' because 'his idea has shifted on a rail on which he is ready to shift it'. And he insisted here again that (a) to have an idea of a regular pentagon and (b) to know what is meant by constructing by rule and compasses, e.g. a square, do not in combination enable you to know what is meant by constructing, by rule and compasses, a regular pentagon. He said that to explain what is meant by 'construction' we can give two series of 'constructions', viz. (a) equilateral triangle, regular hexagon, etc., and (b) square, regular octagon, etc., but that neither of these would give meaning to the construction of a regular pentagon, since they don't give any rule which applies to the number 5. He said that in a sense the result wanted is clear, but the means of getting at it is not; but in another sense, the result wanted is itself not clear, since 'constructed pentagon' is not the same as 'measured pentagon' and that whether the same figure will be both 'depends on our physics': why we call a construction a construction of a regular pentagon is 'because of the physical properties of our compasses, etc.'

In (I) he had said that in the case of Logic and Mathematics (and 'Sense-data') you can't know the same thing in two independent ways; and that it was in the case of 'hypotheses' and *nowhere else*, that there are different evidences for the same thing. But in (III) he said that even in the case of hypotheses, e.g. the proposition that there is a cylindrical object on the mantelpiece, he himself preferred to say that if the evidence was different, the proposition was also different, but that 'you can say which you please'. He did not say whether, in the case of Logic and Mathematics also, he now held that 'you can say which you please'.

(D) He spent, as I have said in the first part of this article (page 256), a great deal of time on this discussion, and I am very much puzzled as to the meaning of much that he said, and also as to the connection between different things which he said. It seems to me that his discussion was rather incoherent, and my account of it must be incoherent also, because I cannot see the connection between different points which he seemed anxious to make. He said very early in the discussion that the whole subject is 'extraordinarily difficult' because 'the whole field is full of misleading notations'; and that its difficulty was shown by the fact that the question at issue is the question between Realists, Idealists and Solipsists. And he also said, more than once, that many of the difficulties are due to the fact that there is a great temptation to confuse what are merely experiential propositions, which might, therefore, not have been true, with propositions which are necessarily true or are, as he once said, 'tautological or grammatical statements'. He gave, as an instance of a proposition of the latter sort, 'I can't feel your toothache', saying that 'If you feel it, it isn't mine' is a 'matter of grammar', and also that 'I can't feel your toothache' means the same as ' "I feel your toothache" has no sense'; and he contrasted this with 'I hear my voice coming from somewhere near my eyes', which he said we think to be necessary, but which in fact is not necessary 'though it always happens'. In this connection he gave the warning 'Don't be prejudiced by anything which *is* a fact, but which *might* be otherwise'. And he seemed to be quite definite on a point which seems to me certainly true, viz. that I might see without physical eyes, and even without having a body at all; that the connection between seeing and physical eyes is merely a fact learnt by experience, not a necessity at all; though he also said that 'the visual field' has certain internal properties, such that you can describe the motion of certain things in it as motions towards or away from 'your eye'; but that here 'your eye' does not mean your physical eye, nor yet anything whatever which is *in* the visual field. He called 'your eye', in this sense, 'the eye of the visual field', and said that the distinction between motion towards it and away from it was 'on the same level' as 'the distinction between "curved" and "straight" '.

However, he began the discussion by raising a question, which he said was connected with Behaviourism, namely, the question 'When we say "He has toothache" is it correct to say that his toothache is only his behaviour, whereas when I talk about my toothache I am not talking about my behaviour?'; but very soon he introduced a question expressed in different words, which is perhaps not merely a different formulation of the same question, viz. 'Is another person's toothache "toothache" in the same sense as mine?' In trying to find an answer to this question or these questions, he said first that it was clear and admitted that what verifies or is a criterion for 'I have toothache' is quite different from what verifies or is a criterion for 'He has toothache', and soon added that, since this is so, the *meanings* of 'I have toothache' and 'he has toothache' must be different. In this connection he said later, first, that the meaning of 'verification' is different, when we speak of verifying 'I have' from what it is when we speak of verifying 'He has', and then, later still, that there is no such thing as a verification for 'I have', since the question 'How do you know that you have toothache?' is nonsensical. He criticized two answers which might be given to this last question by people who think it is not nonsensical, by saying (1) that the answer 'Because I feel it' won't do, because 'I feel it' means the same as 'I have it', and (2) that the answer 'I know it by inspection' also won't do, because it implies that I can 'look to see' whether I have it or not, whereas 'looking to see whether I have it or not' has no meaning. The fact that it is nonsense to talk of verifying the fact that I have it, puts, he said, 'I have it' on 'a different level' in grammar from 'he has it'. And he also expressed his view that the two expressions are on a different grammatical level by saying that they are not both values of a single propositional function 'x has toothache'; and in favour of this view he gave two definite reasons for saying that they are not, namely, (1) that 'I don't know whether I have toothache' is always absurd or nonsense, whereas 'I don't know whether he has toothache' is not nonsense, and (2) that 'It seems to me that I have toothache' is nonsense, whereas 'It seems to me that he has' is not.

He said, that when he said this, people supposed him to be

saying that other people never really have what he has, but that, if he did say so, he would be talking nonsense; and he seemed quite definitely to reject the behaviourist view that 'he has toothache' means only that 'he' is behaving in a particular manner; for he said that 'toothache' doesn't in fact only mean a particular kind of behaviour, and implied that when we pity a man for having toothache, we are not pitying him for putting his hand to his cheek; and, later on, he said that we *conclude* that another person has toothache from his behaviour, and that it is legitimate to conclude this on the analogy of the resemblance of his behaviour to the way in which we behave when we have toothache. It seemed, therefore, that just as to his first question he meant to give definitely the answer 'No', so to his second question he meant to give definitely the answer 'Yes'; the word 'toothache' is used in the same sense when we say that he has it (or 'you have it') as when we say that I have it, though he never expressly said so; and though he seemed to throw some doubt on whether he meant this by saying 'I admit that other people do have toothache—this having *the meaning which we have given it*'.

It seemed, therefore, that he did not think that the difference between 'I have toothache' and 'He has toothache' was due to the fact that the word 'toothache' was used in a different sense in the two sentences. What then was it due to? Much that he said seemed to suggest that his view was that the difference was due to the fact that in 'He has toothache' we were necessarily talking of a physical body, whereas in 'I have toothache' we were not. As to the first of these two propositions he did not seem quite definite; for though at first he said that 'my voice' means 'the voice which comes from my mouth', he seemed afterwards to suggest that in 'He has toothache' (or 'You have') we were not necessarily referring to a *body*, but might be referring only to a *voice*, identified as 'his' or 'yours' without reference to a body. But as to the second proposition, the one about 'I have toothache', the point on which he seemed most anxious to insist was that what we call 'having toothache' is what he called a 'primary experience' (he once used the phrase 'direct experience' as equivalent to this one); and he said that 'what characterizes "primary experience" ' is that in its case ' "I" does not denote a possessor'. In order to make clear what he meant by this he compared 'I have toothache' with 'I see a red patch'; and said of what he called 'visual sensations' generally, and in particular of what he called 'the visual field', that 'the idea of a person doesn't enter into the description of it, just as a (physical) eye doesn't enter into the description of what is seen'; and he said that similarly 'the idea of a person' doesn't enter into the description of 'having toothache'. How was he here using the word 'person'? He certainly meant to deny that the idea of a physical body enters necessarily into the description; and in one passage he seemed to imply that he used 'person' to mean the same as 'physical body', since he said 'A description of a sensation does not contain a description of a sense-organ, nor, *therefore*, of a person'. He was, therefore, still maintaining apparently that one distinction between 'I have toothache' and 'He has toothache' was due to the fact that the latter necessarily refers to a physical body (or, perhaps, to a voice instead) whereas the former does not. But I think this was not the only distinction which he had in mind, and that he was not always using 'person' to mean the same as physical body (or, perhaps, a voice instead). For he said that 'Just as no (physical) eye is involved in seeing, so no Ego is involved in thinking or in having toothache'; and he quoted, with apparent approval, Lichtenberg's saying 'Instead of "I think" we ought to say "It thinks"' ('it' being used, as he said, as 'Es' is used in 'Es blitzet'); and by saying this he meant, I think, something similar to what he said of 'the eye of the visual field' when he said that it is not anything which is *in* the visual field. Like so many other philosophers, in talking of 'visual sensations' he seemed not to distinguish between 'what I see' and 'my seeing of it'; and he did not expressly discuss what appears to be a possibility, namely, that though no person enters into what I see, yet some 'person' other than a physical body or a voice, may 'enter into' my seeing of it.

In this connection, that in 'I have toothache' 'I' does not 'denote a possessor', he pointed out that, when I talk of '*my* body', the fact that the body in question is 'mine' or 'belongs to me', cannot be verified by reference to that body itself, thus seeming to imply that when I say 'This body belongs to me', 'me' is used in the second of the senses which he distinguished for 'I', viz. that in which, according to him, it does not 'denote a possessor'. But he did not seem to be quite sure of this, since he said in one place '*If* there is an ownership such that I possess a body, this isn't verified by reference to a body', i.e. that 'This is *my* body' can't possibly mean 'This body belongs to this body'. He said that, where 'I' is replaceable by 'this body' 'I' and 'he' are 'on the same (grammatical) level'. He was quite definite that the word 'I' or 'any other word which denotes a subject' is used in 'two utterly different ways', one in which it is 'on a level with other people', and one in which it is not. This difference, he said, was a difference in 'the grammar of our ordinary language'. As an instance of one of these two uses, he gave 'I've got a match-box' and 'I've got a bad tooth', which he said were 'on a level' with 'Skinner has a match-box' and 'Skinner has a bad tooth'. He said that in these two cases 'I have . . .' and 'Skinner has . . .' really were values of the same propositional function, and that 'I' and 'Skinner' were both 'possessors'. But in the case of 'I have toothache' or 'I see a red patch' he held that the use of 'I' is utterly different.

In speaking of these two senses of 'I' he said, as what he called 'a final thing', 'In one sense "I" and "conscious" are equivalent, but not in another', and he compared this difference to the difference between what can be said of the pictures on a film in a magic lantern and of the picture on the screen; saying that the pictures in the lantern are all 'on the same level' but that the picture which is at any given time on the screen is not 'on the same level' with any of them, and that if we were to use 'conscious' to say of one of the pictures in the lantern that it was at that time being thrown on the screen, it would be meaningless to say of the picture on the screen that it was 'conscious'. The pictures on the film, he said, 'have neighbours', whereas that on the screen has none. And he also compared the 'grammatical' difference between the two different uses of 'I' with the difference between the meaning of 'has blurred edges' as applied to the visual field, and the meaning of the same expression as applied to any drawing you might make of the visual field: your drawing might be imagined to have sharp edges instead of blurred ones, but this is unimaginable in the case of the visual field. The visual field, he said, has no outline or boundary, and he equated this with 'It has no sense to say that it has one'.

In connection with his statement that 'I', in one of its uses, is equivalent to 'conscious', he said something about Freud's use of the terms 'conscious' and 'unconscious'. He said that Freud had really discovered phenomena and connections not previously known, but that he talked as if he had found out that there were in the human mind 'unconscious' hatreds, volitions, etc., and that this was very misleading, because we think of the difference between a 'conscious' and an 'unconscious' hatred as like that between a 'seen' and an 'unseen' chair. He said that, in fact, the grammar of 'felt' and 'unfelt' hatred is quite different from that of 'seen' and 'unseen' chair, just as the grammar of 'artificial' flower is quite different from that of 'blue' flower. He suggested that 'unconscious toothache', if 'unconscious' were used as Freud used it, might be necessarily bound up with a physical body, whereas 'conscious toothache' is not so bound up.

As regards Solipsism and Idealism he said that he himself had been often tempted to say 'All that is real is the experience of the present moment' or 'All that is certain is the experience of the present moment'; and that anyone who is at all tempted to hold Idealism or Solipsism knows the temptation to say 'The only reality is the present experience' or 'The only reality is *my* present experience'. Of these two latter statements he said that both were equally absurd, but that, though both were fallacious, 'the idea expressed by them is of enormous importance'. Both about Solipsism and about Idealism he had insisted earlier that neither of them pretends that what it says is learnt by experience—that the arguments for both are of the form 'you can't' or 'you must', and that both these expressions 'cut (the statement in question) out of our language'. Elsewhere he said that both Solipsists and Idealists would say they 'couldn't imagine it otherwise', and that, in reply to this, he would say, 'If so, your statement has no sense' since 'nothing can characterize reality, except as opposed to something else which is not the case'. Elsewhere he had said that the Solipsist's statement 'Only my experience is real' is absurd 'as a statement of fact', but that the Solipsist sees that a person who says 'No: my experience is real too' has not really refuted him, just as Dr Johnson did not refute Berkeley by kicking a stone. Much later he said that Solipsism is right if it merely says that 'I have toothache' and 'He has toothache' are 'on quite a different level', but that 'if the Solipsist says that he has something which another hasn't, he is absurd and is making the very mistake of putting the two statements on the same level'. In this connection he said that he thought that both the Realist and the Idealist were 'talking nonsense' in the particular sense in which 'nonsense is produced by trying to express by the use of language what ought to be embodied in the grammar'; and he illustrated this sense by saying that 'I can't feel his toothache' means ' "I feel his toothache" has no sense' and therefore does not 'express a fact' as 'I can't play chess' may do.

(E) He concluded (III) by a long discussion which he introduced by saying 'I have always wanted to say something about the grammar of ethical expressions, or, e.g. of the word "God" '. But in fact he said very little about the grammar of such words as 'God', and very little also about that of ethical expressions. What he did deal with at length was not Ethics but Aesthetics, saying, however, 'Practically everything which I say about "beautiful" applies in a slightly different way to "good" '. His discussion of Aesthetics, however, was mingled in a curious way with criticism of assumptions which he said were constantly made by Frazer in the *Golden Bough*, and also with criticism of Freud.

About 'God' his main point seemed to be that this word is used in many *grammatically* different senses. He said, for instance, that many controversies about God could be settled by saying 'I'm not using the word in such a sense that you can say . . .', and that different religions 'treat things as making sense which others treat as nonsense, and don't merely deny some proposition which another religion affirms'; and he illustrated this by saying that if people use 'god' to mean something like a human being, then 'God has four arms' and 'God has two arms' will both have sense, but that others so use 'God' that 'God has arms' is nonsense —would say 'God *can't* have arms'. Similarly, he said of the expression 'the soul', that sometimes people so use that expression that 'the soul is a gaseous human being' has sense, but sometimes so that it has not. To explain what he meant by 'grammatically' different senses, he said we wanted terms which are not 'comparable', as e.g. 'solid' and 'gaseous' are comparable, but which differ as, e.g. 'chair' differs from 'permission to sit on a chair', or 'railway' from 'railway accident'.

He introduced his whole discussion of Aesthetics by dealing with one problem about the meaning of words, with which he said he had not yet dealt. He illustrated this problem by the example of the word 'game', with regard to which he said both (1) that, even if there is something common to all games, it doesn't follow that this is what we mean by calling a particular game a 'game', and (2) that the reason why we call so many different activities 'games' need not be that there is anything common to them all, but only that there is 'a gradual transition' from one use to another, although there may be nothing in common between the two ends of the series. And he seemed to hold definitely that there is nothing in common in our different uses of the word 'beautiful', saying that we use it 'in a hundred different games'— that, e.g., the beauty of a face is something different from the beauty of a chair or a flower or the binding of a book. And of the word 'good' he said similarly that each different way in which one person, A, can convince another, B, that so-and-so is 'good' fixes the meaning in which 'good' is used in that discussion—'fixes the grammar of that discussion'; but that there will be 'gradual transitions', from one of these meanings to another, 'which take the place of something in common'. In the case of 'beauty' he said that a difference of meaning is shown by the fact that 'you can say more' in discussing whether the arrangement of flowers in a bed is 'beautiful' than in discussing whether the smell of lilac is so.

He went on to say that specific colours in a certain spatial arrangement are not merely 'symptoms' that what has them *also* possesses a quality which we call 'being beautiful', as they would be, if we meant by 'beautiful', e.g. 'causing stomach-ache', in which case we could learn by experience whether such an arrangement did always cause stomach-ache or not. In order to discover how we use the word 'beautiful' we need, he said, to consider (1) what an actual aesthetic controversy or inquiry is like, and (2) whether such inquiries are in fact psychological inquiries 'though they look so very different'. And on (1) he said that the actual word 'beautiful' is hardly ever used in aesthetic controversies: that we are more apt to use 'right', as, e.g. in 'That doesn't look quite right yet', or when we say of a proposed accompaniment to a song 'That won't do: it isn't right'. And on (2) he said that if we say, e.g. of a bass 'It is too heavy; it moves too much', we are not saying 'If it moved less, it would be more agreeable to me': that, on the contrary, that it should be quieter is an 'end in itself', not a means to some other end; and that when we discuss whether a bass 'will do', we are no more discussing a psychological question than we are discussing psychological questions in Physics; that what we are trying to do is to bring the bass 'nearer to an ideal', though we haven't an ideal before us which we are trying to copy; that in order to show what we want, we might point to another tune, which we might say is 'perfectly right'. He said that in aesthetic investigations 'the one thing we are not interested in is causal connections, whereas this is the only thing we are interested in in Psychology'. To ask 'Why is this beautiful?' is not to ask for a causal explanation: that, e.g., to give a causal explanation in answer to the question 'Why is the smell of a rose pleasant?' would not remove our 'aesthetic puzzlement'.

Against the particular view that 'beautiful' means 'agreeable' he pointed out that we may refuse to go to a performance of a particular work on such a ground as 'I can't stand its greatness', in which case it is disagreeable rather than agreeable; that we may think that a piece of music which we in fact prefer is 'just nothing' in comparison to another to which we prefer it; and that the fact that we go to see 'King Lear' by no means proves that that experience is agreeable: he said that, even if it is agreeable, that fact 'is about the least important thing you can say about it'. He said that such a statement as 'That bass moves too much' is not a statement about human beings at all, but is more like a piece of Mathematics; and that, if I say of a face which I draw 'It smiles too much', this says that it could be brought closer to some 'ideal', not that it is not yet agreeable enough, and that to bring it closer to the 'ideal' in question would be more like 'solving a mathematical problem'. Similarly, he said, when a painter tries to improve his picture, he is not making a psychological experiment on himself, and that to say of a door 'It is top-heavy' is to say what is wrong with it, *not* what impression it gives you. The question of Aesthetics, he said, was not 'Do you like this?' but '*Why* do you like it?'

What Aesthetics tries to do, he said, is to give *reasons*, e.g. for having this word rather than that in a particular place in a poem, or for having this musical phrase rather than that in a particular place in a piece of music. Brahms's *reason* for rejecting Joachim's suggestion that his Fourth Symphony should be opened by two chords was not that that wouldn't produce the feeling he wanted to produce, but something more like 'That isn't what I meant'. *Reasons*, he said, in Aesthetics, are 'of the nature of further descriptions': e.g. you can make a person see what Brahms was driving at by showing him lots of different pieces by Brahms, or by comparing him with a contemporary author; and all that Aesthetics does is 'to draw your attention to a thing', to 'place things side by side'. He said that if, by giving 'reasons' of this sort, you make another person 'see what you see' but it still 'doesn't appeal to him', that is 'an end' of the discussion; and that what he, Wittgenstein, had 'at the back of his mind' was 'the idea that aesthetic discussions were like discussions in a court of law', where you try to 'clear up the circumstances' of the action which is being tried, hoping that in the end what you say will 'appeal to the judge'. And he said that the same sort of 'reasons' were given, not only in Ethics, but also in Philosophy.

As regards Frazer's *Golden Bough*, the chief points on which he seemed to wish to insist were, I think, the three following: (1) That it was a mistake to suppose that there was *only one* 'reason', in the sense of 'motive', which led people to perform a particular action—to suppose that there was 'one motive, which was *the* motive'. He gave as an instance of this sort of mistake Frazer's statement, in speaking of Magic, that when primitive people stab an effigy of a particular person, they believe that they have hurt the person in question. He said that primitive people do not *always* entertain this 'false scientific belief', though in some cases they may: that they may have quite different reasons for stabbing the effigy. But he said that the tendency to suppose that there is 'one motive which is *the* motive' was 'enormously strong', giving as an instance that there are theories of play each of which gives *only one* answer to the question 'Why do children play?' (2) That it was a mistake to suppose that *the* motive is always 'to get something useful'. He gave as an instance of this mistake Frazer's supposition that 'people at a certain stage thought it useful to kill a person, in order to get a good crop'. (3) That it was a mistake to suppose that why, e.g., the account of the Beltane Festival 'impresses us so much' is because it has 'developed from a festival in which a real man was burnt'. He accused Frazer of thinking that this was the reason. He said that our puzzlement as to why it impresses us is not diminished by giving the *causes* from which the festival arose, but is diminished by finding other similar festivals: to find these may make it seem 'natural', whereas to give the causes from which it arose cannot do this. In this respect he said that the question 'Why does this impress us?' is like the aesthetic questions 'Why is this beautiful?' or 'Why will this bass not do?'

He said that Darwin, in his 'expression of the Emotions', made a mistake similar to Frazer's, e.g. in thinking that 'because our ancestors, when angry, wanted to bite' is a sufficient explanation of why we show our teeth when angry. He said you might say that what is satisfactory in Darwin is not such 'hypotheses', but his 'putting the facts in a system'—helping us to make a 'synopsis' of them.

As for Freud, he gave the greater part of two lectures to Freud's investigation of the nature of a 'joke' (Witz), which he said was an 'aesthetic investigation'. He said that Freud's book on this subject was a very good book for looking for philosophical mistakes, and that the same was true of his writings in general, because there are so many cases in which one can ask how far what he says is a 'hypothesis' and how far merely a good way of representing a fact—a question as to which he said Freud himself is constantly unclear. He said, for instance, that Freud encouraged a confusion between getting to know the *cause* of your laughter and getting to know the *reason* why you laugh, because what he says sounds as if it were science, when in fact it is only a 'wonderful representation'. This last point he also expressed by saying 'It is all excellent similes, e.g. the comparison of a dream to a rebus'. (He had said earlier that all Aesthetics is of the nature of 'giving a good simile'.) He said that this confusion between *cause* and *reason* had led to the disciples of Freud making 'an abominable mess': that Freud did not in fact give any method of analysing dreams which was analogous to the rules which will tell you what are the causes of stomach-ache; that he had genius and therefore might sometimes by psycho-analysis find the *reason* of a certain dream, but that what is most striking about him is 'the enormous field of psychical facts which he arranges'.

As for what Freud says about jokes, he said first that Freud makes the two mistakes (1) of supposing that there is something common to all jokes, and (2) of supposing that this supposed common character is the meaning of 'joke'. He said it is not true, as Freud supposed, that *all* jokes enable you to do covertly what it would not be seemly to do openly, but that 'joke', like 'proposition', 'has a rainbow of meanings'. But I think the point on which he was most anxious to insist was perhaps that psycho-analysis does not enable you to discover the *cause* but only the *reason* of, e.g., laughter. In support of this statement he asserted that a psycho-analysis is successful only if the patient agrees to the explanation offered by the analyst. He said there is nothing analogous to this in Physics; and that what a patient agrees to can't be a *hypothesis* as to the *cause* of his laughter, but only that so-and-so was the *reason* why he laughed. He explained that the patient who agrees did not think of this reason at the moment when he laughed, and that to say that he thought of it 'subconsciously' 'tells you nothing as to what was happening at the moment when he laughed'.

(F) In (I), rather to my surprise, he spent a good deal of time in discussing what would usually be called a question about colours, namely, the question how the four 'saturated' colours, pure yellow, pure red, pure blue and pure green, which he called 'primary', are distinguished from those 'saturated' colours which are not 'primary'. He drew a circle on the blackboard to represent the arrangement of the saturated colours, with a vertical diameter joining 'yellow' at the top to 'blue' at the bottom, and a horizontal diameter joining 'green' on the left to 'red' on the right. And he seemed to be maintaining with regard to these four colours that they are distinguished from the other saturated colours in the two following ways, viz. (1) that the sense in which any purple is 'between' pure red and pure blue, and in which any orange is 'between' pure yellow and pure red is very different from the sense of 'between' in which pure red is 'between' any orange and any purple; a difference which he also expressed by saying that whereas an orange can be properly called a 'mixture' of yellow and red, red cannot possibly be called a 'mixture' of orange and purple; and (2) that whereas pure red can be properly said to be 'midway' between pure yellow and pure blue, there is no colour which is 'midway' between pure red and pure blue, or 'midway' between pure yellow and pure red, etc. He said that, for these reasons, the arrangement of the saturated colours in a square, with the four 'primaries' at the four corners, is a better picture of their relations than the arrangement of them in a circle.

I say only that he *seemed* to be making these assertions, because he emphasized from the beginning that 'primary' is not an adjective to 'colour' in the sense in which 'black' may be an adjective to 'gown', but that the distinction between 'primary' and 'not primary' is a 'logical' distinction—an expression which he explained later on by saying that, just as sounds are not distingushed from colours by the fact that something is true of the one which is not true of the other, so red, blue, green and yellow are not distinguished from the other saturated colours by the fact that anything is true of them which is not true of the others. He emphasized to begin with that the sentences 'blue is not primary' and 'violet is primary' are both of them 'nonsense', and I think there is no doubt he held that, since this is so, their contradictories 'blue is primary' and 'violet is not primary' are also nonsense, though there is a sense in which the two last are true, and the two former false. In other words, I think he certainly held that 'blue is primary' is a 'necessary proposition'— that we can't imagine its not being true—and that therefore, as he said (page 311), it 'has no sense'. It would seem to follow that if, as he seemed to be, he was really talking about the *colours*, red, blue, green and yellow, all that he said about them was 'nonsense'. According to what he said elsewhere, he could only have been talking sense if he was talking, not about the colours, but about certain words used to express them; and accordingly he did actually go on to say that 'red is primary' was only a proposition about the use of the English word 'red', which, as I said (page 291), he cannot seriously have held. The question I am here raising is the question which I discussed at length in the second part of this article, and I have nothing to add except to give one quotation which I ought to have given there. He actually said, in one place in (II), 'What corresponds to a necessity in the world must be what in language seems an arbitrary rule'. I do not think he had succeeded in getting quite clear as to what relation he wished to assert to hold between what he called 'rules of grammar', on the one hand, and 'necessary propositions', on the other.

(G) With questions about Time he dealt, at considerable length, in two places in (III).

The earlier discussion was in connection with his view that the 'troubles in our thought' which he was concerned to remove, arise from our thinking that sentences which we do not use with any practical object, sound as if they 'ought to have sense', when in fact they have none. And in this connection his main point seemed to be that, since we talk of Time 'flowing' as well as of a river 'flowing', we are tempted to think that Time 'flows' in a certain 'direction', as a river does, and that therefore it has sense to suppose that Time might flow in the opposite direction, just as it certainly has sense to suppose that a river might. He said, in one place, that some philosophers have actually made the muddle of thinking that Time has a 'direction' which might conceivably be reversed. Later on he made a distinction, as to the meaning of which I am not clear, between what he called 'memory-time' and what he called 'information-time', saying that in the former there is only earlier and later, not past and future, and that it has sense to say that I remember that which in 'information-time' is future. This distinction seemed to be connected with one he had made earlier, when he said, that if we imagine a river with logs floating down it at equal spatial distances from one another, the interval between the time at which, e.g., the 120th log passed us and that at which, e.g., the 130th passed, might *seem* to be equal to that between the time at which the 130th passed us and that at which the 140th passed us, although, *measured by a clock*, these intervals were not equal. He went on to ask: 'Supposing all events had come to an end, what is the criterion for saying that Time would have come to an end too, or that it still went on?' and to ask: 'If there were no events earlier than a hundred years ago, would there have been no time before that?' He said that what we need to do is to notice how we use the expression 'Time'; and that people ask 'Has Time been created?' although the question 'Has "before" been created?' has absolutely no meaning.

But he said a good many things in this discussion which I have failed to understand, and I may easily have omitted points which he would have considered of the first importance.

In his second discussion he was trying to show what was wrong with the following statement which Russell made in his *Outline of Philosophy*: 'Remembering, which occurs now, cannot possibly prove that what is remembered occurred at some other time, because the world might have sprung into being five minutes ago, full of acts of remembering which were entirely misleading.' But I cannot help thinking that, in what he said about this statement, he made two quite definite mistakes as to what Russell was implying by it. In order to explain why I think so I must, however, first explain what I take it that Russell was implying.

It will be noted that Russell speaks as if 'acts of remembering' could be 'entirely misleading'; and he seems not to have noticed that we so use the term 'remember' that if an act, which resembles an act of remembering, turns out to be entirely misleading, we say that it was not an act of remembering. For instance 'I remember that I had breakfast this morning' is so used that, if it turns out that I did not have breakfast this morning, it *follows logically* that I do *not* remember that I did: from 'I remember that I had it' it *follows logically* that I did have it, so that 'acts of remembering, which are entirely misleading' is a contradiction in terms; if an act is entirely misleading, it is not an act of remembering. It is plain, therefore, that Russell was using the expression 'acts of remembering' in a different sense from any in which it can be correctly used; and his view could be more correctly expressed as the view that it is *logically possible* that we never remember anything. I say 'logically possible', because when he says 'the world *might* have sprung into being five minutes ago', I think he certainly means by 'might', merely that it is *logically possible* that it did.

Now Wittgenstein pointed out, quite justly, that when Russell says 'The world might have sprung into being five minutes ago' his choice of 'five minutes ago' as the time when the world might have 'sprung into being' is 'arbitrary': Russell's view requires that it is equally true that it might have 'sprung into being' two minutes ago or one minute ago, or, says Wittgenstein, that it might have begun to exist *now*: he actually said that Russell *ought* to have said 'The world might have been created *now*'. And I think it is true that Russell does imply this. But Wittgenstein said that in the statement quoted, Russell was 'committing the precise fallacy of Idealism'. And surely this is a complete mistake! From what I have quoted (page 311) it appears clear that what Wittgenstein regarded as the 'fallacy of Idealism' was some such statement as 'It is logically *im*possible that anything should be real except the present experience'. And Russell's statement certainly does not imply this. It looks to me as if, for the moment, Wittgenstein was confusing the two entirely different propositions, (1) 'It is logically possible that nothing exists except the present experience' which Russell may be said to imply, and (2) 'It is logically *im*possible that anything should exist except the present experience', which he certainly does not imply.

But it seems to me that he also made another complete mistake as to what Russell's view implied; and this was a criticism into which he went at some length. He began by asking us to consider the question 'What is the verification for the proposition "The world began to exist five minutes ago"?' saying that, if you admit no criterion for its truth, that sentence is 'useless', or, as he afterwards said, 'meaningless'. And his criticism of Russell here consisted in saying that 'Russell is refusing to admit as evidence for "the world began more than five minutes ago" what we all admit as such evidence, and is therefore making that statement meaningless'. He compared Russell's statement to the statement 'There is a rabbit between A and B, whenever nobody is looking' which he said 'seems to have sense, but is in fact meaningless, because it cannot be refuted by experience'. But surely Russell would admit, and can perfectly consistently admit, that some of those events, which he calls incorrectly 'acts of remembering' do constitute very strong evidence that the world existed more than five minutes ago. He is not concerned to deny that they constitute *strong* evidence, but only that they constitute *absolutely conclusive* evidence—that they 'prove' that it did. In other words, he is only asserting that it is *logically possible* that the world did not. Wittgenstein seems to me to have over-looked the distinction between denying that we have *any* evidence which Russell does not do, and denying that we have *absolutely conclusive* evidence, which I think Russell certainly meant to do.

But later on Wittgenstein seemed to me to be suggesting another quite different argument, which, if he did mean what he seemed to mean, and if what he seemed to mean is true, would really be a valid refutation of Russell's statement. He introduced again the phrase 'memory-time', saying that a certain order of events might be so called, and then going on to say that all these events 'approach a point such that it will have no sense to say "B occurred after the present in memory-time" '; that 'now' 'should be a point in an

L

order'; and that when we say 'The clock is striking now', 'now' means 'the present of our memory-time', and cannot mean, e.g., 'at 6.7' because it has sense to say 'It is 6.7 *now*'. I think all this suggests that his view was that 'now', in the sense in which we commonly use it, and in which Russell was undoubtedly using it, has a meaning such that part of what we are saying when we say that an event is happening 'now', is that it was preceded by other events which we remember; and, if this is true, it would certainly follow that Russell was wrong in implying that it is logically possible that nothing should have happened before *now*.

(H) I was a good deal surprised by some of the things he said about the difference between 'philosophy' in the sense in which what he was doing might be called 'philosophy' (he called this 'modern philosophy'), and what has traditionally been called 'philosophy'. He said that what he was doing was a 'new subject', and not merely a stage in a 'continuous development'; that there was now, in philosophy, a 'kink' in the 'development of human thought', comparable to that which occurred when Galileo and his contemporaries invented dynamics; that a 'new method' had been discovered, as had happened when 'chemistry was developed out of alchemy'; and that it was now possible for the first time that there should be 'skilful' philosophers, though of course there had in the past been 'great' philosophers.

He went on to say that, though philosophy had now been 'reduced to a matter of skill', yet this skill, like other skills, is very difficult to acquire. One difficulty was that it required a 'sort of thinking' to which we are not accustomed and to which we have not been trained—a sort of thinking very different from what is required in the sciences. And he said that the required skill could not be acquired merely by hearing lectures: discussion was essential. As regards his own work, he said it did not matter whether his results were true or not: what mattered was that 'a method had been found'.

In answer to the question why this 'new subject' should be called 'philosophy' he said in (III) that though what he was doing was certainly different from what, e.g., Plato or Berkeley had done, yet people might feel that it 'takes the place of' what they had done —might be inclined to say 'This is what I really wanted' and to identify it with what they had done, though it is really different, just as (as I said above, pages 304-5) a person who had been trying to trisect an angle by rule and compasses might, when shown the proof that this is impossible, be inclined to say that this impossible thing was the very thing he had been trying to do, though what he had been trying to do was really different. But in (II) he had also said that the 'new subject' did really resemble what had been traditionally called 'philosophy' in the three respects that (1) it was very general, (2) it was fundamental both to ordinary life and to the sciences, and (3) it was independent of any special results of science; that therefore the application to it of the word 'philosophy' was not purely arbitrary.

He did not expressly try to tell us exactly what the 'new method' which had been found was. But he gave some hints as to its nature. He said, in (II), that the 'new subject' consisted in 'something like putting in order our notions as to what can be said about the world', and compared this to the tidying up of a room where you have to move the same object several times before you can get the room really tidy. He said also that we were 'in a muddle about things', which we had to try to clear up; that we had to follow a certain instinct which leads us to ask certain questions, though we don't even understand what these questions mean; that our asking them results from 'a vague mental uneasiness', like that which leads children to ask 'Why?'; and that this uneasiness can only be cured 'either by showing that a particular question is not permitted, or by answering it'. He also said that he was not trying to teach us any new facts: that he would only tell us 'trivial' things—'things which we all know already'; but that the difficult thing was to get a 'synopsis' of these trivialities, and that our 'intellectual discomfort' can only be removed by a synopsis of *many* trivialities—that 'if we leave out any, we still have the feeling that something is wrong'. In this connection he said it was misleading to say that what we wanted was an 'analysis', since in science to 'analyse' water means to discover some new fact about it, e.g. that it is composed of oxygen and hydrogen, whereas in philosophy 'we know at the start all the facts we need to know'. I imagine that it was in this respect of needing a 'synopsis' of trivialities that he thought that philosophy was similar to Ethics and Aesthetics (pages 314-15).

I ought, perhaps, finally to repeat what I said in the first part of this article (page 257), namely, that he held that though the 'new subject' must say a great deal about language, it was only necessary for it to deal with those points about language which have led, or are likely to lead, to definite philosophical puzzles or errors. I think he certainly thought that some philosophers nowadays have been misled into dealing with linguistic points which have no such bearing, and the discussion of which therefore, in his view, forms no part of the proper business of a philosopher.

TWO CORRECTIONS

It has been pointed out to me that I made a great mistake in the third part of this article in speaking of 'Tarski's 3-valued Logic', since the calculus in question was invented solely by Professor J. Lukasiewicz, and Tarski had no hand whatever in its invention. I did not know this at the time, and I think I must have been misled into my mistake by Wittgenstein himself, since, on looking up my notes of the passage in question, I find no name mentioned except Tarski's, which is mentioned three times. Of course I cannot be certain that Wittgenstein did not also mention Lukasiewicz: he certainly did at one point speak of 'they', as if Tarski was not the only person involved: but I think he must at least have supposed that Tarski was partly responsible for the calculus, even if he did not suppose him to be its sole author. I am now informed, on unimpeachable evidence, that Tarski had no hand whatever in the invention. Lukasiewicz invented the calculus and published an account of it in 1920, before he was even acquainted with Tarski.

On looking at my notes, to find what (so far as they can be trusted) Wittgenstein had said on this first matter, I found that I had badly misrepresented him on another. I represent him as saying that Tarski had called the third value in the calculus 'doubtful'. But this is a complete mistake. What he actually said was that Tarski had chosen a particular letter to represent the third value, because he supposed this value to 'correspond' to 'possible', and that it did not in fact so correspond. He said nothing whatever about 'doubtful', but only about 'possible'. The substitution of 'doubtful' for 'possible' seems to have been a piece of great carelessness on my part.